ARCHITECTS OF ANNIHILATION

ARCHITECTS OF ANNIHILATION

Auschwitz and the Logic of Destruction

Götz Aly and Susanne Heim

Translated from the German by A.G. Blunden

Weidenfeld & Nicolson
LONDON

First published in Germany in 1991 by Hoffman und Campe
with the title *Vordenker der Vernichtung*.

First published in Great Britain in 2002
by Weidenfeld & Nicolson

© Götz Aly and Susanne Heim, 1991
English translation © A.G. Blunden, 2002

A CIP catalogue record for this book
is available from the British Library.

ISBN 0 297 84278 1

Typeset by Selwood Systems, Midsomer Norton

Printed by Butler & Tanner Ltd, Frome and London

Weidenfeld & Nicolson

The Orion Publishing Group Ltd
Orion House
5 Upper Saint Martin's Lane
London, WC2H 9EA

CONTENTS

INTRODUCTION

The Third Reich lasted for just twelve years, and more than four times as many years have elapsed since its demise. Yet it continues to shape the world we live in. Its bloodless legacy is woven into the everyday fabric of modern German life, from the legal requirement to register with the local police, and the regulation of the market in agricultural produce, to the Volkswagen car. The designation 'special needs school' is a part of that legacy no less than the abolition of the old German script and the invention of mass tourism. The National Socialist state inaugurated a drive for modernization such as Germany had never seen: at the same time it evolved a machinery of destruction and extermination such as the world had never witnessed. The death of millions and the indescribable sufferings of millions more are the bloody legacy of those twelve brief years.

In recent years the modernizing forces unleashed by National Socialism have been attracting the attention of historians, who have examined the institutions and individuals behind this dynamic process. For the most part, however, historical analysis ends where Auschwitz begins. In this book we set out to uncover the connecting links between the politics of modernization and the politics of annihilation. We shall describe the relationship between the development of certain plans and the perpetration of specific acts in Germany during those years. Their purpose was to impose a new political, economic and social order on the German Reich, and ultimately on the entire European continent – and all within a very short space of time. This undertaking was predicated both on the war and on the taking-away of human rights and property.

Allied to the aggressive ideology of National Socialism, these plans were transmuted into political and military aggression, and increasingly radical projects followed at ever-decreasing intervals – projects for a new European order, for a German Europe: 'lightning wars' (*Blitzkriege*), structural models, campaigns of annihilation, large-scale colonization plans, gas chambers. The year 1941 – when victory seemed at hand, and with it the intoxicating prospect of being able to 'reshape' anything and everything – was also the year in which the German leadership decided to murder millions of men, women and children.

A satisfactory explanation for this is not to be found in the individual personality of a Hitler, Himmler or Goebbels, nor in the hysterical fervour – incited and self-incited – of an entire nation. Nor can it be explained away in terms of the self-perpetuating machinery of exclusion and marginalization that operated in a highly compartmentalized way and with characteristically Teutonic efficiency.

All of these factors played a role, and without them the mass murders perpetrated by the Germans could not have taken place.[1] But behind all this lay certain conceptual models, designs for 'final solutions', which recommended – rarely explicitly, more often than not in sterile scientific jargon – the state-directed mass extermination of human beings as a functional necessity for a long-term programme of social modernization. This is the subject of the present book. In their intellectual abstraction these designs seem strangely at odds with the brutal reality of the death camps. And yet National Socialist Germany was not only possessed of an ideology that consigned to extermination all those who were classed as 'inferior': it had also elaborated detailed theories showing how entire social classes, minorities and peoples were to be 'restructured' and decimated. The ideology and the theory had to come together and intermesh in order to produce Hadamar, Chelmno, Leningrad, Stukenbrock, Treblinka and Auschwitz. And it is certain that with every year that National Socialist Germany continued to exist, millions more people would have been killed by various means – starved, deported, sent to the gas chambers or simply worked to death.

The executive dynamism of National Socialist Germany was generated by the interaction of three forces: the abandonment of moral restraint, the pursuit of a nationalistic and expansionist social utopia and the emergence of a modern technocracy. But it was not the case that some Germans severed all moral ties while others gave themselves up in a spirit of idealism to grand social designs and the pursuit of efficiency. Instead the three components define areas of common ground between the Nazi leadership and the advisory and executive intelligentsia. There is broad agreement on this and many other findings of historical research. This research has not sought to play down the criminal nature of German policy at that time, nor has it relativized the murder of the European Jews. But it does help us to see National Socialism in its historical context – not so that we might safely forget the past, but rather that we might reconstruct it more fully.

Our own understanding, which is supported by our study of the source material, is at odds with received historical thinking. The broad consensus – albeit driven by a variety of motives – is that the murder of the European Jews defies all attempts to explain it in historical-rational terms. Hannah Arendt has underlined this very point: what makes the Holocaust unique, she argues, is not the number of victims as such, but the apparent failure of the murderers to consult their own advantage or interest. The documents adduced in evidence in the present book show this thesis to be untenable. As in the case of the mass murder of the mentally ill in Germany and the slaughter of the civilian populations in Poland, Serbia and the Soviet Union, it is possible to discern utilitarian goals behind the murder of the European Jews. Which in no way diminishes the horror of those murders.

Today Auschwitz is discussed in terms of a 'totally irrational racial hatred', of 'annihilation for annihilation's sake', of the 'self-perpetuating machinery' of German bureaucracy, the 'descent into barbarism' and 'the breakdown of civilization'. What is widely ignored or relativized is the fact that in the eyes of those who paved the way for the 'final solution' the policy of extermination implemented against other population groups, most notably in the Soviet Union and Poland, took its place alongside the murder of the European Jews as part of a grand strategy known as 'negative population policy'.

Our analysis shows that arbitrary acts and self-perpetuating bureaucratic routine played only a minor role; that – on the contrary – the National Socialist leadership sought to maximize the input from scientific policy advisers and used their research findings as an important basis for their decisions – including the decisions to murder millions of human beings.

In the SD ('Sicherheitsdienst': security service) Heinrich Himmler not only had at his disposal a thoroughly unorthodox and highly qualified think-tank equipped with its own data bank, but he also appointed a special 'inspector of statistics', for example, whose chief task was to furnish him with empirical raw data on the social make-up of the SS and for the preparation of colonization plans in the East. In order to decide the future fate of the Warsaw ghetto Hans Frank, the Governor-General of German-occupied Poland, commissioned a report from the Reich Board for Industrial Rationalization (RKW) and adopted its recommendations. Shortly before that the Reich Minister of Finance had personally ordered the Reich Audit Office to carry out a review of the economic viability of the Lódź ghetto, in order to put him in the picture and brief him ahead of further debate and discussion. The heads of the armed forces and government ministries commissioned over 1,600 secret reports from the Kiel Institute of World Economic Studies alone as an aid to planning the economic strategy of the war. Hermann Rauschning documents an early example of this kind of political consultancy in National Socialist Germany from 1934:

> I reported to Hitler what I had seen of Koch's 'planning agency' [Koch was the Gauleiter of East Prussia]. A young academic, Professor von Grünberg, had devised all kinds of fantastical 'model landscapes' for the future. He had had maps drawn up at his institute, marked out with lines of communication, fields of force, lines of force, motorways, railway lines, canal projects. The whole of the East as far as the Black Sea, as far as the Caucasus, was divided up into meticulously planned economic zones. These maps showed Germany and western Russia as a single vast land mass with integrated economic and transport systems. The whole scheme was German-centred, of course – planned and run by Germany, for Germany. In this 'planned economy' Poland had ceased to exist, let alone Lithuania ...[2]

The top leadership of the National Socialist state generally took decisions not simply as they saw fit, but on the basis of detailed memoranda. At the key conference which took place on 12 November 1938 Hermann Göring, for example, declared that he was 'not sufficiently versed' to assess the consequences of 'eliminating Jewish elements from the economy'. He asked for suggestions, found them 'excellent', had decrees drawn up, put them into force. Over a hundred people attended the conference. The vast majority of them were either members of Göring's staff, highly experienced in administrative and economic matters, or representatives of an intelligentsia that advised across the whole range of policy issues – the latter all too easily overshadowed in discussions of National Socialist crimes by the leading lights of the Nazi regime, who appear in contemporary and later accounts as all-powerful, larger-than-life presences.

In his book *Behemoth*[3] the jurist and political scientist Franz Neumann identifies industry, bureaucracy, the Party and the military as the four pillars of the Nazi regime. One reason why these pillars were able to support the increasingly elephantine imperial structure of the German state for so long was that they were tied together and shored up by this network of scientific advisers. The advisers to the men in power sat on a variety of differently constituted and changing committees, made up of ministerial undersecretaries, senior ministry officials and experts of every shade and technical persuasion. Later these men would actually boast of their role as 'crisis managers in the Third Reich'.[4]

In this book we describe the work of these economic experts and professional administrators – the regional planners, statisticians and agronomists, the labour deployment specialists and demographers. We endeavour to analyse their influence on key policy decisions taken in 1940 and 1941. We are looking for evidence of specific responsibility, of the part played by these men in planning and pushing through the murder of millions of people.

Initially many of these experts were distinctly cool towards the new regime, and did not join the NSDAP until well after 1933, if at all. Those who joined did so in order to further their careers, but also because they realized that as Party members they would be better placed to shape and influence government policy. Very different from the ideologists of the 'years of struggle' whom they largely came to supplant, these men advanced slowly at first, but with increasing rapidity after 1938, into the nerve centres of political decision-making; and month by month they acquired growing power as planners to decide the fate of thousands, and ultimately many millions, of their fellow human beings. Up until the end of 1941 their influence grew with each new stage in Germany's expansion. Each time they were less constrained in the way they formulated their proposals and options: each time they could afford to take less account of conflicting social realities in the German Reich and in the occupied territories. Compromise was looked upon as a mark of intellectual laziness, while patently criminal acts were spuriously dignified as historical necessity, 'the price one pays for progress'. SS officers, civil servants, junior academics, business leaders and engineers: they were all impressed by the newly conquered 'expanses' and by their seemingly infinite possibilities, just as they were by the scale of the task that confronted them, and by the opportunity to implement their ambitious plans without any bureaucratic obstacles to speak of.

These young, career-minded technocrats and academics, whose plans and ideas are the focus of the present study, regarded Europe – densely populated and shaped by the complex vagaries of history, full of differences and contrasts – as a drawing-board on which to work out their grand designs. For them eastern Europe was one vast wasteland crying out for 'readjustment' and 'reconstruction'. They wanted to rationalize production methods, standardize products, introduce an international division of labour, modernize and simplify social structures, reduce the number of 'unproductive' people to an absolute minimum. The ultimate aim was to harness large tracts of Europe to the interests of the German economy and the German striving for hegemony. The architects of this policy looked to the new, scientifically based concept of 'demographic economics' (*Bevölkerungsökonomie*) to help them attain their goals as cheaply and quickly as possible. The size and qualitative composition of the population were to be continuously monitored and regulated through government programmes of birth control (and birth promotion), resettlement and extermination.

In the course of the war, as supplies of food, raw materials and capital steadily dwindled, 'human resources' soon became the only economic factor that these planners still had the power to manipulate. As they saw it, the German Reich in 1941 was short of one to two million workers, while at the same time there were 30 to 50 million 'useless mouths to feed' in Europe – people whose labour was not being exploited, and could not be exploited without far-reaching changes in social policy. So the architects of the new order set to work on a grand design for 'adjusting' the ratio between productive and unproductive population groups, between those who worked and those who allegedly worked too little or not at all. In the eyes of these German intellectuals, eastern and south-east Europe lacked a middle class that would guarantee stable social conditions and promote the development of an internal market. At the same time – measured by these standards – these regions suffered from 'overpopulation', with umpteen millions too many people living on the land: poor people, eking out a modest existence and devoid of economic aspirations. They stood in the way of plans to develop a modern economy on the German model, and they had to be removed before any useful gains could be extracted from those who remained. So 'resettlement', 'labour redeployment' and 'evacuation' became the chief policy instruments of the German new order.

Economic disadvantaging, starvation and murder – initially of minorities, later of entire peoples – were programmed in from the very beginning by the engineers of this brave new National Socialist Europe in order to create advantages for the majority, especially the German majority, or at least to guarantee the preservation of the social status quo. This is instanced by the fact that the older generation living today report that they only suffered serious food shortages in Germany after the war, following the collapse of the state that had hitherto 'solved' the problems of food, clothing and housing with the aid of mass expropriation, wars of aggression and gas chambers.

When it came to constructing this new social hierarchy, which meant deportation and death for millions of people, the strategic intentions of the planning elite found a ready accommodation with the racist ideology of the National Socialist regime. Heinrich Himmler formulated this murderous design with brutal frankness: 'The only way to solve the social problem is for one lot to kill the others and take their land.'[5]

We have subdivided the historical material of this book into three phases, the first beginning in 1938, the year in which Austria and the Sudetenland were annexed. We show how from that point onwards, and in close conjunction with the continuing process of territorial expansion, anti-Semitism became an integral part of the plan to establish a 'new order', finding expression in a policy of systematic 'Entjudung' – the 'elimination of Jewish elements'. This was followed in the second phase by the war against Poland, which left that country completely crushed and devastated. We describe the German projects designed to bring about the complete transformation of Poland's demographic and economic structure. The planning experts used the occupied country – comprising the 'annexed eastern territories' and the 'Government General' – as a testing ground for their ideas. Here the 'Jewish question' presented itself to them for the first time 'as a population policy problem on a massive scale', which could not be 'solved' with the hitherto customary instruments of terror, expropriation and enforced emigration. What is significant here is how the respective planning staffs of the SS and the civil administrations agreed on a common strategy. From this it is easy to see how the constructive desire of the German planners to build a better future was the very thing that led ultimately to genocide.

For the third phase we look at the situation as it appeared in 1941. In occupied Poland there was growing conflict between German colonization policy on the one hand and plans for economic development on the other. The war of conquest in south-east Europe was designed to create the military conditions for the creation of a European economic community under Nazi auspices. But here too, according to German economists, 'overpopulation' was hindering the development of a new economic order, and many millions of people were viewed as 'unproductive' and 'surplus to need'. Similarly the plans for the military conquest and colonization of the Soviet Union envisaged a 'reduction' in the population – by whatever means. To this was added the prospect of food shortages, which threatened to undermine morale on the home front. In order to maintain food supplies to population groups who were not categorized as 'inferior', 30 million Soviet men, women and children were to be starved. These plans did not exist in isolation. They were part of the context in which the decision was taken, in the summer of 1941, to proceed with the 'final solution of the Jewish question'. Additional encouragement for that decision came from the reports of German economic experts who concluded that no further gains could be extracted from the dispossessed and starving people in the ghettos. To keep them alive, even under a harsh regime of forced labour, was therefore an unprofitable exercise.

In reconstructing events we need to look also at the biographies of the scientists and academics and senior ministry officials who were involved in framing these plans. Through the careers and personal connections of specific individuals we can see how ideas and suggestions percolated upwards through the hierarchy, and how open and permeable the National Socialist state was in this regard. Furthermore, a knowledge of biographical details and an understanding of middle-ranking institutional structures have an important part to play in the search for new documents and the reconstruction of decision-making processes. Many decisions taken in the key organizations were purely verbal understandings, actioned by word of mouth and never written down. In many areas of the National Socialist ruling apparatus the most important written records were either burned immediately ('Top secret – read and destroy!') or consigned to the flames in the final months of the war. This is what happened in most of the main departments of the SS and in Göring's apparat; the same applies to the reports sent by the security police from the Government General, Heydrich's memorandum on the 'final solution of the Jewish question' and many other documents besides. It is indicative – and one of the specific difficulties of a study such as this – that any mention of the systematic policy of mass murder was evidently taboo even in the secret reports drawn up by the security service.[6]

Biographical details are also important in that they focus attention on the members of an intelligentsia that has gone largely unmentioned, not least because the post-war Federal Republic 'relied heavily during the reconstruction period on the old administrative elites who had previously served the NS regime'.[7] After 1945 the members of this intelligentsia obviously had a vested interest in portraying National Socialism as a period in German political life when their efforts to influence events were repeatedly frustrated by 'the nightmare of madness and tyranny'.

Our theme, by contrast, is the nightmare of a designing rationalism in the service of practical policy-making, which inherently tends towards the abandonment of moral restraint, and as such found in National Socialism its ideal conditions.

CHAPTER 1

'ENTJUDUNG': THE SYSTEMATIC REMOVAL OF JEWS FROM GERMANY'S SOCIAL AND ECONOMIC LIFE

Pogroms and rationalization

On the night of 9 November 1938, the so-called 'Reichskristallnacht' or 'Night of the Broken Glass', pogroms and lootings took place throughout the German Reich. The pretext was the murder of a German Embassy secretary by a young Parisian Jew.

The events of 9 November produced a paradoxical outcome. The high point of one kind of anti-Semitism – the anti-Semitism of the street and the mob – was also its end and the beginning of something quite new, namely a coordinated government policy for the 'solution of the Jewish question'. Over one hundred dead, countless injured, 25,000 arrests, nearly two hundred synagogues destroyed, 7,500 shops smashed and looted: this tally signals the beginning of a new era. Standard methods such as pogroms, boycotts, etc. were now abandoned in favour of a government policy that moved inexorably towards the 'final solution': persecution and discrimination now became the official remit of state institutions. Three days later, on 12 November, at a crucial meeting hurriedly called by Göring in the Reich Air Ministry and attended by a hundred or so ministers and experts, key elements of the later policy of extermination were discussed. These included expropriation, controlled impoverishment, ghettoization, the wearing of the yellow star, a policy of starvation, enforced emigration, forced labour – and at the end Göring pointed to the possibility of 'settling scores in a big way'. The outcome of this meeting was the 'general line of policy to be pursued in future'.[1] The allegedly 'spontaneous anger of the people', which had been allowed free rein for a whole night in an orgy of destruction, looting and murder, was transmuted into a long-term government strategy – a strategy that had been precisely thought through, particularly with regard to its economic consequences.

It was no coincidence that this meeting was summoned by Göring.

As Commissioner for the Four-Year Plan he had been responsible since 1936 for coordinating the economic preparations for war. To that end he had set up the Four-Year Plan Authority staffed by a select group of highly qualified officials, which formed one of the main seats of power in the National Socialist state from 1937 to 1941. On 14 October Göring had already called for action 'to tackle the Jewish question now with every available means, because it is time they [the Jews] were removed from economic life'.[2]

Göring began the meeting on 12 November with the following words: 'Since the problem is essentially a complex economic problem, it is here that we need to make a start.' He specifically rejected any further manifestations of mob violence. 'Gentlemen, I am sick of these demonstrations.' At the end of the day they would do as much damage to the economy as they would to the Jews – and he (Göring) was the man in overall charge of running the economy.[3] He and the others present wanted to see some action at this meeting. The period of dithering, of deciding who was responsible for what, had gone on long enough in their view. As Göring put it: 'I beseech the various departments concerned to take immediate action on Aryanization.' The regional economic administrations were to start with an initiative that would clearly demonstrate the government's intentions to the public at large, namely the closing-down and 'Aryanization' of retail businesses. 'First of all,' said Göring, 'the Minister of Economic Affairs will announce which shops he intends to close down.' It turned out to be most of them. Under the policy of Aryanization they were to be 'eliminated' – wound up, in other words – from the outset. The same principle was to be applied to small and medium-sized manufacturing enterprises. First of all, Göring told his audience, the following questions had to be answered: 'Which factories are not needed at all? Which ones can be shut down? Can they be turned into something else? And if they don't have a future, they must be scrapped as quickly as possible.'

'Aryanization' was not primarily about the compulsory transfer of Jewish firms to profit-hungry 'Aryan' capitalists; in essence it was a state-directed programme of closures and rationalization.[4] It served to mitigate the social impact of the extensive rationalization that took place during these years in the small and medium-sized sector of the economy: in 1937 alone 90,000 Aryan workshops in Germany went bankrupt or simply closed down.[5] Viewed from this perspective, the principal economic benefits of Aryanization were structural in nature. Göring called upon the Minister of Economic Affairs 'to go all out on business closures from the outset', because he was only doing what would have to be done 'anyway' in the next few weeks, namely 'transforming non-essential production facilities into economically vital ones'.

As Commissioner for the Four-Year Plan Göring pursued this programme of business closures and rationalization with the sole objective of preparing the German economy for the coming war. Meanwhile the task of devising ways and means was left to the appropriate experts. Their experiences in Vienna in the six months prior to this meeting would stand them in good stead, for in May 1938, following the 'Anschluss' or annexation of Austria by Germany in March, work had begun on the rationalization of the Austrian economy – with the full involvement of the Four-Year Plan Authority. The chief instrument was the dispossession of countless thousands of Jews and their systematic removal from virtually every sector of the economy. The whole operation was directed not, as one might imagine, by zealous anti-Semites, but by established firms of accountants and auditors.

In the summer of 1938 the economic experts in Vienna had developed a concept that combined wholesale rationalization of the 'backward' Austrian economy with the liquidation of Jewish companies. The politician in charge of this programme was the Viennese Minister of Trade, Commerce and Labour, Hans Fischböck. In the hectic hours leading up to the Anschluss on 11 March 1938 Göring had intervened personally to get Fischböck installed,[6] and had made a point of inviting him to the meeting in Berlin.

Here the following exchange took place on 12 November (reproduced below with minor omissions):

Funk (Reich Minister of Economic Affairs): The crucial question is this: should we assume that the Jewish businesses are going to be reopened again later or not?
Göring: That depends on whether or not these Jewish businesses have a decent turnover.
Fischböck: We've already worked out a detailed plan to deal with this in Austria, Field Marshal. It's been decided that 10,000 of the 12,000 workshops should be shut down for good, and 2,000 should be kept going. And out of the 5,000 retail outlets 1,000 will be kept going, i.e. Aryanized, and the remaining 4,000 shut down. We've done a detailed study of all the different trades to see which businesses are needed to meet local needs, we've

cleared it all with the appropriate authorities, and as far as we're concerned the order can go out tomorrow, just as soon as we get the legislation we asked for in September, which would give us broad powers to revoke trading licences in general, without reference to the Jewish question. It would only take a very short piece of legislation.

Göring: I'll draw up the order today.

Fischböck: If we go ahead we could get rid of the entire visible [Jewish] commercial presence by the end of the year.

Göring: That would be excellent!

Fischböck: So out of a total of 17,000 businesses 12,000 or 14,000 would be closed down and the rest would be Aryanized or transferred to the state-owned trust agency.

Göring: I must say it is a terrific proposal. This means that in Vienna, one of the main Jewish cities, so to speak, we could be shot of the whole lot of them by Christmas or the end of the year.

Funk: We can do the same thing here.

By 'here' the Reich Minister of Economic Affairs meant the pre-1938 German Reich – the so-called 'Altreich' – and in particular Berlin. Just six days later the leaders of Berlin's business community held a meeting in the Chamber of Industry and Commerce 'to discuss the pressing problem of the exclusion of the Jews from the retail trade in Berlin'.[7]

The government order so ardently desired by the economic experts working in Vienna was published on 23 November 1938 in the *Reichsgesetzblatt*. The text of the 'Order for the implementation of the ordinance excluding Jews from German economic life' deliberately omitted any mention of 'Aryanization' as its aim, referring instead to business closures in general. Section 1, Paragraph 1 stated: 'All retail sales outlets, mail-order businesses and sales agencies owned by Jews are to be wound up and liquidated.' Any exemptions required special authorization.[8]

In the second phase of the conference on 12 November 1938 the participants addressed the social problems that would arise as people were put out of business at an accelerating rate. It was at this point that Reinhard Heydrich entered the discussion. He too was able to draw on the experience of Vienna – the experience, to be more precise, of his colleague Adolf Eichmann, who also attended the conference,[9] and who in the space of four months had successfully forced tens of thousands of Viennese Jews to emigrate:

Heydrich: It's one thing to remove the Jews from economic life, but at the end of the day the real problem is how to get the Jews out of Germany. In Vienna we set up a Jewish emigration bureau on the instructions of the Reich Commissioner,[10] through which we managed to get 50,000 Jews out of Austria, while only 19,000 Jews were removed from the rest of the Reich during the same period.

Göring: And how did you manage that?

Heydrich: We arranged it so that rich Jews who wanted to emigrate had to pay a levy to the local Jewish cultural association. That money, topped up with foreign exchange, was then used to get a number of the poor Jews out. The problem was not getting the rich Jews out, but getting rid of the Jewish rabble.

Göring: But look, have you really thought this through? Even if we get hundreds of thousands of the Jewish rabble out, we won't be any better off. Have you asked yourselves whether this route could end up costing us so much in foreign exchange that it is no longer viable?

Heydrich then estimated that the number who could still be forced to emigrate in this way would rapidly fall to a maximum of 8,000 to 10,000 a year. 'So that leaves a huge number of Jews still in the country,' he went on. 'As a result of the Aryanization programme and other restrictions the Jews will become unemployed, of course. What we shall then see is the proletarianization of the Jews that remain.' The conference participants discussed how these people were actually going to live: without work or any means of support, and largely isolated within the community, they would 'effectively end up living in a ghetto', which would create all kinds of new problems in terms of policing and feeding them. At this point the National-Conservative Reich Minister of Finance, Lutz Count Schwerin von Krosigk, spoke for the first time:

'What we really need to make sure of is that we don't end up keeping the social proletariat here. Looking after them will always be a terrible burden. So our aim must be what Heydrich has already said: to get as many of them off our hands as we possibly can.'

By now, however, it was already clear that the foreign exchange needed to finance the emigration programme could never be raised. Germany's export earnings did not cover the cost of importing the 'strategically important' raw materials needed for military purposes, or the food that accounted for 17 per cent of Germany's total

consumption. In order to drive as many Jews out of Germany as possible, despite the country's unfavourable balance of trade, Göring
instructed Heydrich on 24 January 1939 to proceed with the establishment of a 'Reich Bureau for Jewish Emigration'. Modelled on
Eichmann's Vienna initiative, the Bureau served as an umbrella organization for all the agencies involved, and was designed to accelerate
the pace of enforced emigration by coordinating procedures and
cutting out red tape. Strict instructions were issued to 'prioritize the
emigration of poorer Jews'. Heydrich was required to report back regularly to Göring on the work of the new Reich Bureau, and to obtain
his prior approval for any 'fundamental measures'.[11]

At the start of the conference on 12 November Göring had said
that the object was 'to get the Jews out of economic life and drive
them into debt'. After three and a half hours of discussion it was
obvious what the potential social and structural benefits for the
German economy were. It was also clear what problems it would
create for the social services budget and the foreign exchange balance
if a sizeable minority of the country's population were to be deprived
of its livelihood. So in formulating their aims the conference participants had for the moment reached an impasse. At this point Göring
hinted at a 'solution' that prefigured the later policy of extermination. If in the foreseeable future they found themselves embroiled in
a foreign-policy conflict – a war, in other words – then this would also
be the time 'to settle scores with the Jews in a big way'.

The fact that Göring reiterated his veto on demonstrations and
pogroms and committed the conference participants to 'stamping out
special operations [against the Jews] once and for all' is only seemingly a nonsense. The meeting had decided on an alternative to street
violence: for now 'the Reich [had] taken the matter in hand'. On 16
December, acting on instructions from Göring, Ministers Frick
(Interior) and Funk (Economic Affairs) briefed a meeting of Gauleiters
and senior regional government officials who had been summoned to
Berlin to receive the new policy line.[12]

Barely a month later, at the beginning of 1939, the mayor of Berlin
delivered a progress report. In the Reich capital the Aryanization of
the retail trade had 'got off to a brisk start'. Although the pace of
Aryanization had quickened after 12 November, his officials were
managing successfully to vet applicants in terms of their business credentials and aptitude, weeding out the impostors with no knowledge
of the business in question. The Chamber of Industry and Commerce
had advised him on this. 'I venture to hope', continues the 'Special

Report on the Elimination of Jewish Elements from the Retail Trade in Berlin', 'that the closure of two-thirds of all Jewish shops (…) will take the pressure off the established German retail trade.'[13] For every retail business approved for Aryanization (we read) there had been three or four Aryan applicants. In other regions of the German Reich the local authorities responsible for overseeing trade and industry were achieving similar results. In Düsseldorf only two out of sixty-four Jewish businesses were approved for Aryanization. And of the 5,822 Jewish workshops that had existed within Germany's 1937 borders only 345 were transferred to new ownership: all the rest were closed down.[14]

As a result of the 'exclusion of the Jews from economic life' – and specifically as a result of expropriation, professional debarment and the emigration of younger family members – more and more Jews were becoming dependent on public assistance. Their situation was further aggravated, of course, by the fact that Jewish welfare and charitable organizations were also being expropriated, so that they were less and less able to provide for the needs of an increasingly impoverished Jewish population.

Just three days after the conference in the Berlin Air Ministry the Dutch newspaper *Nieuwe Rotterdamsche Courant* commented in the following terms: 'Given the present shortage of labour, it cannot be very long before the pensioned-off Jews are denounced as "idle" Jews and parasites on the German body politic (…) Following the pattern of Russian Bolshevism, the enemies of the ruling regime will be put to work for the state in special forced labour camps.'[15]

In its annual report for 1938 the SD (security service) noted: 'The year under review saw the end of the Jewish problem in Germany, in so far as it can be resolved through legal and administrative process. (…) The only way for Jews to make a living now is to emigrate.'[16] The Foreign Office, meanwhile, spoke of 1938 as the 'year of destiny' for the German and Austrian Jews.[17]

The Vienna project

Following the annexation of Austria Göring, acting in his capacity as Commissioner for the Four-Year Plan, had given orders on 28 March 1938 that 'duly considered arrangements [were] to be made for the proper redirection of the Jewish economy'.[18] The emphasis was on the words 'considered' and 'proper', which were intended as a rebuke and a warning to those Austrian Nazis and anti-Semites who thought to exploit the confusion following 'Anschluss' in order to get rich quickly. Austria's economy was in a sorry state – at least in comparison with the flourishing German economy, which was then riding high on the back of full-scale rearmament: production capacities were not being fully utilized, unemployment was running at 30 per cent,[19] and productivity levels were low compared with Germany. When the customs barriers between Germany and Austria came down and German firms rushed to compete in the new market that had opened up in the south-east, the economy of the country that had been annexed – half willingly, half by force – was weakened still further. The only hope for the Austrian economy lay in a rapid and radical programme of rationalization that would bring the general level of production into line with that of the Reich.

On 23 April 1938 the Gauleiter of the Saar-Palatinate, Josef Bürckel, was appointed 'Reich Commissioner for the Reunification of Austria with the German Reich'. The appointment was made on economic grounds, for Bürckel had already demonstrated his credentials in 1935, when the Saarland was 'reincorporated ' into the Reich after years under French administration. Bürckel had succeeded in turning around a region that was still reeling under the impact of the world economic crisis and bringing about its rapid and painless convergence with the expanding economy of the Reich. A certain Dr Rudolf Gater had prepared the rationalization plans for him on that occasion. Gater had obtained his doctorate in Zurich in 1935 with a dissertation on the economic projections of the Harvard Institute, and was promptly despatched to Saarbrücken by the Reich Board for Industrial Rationalization (RKW). Bürckel was well pleased with the work done by his young expert in industrial rationalization, and in Vienna he availed himself of his services again. By the beginning of May the RKW had already established an 'Austria Office' in the Vienna Chamber of Commerce, with Rudolf Gater as its key staff member.

Since Bürckel used to consult his friend Karl Kaufmann, the Gauleiter of Hamburg, on all economic matters, a group of economic experts from Hamburg were also seconded to the Viennese project. They included the legal adviser to the Hamburg Senate, Dr Walter Emmerich, who served in Bürckel's 'Government and Economic Affairs' department. Emmerich used the 'elimination of Jewish elements from economic life' to create openings for Hamburg import and export firms, who would thus be able to use Vienna as their 'gateway to south-east Europe'. As the avowed champion of Hamburg business interests he saw to it that the Aryanization of the city's export firms was carried out as smoothly and expeditiously as possible. For beleaguered Hamburg merchants hard hit by Germany's isolation from world markets and the shortage of foreign exchange, Vienna was to become the springboard for expansion into southeast Europe. But to begin with, the newly annexed city appeared a thoroughly backward place to Emmerich. He and his colleagues bemoaned an export trade that was 'lacking in the necessary drive', a hopelessly antiquated Danube shipping fleet and the 'fragmentation' of trade, commerce, industry and banking. By Hamburg standards there was nothing that could be called a proper trading company in Vienna, only 'agents' acting for 'the buyers of the big Anglo-Saxon department stores'. Instead there was 'an abundance of small firms engaged in low-volume occasional exports to the surrounding region'. Most of these 'were owned by Jews, of course'. To change this situation completely seemed to Emmerich, Gater and many others a far from easy task, but a rewarding one none the less.[20]

In June 1938, only a month after his arrival in Vienna, Gater drafted a 'plan of action' on behalf of the RKW 'for the Aryanization of businesses in the retail shoe trade'. According to this document, around 250 of the 380 shoe shops in Vienna were owned by Jews. In order to 'tidy up' the retail shoe trade, according to Gater's provisional estimate, some eighty of the Jewish-owned shops would have to be closed. Time was pressing. The businesses in question were being boycotted by customers and suppliers alike. 'Aryan' Austrians interested in acquiring these businesses submitted 'a substantial number of Aryanization applications'. So Gater proposed that applications for the transfer of Jewish shoe shops to new ownership be processed 'under the direction of the RKW'. Having first secured the backing of Fischböck and the Four-Year Plan Authority, Gater wrote in peremptory terms to Bürckel's representative: 'Reference Aryanization of the retail shoe trade (...) Unless we hear from you to the contrary, we shall proceed forthwith to carry out our plan of action for achieving that end.'[21]

The shoe shops – and very soon every other kind of shop as well – earmarked for closure or 'Aryanization' were assessed by the RKW in terms of the following criteria: '(a) Turnover, type of business; (b) Commercial viability, location, competition; (c) Employees; (d) Inventory, stock valuation; (e) Financial standing, assets, liabilities (trade creditors, taxes, rents, wages, social security contributions, etc.; (f) Costs (annual rental, etc.); (g) Profit margin (allowing for actual or anticipated cut in profits); (h) Minimum turnover required for profitable trading; (i) Minimum capital required for the running of the business.'[22]

Applicants for the purchase of a business that the RKW had deemed worthy of Aryanization likewise had to submit to a thorough scrutiny of their business credentials and financial resources.

These early efforts by Gater to 'downsize' Vienna's retail and skilled trade sectors by using racist methods in the pursuit of unabashedly commercial ends must be seen against the background of the rapid growth in power and influence exercised by the RKW generally. On 9 June 1938 the Reich Minister of Economic Affairs presented a draft order 'on the role and function of the Reich Board for Industrial Rationalization', which in effect proposed the nationalization of a supervisory board that had hitherto been funded largely by private industry. The draft order stated that the RKW would be 'given a greater role in future [by the Reich Ministry of Economic Affairs] in the planning and coordination of all major joint initiatives aimed at improving the productivity of the German economy'. An eleven-point programme charted a strategy for 'optimizing the deployment of labour resources' and achieving pre-set targets in the war economy and the central management of raw materials. The 'major manpower resource', it was claimed, lay 'in the very large number of small business enterprises'; finding ways of achieving 'further increases in productivity' here was a top priority. 'Centralized control of the economy is only possible if the country's economic leadership knows at all times exactly what latent manpower resources can be tapped by raising the level of individual productivity. It will be the task of the RKW to establish a clear picture of these resources.'[23]

Gater's activities in Vienna were soon no longer confined to the retail shoe trade. On 3 June 1938 Bürckel's chief administrator, Dr Rudolf Kratz, wrote to the deputy head of the RKW, Dr Fritz Reuter, that the reconstruction and convergence of the Austrian economy could only succeed on the basis of careful planning. It was essential to 'weed out the dead wood in the present set-up'; the whole review had to be conducted 'speedily and thoroughly' – and 'the Reich Board for Industrial Rationalization is charged with the task of carrying it out'.[24] With the aid of a questionnaire the RKW obtained not only the usual facts and figures about the running of the business but also very detailed information about the circumstances of ownership and the 'demographic situation': the 'racial' and national composition of the workforce and proprietors.[25] Gater was proud of the fact that on the basis of the RKW's business census over 80 per cent of Jewish businesses had been shut down and only a small remainder – the most commercially viable enterprises, of course – had been transferred to new German and Austrian owners.[26]

Within Austria the RKW examined every major sector of trade, commerce and industry. By mid-May it was helping to set up the so-called 'Property Transaction Agency', whose staff of 460 carried out the 'Aryanization' or winding-up of Jewish businesses as part of the overall economic strategy for the country. The Property Transaction Agency was headed by the engineer Walter Rafelsberger, who became deputy president of the South-East Europe Society a year later.[27]

Within a few months the total number of retail businesses in Vienna had been halved. In the skilled trades 83 per cent of Jewish businesses were shut down, in industry 26 per cent and in the transport and haulage sector 82 per cent. Out of eighty-six Jewish banks only eight remained. In carrying out the closures the staff of the Property Transaction Agency, the RKW and the Auditing and Trust Company had regard not just to the profitability of the businesses and their economic prospects. They also looked at existing business provision within a particular locality and took account of 'future changes in the urban landscape' and proposed 'road realignment schemes'. Furthermore, an effort was made to ensure that retail outlets and workshops were 'evenly distributed (…) to meet the needs of the local community based on population densities'. Such was the aim: but the reality in 1938 was very different. The planners saw their project as an exercise in 'urban development'.[28]

The 'elimination of Jewish elements' from the Austrian economy went ahead quickly and according to plan. In August 1938 it became Adolf Eichmann's job to ensure that the people who had been robbed of their work, their property and their social rights disappeared as quickly as possible by simply leaving the country. Eichmann was in charge of the newly established Jewish Emigration Bureau in Vienna. It was here that he embarked on his career as an expert in deportations. It soon became apparent, however, that the poorer sections of the socially and economically marginalized Jewish population were staying behind in the city – including those who were the least mobile: the elderly and women with children. They stayed behind for financial reasons, for personal reasons, or because they could not meet the strict immigration requirements imposed by other countries. So by the middle of 1939 there were still 110,000 Jewish people living in Vienna who had to be dealt with somehow by the Property

Transaction Agency. This body had a duty 'to support the Jewish proletariat', using public money from the proceeds of Aryanization. At
the same time these proceeds were also used to fund 'loans to
approved National Socialist purchasers' of Jewish businesses, represented as 'compensation' for the injustices allegedly suffered by 'NS
veterans' in 'Vienna's Jewish-Socialist era'.[29] The loan fund functioned as an instrument of structural policy, and naturally it was also
used to satisfy Aryan cupidity. The less money was spent on supporting the impoverished Jewish minority, the more money was available
for these two purposes. So the search began for ways and means of
offloading as cheaply as possible those who had no money or did not
want to emigrate. At which point the officials involved hit upon a
promising idea: the construction of camps.

In October 1938, acting on behalf of the advisory board of the
Property Transaction Agency that he headed, Walter Rafelsberger
drafted 'a set of proposals for the effective implementation of the
policy for removing Jewish elements from society'. He suggested the
construction of three camps, each holding 10,000 Jews.[30] The inmates
would build the huts themselves, since this would keep the overall
cost down to around 10 million marks, as well as providing work for
the '10,000 or so unemployed Jews who are ready to hand'. The hutments were to be built well away from human habitation, in remote
sandy regions or marshlands. The man put in charge of this project
was Ernst Dürrfeld, who had been drafted in from the Saar-Palatinate
along with Bürckel, and was shortly to become a senior figure in the
administration of Warsaw. One of the principal difficulties he faced
was getting hold of barbed wire to fence in the camp compounds.
Overall responsibility for 'the management of the operation' was to
rest with the Property Transaction Agency. Rafelsberger was already
thinking in terms of some form of 'self-government' for the camps, of
the kind that was introduced in 1940 for the ghettos in occupied
Poland: 'The camp is to be owned and administered by an association
formed from the Jewish camp inmates.' Even the post of 'Commissar
for the Jewish quarter', who would later hold office in Warsaw, was
anticipated here: 'This association will be under the direction of a
commissar.' Rafelsberger wanted 'to exploit the labour of the Jews as
long as they remain in the country' and use them for 'public-service
projects'. For 'the supervision of the inmates in transit camps' it was
suggested that 'Party units be drafted in with the agreement of the
Gestapo'.

In the end these plans came to nothing. But five days after the outbreak of war the mayor of Vienna, Hermann Neubacher, contacted the Reich Minister of Economic Affairs and called for 'drastic action' to be taken against the Jewish unemployed in Vienna. He pointed out that they should be working, but declared that he was not in a position 'to make use of this Jewish rabble'. His suggestion: they 'must be dispersed across the length and breadth of the Reich in labour camps'. 'Such an initiative', he went on, 'would also relieve the pressure on the housing market, which is particularly difficult here in Vienna.' Rafelsberger seconded the proposal the very same day in a letter to Göring. He called for the same measures, but his tone was more strident: he spoke of 'forced labour camps', 'road-building works' and 'Jews in segregated work units'.[31] Negotiations had already taken place between the Reich Autobahn Directorate, the SS and the Ministry of Economic Affairs; these had dragged on for six months without producing any tangible results. In March the SS had announced that it was prepared to employ the Viennese Jews in the brickworks of Sachsenhausen or Mauthausen, but only on condition that they were kept as prisoners and that the cost of constructing the hutments did not have to be borne by the SS. The representative of the Reich Ministry of Economic Affairs, Dr Otto Donner, who soon afterwards moved to the Four-Year Plan Authority as a war economy specialist, supported this proposal with the argument that 'the use of Jewish labour in the *private brick industry* is out of the question. The point is that this is very heavy work, calling for specially selected human resources.'[32]

Within a very short space of time the authorities in Vienna were able to push through a programme of restructuring and rationalization at the expense of a minority, placate and consolidate the 'Aryan' middle-class grass roots, and at the same time export the model of the *Volksgemeinschaft* or national community. And if the Nazified Viennese (petite) bourgeoisie had not profited from the policy and practice of 'Entjudung' in quite the way they had hoped for in terms of 'compensation', at least they did not suffer serious hardship in the course of Austria's economic realignment with Germany. All the same, it sounded like a veiled threat when Rafelsberger announced that the rationalization programme was to be confined to the 'Jewish sector' just 'for the time being'. And indeed 'a structural review and readjustment of the Aryan sector too' was to follow in due course.[33] On 1 February 1939 he summed up the results so far: 'The large number of liquidations and the transfer of businesses to new locations as a consequence of Aryanization have eliminated overcrowding in

many branches of commerce and industry and created better conditions in the others. It has not been possible to carry out a complete
review of all trades, as the Aryan sector of the economy could not be
included in the present restructuring programme.' Nevertheless the
'elimination of Jewish elements from trade and commerce' had
'created conditions in the Ostmark [i.e. Austria] that contribute significantly to the strengthening of the national economy', and as such
were calculated to promote the 'economic integration' of Austria 'into
the Greater German sphere of influence'.[34]

The process of depriving the Jewish minority of its rights and property was referred to here in terms of 'restructuring' – a sociological
rather than a racist concept. Short-term disruptions of economic life,
even declining production figures, were accepted as the price of
achieving the long-term goals of greater competitiveness and a more
efficient economic structure. The regret implicit in the observation
that 'the Aryan sector of the economy could not be included in the
present restructuring programme' shows where things were headed:
forcing the Jewish minority out of business was merely the first (and
very easily accomplished) step in a grand design aimed at reordering
the entire social, demographic and economic life of the country.

So it was that in Vienna racist ideology and economic rationalization came together for the first time. The population at large was
shielded from the social consequences by the dispossession and social
exclusion of a minority.

A textbook example

That the approach pioneered in Vienna was viewed – and subsequently adopted – as a model for other occupied countries is evident
not least from the careers of the men who first developed the
concept. Hans Fischböck was appointed Commissioner for Trade
and Industry in the occupied Netherlands in June 1940, while
Eichmann's 'successes' in Vienna made him the key figure within the
SD for all matters relating to enforced emigration, resettlement and
'evacuation'. Sitting alongside Rafelsberger on the advisory board of
the Property Transaction Agency were the Gauleiter of Vienna, Odilo
Globocnik, a trained engineer and later head of the SS and police in
Lublin; Vienna's mayor, Hermann Neubacher, later to become
Commissioner for Trade and Industry in the South-East; and Hans
Kehrl, who saw himself as a crisis manager in the Third Reich and
represented both the Reich Ministry of Economic Affairs and Göring's

Four-Year Plan Authority on this board.[35] In May 1940 Walter Emmerich joined the government of occupied Poland as Minister for Economic Affairs; a month later he was followed by Gater, who became head of the newly formed 'Office for the Government General' within the RKW. The early memoranda and articles of these two men show the broad measure of agreement that already existed between them. The expropriation of the rights of a minority and the process of economic reconstruction were to go hand in hand, creating a common foundation for their collaboration. In February 1941 Emmerich commissioned the RKW to produce a special report; its subject: 'The economic profitability of the Jewish quarter in Warsaw'. In this report, as we shall show, Gater calculated 'the value of a Jew'. He offered one suggestion for 'balancing the books' of the Warsaw ghetto: 'A situation of undersupply could be allowed to develop, without regard for the consequences.' The RKW still exists in Germany today, except that the 'Reichskuratorium für Wirtschaftlichkeit' has become the 'Rationalisierungskuratorium der Deutschen Wirtschaft' – the Board for Rationalization of the German Economy. And Dr Gater was listed in the German *Who's Who* as one of the Federal Republic's leading experts on rationalization.

On 10 May 1941 the German Wehrmacht invaded the Netherlands. The occupation authority that was installed shortly thereafter was staffed mainly by Austrians, principal among them the Reich Commissioner for the Occupied Netherlands, Arthur Seyss-Inquart – formerly Reich Governor in Vienna. He summoned Hans Fischböck to Amsterdam to become his General Commissioner for Trade, Industry and Finance. In the Netherlands, as previously in Austria, Fischböck saw to it that the 'elimination of Jewish elements from economic life' was not primarily an exercise in lining the pockets of individual Germans – although of course it was that too – but had a serious economic 'ordering function'. In particular he was anxious to ensure that Jewish businesses were not handed over – as had happened in Austria – to persons selected mainly on political grounds, i.e. to indigenous or German National Socialists. Instead the applicants were not only required to pay a fair price for these businesses, but also had to have appropriate business credentials. With the aid of various agencies engaged in the monitoring and control of economic activity,[36] Fischböck's department sought to avoid the 'mistakes' that had been made in Vienna and apply the lessons that had been learned there to the situation in the Netherlands. One of these monitoring agencies was the Audit Office. As of 22 October 1940 all Jewish businesses had to be registered with this organization. Following a period of preparation the process of 'Aryanization' duly began in March 1941, a few days after the general strike in Amsterdam had been crushed.

Erich Rajakowitsch, a close collaborator of Eichmann's, now proceeded to set up a 'Central Bureau for Jewish Emigration' which was likewise modelled on its Viennese predecessor. Only a handful of Dutch Jews were able to emigrate, however. Since the Germans were at pains to maintain a semblance of legality in their pursuit of Aryanization, their immediate aim was to secure the emigration of those Jewish businessmen who could not otherwise be forced to sell up at this stage. The SS proposed that exit visas be issued specifically to the proprietors of those businesses 'that are of special interest to the Four-Year Plan Authority and other agencies involved in the work of economic integration'.[37]

In contrast to Austria, the productivity of the Dutch economy was on a par with that of Germany, so when it came to 'Aryanization' interest focused mainly on the creation of capital links between the two countries (i.e. the investment of German capital in Dutch companies); the rationalization of the economy took second place. Göring had issued an 'Order on the formation of capital links with the occupied western territories' in order 'to create a fait accompli as soon as possible ahead of the peace treaties that will have to be signed'.[38] The Reich Ministry of Economic Affairs set up a separate capital links unit within the special department for 'Preparation and Organization' headed by Gustav Schlotterer.[39] In the case of Holland, and more especially Belgium, the policy was '(to) concentrate on really promising and economically worthwhile projects'.[40] In Holland the list was headed by the four 'global concerns' Shell, Philips, Unilever and Algemeene Kunstzijde Unie, but it also included big players in heavy industry and armaments such as the Fokker aircraft works.[41]

'Aryanization' was not the only means of 'penetrating the Dutch economy with German capital', especially as Unilever was the only one of these concerns that was classed as 'Jewish'. But it did offer the possibility of a 'more broad-based penetration' of the country's economy (through Aryanization of the small to medium-sized business sector), and as such came into its own where the German strategy was resisted or rejected by business owners in the occupied territories. For it was very much in the interests of the Reich Ministry of Economic Affairs that Dutch and Belgian entrepreneurs should respond positively to the idea of capital interlinking. But a positive response was more likely to be forthcoming if 'penetration of the market'[42] was achieved at the expense of Jewish business owners. As in the Protectorate of Bohemia and Moravia, and later in south-east Europe, German firms sought to use 'Entjudung' as a means of gaining a foothold in Dutch markets,[43] with encouragement and 'guidance' from the Reich Ministry of Economic Affairs.

At the same time Fischböck's experts managed to combine Aryanization with a programme of economic rationalization – even in Holland. Of the 21,000 Jewish businesses and workshops registered by the Audit Office, 11,000 were transferred to new ownership and the remaining 10,000 were dissolved, their inventory and stocks sold off to Aryan competitors.

Most of the proceeds from the sale of Jewish firms, houses and property were transferred to the Property Management and Pensions Corporation (VVRA). Fischböck and Seyss-Inquart viewed the VVRA as the 'big pot'[44] in which all the Jewish assets were collected – amounting to 350 million Dutch guilders in all.[45] The persecution of the Jews was also financed from this fund: the security police were reimbursed by the VVRA for expenses incurred in their 'work relating to the persecution of the Jews'. This organization also paid bounty money to informants who revealed the whereabouts of Jews who had gone into hiding,[46] and financed the enlargement of the de Vught transit camp for Jews, the Westerbork camp and the connecting rail link. But then the materials only needed to be rented: when the construction contract was placed in July 1942 it had already been decided that the railway tracks would be taken up again a year later, by which time all of Holland's Jews were due to have been deported.[47] To pay for the construction of the concentration camp in Ommen, the banking house of Lippmann & Rosenthal advanced the sum of 150,000 guilders from the assets of dissolved Jewish associations and foundations. The Jewish Council in Amsterdam received grants amounting to 40,000 guilders from this fund, which contained a total of 11 million guilders. The entire persecution of the Jews in Holland was 'financed from beginning to end with Jewish money'.[48]

While Jewish shareholders and company owners, skilled tradesmen and merchants were dispossessed by the 'Aryanization' of their businesses, ordinary Jewish workers generally lost their jobs. Either they were made redundant when the businesses they worked for were closed down, or they were dismissed by the trustees who now replaced the former owners. In October 1941 Seyss-Inquart published an ordinance that broadly prohibited the employment of Jewish workers except with special permission.[49]

The expulsion of the Jewish minority from Holland's economic life soon left the German occupiers facing the same problem they had encountered in Vienna: the Jewish population very quickly became impoverished and dependent upon welfare. Even if it had been possible to fund the welfare payments from plundered Jewish assets, this would have constituted a debit entry in the balance sheet of 'Aryanization'. The proposals for dealing with the problem had likewise been tried out in Austria already. These required emigrants not only to leave behind a portion of their wealth and assets to fund the care of the poor, but also 'to take a certain number of penniless Jews with them'.[50]

The Four-Year Plan

On 31 July 1941 Hermann Göring wrote to Heydrich and instructed him to prepare 'a complete solution to the Jewish question within the German sphere of influence in Europe'. The order was written under the letterhead of the president of the Reich Defence Council and the Commissioner for the Four-Year Plan. It is commonly claimed that Heydrich took the initiative himself, getting Eichmann to draw up the order and Göring to sign it. Even if this was the case, as Eichmann's later testimony in Jerusalem asserted, the various options for the 'final solution of the Jewish question' had certainly been discussed in Göring's Four-Year Plan Authority as well. In the period from 1938 to 1941 the Four-Year Plan Authority was involved in all the key decisions relating to anti-Jewish policy, the conduct of the war and the policies of expulsion and annihilation in eastern Europe. Its academic staff saw themselves as a coordinating cadre, an intelligent power centre, an elite that drew up plans, inspired and motivated – but wherever possible delegated the implementation of those plans and the associated administrative tasks to other agencies. The Four-Year Plan Authority had been set up in October 1936[51] in order to prepare Germany militarily and economically for the war, and in so doing 'to engage in the political debate aimed at resolving the question of national spheres of influence'.[52] The basis for this was a memorandum drafted by Hitler himself in 1936, in which he set out 'the following mission objectives': 'I. The German army must be ready for action in four years' time. II. The German economy must be on a war footing in four years' time.'[53]

Göring's newly created command centre for economic and social policy was based around a 'small central office' with a permanent staff of little more than a hundred. Their role was to oversee the work of the individual economic departments and to offer suggestions to Göring as appropriate 'for the coordination of individual projects, the remedying of deficiencies and the elimination of danger-points'.[54] It was here – and not by Göring himself – that the crucial directives for the running of the war economy were formulated. Göring was one of the most powerful men in the National Socialist state, and yet he was 'totally dependent on the advice and policies of the "experts" and "advisers"'.[55] At the conference on 12 November 1938 he had described himself as 'not sufficiently versed' when it came to evaluating economic plans in detail.[56]

Göring's function was to make it easier to overcome moral inhibitions and exceed the limits established by legal norms in order to attain political ends. How that was to happen in specific instances, what priorities were to be set and what procedures were to be adopted – such matters were decided by his experts and by the undersecretaries from various government departments, who sat together on the general council of the Four-Year Plan Authority.

The Authority's brief was to create the right conditions for 'an expansion of the German sphere of influence … in order to supplement the country's own economic resources from outside as necessary'.[57] The architects of the Four-Year Plan Authority presupposed two things: 'political action that would extend the boundaries of the national state' and the systematic control and direction of the economy.[58] They saw themselves as an 'economic high command' – and emphatically not as a cumbersome bureaucracy. They were not interested in taking the detailed decisions 'with rule and compass'. Their task, rather, was to oversee the big picture, and to guarantee the necessary 'flexibility of programmes' in the face of the 'frequent abrupt changes of mind by the top political leadership'.[59]

The Four-Year Plan Authority was designed to prepare the German economy for the planned war, to streamline and rationalize it to that end, to ensure an adequate supply of foreign exchange and manpower, and to regulate the relationship between wages and prices.[60] It was to monitor the composition of the population, having regard both to its skills training and qualifications and to its capacity for work duties. And finally it was to make sure that the social charge on the state – i.e. the cost of providing welfare support for people who could no longer work – fell rather than rose.

The ideal of an effective command centre was realized to a very high degree in the Four-Year Plan Authority. Here efficiency and professional expertise counted for more than seniority and the bureaucratic pecking order. So it is not surprising that many of the managers who sat at the levers of power were still very young. Barely thirty years old by the end of the war, most of them moved on to a second career without any difficulty at all. Ten years after the defeat of Nazi Germany they were still so enthusiastic about their failed collective enterprise that one of them could write, on the occasion of a nostalgic weekend reunion of former colleagues: 'My one and only wish is that succeeding generations might once again be entrusted with tasks such as those that we were privileged to fulfil with upright hearts, impassioned energy and painstaking labour.'[61]

Another member of this circle was Otto Donner, born in 1902. He had trained at the Berlin Institute for Economic Research and at the World Economic Institute in Kiel. From April 1940 to 1943 he worked as personal assistant and close confidant to undersecretary Erich Neumann, the man who attended the Wannsee conference as Göring's representative. Throughout this period Donner also headed the research bureau for the war economy within the Four-Year Plan Authority – of which more later. One of his tasks in this capacity was to devise a long-term strategy designed to force south-east Europe into a position of absolute economic dependency. Donner was one of the Four-Year Plan's leading experts on war economies and how to run them. By October 1945 at the latest he was working for the American occupation authorities, who put him in charge of the personnel and administration department of the Economic Division. In 1947 he became a US citizen and a professor in Washington. From 1952 onwards Otto Donner was deputy executive director for the Federal Republic of Germany and Yugoslavia at the International Monetary Fund, and from 1954 until 1968 he was German executive director at the World Bank.

In the summer of 1939, three months before the German invasion of Poland, Donner, then still an assistant secretary in the Ministry of Economic Affairs, calculated the financial requirements of the war. The costs, he warned, could 'escalate to the point where they are not far short of the general national income in peacetime – and they may even exceed it'.[62] But the costs of the war should on no account be financed by inflation, i.e. by simply increasing the money supply. Donner spelled out the facts of economic life: 'The maximum proportion of the national income from employment that the state can use for its own needs is manifestly equal to the difference between the total national income from employment and the subsistence requirements of the civilian population.' From this proposition he derived a 'basic equation for the economy in wartime': '$V_{st} = P - V_z$'.[63] In other words: 'Maximum government consumption = national product – civilian subsistence requirements'. According to this principle, the state could increase its war expenditure in inverse proportion to the financial resources consumed by the civilian population. Thus far Donner's arithmetic and the formula he devised were pretty much a statement of the obvious. But having concluded that the 'additional financial requirement of the war' could not be met by increased economic output, he pointed to 'the need for a drastic curtailment of civilian requirements'. To his mind there was only one question that really mattered: 'How far can the consumption of the civilian population be cut back in the event of war?'[64] One way of cutting back on demand was to lower living standards to the level they had fallen to during the world depression of the early 1930s, which would free up 13 billion Reichsmarks (RM). Donner came up with these figures himself, and called for a propaganda drive to instil the necessary spirit of self-denial: 'The willingness of the nation to tighten its belt and endure privations is directly related to its mental attitude towards sacrifice and struggle.'

The other option for restricting demand from the civilian population was not spelled out by Donner, although it was implicit in what he was saying. This was the option of distributing goods and services in such a way that the productivity of the working population was maintained on the one hand, while on the other those sections of the population regarded as 'useless' or 'racially inferior' had to pay a disproportionately high – and for them rapidly fatal – contribution to the costs of the war.

Similar arguments were invoked to justify the annihilation of the mentally ill and the so-called 'antisocial elements'. The countless thousands of murders that began a few months after the outbreak of war were costed out in terms of the food saved, the hospital beds freed up and the institutional vacancies created. The murder of 70,000 mentally ill patients in the period up to August 1941 yielded a clear profit, according to a statistician who was specifically assigned to do the costings. Projecting the same trend over a ten-year period, the state had saved nearly a billion marks in so-called 'dead costs', freeing up these resources for other purposes, namely the financing of the war.[65] Such methods for selectively 'cutting back on civilian demand' soon became an important regulatory instrument of German financial and social policy in time of war, employed not only against 'surplus' persons in Germany, but also, and in particular, against ethnic minorities and certain population groups in eastern Europe.

As Blitzkrieg yielded victory after victory, culminating in the preparations for the attack on the Soviet Union, the workload and importance of the Four-Year Plan Authority grew with every passing month – to the rapturous delight of its economic strategists: 'In its dynamic forward thrust the Wehrmacht has opened up new horizons for us, giving us freedom of movement and a free hand throughout the major portion of the European continent.' Admittedly this had made their task of economic planning 'easier in some ways, more difficult in others'.[66]

The experts – in this case Otto Donner – saw problems ahead in the form of a deterioration in the food-supply situation. The German war planners had reckoned from the outset with the British naval blockade. The intensive agricultures of Germany, Denmark and the Netherlands were heavily dependent on the import of animal feedstuffs from overseas. At the same time Donner did not believe that the shortfall could be made up by reliance on the backward, inefficient agricultures of south-east and eastern Europe. The reserves of food that existed there 'on paper' could not be tapped during the war because the 'heavy investment of labour and materials' that would be required 'would not bear fruit for many years'. Meanwhile, Donner pointed out, the war was forcing those regions of Europe with a tradition of intensive agriculture to adopt increasingly extensive forms of cultivation. In the long term, therefore, even areas that normally produced a surplus were bound to end up having to import produce.[67] This analysis, as we shall show, formed one of the economic cornerstones of the plans for war against the Soviet Union.

With the outbreak of war the Four-Year Plan Authority began to arrogate more and more power to itself at the expense of the Reich Ministry of Economic Affairs. This established the claim to leadership of the ministerial undersecretaries who sat on the general council of the Four-Year Plan Authority – not ministers, be it noted, but undersecretaries, representing all the key government departments involved in economic and social policy-making. They justified the expansion of their power by the need 'to direct all our resources towards the conduct of an extended war'.[68] Apart from Göring the general council consisted of eight undersecretaries, the Reich Commissioner for Price Setting, General Georg Thomas, who headed the German High Command's War Economy Office, and a representative of the NSDAP. Where necessary, leading experts and senior officials from the Ministry of Finance and the Reichsbank could be drafted in to assist the council. This structure confirmed the supremacy of the undersecretaries, who, unlike the ministers for whom they worked, saw themselves as specialists and technocrats. They reported back constantly to the general council about what was going on in their ministries, and as a body they were also empowered to initiate 'necessary measures'. As members of the general council the undersecretaries actually outranked their own ministers.[69]

The undersecretaries who sat on the general council of the Four-Year Plan Authority were as follows: Herbert Backe (Food and Agriculture), Friedrich Landfried (Ministry of Economic Affairs), Friedrich Syrup (Ministry of Labour), Wilhelm Kleinmann (Ministry of Transport), Friedrich Alpers (Reich Forestry Office) and Wilhelm Stuckart (Ministry of the Interior). The remaining two undersecretaries, Paul Körner and Erich Neumann, represented the Four-Year Plan Authority itself.

At the same time Backe, Landfried, Syrup, Kleinmann and Stuckart each headed their own business unit within the Four-Year Plan Authority, mirroring the remits of their respective ministries. This put them in a position to recruit experts for the work of the Authority from among their own ministerial officials. In this way they were able to underpin their independence from their ministers through personal staff loyalties and thus bypass the ministerial hierarchy.

The de facto chairman of the general council of the Four-Year Plan Authority was Paul Körner, Göring's closest and most intimate colleague. Born in Saxony in 1893, he had joined the NSDAP back in 1926. Since 1933 Körner had been undersecretary at the Prussian Ministry of State, invested with the rank of flight lieutenant in the air force reserve and that of Obergruppenführer (equivalent to a general) in the SS. He acted as Göring's deputy in all important capacities – and as the real chairman of the Four-Year Plan Authority and its general council. It was Körner who from January 1941 onwards began to push for the rapid modernization of German industry. He argued that the size of the workforce was ultimately limited, and that 'the continuing rationalization of German industry and the introduction of modern technology [are] to be seen as a task of the highest importance'. That presupposed adequate research and training facilities, but also 'generous new social policies (...) aimed at maintaining and enhancing the productive capacities of each and every German'. In the general council Körner laboured assiduously to 'reconcile disparate interests with tact and understanding'.[70]

Körner delegated wherever he could, and once plans had been formulated he was always happy 'to leave [their implementation] to the individual departments concerned'. But above all he was a strong believer in the integration of economic and social policy: 'He always had a clear and just appreciation of the social impact of any measures. A profound awareness of the larger social context and an understanding of socio-political necessities were among his abiding characteristics.' After 1939 Körner's workload rapidly assumed 'continental European dimensions': 'From the summer of 1941 onwards Germany was confronted with new economic tasks in the East on a grand scale, in the planning and execution of which the undersecretary – aided by the newly formed "Economic Policy Unit for the East" – was heavily involved.'[71] As Göring's representative he chaired the general council of the Four-Year Plan Authority, which from February 1941 onwards was devising a military and economic strategy that deliberately envisaged the death by starvation of millions of people in the Soviet Union. It was Körner, and not the Minister of Labour technically responsible for such matters, who signed the 'Order concerning the employment of Jews' published in the Reich Law Gazette. The order was dated 3 October 1941, a matter of days before the first deportations of German Jews 'to the East' began. It effectively stripped all those who were due to be deported for forced labour and extermination of any protection under the general labour laws.[72] In 1943 Körner actually visited the extermination camp at Auschwitz.[73] In 1944, when the Four-Year Plan had long since become an irrelevance, the political scientist Franz Neumann, who had emigrated to the USA, named 'Paul Körner, undersecretary in the office for the Four-Year Plan', as one of the National Socialists who 'wield enormous power because they act as a link between the Party and the remaining sections of the ruling class'.[74] The US military tribunal in Nuremberg sentenced him to a jail term of fifteen years. He was pardoned in 1951, and received a state pension until his death in 1957.

The second man behind Göring was Erich Neumann. He was born in 1892, and joined both the NSDAP and the SS in 1933. A lawyer and economist by training, he had gained administrative experience in the Prussian Ministry of Trade and was regarded as a 'quiet worker'.[75] Appointed undersecretary and deputy to Körner in 1938, he dealt with foreign-exchange matters within the Four-Year Plan Authority as well as with 'special tasks of a general economic nature'. As such his remit also included special responsibility for 'Jewish affairs' – i.e. for all economic and foreign-exchange matters arising out of the enforced emigration programme. It was on the strength of this authority that Neumann represented Göring, and hence the general council of the Four-Year Plan Authority, at the Wannsee conference on 20 January 1942.

From the time the Four-Year Plan Authority was constituted the experts who worked there viewed the business of preparing the economy for war not just in terms of long-term structural planning and centralization. When it came to husbanding scarce resources they also made demographic selection into a guiding principle. For years the Four-Year Plan Authority played a pivotal role in the policy of discrimination, marginalization and persecution conducted against the Jewish minority. In March 1938 the Commissioner for the Four-Year Plan for the newly annexed Austria issued a directive stating that 'the Jews [are] to be eliminated from economic life too as quickly as possible'.[76] On 26 April Göring, acting in the same capacity, issued the 'Order concerning the registration of Jewish assets'.[77] On 16 December 1938, five weeks after the Air Ministry conference referred to earlier, a meeting 'on the subject of the Jewish question' took place in the Ministry of the Interior. Its purpose was to commit all levels of the German state administration to the findings of the November 12 conference. It was noted in the minutes that 'the Commissioner for the Four-Year Plan' had now 'taken central charge' of Jewish policy and put in hand the 'expulsion of the Jews from active business life and their transformation to pensioner status', together with 'a large-scale campaign to promote emigration'.[78]

On 24 January 1939 Göring instructed Heydrich to proceed with the establishment of the Reich Bureau for Jewish Emigration. Two days after the capitulation of Poland, on 19 September 1939, the Council of Ministers for the Defence of the Reich and the chief functionaries of the Four-Year Plan, the undersecretaries, together with Heydrich and the heads of the various Reich Ministries under the chairmanship of Göring, debated 'the question of the population of the future Polish protectorate and the relocation of Jews living in Germany'.[79] Two days after that Heydrich issued guidelines for the *Einsatzgruppen* (special units) of the security police on 'the Jewish question in the occupied territory'. As 'the first step towards the final objective' he named 'the concentration of the Jews (...) in the larger towns and cities'. Amongst other things the commanders of the special units were instructed to report back on the Aryanization of Jewish businesses and on the possibility of 'converting businesses to really essential or strategically important production or other work of importance to the Four-Year Plan'. Among the select group to whom this order was copied was undersecretary Neumann of the Four-Year Plan Authority, who was directly concerned with the 'Jewish question'.[80]

On 12 February 1940 Göring chaired a high-level meeting on resettlement policy in the newly conquered 'East'. Those present included 'all the key figures from the Four-Year Plan Authority'. At this meeting Göring criticized the random deportation of people from the 'annexed eastern territories' to the Government General, carried out without clearance from the authorities concerned – particularly as 'the Poles [are] needed as agricultural workers'. These words put Heinrich Himmler (who was also present) firmly in his place in the presence of middle-ranking section chiefs, even though he conceded at this stage, apropos of 'the resettlement of the Jews', that 'this resettlement should be put in hand according to plan'.[81]

Six weeks later he withdrew this concession. On 23 March 1940 Göring prohibited the deportation of Jews to the Government General, thereby ensuring that the arguments of the economic experts – who wanted to turn the Government General into a productive 'satellite of the Reich' instead of a dumping-ground for deportees – would prevail, at least for the time being. Meanwhile, however, the Four-Year Plan Authority had set up its own organization, the Central Trust Agency for the East, which expropriated all Jewish property in the 'annexed eastern territories' with the executive assistance of the SS. The consequence of Göring's decision was that the Jewish minority in the newly annexed Warthegau was shut up in ghettos from now on. Before long the deportation experts were looking around for alternative dumping-grounds: the conquest of France gave fresh impetus to plans to deport the Jewish population to Madagascar.

On 1 April 1940 a meeting had taken place in the Reich Ministry of the Interior at which representatives of the Four-Year Plan and the Ministries of Finance and Food, as well as the head of the Central Trust Agency for the East, had discussed the establishment of the ghetto in Lódź. It was agreed that the ghetto should ideally be viewed as a temporary solution only, and that 'the first priority in any event is to evacuate the Jews from Lódź'.[82] During the summer months the

Foreign Ministry devised a scheme in conjunction with the Central
Office for the Security of the Reich, the Four-Year Plan Authority and
the Ministry of Propaganda, whereby Jews living within the German
sphere of control were to be deported to Madagascar. The Four-Year
Plan Authority was responsible for the economic management of the
project, from the confiscation of Jewish property and assets to the
establishment of a special bank and the calculation of the transport
costs.[83]

Against the background of preparations for war with the Soviet
Union General Georg Thomas of the War Economy Office presented
a memorandum on 13 February 1941 which examined 'the effects on
the war economy of an operation in the East'. He discussed his conclusions – probably that same day – with Göring's undersecretaries
Neumann and Körner.[84] All three men were members of the Four-
Year Plan's general council. At the instigation of another member of
the Four-Year Plan staff, Carl Krauch, who was commissioner for
special aspects of chemical production, Göring sent an order to
Himmler on 26 February 1941 which called for the Jewish population
to be evacuated from the town of Auschwitz. At the same time
Göring prohibited the deportation of Polish construction workers
from this region;[85] for there were plans to establish an industrial
enclave here, mainly for chemical production, at a safe distance from
enemy bombing. On several occasions in May and June the general
council of the Four-Year Plan Authority discussed the problem of
feeding the population of occupied Europe, working on the assumption that 'X millions' of people in the Soviet Union would be deliberately left to starve. On 14 July the Economic Policy Unit for the East,
which reported to Göring and shared many of its staff with the Four-
Year Plan, called for the 'early ghettoization' of the Jews in those
areas of the Soviet Union that had been occupied just a few days previously, in order to 'give the trustworthy local non-Jews a look-in'.[86]
On 31 July 1941 Körner had a meeting with the aforementioned
General Thomas to discuss 'the question of organization in Russia'.
The outcome was an announcement of Göring's decision: 'Quarter
the Jews in barracks and put them to work in segregated work
columns.'[87] At the same time undersecretary Backe confirmed at a
meeting of the Economic Policy Unit for the East that 'only very
limited supplies [are] available' to feed the urban population in the
occupied parts of the USSR.[88] Six weeks later, with logical consistency,
Göring formulated a strategy in which starvation became a recognized method of waging war: 'For economic reasons it is not

advisable to take large cities by storm. It is better to encircle and besiege them.'[89]

In the spring of 1942, following the end of the Blitzkrieg campaigns, the Four-Year Plan Authority was forced to surrender most of its power to Albert Speer's Ministry, which in the face of impending defeat was charged with concentrating all the nation's industrial capacities on the production of armaments and other essential war needs. Prior to this, however, Göring and his team had been reviewing industrial efficiency and mapping out a new programme of rationalization. Göring summed up their aim on 7 November 1941: 'In a nutshell: German industry must be made as efficient and productive as America's.' A number of managers at the Four-Year Plan Authority took on other, equally important posts in the period that followed. It was due not least to this that their policy line subsequently prevailed in all the key planning bodies. The newly formed central planning committee within Speer's Ministry consisted of three men: the Reich Minister for Armaments and War Production Albert Speer, Göring's undersecretary at the Air Ministry Erhard Milch, and Paul Körner again. The head of the planning office at the Four-Year Plan Authority, Hans Kehrl, was put in charge of Speer's planning office.

In contrast to the traditional type of bureaucratic and inflexible ministerial official, these undersecretaries and their assistants were able to combine widely divergent social policy and economic considerations with the 'exigencies of war' and a far-sighted structural policy. In other words, they did not look at things from the usual blinkered departmental perspective. No expedient was taboo for them, provided only that it did not threaten the 'morale' of the German people. Their professional competence and their capacity for interdisciplinary thinking also meant that they could overlook the difference between the planning intelligentsia – i.e. the people who actually came up with the ideas – and the more or less anti-intellectual Nazi leadership, to the point where both groups could get along reasonably well. This made it considerably easier to transgress the limits imposed by morality and legal constraints: force of circumstances legitimized any and every means. The fact that the Wannsee conference was also referred to internally as the 'meeting of undersecretaries' is symptomatic of this tendency. The general tone and the technocratic, 'morality-free' style of argument adopted by this body are exemplified in the minutes of the meeting of 2 May 1941, which laid down the economic principles on which the war against the Soviet Union would be fought. The minutes are cited here in full:

1. The war can only be continued if Russia supplies the food for the entire German armed forces in the third year of the war.

2. Millions of people will undoubtedly starve if the food supplies necessary to meet our needs are extracted from the country.

3. The top priorities are oil-seeds and oilcake, followed by grain; these must be gathered up and shipped out of the country. The available fats and meat will probably be consumed by our troops.

4. Industry will be allowed to resume work only in those sectors where there are shortages, e.g.

> Plants manufacturing vehicles and transport equipment,
> plants supplying basic industrial needs (ironworks),
> textile works,
> selected armaments factories, i.e. only those needed to relieve
> production bottlenecks in Germany.
> Repair workshops for the use of the armed forces will need to
> be opened up in large numbers, of course.

5. Special detachments must be deployed to secure the wide tracts of territory between the main supply routes; the Reich Labour Service or reserve army units could be drafted in, perhaps. It will be necessary to identify those areas that are particularly important and therefore in special need of protection.[90]

Military security, repair workshops, and the death of millions left to starve: the assembled undersecretaries discussed it all in the same breath, and with the same technocratic detachment.

CHAPTER 2

LOOKING TO THE EAST

Ever since the assumption of power by the National Socialists, economic experts had been working not just on the implementation of 'Entjudung' and the rationalization of the German economy, but also on a new economic order for Europe under German control. In the name of this 'new order' they drew up plans for breaking Great Britain's international dominance and curbing France's influence. Their purpose was to reverse the outcome of the First World War, and in particular its economic legacy. The work and ideas of Anton Reithinger are typical of this endeavour. Reithinger was an expert on eastern Europe and head of the economic research department of I.G. Farben. This was the largest department at the company's Berlin head office. Its information-gathering went far beyond the immediate interests of a chemical concern to embrace any social, political and economic data that might be useful for the economic and political domination of other countries. The data and reports proved of inestimable value to German ministries and research institutes. By the outbreak of war at the latest Reithinger's department was operating as a cross between an espionage centre and a political information office, serving various government agencies and the Wehrmacht in addition to the concern's own internal interests.[1]

The collapse of Europe's foreign trade system in the world economic crisis (wrote Reithinger in 1934) 'has put the problem of a general reordering of European trade relations back at the top of the agenda'.[2] This essay was the last in a series of three. In the two preceding pieces Reithinger had looked at Europe's agricultural system and its demographic situation. When he wrote of 'a common destiny shared by the nations of Europe' and of 'a broad communality of vital interests among the nations living in continental Europe', without which a political and economic consolidation of Europe would not be possible,[3] he was referring to the development and entrenchment of a hierarchy: the countries of south-east Europe were to be cast in the role of suppliers of food and raw materials to Germany, permitted to industrialize only to the point where sales of German industrial exports would not suffer in consequence. But before the European agricultural states could undertake 'the intensive production of the agricultural products we lack', Reithinger went on, one problem remained to be solved. Much more serious than the protracted agrarian crisis that had affected the whole of Europe for many years was 'the rural overpopulation of the entire eastern half of Europe'. In eastern and south-east Europe, he wrote, the population density per square kilometre of agricultural land was twice as high as it was in western, central and northern Europe. On top of that the climate and soil conditions there were much less favourable and the land was farmed extensively rather than intensively. For these reasons yields per unit area in eastern and south-east Europe were 'only about a third to a half of those obtained in central and western European countries'. Agricultural productivity per head of the rural population, he claimed, was only one-sixth to a quarter of the figure for central and western Europe. He summarized the overall picture as follows: 'Under these conditions the entire eastern half of Europe is characterized for the most part by extreme poverty and a level of purchasing power among the rural population that is unimaginably low by our standards. This also explains why – in the absence of long-term capital aid from abroad – there has so far been very little in the way of industrial development here.'[4] But the efforts of foreign entrepreneurs to invest in Poland or extend credits to the government would be severely curtailed, not least by the 'unresolved conditions in central Europe' – in other words, the unstable political situation in 1934 – and would in any event be repeatedly undermined by continuing population growth.[5]

I.G. Farben had sent Reithinger on a fact-finding tour to Poland in 1932, and here too he had encountered overpopulation, low agricultural productivity and a lack of purchasing power.[6] In the report on Poland prepared by the concern's economic research department in 1938 the main focus was once again on population issues. According to the report, Poland's population had grown by 27 per cent in seventeen years. This would produce 'an untenable situation in the long term' and the risk of serious 'economic and social upheaval'. 'Possible options for solving this problem' were seen 'in an intensification of agriculture on the one hand and in the siphoning-off of surplus unemployed manpower into an expanding industrial sector on the other. In practice Poland's lack of capital resources presents an almost insurmountable obstacle to the implementation of such a programme.'[7]

Two years later an 'overpopulated' and 'underdeveloped' Poland was forcibly assigned a key role in German plans for a new European order. From the German point of view, the creation of a successful European economic system depended on the modernization and rationalization of the Polish economy, its adaptation to the interests of German capital, the development of the transport infrastructure – but above all on the elimination of rural overpopulation.

Poland on the threshold of industrialization

'Poland: Key to Europe' is the title of a study by the American government adviser Raymond Leslie Buell which appeared on the eve of the Second World War.[8] Poland then stood on the threshold of industrialization. Construction contracts for infrastructure projects and industrial plant would have offered plenty of opportunities for well-capitalized US firms, if the tense internal political situation and the growing threat from Germany and the Soviet Union had not made the country's economic future look increasingly uncertain. According to Buell's analysis, Poland in the second half of the 1930s stood on the brink of civil war. The only way in which the dilemma could be resolved, concluded the American economist, who had travelled to Poland specially from Washington, was by reorganizing the European economy, with Poland as its linchpin – the 'Key to Europe'.

Many of the crisis symptoms catalogued by Buell are described in similar terms in other contemporary studies by British, French, German or Polish writers.[9] On one point in particular they were all in agreement: Poland's biggest problem was 'rural overpopulation'.

Poland had been partitioned and ruled for more than a hundred years by Prussia, Austria and Russia, and it was only after the First World War that a Polish national state came into being for the first time. The individual regions had reached different stages of development, the country lacked an integrated infrastructure, and its traditional trade relations with Vienna, St Petersburg and Berlin were suspended. Only some two-thirds of the population thought of themselves as Polish; the remaining third belonged to one or other of various minorities. In 1919 the Polish parliament had passed a land reform bill under pressure from the farmers, and in order to prevent the Russian Revolution from spilling over into Poland. But in the years that followed, the reforms were only tentatively implemented, and many large landowners simply circumvented them.[10] So there emerged a class of smallholders who had to get by with less and less land as their inheritance became increasingly divided. In the 1930s Poland's agrarian planners – in common with their colleagues in other eastern European countries – regarded National Socialist legislation on the hereditary tenure of farmland as a model of its kind. It was designed to sweep away traditional agrarian structures and replace them with a 'strong farming middle class', which would provide the regime with its loyal, and above all productive, grass roots.[11] The agrarian reform legislation of 1937 represented a first step in this direction.[12] When Buell published his study, 70 per cent of Poland's population were making their living from agriculture. The country's agricultural land was either concentrated in the hands of a few large landowners or divided up into tiny parcels. To call their owners 'smallholders' would already be overstating it. In many cases they had to travel for several hours from home to reach their fields.[13]

According to Buell, four million Polish 'farmers' did not possess any land of their own. For them, their wives and their children, hunger was a daily reality, especially outside the harvest season, when it was almost impossible to find wage work. Polish studies indicate that there was a large element of 'hidden unemployment' in the country's agricultural economy prior to the Second World War. It has been estimated that eight to nine million people, or a third of the rural population (and in some regions as much as a half), could have migrated to the towns and cities without agrarian production being affected in any way.[14]

Before the First World War many people from Poland's villages had emigrated overseas or become migrant workers who found work elsewhere in Europe, particularly in Germany and France. With the reassertion of Polish sovereignty after the First World War and the increasingly restrictive immigration policies practised by countries that had traditionally received immigrants in the past, the opportunities for emigration were rapidly curtailed in the 1920s. At the same time the establishment of a Polish national state combined with racism and economic crisis in Europe to persuade many Polish émigrés and their families to return to Poland.[15] But in the meantime population growth in Poland was accelerating dramatically: between 1921 and 1937 the population rose from 27 million to 34 million.

The majority of the rural population made just enough money to pay their taxes and supply their own needs, at best producing a small surplus for a very limited regional market. Cash barely featured in this kind of subsistence economy. People either made their own household goods or obtained them by barter in the nearest small town.

According to Buell and other economic strategists, a key obstacle to the raising of agricultural productivity lay in the fact that Poland's smallholders would not put their surplus earnings – in so far as they had any – to productive use by reinvesting them in the farm enterprise. Instead, as Buell complained, they squandered the money they made in 'good times' by increasing their own consumption, dispensing hospitality or giving anything they could spare to the poor.[16]

Poland's rural population did not contribute to the accumulation of capital that could have been invested in industry, nor did it buy industrial goods in any significant quantity. Viewed from the perspective of the economic planners, a large section of the Polish population effectively played no part in the economic life of the country – a situation, it was unanimously agreed, that called for 'the urgent restructuring of the country's economy and the solution of the population question'.[17]

The term 'Bevölkerungsfrage' – 'population question' – is not an objective description of fact but a slogan masquerading as science, whose purpose is to maintain the existing power structure and to explain the resulting crises and problems as the product of 'over-population'. Poland was ruled by a comparatively small semi-feudal upper class and an inflated military and state apparatus. The money to finance this ruling elite came from large landed estates, but more especially from an oppressive regime of indirect and direct taxation and a bizarre system of monopoly pricing for matches, tobacco, sugar, salt and brandy. And if the rural population did not feature in the economy as consumers, it was partly because most industrial goods were too expensive for them anyway, given the low prices paid for agricultural produce. So the fact that they clung to a subsistence economy and settled for producing just enough to cover their own needs was also a reaction to a crisis that had been made worse by the government's economic policies – a survival strategy, in other words.

But things did not stop at this passive reaction to impoverishment. As early as 1926 the *Osteuropäische Korrespondenz*, published in Berlin, was complaining about the rising tide of crime fuelled by the poverty and growing political unrest in Poland: 'The condition of the unemployed is indescribably wretched. It was not the much-vaunted Communist intrigues but hunger that drove the unemployed masses to the recent outrages in Stry, Vilna and Lvov, which could only be suppressed in the blood of the rioters. But the Communists did seize control of these disaffected masses.' Even mass arrests of Communists (the paper went on) would not suffice to bring the situation under control. In the countryside, too, unrest was growing and spreading with inexorable momentum. The 'intolerable burden of taxation' had brought economic ruin to the farming middle class, particularly in eastern Poland. 'Agricultural productivity is declining steadily. This is compounded by the unresolved problem of the non-Polish village proletariat in the eastern territories of Poland, which is very often unable to get work on the large estates as a result of the agrarian reforms, but cannot acquire land of its own either because the estates are being divided up among the new settlers coming in from the Polish mother country. So both in industry and in agriculture the conditions that presently obtain are precisely those described in Bolshevist ideology as "the objective preconditions for social revolution in an economically backward country".' In this situation, the writer continued, the Polish economy had a stark choice between two alternatives: 'Either inflation – or a foreign loan. The first must inevitably lead to the outbreak of social revolution, while the second will only serve to avert Poland's internal troubles if the country agrees to accept foreign domination not only in economic matters, but in political matters as well.'[18]

Poland's ruling class opted for the second alternative. In May 1926 Józef Piłsudski came to power in a military coup. In 1927 the new government raised a loan of $62 million in the USA. It had to accept interest rates 'far higher than was normal or supportable'.[19]

Moreover the government had agreed 'to give the Americans total control' over how the money was used.[20] On the back of growing foreign indebtedness the Polish economy now enjoyed a two-year boom, which came to an abrupt end in 1929 when agricultural prices plunged on the world market. Prices for industrial goods, on the other hand, continued to rise sharply in the years that followed.[21] This situation led to growing dissatisfaction within the country, particularly among Poland's rural population. In 1931 the Polish government switched to a rigidly deflationary policy. Hardest hit were the rural smallholders and industrial working class, who saw their standard of living fall still further.

In 1932 the popular Galician politician Wincenty Witos, leader of the Peasant Party and former prime minister,[22] painted a gloomy picture of the situation:

The standard of living in our villages has declined. Even well-to-do households can no longer afford sugar in many cases. And people are even saving on salt. Splitting matches into several pieces, using a flint to strike a spark, carrying glowing coals from one house to another in a bucket – these are everyday and commonplace occurrences in our villages. (...) Tuberculosis has reached epidemic proportions. Despite the winter weather people are walking around without boots; they lack essential items of linen, and are obliged to make do with rags left over from better times. (...) A large proportion of the young adult population cannot find work any more. Their aspirations for a decent life are making them a thorn in the side of their families, a burden unto themselves, and in many cases a dangerous breeding-ground for subversion.[23]

The situation was little better in the towns and cities. In 1935 approximately 40 per cent of workers' families could no longer feed themselves adequately on their incomes.[24] Although the years that followed were marked by an upturn in many areas of the economy, mass poverty continued to increase in Poland. By the spring of 1939, according to Buell's figures, a quarter of the Polish population was living on the brink of starvation.[25]

In 1936 the government approved a programme of economic reform whose centrepiece was the development of a new industrial region in central Poland in the vicinity of Sandomierz.[26] The project was clearly aimed in part at bolstering the country's defence industry, but its main purpose was to transfer large sections of the population out of agriculture and into manufacturing industry.[27] The experiment never got beyond the planning stage. To create jobs in domestic industry for a substantial number of people who were deemed 'surplus to requirement' in the agricultural sector would have required massive investment – and the capital was simply not available. All alternative plans to redirect the rural 'population surplus' into other forms of work, i.e. to relocate them to the towns and cities and find productive employment for them there, fell foul of another structurally conditioned obstacle: the skilled trade and commercial sectors in the towns and cities were already regarded as 'oversubscribed', i.e. by any rational economic reckoning there were already more tradesmen and small traders than were needed to supply the needs of the urban population.

Under these conditions the crisis worsened. In 1936 the rural population embarked on a series of violent protests against the rising tide of impoverishment and destitution. The demonstrations began in Galicia and spread throughout central Poland; according to newspaper reports 120,000 smallholders took part,[28] and very soon they were joined by sections of the urban working class. They demanded that the estates of the large landowners be broken up and redistributed. When the situation grew even worse in 1937, following a failed harvest, the Galician farmers responded with a ten-day strike. They boycotted deliveries of food to the towns and blocked the access routes. Workers in Cracow organized sympathy strikes. The authoritarian Polish regime reacted true to form. The leaders of the People's Party were arrested[29] and the police were ordered to put down the disturbances in the villages by force. 'A series of armed clashes took place, in which the number of dead undoubtedly exceeded the figure of forty-two claimed by the government.'[30]

Economic crisis and anti-Semitism

In this situation of social crisis the political right in Poland began to wield a growing influence, and with it the forces of anti-Semitism. While the popular perception was that rural overpopulation lay at the root of Poland's economic ills, the view that the large Jewish minority was the main obstacle to a solution of the problem began to gain currency. This minority was blamed both for the structural crisis as such and for the widespread social unrest, since it was commonly supposed that a disproportionate number of agitators, both Communists and members of the Bund,[31] were Jews. At the instigation of the right-wing parties the Polish parliament, the Sejm, debated this 'problem' and 'possible practical solutions' on a number of occasions at the end of the 1930s. In December 1938 117 members of parliament – more than a quarter of all MPs – signed a declaration calling for action. The *Deutsche Allgemeine Zeitung* reported on its content: 'A radical reduction in the number of Jews is needed to satisfy the pressing economic, social and cultural requirements of the Polish nation. The Jews are an element that weakens and impedes the normal development of Poland's national energies. In particular the Jews are hindering the establishment of economic independence for the Polish population in town and country.'[32] Although Poland's Jewish minority had settled in the country centuries before, these and similar pronouncements set them apart from the Polish population and excluded them from the life of the nation.

In the 1930s there were three million or so Jews living in Poland, making up approximately 10 per cent of the total population. Only around 7 per cent of these lived on the land[33] – a consequence of the discriminatory anti-Jewish policies of the nineteenth century that had banned them from acquiring, renting or managing farmland.[34] The new Polish state had made the situation worse by depriving Jewish villagers – particularly those engaged in trade or commerce – of their livelihoods. 'By creating a series of government monopolies for brandy, salt and tobacco the state was able to select its preferred vendors, and it used this influence to oust the Jews completely from their previous line of business.'[35] In order to pacify the farmers, the government announced a moratorium on debts. While the banks to whom the farmers owed money were underwritten by the national bank, the government announcement spelled ruin for thousands of traders – most of them Jewish – who could not recover their outstanding debts from the farmers. Through such seemingly neutral, but at bottom anti-Semitic measures the government sought to aggravate the conflicts of interest within the population and turn the crisis against the Jews.[36]

The majority of Poland's Jews worked in commerce or the skilled trades. For the most part they were self-employed, often running tiny businesses, stalls or workshops from which the owner could barely make a living. According to official statistics, 44.4 per cent of the Jewish working population were engaged in trade or transport and haulage, and 33.8 per cent in the skilled trades and industry. The Jewish industrial workers were employed for the most part in small-scale enterprises, where frequently the entire workforce was Jewish – thus avoiding the loss of two working days a week through the need to respect both the Sabbath and the Sunday.[37] Most Jewish traders did not sell their goods through shops as such – not as visitors to Poland from western Europe would have understood the term. Instead they worked the streets, selling from handcarts, hawker's trays, market stalls, or straight out of their coat pockets. They bartered or sold all manner of household goods, new or second-hand, complete or incomplete. Cobblers, tailors, tinkers or knife-grinders frequently set up their workshops in the single room where a family of four lived, or else they carried their tools around with them. For many Jews, children as well as adults, necessity had been the mother of invention, reviving trades that had long since disappeared from other parts of Europe – the water-carrier, for example.

There was not a lot of money to be made from such business

enterprises; but the concentration of Jews in certain branches of the economy prompted a series of anti-Semitic hate campaigns in Poland in the 1930s. The skilled trades and commerce, it was said, had been 'taken over by the Jews', and because the Jewish minority held a virtual monopoly in these areas it was able to dictate prices to the rest of the population. But more than anything else, the Jews were keeping the rural population out of the towns and cities. And the Jewish stranglehold on the skilled trades and commerce was denying young Poles the opportunity to get established in these areas themselves. This in turn, it was claimed, was stifling the development of a Polish middle class. Yet the latter was of paramount importance for the country – as 'a national and patriotic element (...), ever ready to defend the state against any danger that might threaten it'.[38]

Against the background of propaganda like this, an economic boycott directed against the Jewish population was organized in 1936 with the backing of the government and the Catholic Church. Christians who did not go along with the boycott were denounced by name in the right-wing press. Very soon there was a sharp decline in the number of Jewish shops.[39] Jews lost their jobs, and many of them lost their homes in consequence: all in all, material hardship was making the position of the country's Jewish communities increasingly desperate.

But the Polish middle class desired by some as a 'patriotic element' failed to materialize, despite the campaign to discriminate against the Jews. One newspaper in Vienna suggested reasons for this: 'Since the surplus [meaning the "surplus population"] from Poland's villages does not have the opportunities for emigration that it once had, and industry, as we know, cannot absorb them all, anti-Semitic groups propagated the notion that the peasant farmers should wrest the market trade, so widespread in Poland, from the grasp of the Jews. (...) But as this is a trade with minuscule returns, from which even the Polish Jew, with his modest needs, can scarcely make a living, it is a battle for a lost cause.' The market trade in Poland (the article continued) 'is doomed to disappear, regardless of who controls it, the moment that Poland starts to modernize its system of goods distribution', and the anachronistic struggle for the 'Polonization of trade' was therefore only an attempt 'to get around the dangerous issue of agrarian reform'.[40]

However, the Polish right was intent not only on ousting the Jews from the market trade in agricultural produce, but also on ending the 'burden imposed by the Jews as an element in economic life' in general.[41] Poland's universities developed into strongholds of anti-Semitism. 'Students are organized along right-wing and anti-Semitic lines. Since the call for restricted admission' – meaning a general restriction on the admission of Jewish students to university – 'is naturally opposed by the government, there has been widespread rioting. In the lecture halls there are now separate benches for Christians and Jews.'[42] A substantial portion of the student body and a number of Christian professors stood out against this tendency, but for many years Polish universities operated an unofficial system of admission restrictions which resulted in a decline in the number of Jewish students from 20.4 per cent of the student body in 1928–9 to 9.9 per cent in 1937–8.[43] The increasingly aggressive hate campaign led eventually to numerous pogroms. According to reports in Polish newspapers pogroms took place in over 150 Polish towns and cities in 1935 and 1936 alone, resulting in hundreds of deaths.[44]

Starting from the initial focus on the economic function of the Jewish population, their existence *per se* gradually came to be seen as a 'problem'. In political debate the general economic crisis, so-called 'overpopulation' and the 'Jewish question' were frequently mixed up together, prompting a search for appropriate 'solutions'. From 1936 onwards the Polish government, supported by the extremely active Polish Maritime and Colonial League, demanded access for Poland to overseas colonies. The fact that the new Polish state established in 1918 incorporated territory formerly belonging to Germany formed the basis of Poland's claim to a proportionate share in Germany's colonies. The government also pointed to 'severe overpopulation' and a shortage of raw materials to justify its demands, which it paraded with increasing frequency in negotiations with foreign politicians and at the League of Nations. If Poland were to acquire these colonial territories – so the argument ran – 'it could fill them up in part with its surplus rural population, which would certainly include a proportion of Jews consistent with the average for the population as a whole. This would create a healthy economic structure and an opportunity for Poland to solve the Jewish question at home.'[45]

A Polish claim to colonial rule in the normal sense was not under discussion here. Instead the government was taking a neo-colonialist stance in demanding licensing agreements and rights of use for countries that it saw as a reservoir of raw materials and land for settlement. The colonial powers recognized that Poland's wishes were justified in principle – which did not mean that they were prepared to grant them. On the one hand they had no intention of relaxing their restrictive immigration laws, thereby making it possible for Polish Jews to emigrate to western Europe or the United States. On the other hand Great Britain, France and the USA all feared a further destabilization of Poland caused by the unresolved 'population question'. What gave rise to their concern was not just the amount of British, French and US capital tied up in the Polish economy: all three countries also looked upon Poland as their acting representative in eastern Europe, looking after their interests in the region by curbing both German and Soviet Russian expansion.

The view that there was a 'Jewish problem' in Poland gradually gained wider currency. In the summer of 1937 a Polish delegation travelled out to the then French colony of Madagascar to investigate the possibility of resettling Polish Jews there.[46] In December of that year the Polish Foreign Minister, Józef Beck, had discussions with his French counterpart, Yvon Delbos, on the Madagascar project.[47] The French government took a cool, but not unsympathetic view of the Polish request.

The Polish government formulated its appeals to the colonial powers and the League of Nations in ever more strident and aggressive tones, but met with no response. In the continuing debate about Jewish emigration, populist anti-Semitism became increasingly bound up with fundamental issues of economic policy. The 'Jewish question' soon became the subject of parliamentary discussions[48] and foreign trade negotiations. The biggest obstacle to the resettlement of the Jews overseas, it was claimed, was the foreign-exchange issue. The government wanted as many Jews as possible to emigrate, but it also wanted to prevent the few wealthy Jews among them from taking their wealth – in the form of valuable foreign exchange – out of the country.

In March 1937, therefore, the Polish government, like the German government a few years before,[49] had signed a transfer agreement with the Jewish Agency for Palestine that was designed to facilitate the export of capital from Poland to Palestine. 'Jewish emigrants paid the amounts to be transferred into a Polish clearing account in Warsaw and received the proceeds in Palestine when Polish exports to Palestine exceeded the value of Palestinian goods supplied to Poland.'[50]

In April 1939, when political tensions in Europe were rising as Germany prepared for war, Great Britain and France sought to secure the goodwill of the Polish government. A mutual defence pact and a credit for Poland to the value of 20–30 million pounds sterling were designed to help things along. In addition the British government agreed to accept 50,000 Polish Jews a year as immigrants into the British Dominions.[51] On a visit to London by the Polish foreign minister Józef Beck it was agreed that wealthy Jews who wanted to emigrate should deposit 80 per cent of their assets with a credit cooperative in Poland. The remaining 20 per cent was the 'price' they paid for being allowed to emigrate in the first place. This fund would later be used to finance the emigration of the Jewish lower class.

The idea was to issue the Jews with promissory notes in respect of the four-fifths of their assets that had been effectively confiscated. Following their emigration to Palestine or to 'some of the "empty spaces" of the world', they would set up firms with the approval of the aforementioned credit cooperative and 'all the parties concerned', these firms to undertake the export of raw materials from the 'empty spaces' to Poland. The promissory notes would gradually be redeemed against the value of these exports, and at the end the Jewish entrepreneurs would be reimbursed in foreign exchange for the 80 per cent of their assets they had 'deposited' prior to emigration. Such an arrangement would not have cost Poland any more in foreign exchange than it would have spent anyway on importing raw materials. Wealthy Jewish businessmen would set up companies abroad as 'pioneers of Jewish emigration'; these companies would then provide employment for poor Jews subsequently deported from Poland. So under the terms of this plan, for which it was hoped to win the backing of 'world jewry', and in particular of Jewish financiers in the USA, the Jewish population would not only be evacuated from Poland, but would also be engaged in exploiting new sources of raw materials for their 'mother country'. And because the newly established enterprises employed only Jewish émigrés, and were in any case located in these so-called 'empty spaces', their activities would not impinge on the economies of other countries.[52] As the available options for emigration were progressively narrowed down by governments in their pursuit of power politics, the fiction of the world's 'empty spaces' to which the 'surplus humanity' would supposedly be deported acquired a growing propaganda significance.

So by 1939 the ongoing discussion in Poland and in the international arena about the issues of migration, overpopulation and the transfer of population groups had thrown up all the key sociopolitical and economic arguments that would later influence the deliberations and decisions of the German occupying power in Poland.

German research on eastern Europe, 'overpopulation' and the 'Jewish question'

If Poland in the 1930s had been the 'Key to Europe' for the American economist Buell, to the German intellectual observer of that time it functioned as a buffer zone between 'civilized western Europe' and the 'primitive East'. Few indeed were the accounts of travels in Poland that failed to deplore the 'appalling lack of hygiene' or to look down upon the supposed 'low level of culture' and the widespread illiteracy.[53] A characteristic feature of Poland's small towns was 'the very high proportion of wooden houses, which are in fact the principal form of housing, even in urban settlements'. And because 'all the settlements have a large proletarian element made up mostly of east European Jews' they are 'ill-equipped to fulfil the cultural and political functions of European towns and cities'.[54] In Galicia the same observer, who was 'astonished, not to say dumbfounded' by his impressions, noted an illiteracy rate of 50–60 per cent, while eastern Poland struck him as 'still prehistorically primitive'.[55]

To another German specialist on Poland the country's villages and towns seemed grey and drab, and he missed the neat front gardens of the Germans. 'Four-fifths of the Polish population live in these villages and towns. They know nothing else. (...) Centuries of serfdom have robbed them of the strength to become masters of this land.'[56]

As German–Polish relations progressively deteriorated on the eve of the Second World War, German commentators sounded off in increasingly venomous tones about 'Polish delusions of grandeur', accusing the government of indulging in ambitious schemes for industrialization and making brazen foreign-policy demands when it was not even capable of solving the country's most pressing domestic problems. To the extent that German intellectuals writing about Poland in the 1930s and early 1940s found anything to admire about the country, or anything positive to say about it at least, they attributed it to German drive and enterprise, or to the pioneering spirit of their Teutonic forebears in earlier centuries.

But this brand of rabidly Germanocentric propaganda was only one way of approaching the 'Polish issue'. Another way was through German academic research on eastern Europe. One of the leading centres of this research was the Institute of East European Economic Studies in Königsberg. Its director since 1 March 1933 had been a Dr Theodor Oberländer, only twenty-seven years old at the time of his appointment, and a practised propagandist for German expansion in the East.

The studies on Poland published by the Königsberg Institute under his direction were initially fairly moderate in tone, in keeping with their academic pretensions, and were undertaken for the purpose of collecting and collating data and analysing socio-economic structures. But as time passed the Institute's academics began increasingly to overlay their analyses with the racist paradigms of National Socialism. A typical example is the joint study published by the Polish Department at Oberländer's Institute in 1937 under the title 'Poland and Its Economy'. After the Germans had done the real work of 'colonizing the East', it was claimed, they had been ousted from their positions by 'the Jews'. The latter, 'following the flourishing trade routes, particularly in the 13th and 14th centuries, (...) had established themselves in the towns, where, protected by royal warrants, they had exercised significant economic influence at a very early stage. Multiplying rapidly, the Jews now moved into towns emptied of Germans (...) and effectively took control of the local economy.'[57] The book's editor was the head of the Polish Department at the Institute, Peter-Heinz Seraphim. He and Oberländer had worked together on developing the idea for the book, whose purpose was to 'marshal the salient facts about Poland with scientific objectivity and organize them under key headings'. More than half the book consists of maps and charts, which show not only Poland's centres of industrial production and mineral deposits, but also its population structure – broken down according to religious faiths and ethnic groupings, with a separate map showing 'the most important Jewish towns in Poland'.

In common with other contemporary publications this book points to rural overpopulation as one of 'the most pressing and important issues for Poland': 'In the case of Poland we are dealing with a rurally overpopulated region whose agriculture is largely dependent on an inefficient system of smallholdings.'[58] So widespread is this form of land management (the writer continues) that it 'threatens to damage the agrarian economy and the economy of the country as a whole', because instead of 'proper full-time farmers' it is creating a huge agricultural proletariat 'that is barely able to eke out the most basic existence from its agricultural activity'.[59] Seraphim shared the view that Poland lacked a middle class with the purchasing power to create a market for industrial goods. Poland's farmers, he believed, had 'withdrawn wherever possible from the economic mainstream', and the smallholders were living 'in a kind of "closed household economy"'.[60]

Oberländer had made an intensive study of the problem of rural overpopulation in Poland two years previously. Published in 1935, his book is still regarded as a standard textbook on the subject.[61] He warned that the 'pressure of overpopulation' and the lack of capital in Poland would create internal tensions that would make the country ripe for an agrarian revolution on the Russian model. This development could only be countered by comprehensive agrarian reform and by the provision of 'relief valves' (in the form of alternative employment opportunities, for example). Oberländer's academic study found its complement in Königsberg in the publications of his deputy, Professor Peter-Heinz Seraphim. In a manner of speaking the complementary nature of their work was based on a natural division of labour.[62] Seraphim had studied economics, and it was as an economist and a student of eastern Europe – as he himself wrote in 1938 – that he had become an expert on the 'Jewish question'. Later on he worked at the 'Institute for the Study of the Jewish Question' in Frankfurt, where he edited the virulently anti-Semitic journal *World Struggle: the Jewish Question Past and Present*. In 1938 Seraphim published his book *The Jews in Eastern Europe*, which quickly established itself as a standard work.[63] It was one of the most important studies published by the Königsberg Institute of East European Economic Studies under Oberländer's direction. While Oberländer had looked in general terms at the overpopulation from which Poland in his estimation suffered, Seraphim linked the 'population question' with the 'Jewish question'. This is reflected in the various expressions freely used by Seraphim, expressions such as 'Judenballung' ['concentration of Jews'], 'Verjudungsprozess' ['Judaization'], 'Judendichte' ['density of Jews'], 'judenreich' ['full of Jews'] and 'judenfrei' ['Jew-free']. Seraphim speaks of the 'degree of saturation with Jews in the Russian towns and cities', and of the fact that Russian governments 'offloaded' their 'Jewish population surplus' in Congress Poland. The text is illustrated with photographs of various 'Jewish types' and accompanied by maps that show the 'density of Jews' in specific towns and countries.

Over more than seven hundred pages Seraphim describes the 'penetration' of the Jewish population into eastern Europe from around AD 1000 onwards, and more especially its 'infiltration' of trade, commerce and money transactions. Agricultural labour, on the other hand, was something that the majority of the Jewish 'interlopers' had always avoided: 'The reason for this is that the Germans were genuine farmers, (...) while the Jews belonged to a proletarianized urban underclass for whom the move to the countryside was a pretext for evading military service and local taxes, and who were not only unaccustomed to agricultural labour but actually refused to undertake physical work of this kind.'[64]

Seraphim constantly bemoans the lack of citizenship among his 'research subjects'. The Jews, he claims, evade military service and dodge their taxes, refuse to send their children to state schools, undermine the morality of officials by bribery and sabotage all attempts to relocate them in the agricultural sector and transform them into 'useful members of society'. Seraphim also takes them to task for 'an almost insuperable aversion to any form of government survey', meaning national censuses.

Among Jewish women, claimed Seraphim, 'the aversion to physical labour, notably factory work, which is an obvious choice for ordinary women', was even greater than it was among Jewish men. 'Tradition and the widespread survival of the patriarchal family unit are also factors here. This is why the proportion of Jewish women in paid work is less than half the figure for non-Jewish women.'[65] It was also primarily due to the women that 'the birth rate within the strict Jewish community', particularly in eastern Galicia, was 'relatively high'.[66] Only growing assimilation into the large cities could make the Jewish population receptive to a 'rationalization of their reproductive behaviour'.[67]

But when a Jew abandoned his religion to embrace a different creed – socialism, for example – then such a change of world-view [Weltanschauung] was far more dangerous, according to Seraphim, than it would be in a non-Jew. For 'the Jew' was 'infinitely more prone to rootlessness', and was therefore apt to become more radical, more fanatical and more ruthless than, say, a non-Jewish socialist. Seraphim repeatedly makes the point that the Russian revolutionaries numbered a high proportion of Jews among their ranks, so that fear of the spread of the Jewish minority in eastern Europe was tantamount to a fear of the spread of revolution itself.[68]

According to Seraphim's analysis, however, the 'Jewish question' only became a really pressing issue with the impoverishment of large sections of the Jewish population in the late nineteenth century and the subsequent mobilization of these masses during the First World War. Around 1800, he estimates, the Jewish population in eastern Europe totalled some two million; by 1900 their numbers had risen to over seven million.[69] In other words, there had been 'a multiplication in the number of Jews [in eastern Europe] such as had never before been seen in the history of Jewry'.[70] Seraphim noted an increase in Jewish migration towards the end of the century: 'In the 1880s and 1890s we see the clear beginnings of the movement towards the urbanization of the Jews in eastern Europe. The process of industrialization in western Russia and Congress Poland, the consequent expansion of trade in the towns and cities, the growth in credit business – all this drew the Jewish population into the towns and cities in large numbers', where in the truest sense of the word a 'reserve army of the impoverished' had come into being.[71]

The closer Seraphim gets to his own times in his account, the more dramatic his portrayal of the 'Jewish question' becomes. To ignore the problem – so his analysis sets out to demonstrate – would be to invite a social cataclysm of European proportions. 'The Jewish area of settlement in eastern Europe, which had been firmly established and clearly defined for many centuries, was thrown into a ferment and a state of dissolution in the first three decades of the 20th century.'[72] This process had serious consequences primarily because the growth in the urban Jewish population went hand in hand with an increase in poverty. According to Seraphim, 60–70 per cent of Poland's Jewish minority in the second half of the 1920s were so poor that they either paid no tax at all or were taxed at the lowest rate. While the spread of capitalism and industrialization had initially stimulated the 'process of urbanization' and offered Jews migrating to the city from the countryside the prospect, at least, of a new life, migration was now outpacing economic expansion. The Jews migrating to the city from the land could no longer be absorbed into the urban economy. In Seraphim's parlance: they 'crowd' into the large cities, where they 'swamp the commercial sector, infiltrate the liberal professions and swell the ranks of the proletariat'.[73]

This process was further accelerated by the world economic crisis and by the restrictive immigration policies of those countries that had admitted Jews from eastern Europe in earlier years. 'The social impoverishment of large sections of the Jewish population in Poland is an undoubted fact.' Although the numbers cannot be precisely established (writes Seraphim), estimates suggest that 'possibly as many as 30–40 per cent of the total Jewish population belong to this impoverished and downwardly mobile social underclass'.[74] For eastern Europe as a whole Seraphim puts the number of impoverished Jews at 3.1 million, 'i.e. 43 per cent of east European Jewry'.[75]

In this mental climate the 'social question' – the problem of 'overpopulation' and impoverishment – becomes synonymous with the

'Jewish question'. And finding a solution to this problem, as Seraphim pointed out in each successive publication, was of crucial importance for the future development of eastern Europe. 'This problem of overpopulation,' he writes in April 1939 in the *Frankfurter Zeitung,* 'is one of the key issues facing Poland today, and finding a solution to this problem is a challenge that Poland's economic policy-makers have so far failed to meet. The attempts to relocate people in the wake of the so-called agrarian reform and the phenomenon of industrialization (...) are both linked to this population pressure. Similarly the Jewish question is aggravated by the fact that the present generation of farmers' sons, unable to remain on the land as a consequence of rural overpopulation, are beginning to migrate to the towns and cities, where they find that nearly all of the trade and commerce, as well as the skilled trades and most of the liberal professions, are already in Jewish hands.'[76]

A year after this book was published with the aid of a grant from the Secret Prussian State Archive, the Germans invaded Poland. Oberländer and Seraphim were both serving as officers in the military by now: posted to Cracow in 1940, they began to submit proposals for dealing with the overpopulation problem – a problem they had previously linked with the 'Jewish question'.

CHAPTER 3

DEMOGRAPHIC ECONOMICS – THE EMERGENCE OF A NEW SCIENCE

'In large areas of eastern Central Europe, rural overpopulation is one of the most serious social and political problems of the present day. (...) In Russia it was one of the key factors that made the Bolshevist revolution possible.'[1] Such was the conclusion reached by the social historian Werner Conze in 1939. According to Conze, overpopulation led to 'a state of total impoverishment' and created 'a hotbed of permanent tension and revolutionary unrest'. This dangerous condition was particularly far advanced in Poland – 'the clearest example can be seen in Galicia'.[2] These remarks had been prepared for the XIV International Congress of Sociologists, which had been due to begin in Bucharest on 29 August 1939, but was postponed indefinitely two weeks beforehand. The central theme was to have been 'Town and Village'. The papers submitted were printed and published only a few months later – a measure of their importance. The stated aim of the Congress was the 'planning of a lasting order'.

In 1943 the Reich University in Posen appointed Werner Conze to a professorship. Ten years later he was one of the founders of the *Vierteljahrshefte für Zeitgeschichte*, and remained one of its co-editors until his death in 1986. The journal was founded in 1953 for the principal purpose of 'vigorously addressing the National Socialist period in our history, mindful of the undeniable responsibility that rests with German science in particular'. In the first year's issue of the *Vierteljahrshefte* Conze published a text that had presumably lain in his drawer for a number of years. This was an essay on the demographic 'structural crisis in eastern Central Europe'. Although the writer confined himself here to the period up until 1936, he again saw 'the pressure of overpopulation' as the root cause of poverty, crisis and rebellion. And in contrast to western Europe there was no adequate 'outlet' at that time for the surplus population of eastern

Europe. Writing in 1953, Conze explains why this was so: 'Industry offered very little scope for making a living; trade and commerce in the small towns and villages were in Jewish hands, with virtually no spare capacity – in fact many trades were over-subscribed already.'[3]

In 1939 Conze had been more explicit in his arguments – and more forthright about the possible consequences. Among the measures that might prove 'extremely effective and helpful' in alleviating the distress of overpopulation he included 'the removal of the Jews from the cities and small market towns in order to create jobs for the rising rural generation in commerce and the skilled trades'.[4]

Unemployment in the towns and cities, poverty and 'underemployment' in agriculture, 'backwardness' and low productivity: since the 1930s all these phenomena had been understood by demographers as the consequence of a steadily growing human population surplus, which was inhibiting, or even blocking, economic development. In the case of Poland, Oberländer had pointed out early on that there was a danger of revolution on the Russian model if no means could be found to 'siphon off' the surplus population from agriculture. A similar fate was predicted for other countries in the late 1930s, particularly the countries of south-east Europe.

According to this analysis, these countries were exerting a 'population pressure' on Germany's borders. In concrete terms this meant that Polish workers from the border regions (for example) were looking for work in Germany that was not to be had in Poland – or if it was, only on less favourable terms. German demographic specialists categorized this as an 'infiltration' of Germany by Poles (as opposed to the Germanic 'settlement' of Poland in earlier centuries), which could well become 'a social and national threat', especially if allowed to take place in an uncontrolled, or indeed illegal, manner.

According to this received scientific wisdom, the social stability of the continent and the revival of its economic fortunes depended on a 'relief of the population pressure'. This meant, however, that finding a solution to the 'overpopulation problem' became an issue of central importance in German plans for Europe.

Looking back, the economist and sociologist Carl Brinkmann believed that 'excessive population pressure' had been a continuing problem for the whole of Europe, and in October 1942 he identified it as a primary cause of the war: 'It is widely recognized that the present world war is in large part a consequence of the population pressure created by the monopolistic actions of overseas countries in closing their doors to immigration by the overflow from Europe's (and Japan's) agrarian populations.'[5]

The theory of optimum population size

The growing interest in demographic analysis had led specialists in this field to the 'surprising discovery' that they could 'frequently (...) categorize large land masses that are extremely thinly populated in themselves' as 'overpopulated', provided they were viewed in the appropriate terms.[6] For 'overpopulation' did not mean that the absolute population density per square kilometre had to be particularly high as such: instead, according to Oberländer, the term connoted 'deviation from a hypothetical population norm or optimum population size'. The optimum was a population size that allowed the maximum possible return to be extracted from the economic resources of a country. If the population remained below this optimum size, these resources would not be exploited to their full capacity; if it exceeded the optimum, then this 'population surplus' would start to become 'a burden on the national economy'. People who had contributed little or nothing by their own labour to the creation of the country's wealth would be sharing in that wealth. Consequently they would be consuming the theoretically possible surpluses that could otherwise have been invested in increasing the national income or promoting industrialization. In Oberländer's view, any deviation from the optimum population size must necessarily lead to 'symptoms of social and economic disease'.[7]

The theory of optimum population size had already been formulated by some economists at the start of the century.[8] Paul Mombert had particularly distinguished himself in this regard. He developed the so-called 'Mombert formula', a mathematical equation for calculating the relationship between population size – *Volkszahl* – and economic resources (or 'feeding capacity' – *Nahrungsspielraum* – as he termed it). This stated that 'the feeding capacity is equal to the population size multiplied by the standard of living (*Lebenshaltung*)', or 'N = V × L'. The term 'Nahrungsspielraum' referred not to the available agricultural land or indeed to any kind of 'space in the geographical sense', but to the feeding capacity of a given area. The formula applied regardless of whether the population in question earned its living from agricultural production, the sale of raw materials, the sale of industrial products, or any combination of these three possibilities. The concept on which the Mombert formula is based is an extremely simple one: if the population grows in size, then in order to feed the extra mouths either the standard of living has to fall or the 'feeding capacity' has to be increased. As long as one is dealing with abstract quantities, 'V', 'L' and 'N' can be divided and multiplied at will. The later function of the formula, which Oberländer adopted as 'irrefutable' and to which he made repeated reference in his own calculations of population surpluses, lay in the reduction of complex social processes and conflicts to mathematical formulae.[9] This reductive approach enabled planners to get a seemingly 'logical' handle on the messy stuff of reality: put into an equation, where they could be multiplied and divided, the social conflicts and crises associated with industrial development – so the formula suggested – could be converted mathematically into a population problem. To satisfy the equation it might be necessary to reduce the population size in order to achieve a higher standard of living for a given 'feeding capacity'. In practical terms, this translated in the 1920s and 1930s to the demand for colonies and increased emigration opportunities. But when, as in wartime, living standards and 'feeding capacity' were both reduced as a result of the destruction of economic resources, one way of compensating for this was to 'lower population numbers' accordingly. Viewed in these terms, the 'normal' casualties of war and the deliberate killing of people both worked in the interests of maintaining economic equilibrium.

By invoking the theory of optimum population size, any or all of the attendant ills of an economic crisis – be it poverty or unemployment, lack of capital or raw materials, an absence of markets or low labour productivity – could be expressed as a population excess or deficit.

Expressed in such terms, the annexation of western Poland was an 'extension of feeding capacity' for the German Reich, the campaigns of mass murder were a 'reduction of population numbers', and the plundering of food in the German-occupied areas of Europe was a 'lowering of living standards' that served to offset the growing restrictions on Germany's own 'feeding capacity'. The recruitment of forced labour brought about the desired 'lowering of population numbers' in occupied Poland. More than that: it also compensated temporarily for the departure from 'optimum population size' within the Reich that had resulted from the conscription of German males for military service. Viewed in these terms, the population of a country is just one of a number of economic factors – albeit one that can easily be modified by the use of political and military force.

Paul Mombert, the man who devised this population equation, was born in 1876 and appointed to the chair of economics at the University of Giessen in 1922. In 1933 he was forced to retire as a 'non-Aryan'; he died in December 1938, having been briefly held in custody by the Gestapo. Like the economists and demographers who cited him as an authority, Mombert was also interested in calculating the optimum labour output, and he too saw the size of the population as a variable. But he certainly did not intend the formula named after him to be put to the kind of use outlined here. In 1926 he spoke out forcefully against the notion that an imbalance between 'feeding capacity' and population size might be redressed 'from the population side', pointing out the 'massive loss of manpower resources' that 'emigration on a large scale [would] entail for our nation'.[10]

To adherents of the optimum theory, Germany too was 'overpopulated' during the world economic crisis. And as early as 1932 the demographic economists were calculating the burden imposed on the economy by those people who could not be productively employed. In his book *Bevölkerungsentwicklung und Wirtschaftsgestaltung* [Population Trends and Economic Management] Mombert reviews the debate then going on among his professional colleagues, who had calculated that it cost RM 10,000 to bring up each person in the country. Given that there was a 'population surplus' at that time of 400,000 people, this meant that RM 4,000 million were tied up in the raising of surplus people, instead of being available for productive investment in 'extending the country's feeding capacity', i.e. in an expansion of the economy. On top of the direct costs of bringing up a child (and here Mombert is quoting the remarks of a colleague), 'a working capital of DM 20,000 is also required for every supernumerary German who has to be fed'.[11] From this it was concluded that a decline in population numbers would allow more capital to be accumulated. If this 'cannot be put to work at home, then it looks to go abroad, as we know from experience'.[12] Here Mombert was outlining the possibility for the countries of western Europe – 'if population growth can be halted', a problem that demographers had been wrestling with in vain for at least twenty years – to export capital on a long-term basis, as France was already doing. Admittedly when Mombert had spoken of exporting capital in 1932 he was thinking in terms of financing colonization projects in Africa. But at the same time he had outlined a more general model for accumulating capital more quickly, namely through a 'cessation of population growth'.

For the German scientific experts in positions of power in occupied

Poland, this, as we shall show, was the solution to the problems analysed by Oberländer, Werner Conze and numerous other academics. A 'reduction of population numbers' would serve both to relieve the 'population pressure' and accumulate the capital needed for the modernization of the economy: otherwise occupied Poland would 'become a burden on the German-controlled sphere of influence'. The fact that most of the people in the country were not working at German levels of productivity (were 'under-used as a labour resource or not used at all'[13]) was soon being described in terms of every second person in Polish agriculture being so much 'dead ballast'.

Such at least was the view of Helmut Meinhold, who in 1941 was a 28-year-old economist working at the Institute for German Development Work in the East in occupied Cracow. The experts' reports and recommendations drafted here were frequently acted upon within a matter of days or weeks by those in charge of running the economy. In 1941 Meinhold wrote a paper on 'the industrialization of occupied Poland', which also dealt at length with the 'population question'. In order to calculate the extent of 'overpopulation' he borrowed from Oberländer not only Mombert's formula, but also the criteria that were used to measure the 'population surplus'. In his 1935 book on the rural overpopulation of Poland, Oberländer had shown that one could measure it either in terms of how many people could be fed from the available land for a given level of productive resources (the 'consumption index'), or in terms of how much manpower could be productively employed on the available land (the 'labour index'). The 'physiological subsistence level', on the other hand, was 'too variable a quantity in terms of race, occupation and culture to provide any kind of meaningful benchmark for a scientific study'.[14]

Six years later Meinhold stated that 'the purpose of studying overpopulation' was 'generally to measure the productivity of labour', and this 'with a view to maximizing labour productivity within the European sphere of influence'.[15] He was in no doubt, therefore, that the extent of overpopulation had to be calculated in terms of the 'labour index'. But the results were very different depending on the level of economic performance one took as a yardstick: a calculation based on the 'backward' and 'inefficient' Polish economy, for example, yielded far fewer 'surplus' people than one based on the 'superior' German system of labour organization, or indeed on a hypothesized 'maximum level of labour productivity within the European sphere of influence'. In the first case one would simply have calculated the hidden unemployment – the 'inadequate utilization of manpower' in relation to the actual state of labour organization. But since Meinhold – and he was only one of many – undertook his calculations precisely in order to bring about the restructuring of the Polish economy and its convergence with the newly defined economic norm for German-occupied Europe, he started from the premise of a rationalized agricultural economy. Such a thing did not exist in Poland, of course. Depending on whether he measured conditions in Poland by the 'optimum standards of labour productivity in the Reich' or used a 'somewhat higher level of manning in agriculture' as his yardstick 'for the present',[16] he concluded that 3.75 million persons (by German standards) or 2.56 million (by Polish standards) who were then employed in agriculture in the Government General (the 'rump' of Poland, which had been reduced to about a third of the country's original size as a result of German and Soviet annexations) were surplus to requirement. If one also included children and old people, one arrived at a total 'surplus population' figure of 5.83 million or 4.5 million respectively.[17] Based on this calculation by Meinhold, 'every second person in Polish agriculture', as already cited, 'represented nothing but dead ballast'.[18]

Oberländer regarded the voivodeships in southern Poland – formerly Austrian Galicia – as especially problematic, and had calculated that rural overpopulation here was running at 50 to 75 per cent. For the region of Kielce the quota of 'surplus people' was around 75 per cent, while for the Cracow and Lvov regions the figures were 66.5 per cent and 62.3 per cent respectively.[19]

Such calculations were undertaken not only for occupied Poland. The aim indeed was to 'cleanse' the entire territory of German-occupied and dominated Europe from the scourge of overpopulation, and to bring it up to the new, higher standards of labour organization. In Meinhold's estimation the majority of the agricultural population in south-east Europe was likewise 'still stuck' in a system of closed household economies, producing most of their own food and household goods – and producing very little for sale on the open market. 'In the event of a radical solution to the agrarian labour problem,' wrote Meinhold in 1941, it would be possible to 'mobilize 12 to 15 million workers' in south-east Europe.[20] And that wasn't all: these workers also had families, so that 'something like 50 million people would be taken out of the more or less closed household economy in which they had been living.'[21]

In 1943 Oberländer analysed rural overpopulation in southern and eastern Europe. Using comparative data collected for Germany and Denmark, he calculated a target value for the productivity of agricultural labour and the size of workforce that would be needed in south-east Europe to achieve that value. According to his calculations, the ratio between 'those people who are productively engaged in agriculture' and 'those who are simply "extra mouths to feed"' was 1:0.6 in Romania, 1:0.7 in Bulgaria, and as high as 1:1.09 in Yugoslavia. To these scientists and academics the unemployed in south-east Europe, as in the Government General, were 'a continuous drain on resources that prevents the healthy formation of capital'.[22]

But they did not stop at simply calculating the figures. In their scientific writings Oberländer and Meinhold both maintained that a 'reduction in population numbers' was a prerequisite for the formation of capital. 'By the same token,' says Meinhold, 'overpopulation amounts to an actual erosion of capital',[23] for the simple reason that all those 'extra mouths to feed' consume the surpluses generated by those who are 'productively engaged' and thereby prevent their reinvestment. Meinhold's colleague at the Institute for German Development Work in the East in Cracow, Hans-Kraft Nonnenmacher, portrayed the problem as a 'vicious circle' that had to be broken. Nonnenmacher outlined his thinking in terms that would not be at all out of place today:

> The faster overpopulation rises, the less chance there is of eliminating it – and the more the consequences of overpopulation will contribute to its further growth. For as the productivity of labour continues to fall, the population is no longer in a position to save the money needed to increase the capitalization of business and industry. But a higher level of capital-intensity is a precondition for the creation of new employment opportunities, in agriculture itself and in industry, which would gradually grow and develop if the savings ratio were increased. We are faced here with a vicious circle, which is leading to a steadily worsening impoverishment of the population. This manifests itself in many different ways, and the further consequences arising out of this situation are many and various.[24]

Nonnenmacher describes overpopulation as a condition that will continue to get worse in the absence of outside intervention. In theory it is possible to control economic development *either* by injecting capital *or* by reducing the size of the population. In his first sentence, however, Nonnenmacher clearly places the emphasis on overpopulation. Scientists and academics like him represented the 'vicious circle' of overpopulation and inadequate capital formation as a kind of natural disaster, from whose baleful consequences the economic life of the occupied territories could only be protected if German economists calculated the supposed imbalance between population numbers and 'feeding capacity' and specified the appropriate corrective measures. But German standards of labour productivity could not be imposed on Poland without recourse to despotic methods. A Polish peasant family did not refer to some abstract labour index to determine whether or not it could make a living from agriculture. And despite the poverty on every side, nobody thought to draw a distinction between the 'productively engaged' and 'extra mouths to feed' – nobody apart from the economists and political planners, that is. The German experts had sweeping powers and resources at their command. They combed the occupied territories in search of unused manpower and 'Ballastexistenzen' [meaning people who are – quite literally – 'a waste of space']. And they did so in the knowledge that their ideas were seconded by an executive that was willing and able at any time to adjust the size and composition of the population by forcible means. With capital shortages in the Reich now made worse by the war, they ruled out any prospect of a German 'development credit' for Poland from the outset. Instead their restructuring plans were predicated on the principle that all Germany's ambitions for world power, including the military occupation of conquered territories, were to be financed by the subjugated peoples.

No matter what point of departure these economists took for their analysis, they always came back to the same – and in their terms unavoidable – conclusion: they portrayed every economic and social problem as a consequence of overpopulation. And implicit within this was the way forward to a solution of the 'problem': the 'oppressive burden of overpopulation' had to be reduced.

As early as 1942 Franz Neumann passed succinct judgement on this thinking: 'To blame unemployment on overpopulation is pure demagogy, designed to mask the inner contradictions produced by capitalism.'[25]

'Overpopulation' in the Soviet Union

In whatever terms rural overpopulation was described and explained, Oberländer and his colleagues basically worked on the assumption

that Poland and south-east Europe needed to catch up with developments that had already taken place not only in western Europe, but
also in the Soviet Union. This meant that the 'backward' agricultural
industry in these countries had to be rationalized, and that a proportion of the landless rural population should be drafted into manufacturing industry. The Soviet Union had already taken this step at the
beginning of the 1930s, and thereby, as Oberländer wrote, 'caught up
with the trend in western Europe to reduce the size of the rural population by undertaking a massive purge of peasant farmers in the name
of collectivization'. Enforced collectivization under Stalin, he wrote,
had amalgamated 25 million smallholdings into 250,000 collective
farms, and 'within a relatively short space of time the individual
smallholding' had simply disappeared. At the same time industrialization had 'alleviated the population factor'.[26] In the elimination of
millions of Soviet peasant farmers Oberländer saw the successful
attempt 'to establish a balance between feeding capacity and population numbers'. His barely concealed admiration for Soviet strong-arm
methods presumably had something to do with the fact that Stalin's
agrarian policy had dealt with the problem of rural overpopulation in
the Soviet Union in very short order – virtually within a decade, in
fact.[27]

Following the October Revolution, the Bolsheviks had initially
reintroduced an old Russian system of land distribution, the so-called
mir system, in order to strengthen their power base. Abolished a
decade earlier by Stolypin's agrarian reforms,[28] this system favoured
families with large numbers of children, and at the same time put
economic checks on migration from the land to the towns and cities.
The result was that the land owned by the commune had to be
divided up between more and more people.

In the early 1920s the Soviet government sought to accumulate
capital from the agrarian sector for the development of the country's
industry. To this end it kept the price of industrial goods and taxation
levels relatively high, while prices for agricultural produce remained
low. But – just like capitalist Poland – the gap between industrial and
agricultural prices encouraged peasant farmers to keep their produce
for their own consumption rather than selling it on.

When the grain bought up by the government in 1927–8 fell well
below the projected figures, despite a good harvest, the government
reintroduced the compulsory delivery of agricultural produce. It had
used similar tactics to incite the peasant population against the new
Soviet power during the period of War Communism. In the 1920s

Soviet economists shared the view that large tracts of the Soviet Union were overpopulated – although their estimates of how many people constituted 'too many' were as widely divergent as their ideas about how to solve the problem.[29] Together with an intensified programme of industrialization, mass resettlement was seen as an effective method, not least because it would also open up hitherto undeveloped regions in the east of the country to economic exploitation. Initially people were encouraged to resettle in Siberia by offers of government aid. But when this failed to have the desired effect, the authorities resorted once again to forcible methods.

The year 1929 marked the beginning of the wholesale elimination of the kulaks as a class – the process described by Oberländer as 'a massive purge of peasant farmers in the name of collectivization'. Between then and 1932 millions of Soviet peasant families were dispossessed and divided into three groups. The first group was either summarily murdered or imprisoned, the second was deported to Siberia and the third was 'merely' banished from the district. This last group could be absorbed into a kolkhoz or collective farm after a probationary period of three to five years. The majority of kulaks belonged to the second group. In the Russian Soviet Republic alone an estimated 820,000 families – some four million people – were deported.[30] Many of them – the exact number is not known – died in transit. To escape the terror many people fled from the countryside into the towns and cities, where they tried to find work illegally in industry.

The black-earth region of the Ukraine, the 'bread basket of the Soviet Union', was regarded as particularly 'overpopulated'. The Ukraine played an important economic role, most notably as an exporter of grain. After the population had already been severely decimated by the elimination of the kulak class, something like a fifth to a quarter of the population fell victim in 1932–3 to the government's policy of deliberate starvation.[31] The cause of the famine was not failed harvests or natural disasters, but the abnormally high delivery quotas for grain imposed on the farmers. Until this quota had been met, keeping back even small amounts of grain for one's own use was punishable by severe penalties. The starving populace tried once more to flee the countryside and seek refuge in the cities, but special units of troops were deployed to prevent them. According to new Soviet estimates, a total of nine million people died as a result of resettlement and famine[32] – the consequences of a policy designed to rationalize agriculture at any price in order to create the necessary conditions for industrialization.

Contrary to the official political line, the drive to eliminate the kulak class was directed not only against well-to-do peasant farmers who were accused of exploiting poorer villagers, but also – soon enough – against families on tiny smallholdings who barely had enough to live on themselves. So collectivization was not the great achievement born of the class struggle that the Soviet Communist Party made out, but an attempt, as ruthless as it was successful, to eradicate rural overpopulation by various means and to accumulate capital in order to impose a modern economic structure on the country in the shortest possible time. Oberländer was in no doubt 'that the Soviet Union has embarked on the path of industrialization under the pressure of agrarian overpopulation, and in so doing has taken one of the paths by which agrarian overpopulation may be combated'.[33] Dispossession, famine, resettlement and mass murder were evidently viewed in the Soviet Union, as they later were in German-occupied Poland, as necessary and legitimate methods for 'correcting' the country's demographic make-up. In the Soviet Union this 'correction' was justified in terms of the 'laws of the class struggle', while in the German plans for a new European order it was justified by racist arguments. In their semantic parallelism the German terms 'Entkulakisierung' and 'Entjudung' ['the elimination of the kulak class' and 'the elimination of Jewish elements'] point to a certain similarity in the two programmes, while at the same time identifying their differing ideological thrust. When Oberländer cited the Soviet Union as a model and exemplar in his study of 'Ostmitteleuropa', he put the ideological baggage to one side and reduced both programmes to a common denominator of population policy: the eradication of population groups who were classed as 'extra mouths to feed'.

From emigration to 'resettlement in the name of the new order'

Once the economic situation had been formulated in terms of 'population pressure' and 'Ballastexistenzen', it was only a small step for the German rulers of occupied Europe to redress this 'deplorable state of affairs' through a combination of planned resettlement, social 'restructuring' and economic marginalization. While Oberländer had proposed emigration and 'seasonal migration' (to get harvesting work, for example) as 'relief valves' for overpopulation – both options, as he himself had admitted, that were of little practical relevance by the mid-1930s[34] – his colleagues saw completely new possibilities for economic action on a European scale after the start of the Second World War, and in particular after the German attack on the Soviet Union. The enforced deportation to the Reich of Polish forced labourers, euphemistically termed 'itinerant workers' by Meinhold and his colleagues, was intended both to alleviate the labour shortage in Germany and to reduce the overpopulation in Poland's agricultural sector. In 1941 Meinhold argued that 'the continuing military advance to the East' had opened up a new possibility for solving the overpopulation problem: the entire Polish population could simply be 'resettled much further to the East'.[35]

The resettlement of entire peoples or large population groups was already being taken for granted by the German economic planners. Likewise the 'reduction of population numbers' was by now an integral part of the master plan for occupied Europe – whether the 'excess population' was to be 'siphoned off' into supposedly empty regions (Meinhold) or deported to Germany for forced labour. 'The economy of German-occupied continental Europe in the future', we are told, was to be 'an economy of full employment', and that included 'the migration of labour within Europe'. Not only population numbers, but also the social make-up and mobility of the population were to be controlled, and new standards were set for discipline in the workplace. The era of the liberal world economy, with its free movement of labour and mass emigration from Europe to countries overseas, was seen as a thing of the past. Social peace would be forcibly established through population policy and planned resettlement. 'The future belongs to migration under the guiding hand of the state – a strictly controlled migration, designed to serve the best interests of the nation as a whole.'[36] Writing in November 1941, the economist Karl C. Thalheim cited the 'huge mass movements' of Jews, 'which will help to bring internal peace to Europe', and the 'resettlement operations in Central Europe' as two examples of such state-controlled migration.[37] By now the forcible resettlement of millions of people as an instrument of demographic engineering was accepted as standard practice. Himmler's inspector of statistics, Richard Korherr, saw in the German resettlement policy for the East 'a mighty 20th-century exodus, a planned migration of peoples' that would 'clear the decks'. He envisaged a number of methods for directing 'migratory movements' within the German Reich, including compulsory labour service, the regeneration of old urban areas, housing and land policy and 'the migration of some 400,000 Jews, other emigrants and a large number of Czech nationals (...) from the Sudetenland into the Protectorate'.[38]

In an essay on resettlement movements in Europe published in 1942, Professor Karl C. von Loesch identified twelve different types of resettlement. These included the relocation of people to border regions for defence and security reasons, 'population exchanges' and 'enforced resettlement', 'resettlement in the course of withdrawal', 'resettlement in the service of reconstruction and reorganization' and the early resettlement of 'recently devastated areas'.[39] Loesch was another who believed that 1939 had ushered in a 'new phase in European resettlement movements'.

According to the demographic economists, the new era in resettlement was characterized not only by state control of migration movements, 'migration under the guiding hand of the state', designed to 'bring peace to Europe', but also by the attempt to redefine social hierarchies. In this concept, existing differences and grievances between population groups were deliberately exploited to place migration 'under the guiding hand of the state' and to control the movement of labour within German-occupied Europe. Discrimination against minorities was used as a deliberate instrument of population policy: it created the freedom of movement necessary to redistribute populations 'in strict accordance with the interests of the nation as a whole'.

On the lowest rung of the hierarchy was the Jewish population. Back in 1938 Peter-Heinz Seraphim had pointed out that the 'Jewish question' in eastern Europe amounted to a 'population policy problem on a massive scale'. For him and his kind, the war represented an 'opportunity' for the wholesale 'reordering of existing population structures', so it seemed to follow that the time had come to 'resolve the Jewish question' as well. The first step was to exclude the Jews from economic life. The dispossession and ghettoization of the Jewish minority was intended to make room in the towns and cities of eastern Europe for the rural population that was to be 'liberated' from the land. But that in itself did not improve the situation – on the contrary: the economic exclusion of the Jewish minority simply made them more destitute. And once again the wishful thinking of the planners beat a path where action would later follow. In calling for 'solutions' and 'relief' they anticipated in thought the mass murder that was to take place in reality. The following words were written in November 1940, just as the Warsaw ghetto was being closed, by Heinrich Gottong, a racial researcher at the Institute for German Development Work in the East and a man well-versed in the practicalities of resettlement: 'The events of the war and their consequences have placed tight constraints on the lives and living conditions of the Jews. Jewish workers have been replaced by Aryans in many businesses, so that as well as being physically confined they are now subject to economic and social restrictions that will become increasingly acute. The mounting pressure of these restrictions will have to be relieved somehow, and a solution found.'[40] Implicit in Gottong's remarks was the recognition that this 'population pressure' had been created in part by German occupation policy in the Government General and the programme of social 'restructuring'.

So the alleged necessity for relieving large tracts of territory from a 'population pressure' was self-imposed in a twofold sense: on the one hand by the theoretical calculation that applied German standards of labour productivity to the land, and on the other hand by the practice that simply deported people en masse, herded them into ghettos, and thus created the pressures of physical, economic and social confinement in the first place. Theory and practice alike led the German social planners in the Government General to devise ever more radical plans for the restructuring of the country's economy and society.

In the 'new era' there were to be no uncontrolled population movements and the population would not be allowed to exceed its optimum size, as this would only fritter away capital on the feeding of 'useless mouths'. What it also meant, however, was that impenetrable and inefficient economic structures, to which the Germans gave labels such as 'underemployment', 'hidden unemployment' and 'retreat into self-sufficiency', were now to be replaced by the clear-cut distinction between those who were merely 'extra mouths to feed' and those who were 'productively engaged in economic activity'. But who would be classed as 'productive' and who as 'unproductive' was a matter for the state to decide. So at this point racism and demographic economics came together: dispossession and ghettoization forced the Jewish population into the position of being 'surplus to requirement'. Viewed in these terms, they were a 'burden' on the occupied territories, and as such they stood in the way of German plans for the economic restructuring of Europe's underdeveloped regions. These plans were all about efficiency, and in the political climate created by National Socialism they could most easily be implemented against the Jewish minority. The Jews were discriminated against anyway – and by now they were socially and economically isolated as well.

CHAPTER 4

WAR AND RESETTLEMENT

'The break-up of the old order'

> 'Since the start of the war and with the victory of our arms, the old order in Europe is breaking up. (...) The principles of a healthy ethnic and geographical order, which have remained mere theory in the absence of the freedom to plan and organize, are now close to being put into practice.'   (Konrad Meyer)[1]

Five weeks after the outbreak of war, on 6 October 1939, Hitler proclaimed his intention of 'creating a new ethnographic order' in Europe. This he proposed to achieve through 'a resettlement of nationalities'. The outcome of this process was to be 'the emergence of clearer dividing lines'. At the same time Hitler announced that 'efforts [would be made] to clarify and settle the Jewish problem'.[2] The very next day Hitler made Himmler responsible for organizing the logistical side of this violent expulsion of whole peoples. Himmler promptly styled himself 'Reich Commissioner for the Strengthening of German Nationhood' [Reichskommissar für die Festigung deutschen Volkstums, or RKF], and set up an office of the same name that was to prepare and carry out the task of population redistribution with which he had been personally charged. Within a few months Himmler's small office had grown into a powerful, wide-ranging institution that set the tone of policy, underpinned by a whole network of banks, limited companies, planning groups, an 'industry start-up and advisory agency' and regional planning staffs. All these bodies were armed with the authority to issue instructions to existing institutions. Between them they employed many thousands of people: SS men, social workers and community liaison staff, architects, auditors, administrators, agronomists, bookkeepers...

All these different skills and activities were harnessed to a single purpose: to organize resettlement policy in the annexed regions of western Poland – or the 'reincorporated eastern territories', as they were viewed from a German perspective. People were dispossessed and driven from their homes, others were drafted in to replace them. The RKF wound up many businesses, amalgamated others, handed them over to new owners. It made credit available, planned new roads, communications and energy supply systems, reorganized entire villages and towns and set itself the task of 'completely changing the face of the countryside'.[3] The first prerequisite for this was that the Reich Commissioner for the Strengthening of German Nationhood should 'transplant entire ethnic contingents', as Himmler put it.[4]

The RKF combined racial, population and structural policy in a comprehensive and unified concept for 'German reconstruction in the East'. The simplest and cheapest 'solution' was a population policy that was as deliberate as it was brutal. Founded on the racist norms of National Socialist society, it developed these into a practical instrument of social engineering. The resettlement of whole population groups created freedom of movement for the realization of vast projects, allowed the necessary funding to be 'released' and cleared the way for the attempted construction, by force and at the expense of other people, of a society that was to be a model of efficiency in its social and economic organization and infrastructure. So the work of the RKF was centred around population policy, both positive and negative: its victims were discriminated against and 'eliminated', its beneficiaries were privileged and promoted. It was a political instrument that had been applied since the earliest days of National Socialist rule in the form of compulsory sterilization on the one hand and carefully targeted birth promotion on the other – and it was absolutely predicated on the denial of the principle of equality.

The RKF main office in Berlin, the central staff office, was run by SS Gruppenführer Ulrich Greifelt. In the 1920s he had been a successful business manager, but from 1933 onwards he worked full-time in the SS administration.[5] Tellingly, the trained economist Greifelt had 'no idea' about issues of nationhood 'and had never done any work relating to nationhood'.[6] But he possessed other qualities that marked him out for the new post. As Himmler's special adviser on economic questions and head of the Four-Year Plan Office on Himmler's personal staff from 1938 onwards, Greifelt had functioned as 'a kind of liaison officer between Göring and Himmler'[7] – so maintaining a rapport that must have been absolutely pivotal to the programme of expropriation, economic reconstruction, deportation and resettlement.

The Four-Year Plan Office had originally been set up by Himmler to ensure an adequate supply of labour for the German economy. At the time, at the end of 1938, there was already a shortfall of half a million workers, mainly in agriculture. Greifelt planned to solve the problem with the aid of the '30 million German citizens and ethnic Germans living abroad (...) who are currently putting their labour, their expertise and knowledge, their blood and their progeny at the disposal of foreign states'. Their repatriation was intended to solve the problem of labour shortage, and therefore had 'very little to do with ethnic policy from the outset, but a good deal to do with economic considerations'.[8] With Himmler's backing, Greifelt deliberately and openly took up a position that was 'directly opposed to the official German policy line on ethnic matters' – official up until the start of the war, that is – whereby Germans living abroad were not to be repatriated, but were instead to be functionalized as 'guardians of the German ideal' in the world at large.[9] It was Greifelt's Four-Year Plan Office, too, that had taken action in 1938 against 'socially undesirable' and 'work-shy' Germans, sending 'well over 10,000' of them to concentration camps, as Greifelt himself noted.[10]

The institution of the Reich Commissioner for the Strengthening of German Nationhood is generally regarded as a hotbed of the most bigoted ethnic racism. In fact it was staffed by intellectuals for whom economic considerations invariably took priority over so-called racial policies. And this was plainly how Himmler wanted it: speaking about resettlement policy in the East, he referred to 'economic zones that are being managed in accordance with a clearly defined plan'.[11] So it was only logical that in 1939 he should transform the Four-Year Plan Office into the central staff office and administrative nerve centre of the Reich Commissioner for the Strengthening of German Nationhood. Greifelt made it his business to see that 'in the office of the Reich Commissioner matters of industrial and economic planning' received 'the attention merited by their great importance'.[12] He was among those invited by Heydrich on 29 November 1941 to attend the Wannsee conference, though in the event he was unable to do so.[13]

Greifelt's deputy, SS Obersturmbannführer Rudolf Creutz, also came from a business background, having done his commercial training in Hamburg and Vienna. In May 1945, as American troops were closing in on the RKF headquarters, which had been evacuated to Schweiklberg near Vilshofen in Lower Bavaria, Creutz tried to destroy all traces of the criminal resettlement programmes, burning the files of the central staff office. At the Nuremberg trials he was sentenced to fifteen years' imprisonment, while Greifelt received twenty years. Greifelt died in prison in 1949, Creutz was pardoned in 1955.[14]

The key departments within the central staff office of the RKF were the 'planning office' (also called the 'central planning department') under Konrad Meyer, 'the central land office', and the 'office for matters relating to the distribution of human resources' (later known as the 'office for the deployment of human resources'). However, the power wielded by the RKF did not derive solely or even primarily from its own agencies, but from the fact that all other institutions involved in any way with deportations and the work of 'Germanizing' in the annexed eastern territories were either directly subordinated to the RKF, or obliged to yield to it in any conflicts of jurisdiction.

As an organization that reported directly to Himmler, the RKF enjoyed 'not only the authority to issue instructions to all central offices and other agencies of the SS, but also strict power to command, even though these agencies were not working exclusively for the RKF, and indeed for the most part were doing relatively little on its account'.[15]

The western regions of Poland annexed in the wake of the German invasion – covering an area as large as Bavaria and Schleswig-Holstein put together, and with a population of nine and a half millions – were to be 'Germanized' as quickly as possible and their economic systems adapted to the needs of the German Reich. To that end the planners at the RKF proposed to expel the Jewish population and a portion of the native Polish population from these territories and to deport them to the central provinces of the former Polish Republic, crushed by Germany with the assistance of the Soviet Union – the so-called 'Government General'. The houses, farms, shops and work-shops of the deportees were either closed down, demolished or allocated to ethnic Germans 'repatriated' from the Baltic states, from Soviet-occupied eastern Poland and later from Romania.

The Reich Commissioner for the Strengthening of German Nationhood was thus creating not just a new 'ethnographic order', but also a new economic and social order. While its activities were mainly concentrated in the annexed eastern territories, it was not long before the local representatives of the RKF were at work in all German-occupied or annexed territories, where people were sorted into categories – 'persons of German origin', 'persons suitable for Germanization' or 'members of a dependent minority race' – and the various ethnic and minority groups were displaced and resettled.[16] In being thus categorized, people were either confirmed in their civil and social rights – or summarily stripped of them. Those judged 'suitable for Germanization' received adequate supplies of food, and the men were quickly conscripted into the Wehrmacht. Those who were classed as 'belonging to a dependent minority race', on the other hand, not only forfeited immediately all claims to a pension, but henceforth belonged to a population group without human rights that could be shunted around at will.

On 30 October 1939 Himmler issued an order for the following resettlement operations to be carried out in the period between November 1939 and February 1940: '(1) From the former Polish, now German provinces and territories: all Jews. (2) From the province of Danzig-West Prussia: all Congress Poles. (3) From the provinces of Posen [later known as the 'Warthegau'], South and East Prussia and Upper Silesia: a yet to be determined number of particularly hostile Polish nationals.'[17]

A so-called 'immediate-action plan' called for the deportation 'by the beginning of the census on 17.12.39' of 'a sufficient number of Poles and Jews to make room for the incoming Baltic Germans'. This plan applied only to the Warthegau. Looking further ahead, a long-term plan set forth future resettlement operations for the whole of the 'eastern provinces'. 'The clearances under the long-term plan (...) will take place on the basis of the census records.'[18] However, the idea was not simply to replace the Jewish and a portion of the non-Jewish population in the annexed eastern territories with ethnic Germans, but at the same time to reduce the population density. The planners judged that this would allow them to amalgamate groups of farms and so create more profitable economic units. In order to achieve this the RKF decreed that for every ethnic German moving into the area at least two Poles or Jews must be expelled; in many regions the figure was much higher. The whole process relied on meticulous forward planning. In December 1939 a report by senior SS and police commander Warthe stated: 'The critical factors determining the number of evacuees from each district are the ethnic composition of the local population, its political complexion and its socio-economic structure. (...) It should be borne in mind that we are not dealing here with some indiscriminate mass deportation, but with a very specific group of persons who first have to be identified and documented and then taken away.' For every person who was to be deported the German authorities filled out an 'evacuation card'. This card then went the rounds of the 'ethnic German index, the deferral index, the

Ukrainian and Russian index and the transport index', where it was
carefully checked against the records held by each. In addition a
special commission examined the deportation application and made
a final decision.[19]

According to a report on the 'resettlement of Poles from the new
Reich territories', prepared by Eduard Könekamp as an observer at the
German Foreign Institute in December 1939, a routine had quickly
been established:

> As ethnic Germans from the Baltic states, Volhynia and Galicia
> come pouring into the new Reich territories, particularly the
> Warthegau, an equivalent number of Poles from matching occu-
> pations are being evacuated at the same rate. Depending on the
> number of German farmers, traders, skilled tradesmen, etc., who
> are registered with the immigration offices, a corresponding
> number of jobs, houses and farms previously held or occupied by
> Poles must be made available for them. If, for example, an incom-
> ing batch of immigrants from the Baltic states contains twenty
> German master bakers, then twenty Polish bakeries in Posen and
> the rest of the Warthegau must be evacuated.[20] The German
> immigrants then move into these premises (...) Initially the evac-
> uation of residents from the towns was not carried out selective-
> ly, but simply block by block. This often meant that railway
> workers and other persons working in vital industries were evacu-
> ated, causing economic disruption. Today evacuations are carried
> out on the basis of specially prepared lists. Polish intellectuals are
> evacuated as a matter of priority. Polish agricultural workers,
> domestic staff and factory workers are allowed to remain.[21]

On 30 January 1940 a conference convened by Himmler and
chaired by Heydrich reviewed the first phase of the resettlement programme and discussed how all 'the agencies involved' might best
coordinate their efforts. These agencies included the RKF itself, the
commander (and the inspectors) of the security police and the SD,
the senior SS and police commanders in the annexed eastern territories and the Government General, the 'Ethnic German Agency'
[*Volksdeutsche Mittelstelle* or 'VoMi'][22] and the Central Trust Agency
for the East.[23] The Central Office for the Security of the Reich had no
less than nine representatives around the table. Adolf Eichmann was
present, as was the economics specialist and head of the SD in
Germany, Otto Ohlendorf. Heydrich told the assembled delegates

that apart from the 87,000 Poles and Jews who had been deported in order to make room for ethnic Germans from the Baltic states, an 'uncontrolled' and so-called 'illegal' emigration had taken place. By this he meant the mass exodus of people trying to escape the German terror. Heydrich also reported on the especial zeal displayed by his officials, who had ensured 'that in the evacuations carried out to date the original quotas have not only been met, but have been exceeded'. He gave notice of further deportations in the 'very near future': '40,000 Jews and Poles to facilitate the relocation of Germans from the Baltic States' and '120,000 Poles to facilitate the relocation of Germans from Volhynia'. He also announced the deportation of the entire Jewish population from the 'new eastern districts' (Ostgaue) – some 450,000 people – and of the 30,000 or so 'gypsies' from the German Reich.[24] But the limited transport capacity of the German railway system – the Reichsbahn – and food shortages in the Government General were thought likely to cause problems in this regard.

For future reference it should be made clear here that Section IV in the Central Office for the Security of the Reich was responsible for all resettlement operations, and not just for the 'Jewish transports'. On 21 December 1939 Heydrich had issued the following instructions regarding the 'clearance of the eastern provinces': 'It is necessary for practical reasons to have all security-related matters handled by a central agency while the programme of clearances in the eastern territories is being implemented. As my special adviser in charge of Section IV at the Central Office for the Security of the Reich I have appointed SS Hauptsturmführer Eichmann, with SS Hauptsturmführer Günther as his deputy. The offices of this special department are located in Berlin W 62 at Kurfürstenstrasse 115/116.'[25] By 8 January 1940 Eichmann was already chairing his first meeting with representatives of various ministries on the subject of the 'evacuation of the Jews and Poles in the very near future'.[26]

Expulsion and Germanization

The RKF was not in the business of categorizing the people affected by its plans in blanket racial terms. The population specialists at the RKF made a very clear distinction between population groups that they defined as superfluous and replaceable, and those that they regarded as 'racially undesirable' but not replaceable – not in the short term at least. This method of sorting and classifying

populations differed essentially, however, from Hitler's declared principle of creating clearer 'ethnographic dividing lines' – a principle
that the experts very quickly subverted in practice. It continued to
apply without restriction to the Jewish population and to gypsies, but
not to other 'dependent minority races'. The 'eligibility examiners' –
not 'racial examiners', be it noted – singled out those from the
'dependent minority races' whom they deemed 'suitable for
Germanization'. In making its selections, the RKF was guided far
more by the perceived economic benefits than by a fundamentalist
interpretation of Nazi ideology. Just how close those within the RKF
saw the relationship between the social question and general population and racial policy aims is documented by a report on the expulsion of a portion of the Alsatian population. The key passage strikes a
somewhat shrill note:

> The expulsion operation in Alsace was carried out in the period
> between July and December 1940, and 105,000 persons were
> expelled as a result or prevented from returning. These persons
> consisted in the main of Jews, gypsies and members of other
> foreign races, criminals, antisocial elements and the incurably
> mentally ill, plus Frenchmen and Francophiles. The patois popu-
> lation[27] was scoured by this wave of deportations just like the rest
> of the Alsatian population.

The aim had been 'to purge [Alsace] of all foreign, diseased and unreliable elements'. The operation had apparently been expressly authorized by the Führer. But as the first wave of deportations had not been
sufficiently comprehensive, a second 'must be prepared as soon as
possible'. It was to embrace the following population groups: '(a)
Coloured persons and their descendants, negroes and coloured half-
castes, gypsies and their descendants, Jews from half-Jews upwards,
Jewish mixed marriages; (b) members of dependent minority races
and their descendants; (c) the patois population; (d) antisocial
elements; (e) the incurably mentally ill.'[28]

This list reflects both the thinking behind a racist and preventive
social policy of 'ethnic cleansing' and the utilitarianism that drove the
campaign of euthanasia. At the same time the RKF proved extremely
flexible when it came to accommodating overriding economic and
socio-political goals. This flexibility allowed it to adapt its approach to
individual circumstances; the procedures adopted varied from one
region to the next, and were never dictated by rigid principles.

As early as November 1939 a special dispensation was already in place for Upper Silesia, decreeing that 'all parts of Upper Silesia where there are thought to be coal deposits (...) will initially be exempted completely from the evacuation measures on economic grounds'.[29]

> I estimate [wrote a resettlement expert in November 1940, describing his assignment in the annexed province of Lorraine] that the evacuation will take 12 to 14 days and that a total of 60 to 70,000 people will be moved out. This probably amounts to around one-third of the French-speaking population of Lorraine. Essentially only farmers, skilled tradesmen and independent professionals are being evacuated. The industrial workforce of the area around Thionville, which is like a smaller version of Upper Silesia, will remain in its entirety; in its composition it represents an ideal mix of European and African stock (...). There are Berbers here, Africans, Algerians, Italian anti-fascists, Poles, Czechs, Slovaks, Jews, even some Indo-Chinese, with a few Germans and Frenchmen here and there. The task of resettling this area has been assigned to Gauleiter Bürckel, who will be drawing the new settlers solely from the population surplus in the Saar-Palatinate.[30]

So the author of this report was guided by a number of different criteria. He took account of the regional structure and current manpower requirements, and he also included in his calculations the 'population surplus' in neighbouring regions. The early deportation of the Jewish population from Baden and the Palatinate to southern France (on 22 October 1940) was part of the policy of evacuation and resettlement pursued by the RKF in Alsace-Lorraine. This reflected what was happening in the annexed eastern territories and the adjoining regions of the German Reich. In the annexed territories of the West, too, the deportation of the Jewish minority went hand in hand with the evacuation of tens of thousands of families belonging to the 'dependent minority races'.

The entire procedure had been approved, and doubtless also modified, by Göring's Four-Year Plan Authority, the highest economic planning agency in the land:[31] 'By order of the Reichsmarschall [i.e. Göring] the following categories of persons are exempted from deportation: workers in factories and iron and steel works, employees and officials of the railways, postal services and canals, plus agricultural and forestry labourers owning less than 1.5 hectares of land. Also exempted are doctors and pharmacists. So basically it is the agricultural population, skilled tradesmen and small traders who will be deported to France.'[32]

The social and occupational criteria around which the deportations were organized played an even more central role in the process of Germanization. As the term itself suggests, Germanization was not about 'repatriating' families who had thought of themselves as Germans for generations past, but about dividing the subjugated peoples into 'useful' and 'useless' groups. It was also about offering the option of collaboration to individuals who were willing to conform and to those who were particularly needed. It was about pursuing a brutal and calculated policy of divide and rule, and destroying ethnic cultures and identities. Quite simply, Germanization meant the 'creaming-off' of 'human resources' for the social and economic 'rebuilding of the Reich' and the conduct of the war. The threat of starvation, dispossession and possible deportation was used to 'soften up' the subject populations and make them 'more receptive' to Germanization. Persons who were deemed unsuitable for Germanization were thereby cleared for deportation.

The 'guidelines for the Germanization of Polish families' issued in March 1942 state: 'The Germanization of families of other nationalities is not primarily intended to swell the ranks of the German nation by incorporating persons of predominantly Nordic-Dinaric blood, but rather to sap the quality of the leadership caste in the foreign ethnic stock.' Experience has shown (the author continues) 'that particularly among the leaders of the Polish insurgents and resistance movement there is a high preponderance of Nordic blood, which predisposes them to play a more active part in events than the more fatalistic Slavic elements'. And then he goes on: 'For this reason in particular the more racially valuable strains should be creamed off from the Polish nation.' Only the Reich Commissioner for the Strengthening of German Nationhood, the NSDAP and the SD were able to recommend the Germanization of persons belonging to 'dependent minority races'. The eligibility criteria were as follows: 'The family must stand out from the rest of the Polish population *and* [the writer's own emphasis] the ethnic German population by virtue of its general demeanour, diligence, cleanliness and healthiness, even if it is living in impoverished circumstances.' Furthermore, families deemed 'suitable for Germanization' must not only stand out from the average of the indigenous population, but must also 'be above the average for the equivalent social class in the Reich'. Factors rated highly by the RKF included the desire to better oneself and the willingness to conform – rather than any characteristics relating to national origins. On this point the guidelines are quite specific: 'A poor knowledge of German, or a political past, are no impediment.'[33]

The mentally ill, social misfits, active Communists, persons living in so-called mixed marriages and other maladjusted types could not become Germans. To qualify for this 'privilege', candidates must be given a clean bill of health – medically, genetically and politically. Without this such persons were classed as 'racially undesirable' – even if they were ethnic Germans.[34]

Moreover the general policy was not to Germanize persons over the age of forty-five. The reason given was as follows: 'The German nation would burden itself with such persons, not simply in demographic terms [the "mortgage of death", according to the demographer Burgdörfer], but also in purely social terms. The persons concerned are capable of fully productive work only in very few instances, and since they are unlikely to produce further offspring they constitute an unnecessary burden on the body of the nation.'[35]

The social utopia envisaged by the RKF was not dictated primarily by a sentimental German nationalism. Its supreme goal was to establish a German-speaking master race on the one hand, and on the other hand to eradicate, or at least enslave, large groups of so-called inferior peoples. And through the 'creaming-off' of so-called 'superior' elements the social fabric of these peoples was to be destroyed. At the same time the demographers at the RKF had it in mind to replace their own 'inferior' population inside the German Reich with these newly acquired 'human resources': after all, plans were already being made to eliminate more than a million 'antisocial elements', 'misfits' and 'idlers' from the Reich.[36]

Himmler regarded the policy of Germanization as part of that strategy he had summarized in a memorandum of May 1940. In contrast to his early decrees he now embraced Germanization as an effective instrument of social restructuring. For in the meantime it had dawned on the National Socialist leadership too that the manpower needed for the far-reaching imperialistic plans of the German Reich could not be supplied from their own population alone. Under the title 'Some thoughts on the treatment of the dependent minority races in the East' Himmler's memorandum called for the population in the East to be 'broken up into countless small fragments and particles'[37] – a policy expressly endorsed by Hitler. In future Polish children should only have four years of primary schooling, learning 'simple arithmetic allowing them to count to a maximum of 500'.

Their 'highest precept', Himmler avers in his memorandum, must be 'to obey the Germans and to be honest, hard-working and well-behaved'. However, these much-quoted remarks did not apply to *all* Polish children. Himmler planned to use this process to sift out those Polish families who wanted a better education for their children, exploiting their aspirations as a criterion and lever for Germanization. This was the context in which Himmler now went on to discuss the methods for 'sifting and screening young persons':

> Parents who wish from the outset to give their children a better education, both at primary school level and later on at a secondary school, must submit an application to the senior SS and police commander. The application will be decided primarily on the basis of whether the child is racially pure and matches up to our requirements. If we acknowledge the child as being of our blood, it will be explained to the parents that the child will be sent to a school in Germany, where he or she will remain for the duration (...) The parents of these children of good blood will then be given a choice: either they must give up their child – making it unlikely that they will produce any more children, and thus banishing the risk that this subhuman race in the East might acquire, through such persons of good blood, a leadership caste that would be a threat to us precisely because it is our equal – or the parents must undertake to move to Germany and become loyal citizens of the Reich. Their love of their child gives us a powerful hold over them, in that the child's future and education depend on the loyalty of the parents.

When these children, with or without their parents, had arrived in Germany, Himmler insisted that they were 'not to be treated like lepers' but 'accepted and integrated into German life after changing their names'. If these measures were 'systematically implemented', after ten years or so there would only be an 'inferior population' living in Poland: a 'leaderless nation of workers', destined to collaborate, under strict supervision, in the 'eternal civilizing deeds' of the German nation.[38]

A few weeks after drafting this memorandum Himmler estimated that approximately one-eighth of the total Polish population could be Germanized in this manner.[39]

The concept was extended with the onward march of German military aggression: 'There are still a few Goths left in the Caucasus and the Crimea,' observed Himmler in 1942 – and he intended to 'bring them out and make them into true Germans'. 'After the war', he continued, he would 'despatch SS commanders to every country to bring out the good blood from the indigenous population via the children. The SS commander would turn up in plain clothes and present himself as a helpful, caring man, showing kindness to the children, telling them about free school places, and then bringing them back to Germany with him.'[40]

The fact that Himmler's plans for Germanization applied primarily to children in the first instance had to do with his belief that young persons should be nurtured and encouraged solely on their merits, without regard to their social origins and the old social hierarchies and class structures. They would then, so Himmler presumed, be especially loyal to Nazi ideas and thinking. Naturally the desire not to create a society top-heavy with elderly people also played its part here: through the relocation of children and juveniles from 'dependent minority races' to the German Reich the population structure would shift in favour of young persons with a healthy capacity for work, and a more favourable ratio between productive labour and welfare costs.

On 12 September 1940 Himmler issued a decree regulating the 'future composition of the population' in the annexed eastern territories.[41] According to this the people living there were to be divided into the following four categories: 'A' = 'German nationals', i.e. 'true' or 'fully-fledged' Germans; 'B' = 'persons of German origin who must be taught to become fully-fledged Germans again, who therefore possess German nationality but not, initially, the rights and status of full Reich citizenship'. Persons in this category were 'generally' to be deported to the German homeland – the pre-war Reich – for 're-Germanization'. This course of action was mandatory, however, for category 'C' persons, defined as 'valuable members of the dependent minority races and German renegades who possess German nationality subject to revocation'. By far the largest category was 'D', into which the Reich Commissioner for the Strengthening of German Nationhood placed all those 'foreign nationals who do not possess German nationality'. Of these eight million or so Polish men and women the authorities were to 'sift out' those 'who constitute a valuable addition to the population of the German nation'; their number was fixed in advance by the decree at 'a maximum of one million persons'.

In the same decree, and on the basis of these categories, Himmler ordered the introduction of a further system for classifying the population, the so-called 'Deutsche Volksliste' [DVL – German National List]. This divided the Germans and those deemed 'worthy of Germanization' – essentially the persons assigned to categories A, B and C – into four 'classes' and conferred upon them differing sets of civil and social rights. Classes 1 and 2 were for those who had 'actively engaged in the struggle for nationhood', or who had at least 'demonstrably preserved their German language and way of life'. 'Persons of German origin who had entered into relationships with the Poles over the years (...) but whose conduct indicates that they have the potential to become full members of the German national community' were assigned to class 3. Included among their number were members of the dependent minority races who were married to Germans – albeit only if the ethnic experts judged that the German element was dominant in such a 'mixed marriage of nationalities'. What this meant in practice was that the ménage had to conform to German notions of orderliness and show a willingness to achieve and to better itself. The last class was reserved for so-called 'renegades', said to be 'persons of German origin who have been absorbed politically into Polish society'. Members of the first two classes were to be 'deployed for the work of reconstruction in the East', while those placed in classes 3 and 4 would be 'brought up as fully-fledged Germans – or re-Germanized, as the case may be – through an intensive programme of education in Germany over a period of time'. (This normally meant deporting the persons concerned for forced labour on German farms.) Those assigned to class 4 of the German National List, together with 'racially valuable members of dependent minority races (Ukrainians, Great Russians, White Russians, Czechs and Lithuanians)' were to be given German nationality subject to revocation.[42] They were kept under close surveillance by the security police. As a reward for conformity and good behaviour they might hope to receive German citizenship after a few years. 'Those who decline to be re-Germanized', it was tersely noted, 'will be subject to action by the security police'. In other words, they would be placed in a concentration camp or murdered. As Himmler noted in a jotting: 'All Germanic blood to us – or be wiped out.'[43]

For the annexed eastern territories, a total of 977,000 people were registered in classes 1 and 2 of the German National List, while those registered in classes 3 and 4 numbered 1,928,000; together they amounted to approximately one-third of the population. Two-thirds of those registered were placed in class 3 of the List. All the remaining members of the 'dependent minority races' – i.e. the majority that did not qualify for the List – were classed as 'client subjects of the German Reich, with limited native citizens' rights'.[44] They were effectively without rights in the face of harassment by the authorities, and they could be deported at any time. But if they displayed evidence of good behaviour they might be rewarded with promotion to the lower ranks of the Germanization hierarchy. These arrangements did not apply to Jews or gypsies.

The numbers of those selected for Germanization varied considerably from one region to the next. This did not reflect the arbitrary whims of individual Gauleiters, but the agrarian and industrial policy aims of the RKF for each region. And when the shortage of manpower became acute in the last two years of the war, the RKF dramatically increased the quotas for Germanization.[45] In the technical jargon of the population planners this process was also known as *Umvolkung* – 'ethnic conversion'.

Resettlement in annexed western Poland

To confiscate and then administer agricultural land in the annexed eastern territories the RKF set up a special department known as the 'central land office'. This agency was supported by regional land offices, which had been established after the invasion of Poland to assist local units of the SS Central Office of Race and Resettlement in 'exercising the rights of the Reich on land belonging to Polish nationals'.[46] The regional land offices were taken over by the RKF at the beginning of 1940. They were now used to push through a 'land reform' designed to serve German interests by supplementing the terror tactics of expulsion with a systematic reordering of the conditions governing land tenure. Special maps were drawn up in the land offices. They were used to locate and identify agricultural property earmarked for confiscation. On these maps, land and soil quality were correlated with 'ethnic grouping', so that one could tell by looking at the map 'which types of land were occupied by German farmers and which by Poles'.[47] The purpose was to ensure that any better-quality land still owned by Poles was now handed over to Germans. But the Polish farmers were to be evicted even from the poorer-quality land, as these areas were designated for afforestation or 'landscaping'.[48]

As soon as the land had been confiscated and arrangements were in place for deportation and resettlement, the RKF's resettlement units went into action. The staff of these units were responsible for installing the incoming ethnic Germans in 'their' new farms and houses. The transit camps in which they had been temporarily housed up until then were often former mental or nursing homes that had been cleared by murdering the inmates under the 'euthanasia' programme. Now the ethnic Germans were given apartments and houses from which Polish and Jewish families had previously been evicted. The realities of resettlement are described in many surviving reports; a small selection is cited below.

A certain Mr Schick, employed in the Katowice Trust Agency, describes a resettlement operation that he was invited to observe by the SS:

> On Sunday 17 May 1942 the SS resettlement unit, together with the local police battalion, carried out the eviction of some 700 persons in Todygowicz and installed new settlers in their place. (...) The evicted Poles were given just half an hour to vacate their properties, and consequently took just the bare essentials with them such as clothing and linen, while the furniture, carpets, household articles, sewing machines and pianos stayed behind. The incoming settlers were supplied with new furniture by the NSV, and will sell on the furniture left behind by the Poles.[49]

Walter Quiring, a colleague of the Dr Könekamp of the German Foreign Institute in Stuttgart who was mentioned earlier, supplies a number of important additional details in his own account: 'The evacuated Poles are taken first of all to transit camps in Litzmannstadt [= Lódź]. Here they are processed and classified according to racial group. Approximately 8 per cent of the total – those belonging to racial groups I and II – are taken back to Germany to be assimilated. A further 15–20 per cent are also sent to Germany for labour service, while the rest are sent east into the Government General.'[50]

In 1946 Franciszka Jankowska, a Pole, gave the following account of her expulsion:

> On 23 April 1940, it was a Tuesday, at 4.00 a.m., when we were all still asleep, two uniformed Germans entered the room. They ordered us to get dressed at once and leave the house. We were terrified, and suspected that we were being deported. Suddenly I noticed smoke in the room. I grabbed my two youngest children

and got them out of the house. The children were only dressed in their nightshirts, I had taken them straight from their beds. The fire spread rapidly. The Germans began to fire on the burning house, shooting into the flames, I'm sure they were trying to kill my husband. I learned from our neighbour, Jacub Pszczólkowski, that my husband didn't get away, but was killed. I and my four children were taken along with other evacuees to a camp in a factory in Lódź. When we left the camp they gave us 20 zlotys each. I had no way of supporting myself and my children, and so was dependent on charity aid from the local population.[51]

Eduard Könekamp, who was mentioned above, describes an evacuation operation of this kind from a German perspective:

In the camp on the very outskirts of the town about 20 buses came in one after the other, bringing a total of 700 evacuees. They came piling out of the vehicles, laden with suitcases, rucksacks, bundles tied up in sheets, prams and children's toys, eating utensils, coats and blankets. It rained incessantly. We were standing around in a sea of mud. A few lamps cast their dim light over the scene. Children, rudely awoken from sleep and distraught, were crying. We saw old women in their eighties and nineties. A man wearing the ribbon of the Iron Cross (second class), a German secondary-school teacher who had chosen to work in Poland – and we saw our countess, ladies in half-veils and fine furs. An implacable but just fate was here being visited upon individual Poles, and upon the ruling class in particular.[52]

In the wake of these brutal evacuations, incoming ethnic Germans were installed as soon as possible. The process is described by Walter Quiring:

I was particularly impressed by the way the resettlement in Janowice (in the Lentschütz district) was organized. The resettlement unit sent a car for me at 4.30 a.m. (...) Our first destination was the transit camp in Zgierz. Parked outside the gate was a line of brown buses normally used to take German workers on vacation trips. The luggage was just then being put on board. The new colonists were sitting in a school hall eating their breakfast. The head of every family had a piece of white paper hung around his neck with the number of his farm written on it (and already the numbering ran from 1441 upwards). I talked to the new colonists. One of them, Selent, had taken part in the Manchurian campaign in 1904–5. His family had been sent to Siberia in 1915, while he served at the front with the Russian army. After the war he went to America for a few years, to make enough money to build up his farm in Volhynia again. (...) We leave with the second group. The people are put on the buses in the order of their farm numbers. (...) At a farm halfway there we meet up with the police unit of 50 or so men who have been working there during the night. Janowice comes into view up ahead. (...) Then the first carts arrive. No. 1441. A pale, elderly farmer in a poor state of health. 'This here is your farm,' the SS man tells him. It's a small, blue-painted Polish cottage. It seems to me that the farmer turns a shade paler. He slowly approaches the high wooden gate. His wife stays on the cart, as if rooted to the spot. 'And the second farm over there, the neighbouring one, that's yours as well...' continues the SS man. 'Now that's more like it,' he seems to be thinking. I accompany the people as they tour the house. They wander slowly from room to room, examining everything closely. Nobody says a word. Now and then the farmer points to an object and says to his wife, 'Look!' We wish the people good luck and go over to the next house.[53]

The practical implementation of the resettlement policy involved both the Party and the Central Office for the Security of the Reich. The NSDAP was represented on the ground by the Ethnic German Agency [VoMi], which had been set up in 1936 with the object of integrating ethnic Germans living abroad more effectively into German political life.[54] The VoMi was headed by SS Obergruppen-führer Werner Lorenz.[55] As soon as the 'repatriations' of Germans living abroad began, the establishment of the VoMi was steadily expanded. By June 1941 it had been promoted to the status of an SS *Hauptamt* or central office.

The Central Office for the Security of the Reich [Reichssicher-heitshauptamt or RSHA] exercised control over resettlement policy through two institutions: the Einwandererzentrale (EWZ) [Immigration Bureau], responsible for the repatriation of ethnic Germans from abroad, and the Umwandererzentrale (UWZ) [roughly, 'Resettlement Bureau'], responsible for the expulsion of the indigenous population. The key posts in both organizations were occupied by SD personnel. The EWZ was headed by SS Standartenführer Dr Martin Sandberger,[56] who was also deputy Gruppenleiter in the RSHA and later gave the order for mass shootings of civilians in the Soviet Union.[57] The head of the UWZ, in charge of deportations, was Adolf Eichmann.

Despite the bewildering multiplicity of agencies and organizations involved in the administration of ethnic policy, in practice the chain of command was much more direct than might be supposed. In many cases the same 'ethnic experts' would be employed by several institutions, which facilitated coordination, or else several different agencies and committees would be headed by the same specialist. So for example the head of the UWZ's office of health, the physician and SS Obersturmbannführer Ernst Fähndrich, was simultaneously in charge of the RKF's department for the deployment of human resources. He also liaised between the central staff office of the RKF and Heydrich. His duties at the UWZ included supervising the medical examination of persons in the resettlement transit camps and undertaking the 'final medical assessment of the families'. As head of department at the RKF he chaired a conference on 30 October 1940 (for example), which was attended by representatives of the Foreign Office, the RSHA (Eichmann), the VoMi and the German Resettlement Trust Company. The subject up for discussion was how to treat Jewish 'Reichsangehörige' [second-class Reich citizens – as distinct from 'Reichsbürger'] who were living in the 'Protectorate' or the Soviet Union, given that 'the Reich has an interest in not allowing assets that are currently in Jewish hands to be seized by the Soviet Russians'.[58]

In October 1939 the RKF had founded the German Resettlement Trust Company [German acronym: DUT] for the purpose of 'administering and safeguarding the property rights' of ethnic Germans who were resettled in conquered territories. Its activities were 'many and various', but according to its charter the Company was primarily concerned with 'the orderly transfer of settlers' assets from the country of origin to the new settlement area'. By the end of 1940 half a million Germans living abroad were 'on their way home', and as such were under the care of the DUT. The Company's last annual report (for 1943) ends with a balance-sheet total of half a billion Reichsmarks. By 31 December 1942 its 1,700 employees had provided for the needs of exactly 806,106 settlers, handing over to them 'confiscated Jewish properties and assets' or leaving them furniture and household goods 'previously owned by Poles and Jews'.[59] Any additional household goods required were commandeered by the RKF from other sources – the Lódź ghetto, for example, where the RKF also continued to have new furniture made up until 1944.[60]

The whole system worked as follows. The Foreign Office concluded bilateral agreements with the Baltic republics, the Soviet Union and Romania governing the resettlement of ethnic Germans. The RKF then resettled these German families – whose forebears had emigrated to eastern and south-east Europe in previous centuries – in the annexed territory of western Poland. The property they had left behind in their old homeland was valued by the DUT, and the government of that country had to make a lump-sum payment of equal value to the German Reich, usually in the form of deliveries of raw materials or food. In theory the German government should then have reimbursed the resettled families for the assets they had left behind. In practice the government pocketed the revenues from the resettlement trade and 'compensated' the resettled families with the stolen property of the displaced Jewish and Polish population. So the German state and the Four-Year Plan Authority, which was responsible for imports of raw materials and food, made a tidy profit from this triangular transaction, which was based on expulsion and deportation. The negotiations over a resettlement agreement with Romania may serve as an example. In this instance the Foreign Office valued the assets left behind by the settlers in Romania at approximately 50 million Reichsmarks, for which the Romanian government was expected to make payment-in-kind by supplying oil to an equivalent value. At the end of 1942 the RKF reported to Hitler 'on the status of the resettlement programme': 'To date the work carried out by the Reich Commissioner has cost approximately 770 million Reichsmarks of public money. An additional 225 million Reichsmarks has been spent through the German Resettlement Bank on renovating and equipping the farms taken over by the settlers in the annexed Eastern territories. By and large the costs of resettlement have been met by utilizing the property and assets formerly belonging to the ousted dependent minorities, without payment of compensation – and without recourse, therefore, to public money.'[61] Some of these millions in profits are disclosed in the balance-sheet total of the DUT. At the same time the DUT functioned as a bank dealing specifically with the financial aspects of resettlement.[62] It gave loans to the incoming colonists to help them get started, and made sure that the new property allocated to them was broadly equivalent to what they had left behind.

The DUT and RKF collaborated closely with the Central Trust Agency for the East (Haupttreuhandstelle Ost = HTO). While the RKF was responsible for confiscating and reallocating agricultural holdings and forestry land, the Central Trust Agency for the East performed the same function vis-à-vis commercial and industrial assets. The latter body was set up by the Four-Year Plan Authority and remained a permanent fixture as a self-contained 'business unit' within the parent institution.[63] The Central Trust Agency for the East administered the businesses it confiscated on a temporary basis and made them over to new owners; but only, of course, if its auditors rated them as 'a paying proposition' when measured against German criteria of productivity. To administer urban real estate the Agency set up a separate limited company, the GHTO. So by extending its reach through the Central Trust Agency for the East the Four-Year Plan Authority was able to bring industry and commerce and urban real estate under its control, and in this way became directly involved in countless deportation operations and expulsions of Jews. The RKF selected the new owners for confiscated businesses and properties, was sometimes involved in hiring new workers for the expropriated firms and supplied new tenants and landlords. The Central Trust Agency and the RKF also undertook joint public relations initiatives.[64] But above all else the Central Trust Agency for the East combined hard-headed economic interests with practical resettlement policy. Its 'entire work' was 'placed in the service of strengthening the war economy of the German Reich' and implementing the 'principles of the Four-Year Plan'.[65]

'Rationally deployed in concert'

Population and structural policy initiatives were drafted by a special planning office within the RKF. As head of this office Himmler had appointed Professor Konrad Meyer, an agrarian and regional planning expert from Berlin. He advised Himmler on all matters relating to agrarian and resettlement policy, bringing to his work 'an exemplary blend of professional expertise and National Socialist leadership qualities'.[66] Meyer's rise to prominence coincided with the emergence of town and country planning as a new discipline at German universities. As a full professor at the University of Berlin and director of the Institute for Agrarian Policy Studies he headed the Reich Working Party on Regional Planning [German acronym: RAG] from 1936, when it was set up in conjunction with the Four-Year Plan, to 1940. The RAG developed town and country planning into a scientifically accredited political instrument of state planning. It acquired substantial influence, and Hitler eventually placed it under the wing of the

Reich Ministry for Religious Affairs, which reported directly to him. Also assigned to the Ministry was the Reich Office of Regional Planning, which was directly under Hitler's control. A personal decree of the Führer granted the Reich Office extensive powers for 'the overall strategic planning and ordering of German-controlled territory'.[67]

Meyer firmly believed that 'planning is central to National Socialist policy'. While it had been viewed with scepticism for a number of years, it was now 'an expression and part-manifestation of our National Socialist system of leadership': 'It seeks to create a healthy body politic through the total ordering of territory and economic activity.' In his keynote address of 1941 he elaborates further:

> Our planning enterprise can only prosper with the scientific col-laboration of, and in close, enduring association with, the univer-sity establishment. I am not talking about a value-free science, with no preconceptions – that sort is of no value at all for our purposes – but a science that sees its raison d'être in serving the people and embracing the forces of blood and soil. For the work of planning we need a scientific approach that seeks not so much to abstract and generalize its knowledge as to relate its findings to concrete situations; not a backward-looking science that is content merely to record past events, but a forward-looking science that plays a constructive part in shaping events as they unfold. (...) National Socialism entered the arena vehemently rejecting the liberal principle of self-regulation and the free play of forces. In the pursuit of its revolutionary aims it has elevated the ordering and rational planning of every area of the nation's life into a ruling principle. The 'laissez-faire, laissez-aller' approach has deliberately been abandoned in favour of the call for individual powers to be conjoined, to be rationally deployed in concert, and to be harnessed to the higher idea of the common national good that now commands our loyalty.[68]

In the summer of 1942 Meyer was made planning commissioner for the reorganization of settlement and land use to the Reichsleiter for Agrarian Policy, the Reich Minister for Food and Agriculture and the Reich Farmers' Leader, as well as head of the colonization com-mittee for the occupied eastern territories.[69] His task was to prepare the outline planning framework for all the authorities involved, to harmonize the plans submitted by the individual institutions[70] and to coordinate these with the resettlement programmes of the SS. From 1943 onwards his deputy in the regional planning department of the Reich Ministry of Food and Agriculture was SS Untersturmführer Friedrich Kann, a trained land economist who worked as a resettlement expert in the SS Central Office of Race and Resettlement. Kann also represented the Reich Farmers' Leader in the planning department of the RKF.[71]

In practice, the RKF relied from the outset on the resources of nearly every civilian and scientific planning institution. Meyer arranged for a 'close collaboration' between the Reich Office of Regional Planning and the planning department of the RKF. The two agencies were to 'coordinate their activities on an ongoing basis' both at the central and at the departmental level.[72] The collaboration between the civilian Reich Office of Regional Planning and the Reich Commissioner for the Strengthening of German Nationhood, with its special executive powers, had a mutually energizing effect on the work of both institutions.[73] It created a situation in which the planners felt increasingly empowered to pursue the remorseless logic of their own thinking, and in which their schemes became increasingly ruthless in consequence.

As early as January 1940 the planning department of the RKF published a preliminary discussion paper on 'the reconstruction of the eastern territories' – marked 'For internal distribution only!' It outlined how the annexed territories of western Poland were now to be conquered and subjugated from within. In the wake of Blitzkrieg the country would now be forcibly Germanized by deploying the instruments of long-term population policy and regional planning: 'On the field of battle the Wehrmacht has created the foundations of a new order, but the battle is not yet over. (...) Indeed, the battle only begins in earnest when the guns fall silent.'[74]

The planners at the RKF proposed to raise the German population quota from 11 to 50 per cent, increasing to 70 per cent on agricultural land. On the eastern frontier they proposed to erect a 'defensive wall of ethnic German stock in the shape of a belt of Germanic farms echeloned in depth'. The land economist Meyer pondered at length on the structure of agricultural settlement and land tenure, and even on the numbers of cows, pigs, goats and chickens that would be allocated to the 'new farmers'. He also had detailed plans drawn up for the electrification of the new villages and the 'extensive use' of electrical appliances.[75] In the towns and cities Meyer envisaged a 'complete rebuilding of the urban fabric and an increase in the proportion of the population living in small and medium-sized towns'. The 'General Principles' of this plan reveal the contempt for human life with which its architects proceeded:

> The following assumes that the entire Jewish population of this area, numbering some 560,000 people, has already been evacuated or will be leaving the area in the course of the winter. To all intents and purposes, therefore, we can assume a total population figure of 9 millions. (...) The restoration of the status of 1914 would mean first of all that the 1.1 million Germans now living in this area would need to be increased by 3.4 million to bring the number up to 4.5 million, while 3.4 million Poles are progressively deported. (...) For general demographic and economic reasons the reconstruction programme as a whole will be planned on the basis of an average population density of 100 persons per square kilometre, which is in fact the current average – although that number conceals an overcrowded agricultural sector. (...) For this reason, therefore, the eastern territory must be developed as a mixed agrarian-industrial region with a social and economic structure similar to that of the most prosperous parts of Bavaria and our north-western province of Hanover.[76]

This plan had implications for the planned density of settlement, as became apparent in the guidelines for 'colonization and evacuation in the annexed eastern territories for 1941': 'According to present calculations the evacuation of the newly annexed province of Danzig-West Prussia should proceed on the basis of 2 persons being evacuated for every one new arrival (...) In the Warthegau 2–3 Poles are to be evacuated for every incoming colonist, in Upper Silesia 4–5 Poles, and for every incoming skilled tradesman and urban settler 3 Poles must be evacuated.'

In planning the resettlement of the annexed eastern territories the Reich Commissioner for the Strengthening of German Nationhood was the first organization to put into practice a new regional planning model that still forms part of the standard repertoire of town and country planning departments today. This was the paradigm of 'central places', as developed in 1933 by the geographer Walter Christaller, who first applied his theory to southern Germany. With the aid of this theory, administrative and utility supply services in 'rural regions' were to be structured hierarchically and coordinated with each other in the interests of greater efficiency. This model, which is now accepted orthodoxy, envisages the following structure: one community is designated as a 'main centre', around which a number of 'intermediate centres' are established within a certain radius, each of which is surrounded in turn by a series of 'subcentres'. Depending on their 'degree of centrality' (calculated originally in terms of the number of telephone connections), these communities are then allocated a varying mix of production facilities, business enterprises and workshops, transport and administrative facilities, service enterprises and – where appropriate – schools and hospitals.[77] Since 1940 Christaller had been working in conjunction with the 'strategically vital research programme "Deutscher Osten" [German East]' to put his model into practice for the conquered eastern territories.[78]

On the basis of this system the existing order of things was ripped up on the drawing-board, so to speak, and a new territorial order was conceived in its place in which human beings were simply one factor among many others – and one that could be as readily altered and manipulated as any other: 'Where a region is uniformly served by a series of evenly distributed central places of a certain size and importance, these central places will be spaced an equal distance apart, so that they form equilateral triangles. These triangles will in turn form regular hexagons, with the central place in the middle of the hexagon assuming a greater importance. (...) The aim of regional planning, however, is to introduce order into impractical, outdated and arbitrary urban forms or transport networks, and this order can only be achieved on the basis of an ideal plan – which in spatial terms means a geometric schema.' For Christaller, 'spatial anarchy' must give way to 'spatial laws' and 'spatial hierarchy'. As he plotted his web of triangles and hexagons on the map he came across places where it seemed 'absolutely essential' to him 'to create a town of at least 25,000 inhabitants here'. And since there was nothing at all at the designated spot, the logic of Christaller's planning geometry left him no other option 'but to build a new town here from scratch'. Three other towns he proposed to 'downgrade to the appropriate size'. Between Radom and Kielce there should be a city of 300,000 people, while Upper Silesia needed 'a Düsseldorf or Cologne' of 450,000 inhabitants to provide a 'cultural centre' – and at the same time to 'serve as a link between Breslau and Vienna'.[79]

Konrad Meyer was responsible for the RKF's regional planning activities in the Reich and in the occupied countries. But even as the German attack on the Soviet Union was being prepared, he was already making plans for territories that the Wehrmacht had not yet conquered. In 1941 he and his planning staff produced the notorious 'General Plan for the East', which divided Poland and the entire Soviet Union into colonization and evacuation zones. Under this plan, not hundreds of thousands of people but over 200 millions would become the objects of regional planning and Germanization: the vast majority would become the victims of enslavement, deportation and extermination.

Atomization and social hierarchy

The fundamental reshaping of the population profile and the continuous selection of people, or 'settler material', as the RKF jargon had it, were intended to secure lasting German control over the newly conquered territories of eastern Europe. Gerhard Ziegler, a regional planner in Silesia, reported on the work of the RKF in the Warthegau following a tour of inspection: 'The backbone of the colony is formed by the Silesians and Pomeranians already established in the Warthegau, with new settlers being drafted in to swell their numbers and strengthen their social ties. (...) The best colonists in terms of their ethnic origins and attitude will be given land in the East and along the exposed western frontier. Galicians are the best, but they are also the most finicky and demanding. Volhynians are more reliable. (...) The wholesale transplanting of village communities is avoided on principle. But nor are they simply broken up; instead they are relocated in blocks of settlers, each one consisting of around 10 families (...) next door to each other wherever possible.' In this manner 'completely new cells of colonization' would be formed and 'settlers of common stock' would grow accustomed to other 'stocks' and marry into them. Himmler gave orders that only a quarter of the villages were to be populated by resettled Germans living abroad, so that 'the rest can be filled up later with settlers from the Reich homeland'.[80]

In the meantime the incoming Germans from abroad were housed temporarily in camps, where they had to wait until new 'places of settlement' were allocated to them. In Lódź, where the central transit camp for incoming settlers was set up in a 'fenced-off former Jewish weekend holiday village',[81] a 'development unit' staffed by 'something like 1,000 men' – students,[82] members of the Ethnic German Agency and representatives of the SS (including Josef Mengele[83]) – worked to record and classify the 'settler material' in terms of their racial origins. The colonists were divided into various categories depending on their home communities abroad, their social structure, their property status, their 'political complexion' and their state of health, and were redistributed accordingly. 'Class 3 communities are broken up on principle, while Class 1 villages of outstanding merit are transplanted wholesale and relocated intact.'[84]

Based on various reference figures and 'target profiles', the regional planners calculated the optimum 'population structure'. Depending on the quality of the land and soil, they laid down the number of persons per square kilometre who were to be employed in agriculture. This in turn allowed them to calculate the optimum number of 'non-agricultural workers'. Their yardstick was the 'recommended village size of 400–500 inhabitants as advocated by the Reich Commissioner', although it was conceded 'that it may be necessary on occasion to depart from the guidelines because of the natural features of the landscape and an existing pattern of settlement that is worth preserving'.[85]

Where the development of small and medium-sized business enterprises was planned for the new settlement zones, the appropriate professional and trade associations were entitled to make their views known.[86] Strict rules were laid down for the setting-up of new workshops and commercial enterprises. Before a settler was granted permission to establish a new business, the regional Chamber of Trades and Crafts or the Chamber of Industry and Commerce had to be consulted, along with the RKF, the Central Trust Agency for the East and the resettlement officer at the German High Command.[87]

So the categorization of people was not just the principle on which the RKF's whole operation of forced evacuation and Germanization was founded. It was also used to grade ethnic Germans – from South Tirolese to Volhynian Germans – as 'settler material' of varying quality, on which basis they were then given preferential treatment (or discriminated against, as the case might be) and eventually 'relocated' under widely varying conditions, but wherever possible in mixed ethnic groupings. Following the occupation of the western Soviet Union, the RKF summarily returned 'poor-quality settler material' – mainly people on welfare and those 'who could not be used in the Reich', or in the language of the RKF, 'not the most serviceable elements' – to their Soviet districts of origin.[88]

Here we can see how people were brutally uprooted from their established life and circumstances, and how every effort was made to eradicate their traditional ties. The 'formation of their new environment' was an entirely artificial exercise, their social make-up shaped

by the theories of social science. Behind all this lay the intention –
completely at odds with the image projected by Nazi ideology – of
creating a social structure within which the individual would be a
highly mobile and available commodity: disengaged from tradition
and familiar surroundings, owing allegiance only to the National
Socialist state, capable of adapting to the rapid pace of change in a
modern industrial society.

This policy of social atomization also extended to categorizing the
population of the German Reich according to certain predetermined
criteria. Meyer's planning department believed that the restructuring
of the social pyramid in the East should react upon social conditions
within the Reich. What this meant in specific terms is illustrated (for
example) by the 'Guidelines for the evaluation of genetically sound
stock' of 18 July 1940.[89] This document had been prepared and published by the department of public health and social welfare at the
Reich Ministry of the Interior, which at that time was also jointly
responsible for the programme of compulsory sterilization and the
murder of psychiatric patients. There was a very close relationship
between these guidelines for evaluating the genetic credentials of the
German population and the policies practised by the RKF – and the
so-called 'new farmers', who were to colonize the newly conquered
territories, had a special role to play in them.

The guidelines proposed to divide the German population into
four distinct categories. The lowest category consisted of 'antisocial
elements'. These persons and their children – the guidelines made no
mention of 'families' – were to be 'excluded from all forms of assistance and social support'. The Ministry did at least concede the use of
the term 'family' in discussion of the next-highest category, 'which
cannot be regarded as a valuable addition to the national community, but which [would] probably not constitute a serious burden upon
it'. This group was 'well below the norm in terms of industry and productivity', however. The directive therefore rated this category of
Germans as 'passable' – but no more than that. Existing welfare benefits would not be stopped, but new ones would not be granted. So
'measures designed to promote better health' – referring primarily to
sick-leave taken in health resorts for the treatment of tuberculosis –
would be considered only in isolated cases. The authors of these
guidelines had doubtless not excluded the possibility of simply
killing off 'antisocial elements'. For while they specifically discussed
compulsory sterilization in connection with the 'passables', there is
no mention of the subject in relation to the 'antisocial elements'.

Ranking next above these two categories was the large grouping described in the guidelines as the 'average population'. And enthroned in splendour above them was the select category of 'genetically high-grade' persons. To qualify for this privileged status it was necessary for the 'majority of family members' to demonstrate a record of 'work achievement and upward social mobility' – rather than exhibiting any outwardly 'Germanic' characteristics. The conclusion is unavoidable: the 'genetically sound stock' in the title of the guidelines refers to something else. There is no mention in the text of hereditary disposition or health as qualifying criteria. Instead the guidelines are expressly concerned with a social reorganization of the German population, and with the possibility of controlling its social structure – like the project in the East, but much smaller in scale, of course, and more cautious in its approach. For the population group defined as 'average' these guidelines – and this is likewise a characteristic feature of National Socialism – opened up the possibility of social betterment, a chance to make a life for themselves beyond the traditional class barriers.[90] But for that the state needed room for socio-political manoeuvre. And since this could not be created through a fundamental change in the system of property ownership, it was carved out at the expense of the people in the newly conquered territories, who were expelled, dispossessed and discriminated against.

The socio-political goals of the new order were publicly outlined by Konrad Meyer, albeit veiled in ideological jargon. In an article entitled 'The East as a Challenge and Obligation for German Nationhood' he concludes: 'So the task before us is one of drawing together and consolidating the positive forces and eliminating the forces hostile to order, of selecting carefully on the basis of national and ethnic criteria and the principles of hard work and achievement, so that the specific characteristics of the race are strengthened and valuable new elements are progressively introduced.'[91] The whole concept met with Himmler's unreserved approval. In particular he admired its scientific credentials: 'The resettlement is taking place on the basis of the latest research findings and will produce revolutionary results, because it is not only transplanting entire ethnic groups, but the landscape itself will also be totally restructured.'[92]

Planning district Auschwitz

Everywhere in the annexed eastern territories the expulsion of local populations was fundamental to the German plans for a new order.

But it was also the German intention to integrate slave labour and extermination into this 'development model' on a long-term basis. Upper Silesia is a prime example. With its large coal deposits, and because it was initially considered safe from air attack, this region was of considerable strategic importance for the German war economy. Plans for the future development of the region dubbed 'the second Ruhr' envisaged not only a radical social 'restructuring' of the population, but also the expansion of the Auschwitz concentration camp.

In September 1940 Dr Fritz Arlt[93] was appointed Himmler's representative for 'the strengthening of German nationhood' in Upper Silesia – the same Dr Arlt, the sociologist and demographic expert, who had previously worked for the Racial Policy Offices of the NSDAP in Leipzig and Breslau, carrying out a census of the local Jewish population and setting up 'registers of persons of foreign race'. As we shall see in Chapter 6, his most recent assignment had been in the Government General. Now Arlt was based in Katowice. Here he took over from a predecessor regarded as incompetent by Himmler, and immediately set about achieving 'an absolute centralization based on a clear understanding of the present position'.[94] In parallel with this he headed the Racial Policy Office of the NSDAP in Upper Silesia, where he also founded a 'Main Office for Practical Population Policy'.[95] Arlt's role as head of the RKF outpost in Upper Silesia was 'quickly defined':

> Our task is to Germanize the reconquered eastern territories over the next few years both in terms of their landscape and of their population. To that end we shall evacuate Poles and Jews to the Government General. (...) We (have) towns with a preponderantly – up to 80 per cent – Jewish population, such as Sosnowiec and Bedzin, while elsewhere – notably in the northern part of our territory – the population is uniformly Polish. The work is made more complicated by the fact that in carrying out the evacuations we must have regard to the needs of the armaments industry that is such an important part of our regional economy, i.e. Poles working in this industry are not to be deported. In a complicated procedure these Poles will be resettled internally, while other surplus and unproductive persons ['Ballastexistenzen'] will be substituted for them and deported in their place.[96]

In conducting such activities Arlt was well served by his close connections with the SD, which were described in these terms by the chief of staff of the security police and SD in Katowice:

In order to bring the planning, preparation, implementation, etc. of the evacuation and resettlement operations for the Upper Silesia district under centralized control, the Katowice Resettlement Bureau was set up under the aegis of the chief of staff of the security police and SD. The task of building up and leading the new organization was entrusted to SS Obersturmbannführer (Horst) Barth. Working in conjunction with the Special Office of the SD's Katowice sector, which is also headed by Obersturmbannführer Barth, and the office of the representative of the Reich Commissioner for the Strengthening of German Nationhood [headed by Arlt], the Katowice Resettlement Bureau is accordingly charged with the following tasks:

1. to identify those persons in the district of Upper Silesia who can be considered for evacuation at a later date (Special Office); 2. to identify those persons whom it is essential to exempt from such measures for the present on economic and political grounds (…); 4. to carry out the evacuation with the assistance of the local constabulary; 5. to make arrangements for the evacuees to be housed in (…) camps (…); 7. following the evacuation, to permit the representatives of the SS Central Office of Race and Resettlement in Berlin to select persons who meet their requirements; 8. to enable the employment offices to select persons suitable for short-term employment in the Reich; 9. to make arrangements for the remaining Poles and Jews to be transported to the Government General.[97]

In Upper Silesia, Arlt and his staff of around 150 were confronted with a dilemma. On the one hand, a substantial number of ethnic German farmers were to be relocated to the region, in the expectation that their loyalty to the state would be equalled by their willingness to beget children for the state. On the other hand, it was necessary to have a sufficient supply of manpower available for work in industry and mining. The latter – and on this point there was never any doubt – were to be recruited as before from the local Polish population. And so Arlt and the SD summarily designated a large section of the indigenous population of Upper Silesia as so-called 'Wasserpolen' [watermen Poles], politically unreliable, but described as a 'hybrid German-Polish class'. Since the Polish peasantry in particular met all attempts at Germanization with passive resistance, whether from religious, national or political convictions, it seemed 'expedient' to Arlt to 'channel the rural Wasserpolen into industry and to replace them with German farmers'.[98]

After an initial process of 'selection' these people were to be Germanized exactly like their forebears, who had emigrated to the Ruhr seventy-five years earlier. As the Polish smallholders were driven from the land and 'sucked' into the industrial cities of Germany, they would be proletarianized, progressively losing their social and cultural identity and becoming Germanized by a process of 'social restructuring'. For – so Arlt probably reasoned – the alienation resulting from industrial labour would finally break their resistance and their traditional ties.

Responding to current manpower shortages, the RKF was 'liberal' in its application of the criteria for Germanization in Upper Silesia. Hence the fact that Himmler could complain, in January 1944, that in Upper Silesia 'even overtly negroid types have in some cases been included in the National List [Volksliste]'.[99]

The policies pursued by demographic specialist Arlt were designed to make social structures more transparent and in particular to establish 'a clear separation between rural peasants and industrial workers'. Measured by Arlt's criteria, agricultural overpopulation was a problem in Upper Silesia as it was elsewhere, with an excessive number of small farms and smallholdings: 'Subsistence-level farms, where owners must inevitably become proletarianized, or else earn a living (...) by working in a factory, taking seasonal work on large estates or hiring themselves and their carts out to industry by the hour.'[100]

Because he refused to give up his independent way of life and become a totally dependent industrial labourer, such a smallholder 'must needs become a poor worker', according to Arlt, 'or else his great expenditure of labour must undermine his physical strength before his time. This blend of modern industrial labourer and traditional Upper Silesian serf is the reason for the premature ageing of our men and women in the industrial region, and for the stunted physical development of the children.' This 'labour force tied to smallholdings' also appeared politically suspect to Arlt.[101] Using the familiar methods – resettlement, Germanization and the amalgamation of small farms into larger units – he planned to remove such elements of uncertainty and establish a clear distinction between farmers and agricultural workers. The farms allocated to the new German farmers by the RKF averaged 20–25 hectares in size. Industrial workers and miners, on the other hand – or their wives and children – were to be given no more than an acre [*Morgen*] of allotment to cultivate – just so much as a worker 'can tend in his spare time without using up the energy he needs for his labours in the mine or factory, thus avoiding the risk of premature ageing'.[102]

In order to realize his vision of a socially pacified society in Upper Silesia, Arlt planned to expel hundreds of thousands of people and to draft in new settlers to take their place. He proposed the destruction of entire villages, or the creation of new ones somewhere else:

> The redrawing of agricultural boundaries will result in the disappearance of a number of villages and settlements. Strategic planning measures such as the construction of autobahns, dams, new industrial plants, etc. will have a similar effect, so that the location and distribution of villages will have to be completely replanned and the entire system of settlement in the district's agricultural sector reorganized in line with the views of the SS Reichsführer in his capacity as Reich Commissioner for the Strengthening of German Nationhood.[103]

In Upper Silesia, as elsewhere, the responsibility for making villages disappear from the map rested with the regional planners. Because they worked to a brief laid down by the RKF, the various institutions involved effectively worked as one. The regional planner was simultaneously the 'general head of section for regional planning matters', and in this capacity he was also 'charged with representing the interests of the central planning department of the RKF…'[104]

The regional planner for Upper Silesia was Gerhard Ziegler, an engineering graduate who was on close personal terms with representatives of the central planning authorities in Berlin.[105] Before he took up his appointment in Katowice he had worked for nearly four years in the Reich Office of Regional Planning in Berlin.[106] He agreed to maintain a 'close and ongoing collaboration' with Konrad Meyer and Fritz Arlt: 'Consultation will take place on all important planning projects. Copies of all important correspondence and planning documents will also be exchanged.'[107]

Ziegler and Arlt were in complete agreement about the oft-lamented structural problems of Upper Silesia. They were also equally ruthless in the way they drew up and pushed through their plans. Ziegler described the economic and demographic structure of Upper Silesia as predominantly 'poor and unsatisfactory'. On the province as a whole his verdict was damning. In his academic jargon, Upper Silesia consisted of 'demographically deficient areas, devastated expanses, areas of agricultural or industrial overpopulation or areas of poor climate'.[108] 'Despite fertile soil conditions and an abundance of raw materials' it was 'the poorest province in the Reich'; much of the wealth it produced was being 'creamed off by outsiders', and its production resources were not being utilized to anything like their full capacity. In his eyes, the internal economy of the region was far too weak, handicapped by the general absence of a 'small business sector capable of seizing the initiative'. The situation was especially dire in his view in the area around Sosnowiec, which had already been designated as an 'eastern redevelopment zone'. This was also where the largest Jewish communities in Upper Silesia were located. When Ziegler decided that the region was to be '80 per cent renewed', this was made all the easier by the fact that the deportation of the Jewish population could be factored into his plans from the beginning. In other parts of the province, too, he proposed to combine 'the destruction of old towns with development plans for new ones'. To this end he drew up plans for absolutely everything. There were plans for the central control of industry and the development of industrial land, plans for the development of coal-mining, electricity and water supply and iron production, a village development plan, plans for the production of food and semi-luxury goods, settlement plans, urban development plans – to name but a few. Overall he judged the future prospects for Upper Silesia to be 'very good', on condition that the development of the region was properly directed: 'It will require a huge amount of work over a long period of time (...) Our task is that of a military general staff: we have to remain flexible in the face of new challenges, not wedded to rigid plans, but with our basic strategy in place.'[109]

In May 1942 Arlt again summarized his 'proposals for a solution' in the District Chamber of Labour for Upper Silesia. 'For the final solution' – meant here in the general sense of a demographic 'new order' – the key measures he proposed were 'the clear separation between rural peasants and industrial workers, the reorganization of agricultural holdings into larger units, a programme of afforestation and a resulting 80 per cent reduction in the size of the rural proletariat'. It was also his intention 'to replace muscle power by machines', to 'rationalize the skilled trades and commerce through mechanization and amalgamation' and to introduce 'mechanization and electrification into agriculture'. 'For the transition' Arlt proposed the following measures: '1. Evacuation of all dependent minority races who are not vital to the war economy; 2. Residential segregation through the creation of special reservations for dependent minority races; 3. Immediate amalgamation of agricultural smallholdings and small businesses owned by dependent minority races to form larger units; 4. Drafting-in of the dependent minority races for labour service at designated locations (thus freeing the countryside from dependent minority races).'[110]

These proposals for the 'transition' had already been tried out for more than a year in the industrial district around Auschwitz. It is safe to assume that this was not an isolated or atypical case, but a model or pilot scheme that was followed with great interest by those in authority in Berlin.[111]

The planners were particularly interested in the region around Auschwitz because they wanted to construct a completely new, modern industrial centre there. The many thousands of labourers who would be needed – those who were not inmates of concentration camps – would be housed, depending on their ethno-political status, in 'reservations' or in 'satellite housing developments'[112] to be built at a later date, while for German skilled workers there would also be 'owner-occupied housing'.[113] The conditions for an industrial development project of this kind were ideal: large deposits of coal, ample supplies of water, excellent access by road and rail. The construction of the I.G. Farben works for the manufacture of 'Buna' or synthetic rubber, which would provide employment for a projected 15,000 people,[114] had already been scheduled. Accommodation would have to be provided for 60,000 people just to house the employees of the works and their families. Additional living quarters would be needed for the employees of the various service industries springing up around the plant, bringing the total housing requirement to 75,000–80,000 people.[115] Hitherto 'Old Auschwitz' had been home to just 12,000 people.[116] On 16 January 1941, when plans for the construction of the I.G. Farben plant in Auschwitz were still under discussion, Otto Ambros, who sat on the board of the concern, announced that if plans for industrial development went ahead 11,000 people would be evacuated from the town of Auschwitz, 'so that the town would be at the disposal of the plant's workforce'.[117] In nearby Brzeszcze coal-mining operations had been taken over by the 'Hermann Göring Works Corporation', and output had already doubled. The proposed construction of a sulphur-processing plant, a long-distance gas pipeline and a high-capacity power station would further increase the productivity of the mines and factories.[118] Coking works and coal-processing industries were also planned.[119]

At the heart of this industrial district lay the 'German town' of Auschwitz, which was to be remodelled to a design drawn up by the architect Hans Stosberg.[120] The concentration camp was sited in the immediate vicinity.

As early as November 1940 Fritz Arlt had called for 'an enlargement of the Auschwitz concentration camp', and had submitted plans to the RKF central staff office in Berlin. The camp commandant, Rudolf Höss, had sought and obtained Himmler's approval for the expansion plans shortly thereafter.[121] In addition to Höss, those involved in discussing where to relocate the camp perimeter included planning professionals Udo Froese and Gerhard Ziegler and the architect Hans Stosberg. Some of their meetings took place in the camp commandant's office.[122] The only area of disagreement arose when the discussion turned to the impact of the proposed camp expansion on landscape planning. District and regional planners pointed out that the expansion of the camp would inhibit the development of the town of Auschwitz and the industrial facilities, and would interfere with highway planning and traffic flows within the region. Other objections were raised on environmental and aesthetic grounds: any expansion of the concentration camp meant that the plans for the new railway station would also have to be revised, necessitating the construction of 'ugly railway embankments' that would 'ruin an otherwise delightful stretch of countryside'.[123]

However, the selection and deportation of population groups were essential to the development of Auschwitz as an industrial district. On that point, at least, everyone was in agreement, from the regional planners on the ground and the officials at RKF headquarters in Berlin to the managers of I.G. Farben.

How the sorting, utilization and resettlement of the indigenous population of Upper Silesia were to proceed in practice was laid down in precise terms by the SS Relocation Office South, of which Arlt was in charge. In a project paper on the 'options for resettlement in 1941' we read:

> (1) All Poles living in the eastern territories will be examined by the responsible employment offices to ascertain their fitness for work. Their findings will be communicated to the Relocation Office, whereupon the persons concerned will be classified as either (a) productive Polish families or (b) unproductive Polish families. By 'productive' we mean those workers who can be

employed in any sector of the war economy, i.e. not just in manufacturing industry as such, but also in the construction of the
necessary buildings and factory facilities. Naturally the families of
these workers will have to be included in the reckoning, and
there is no way round this. Unproductive Poles include those
who could never be integrated into a work process relating to the
war economy, together with antisocial elements and the sick.[124]

'Interested industrial parties'[125] had apparently already 'indicated
those industrial districts in the Upper Silesian area that should
undergo rapid expansion in the immediate future'. The 'concentration of workers from the dependent minority races' in 'Polish reservations' all around these 'future industrial centres' must therefore be
put in hand: 'i.e. all available villages and buildings within conve-
nient travelling distance are to be given over entirely to the housing
of Polish workers and their families. All unproductive Poles and Jews
must therefore be removed from this area first.' A sketch diagram was
attached, showing how the 'productive Poles' were to be screened
from time to time to weed out all those who were unable or unwilling
to work. The 'train of unproductive Poles and Jews'[126] was then to be
deported by all available means to the Government General, and sent
as far east as possible. Any attempts to return were to be forestalled
'by an appropriate strengthening of police powers'.[127]

Once the rightful owners had been evicted, the 'train of German
settlers'[128] could move into their properties. The author of the planning paper, Hans Butschek, head of the RKF Relocation Office South,
was adamant that the entire Jewish population and all Jewish farmers
must either be deported east to the Government General or confined
to the labour reservations: 'for experience has shown that when
German colonists live alongside Polish persons, the latter exercise an
enormous and damaging influence on the German way of life.'

This planning paper was drafted in January 1941 at Arlt's request.
The 'options for resettlement' outlined in the paper did not go unno-
ticed. In so far as they relate to the selection of the industrial workforce, they reappear both in an RKF order dated 4 February 1941[129]
and in a letter from Göring to Himmler of 18 February. Göring called
for the implementation of 'population policy measures for the Buna
works at Auschwitz in Upper Silesia': 'Speedy evacuation of the Jews
in Auschwitz (...) in order to make their homes available for the construction workers engaged on the Buna works project. (...) Temporary
exemption for Poles' living in Auschwitz and the surrounding area

'who could be employed on construction work' and the 'provision of the maximum possible number' of workers from the concentration camp for the construction of the factory.[130] Following receipt of this order from Göring, Himmler issued appropriate instructions to his subordinates on 26 February 1941.[131]

Two days later a further decree on the same subject was issued by the Reich Ministry of Labour. The employment office in Bielitz responsible for the Auschwitz area undertook to recruit the workforce for the I.G. Farben Buna works. A meeting took place with the head of the Gestapo central office in Katowice, representatives of the SS Reichsführer and the RKF Relocation Office South, at which all 'outstanding problems were discussed at some length'. The employment office said it would 'prepare a record of all persons fit for work in card-index form' and communicate the results to the Gestapo, 'who will then exempt these persons from deportation for the present'. The Relocation Office was represented at this meeting by its head, Hans Butschek, author of the planning paper referred to above. He promised that as soon as he received the appropriate instructions he would 'take immediate steps (...) to evacuate the Jews from Auschwitz and deport them as far as possible to the Government General'.[132]

By mid-March 1941 at the latest it was clear even to Butschek that there was no realistic possibility of 'deporting Poles or Jews to the GG': 'Any trains or columns that are despatched to the GG will simply be turned around and sent straight back out' was the view expressed at a conference in Berlin that Butschek had attended.[133] So instead of deportations to the Government General, 'appropriate measures' were now taken within Upper Silesia in order to continue with the resettlement programme despite these organizational difficulties. To put it another way: the resettlement specialists were not at all disposed to abandon the idea of mass deportations – even though the problem of where to send the deportees remained completely unresolved. What was clear, at least, was that they would never be accepted anywhere outside Upper Silesia. This suggests that the 'appropriate measures' that were to be taken 'within the district [Gau]' could have referred to the extermination of 'unproductive persons' on the spot. To begin with, the Germans probably had some kind of 'passive' physical annihilation in mind, as hard labour on the construction of the industrial complex, hunger and privation took their toll. Only later would they turn to gas. It is not improbable that the decision to enlarge the capacity of the Auschwitz camp to 130,000 prisoners was taken in the light of these deliberations.

On 1 March 1941 Himmler paid his first visit to the camp. He promptly issued orders for the enlargement of the main camp to house 30,000 prisoners; for construction to begin on a second camp to house 100,000 'prisoners of war' on the site of the village of Brzezinka (Birkenau); and for 10,000 prisoners to be made available for forced labour on the I.G. Farben construction sites.[134] (In our view, the use of the term 'prisoners of war' is less an indication of the specific purpose for which the camp was enlarged than a formula for justifying the supply of the necessary construction materials as 'vital to the war effort'.) On 14 March 1941, two weeks after Himmler's tour of inspection in Auschwitz, a meeting took place in Arlt's office in Katowice. The subject for discussion was 'Readjustment of resettlement measures'. At this meeting the proposals for population redistribution put forward by Butschek were discussed in the light of the orders issued by Himmler and Göring, and the different agencies involved were assigned their tasks. In addition to district planners, police officials and resettlement experts the meeting was also attended by the head of the regional SD and the 'special commissioner for the labour deployment of dependent minority races', Albrecht Schmelt. The secret minutes of the meeting have survived:

> Those present indicated their acceptance of the following proposals: In order to have the necessary labour resources ready to hand, reservations will be set up for the dependent minority races within a radius of approximately 15 km around the planned industrial facilities. These reservations will also serve as catchment areas for the industries to be established here. The precise location of the reservations will be mapped out in consultation between the office of the district planner for Katowice [= Udo Froese] and the representative [of the RKF] in Katowice [= Arlt]. Auschwitz was used as an example to explain how the process would work in practice. (...) As far as possible the reservations are to be cleared of Jews and useless persons ['Ballastexistenzen'] unfit for work.[135]

At this conference the economic restructuring of Upper Silesia, which had been planned and discussed for more than a year, and the resettlement programme that was already under way, were coordinated with the needs of industry. While it was primarily in the interests of I.G. Farben and other industrial concerns 'to have the necessary labour resources ready to hand', the RKF planners and their regional planning colleagues, working in conjunction with the police, focused from the outset on creating a new demographic and economic structure for the long term that would fit Upper Silesia for its designated role as Germany's 'second Ruhr'. As well as the 'social restructuring' of the rural population this also involved the establishment of a hierarchy of 'necessary labour resources' for industry, with German skilled workers at the top, dependent minority races living in reservations in the middle, and concentration camp prisoners at the bottom. The weeding-out and murder of Jewish men and women and of 'useless persons unfit for work' were to become part of the regime at the Auschwitz industrial complex – not just a one-off 'measure', but a regular, ongoing practice. In 1943, when millions of European Jews had already become the victims of mass murder, the planners were still working on the assumption that the concentration camp would remain in existence as an integral part of the industrial region for another ten to twenty years at least.[136]

'What we accomplished was tremendous!'
A biographical postscript

When the end of the war came, the technocrats who were responsible for the crimes committed in the name of the 'new order' in the annexed eastern territories were obliged to clear their desks in Berlin, Auschwitz or Katowice. But sooner or later they all found work again in their chosen professions.

By September 1945 Gerhard Ziegler was back at work again in regional planning – not 'in the East' this time, but in Württemberg. In 1962 he was appointed to an honorary professorship at the Technical University of Stuttgart, and in 1966 he was awarded the Federal government's Grand Cross of Merit. Shortly before his death on 15 April 1967 he wrote an autobiographical memoir. Writing about his work as a regional planner in the industrial district of Auschwitz, he recalls with pride 'the huge drive to develop an industrial base in Silesia, far from the theatre of war – an area mainly given over to the mining of coal and ore. What we accomplished and put in place was tremendous, though hardly anybody remembers it now. Best of all, we cleared the area without destroying anything. So today the Poles can build on the foundations that we laid.'[137]

Professor Konrad Meyer was acquitted by the American military court in Nuremberg.[138] In 1956 the Technical University of Hanover appointed him to a chair in the Faculty of Horticulture and

Landscape Design.[139] Meyer organized the 'integration' and disper-
sion of refugees. He and his colleagues from the time of the 'general
resettlement plans' were responsible for rationalizing the regional
structure of the Federal Republic. Konrad Meyer died in 1973. His colleague Erhard Mäding, an administrative planner with the RKF,
resumed his career in the Federal Republic as a local planner and
landscape conservation officer. Among the organizations that made
use of his services were the Institute of Regional Planning Studies in
Bonn and the Society for the Protection of German Forests. Hans
Stosberg, the former town and regional planner of Auschwitz, now a
Social Democrat, became the respected architect of post-war reconstruction in Hanover. Among those who helped to transform
Frankfurt am Main into a modern metropolis in the 1960s was Udo
von Schauroth, another former planner with the RKF.[140]

The career path of Meyer's colleague Walter Christaller was not
quite so smooth. Christaller had joined the SPD in 1923, and in 1933
he went into hiding in France. Konrad Meyer brought him back to
Germany, securing research contracts for him and giving him a key
role in his planning project for the conquered eastern territories. In
1940 Christaller joined the NSDAP, and in 1945 he became politically
active to the left of the SPD – which created problems for him in
terms of career advancement. In 1959 he returned to the SPD fold. In
1968 the Ruhr University in Bochum awarded him an honorary
doctorate 'for his internationally recognized services to human
geography and regional planning'.

After 1945 Dr Fritz Arlt developed the Missing Persons Service of
the German Red Cross – a natural enough progression, given that the
Ethnic German Agency [VoMi] had found itself organizing columns
of German refugees at the end of the war. In 1954 Arlt joined the
German Industrial Institute in Cologne, where he rose to become a
member of the governing board and head of the department for 'edu-
cational work and socio-political questions'. Under the motto
'advancement through selection based on merit' he became a committed advocate for the expansion of Germany's 'second way' in education [an alternative route to higher education through evening
classes and correspondence courses]. His deputy from 1955 to 1973
was Dorothee Wilms, who later became a government minister. Arlt
also worked as a 'business consultant advising on corporate organization, information systems and personnel management'. The German
Trade Unions' Federation (DGB) found him very open-minded and
approachable in their dealings with him. In 1968 he took up the

cudgels on behalf of Germany's rebellious students before an audience of young businessmen. Among the causes of their protest he identified the 'failure to come to terms with Germany's political past since 1933', a past that must neither be 'demonized wholesale' nor 'glorified'. A judicial inquiry into Fritz Arlt's past was abandoned by the public prosecutor's office in Dortmund in 1966.

CHAPTER 5

LIVING LIFE AS A MEMBER OF THE MASTER RACE

'Baedeker's Government General'

The idea for a little red-bound book that appeared in 1943 had come from the Governor-General of German-occupied Poland, Hans Frank – an idea 'greeted with enthusiasm' by the publisher. This slim volume introduced the reader to the 'work of reconstruction and development' that had been 'completed or put in hand during the past three and a half years', and furnished him with the wherewithal 'to see the country and the people as they really are'. Since so much in the 'newly explored territory' was still evolving or even 'subject to constant change', the editor could not vouch for the accuracy of every particular, and therefore invited readers to write to him with suggestions for corrections or improvements.[1]

Such was Karl Baedeker's introduction to the latest volume in the series of travel guides that had made his name a byword in Germany: 'Baedeker's Government General'.

The publishers had included three maps and six city plans in the 246-page book. Among his practical travel tips Baedeker had this to say on the subject of language: '... as a German one will speak Polish or Ukrainian only when it is absolutely necessary', especially since – according to the guide – there was really no such thing as a Polish language, but only 'a collection of dialects'. Learning the language was in any event 'difficult for a German, to whom the Slavic world is quite alien'. None the less, a few lines later Baedeker notes that Polish contains 'several thousand loan-words' of German origin, which point 'to the German foundations of the culture'. The Ostbahn [Eastern Railway] cosseted the traveller with all kinds of special facilities: 'Separate ticket counters, waiting rooms, platform barriers and trains are provided for German passengers.' The Deutsche Post Osten [German Post Office for the East] sold postage stamps that were regarded as 'of special artistic interest', while at the same time

Baedeker pointed out to the new arrival that 'conditions within the country' had 'necessitated the introduction of a separate postal service for official communications', which guaranteed that letters would pass 'through German hands only'.

As far as the roads and highways were concerned, conditions were 'for the most part extremely bad during the Polish era', although in the meantime 'many stretches, first and foremost the east–west trunk routes, connecting the region with the Reich' had been upgraded 'under Germany's highway construction programme'. Because of the many horse-drawn vehicles on the roads, breakdowns caused by horseshoe nails were frequent, and Baedeker advised motorists to carry 'a tyre repair kit and a good-quality tyre pump'. They were also advised to exercise a certain amount of caution: 'When travelling on long, isolated stretches of road or travelling at night, it is advisable at the present time to carry a weapon.' For the holiday-maker at that time there was a choice of five 'state-owned spas in the Government General (all under German management)'. The hotels listed in the guide were likewise 'all under German management'. There was also a section on 'Entertainment and Sport'. German cabarets, municipal theatres, smart city bars, chamber music and the Government General Philharmonic – occasionally under the baton of Wilhelm Fürtwängler – cinemas showing exclusively German films, German libraries, museums, horse-racing in Lublin and Lvov...They were starting to make themselves at home, albeit with a pistol tucked into their belt.

The guidebook also enlarged on the 'landscape, inhabitants and economy'. The Government General was said to be 'the heartland, effectively, of the area inhabited by the Polish population', to which Galicia – 'differing in its general mentality, cultural vigour and entrepreneurial spirit' – was 'added' on 1 August 1941. The Carpathian Mountains were said to form a natural barrier to the south, the eastern frontier was an 'unmade marginal boundary'. As for the other frontiers, the guidebook made little attempt to conceal the fact that they were the arbitrary consequence of Germany's appetite for plunder: 'In drawing the boundaries to the north and west, the Greater Silesian industrial region and the textile district around Litzmannstadt [Lódź] were given special consideration as territories immediate to the Reich.'

'The population structure,' according to Baedeker, 'is one of the biggest problems for the reconstitution of the region. Its effects on agriculture, the food supply, mechanization and the growth of the economy in general can only be described in the following terms: the lack of progress resulting from centuries of Polish mismanagement, which also left a huge proportion of the country's wealth in the hands of the Jewish mercantile class, led in central and southern Poland to the proletarianization and impoverishment of broad sections of the population and a general state of technical backwardness at every level of industry and commerce, which can only be reversed through the initiative of Poland's neighbour, the German Reich.'[2]

At that time, so the travel guide informed its readers, the population density in the Cracow district was 137 persons per square kilometre, 88 in the Lublin district, 118 in the Radom district, 192 in the Warsaw district and 119 in the Lvov district. The situation was catastrophic, especially as 'the population increase up until the last was very great'.

On the subject of 'Ethnic Groupings and Settlement', Baedeker reported that the Government General took in 142,000 square kilometres of territory, or 37 per cent of the total area occupied by the former Polish state. Seventy-three per cent of its 18 million inhabitants were Poles, 17 per cent were Ukrainians and 0.7 per cent Germans. And the Jews? Baedeker refers to them in 1943 in the past tense: the highly centralized structure of former Poland (he writes) had resulted in a 'massive concentration' of 1.25 million people in Warsaw, 'of whom 0.4 million *were* Jews'. Cracow, Baedeker notes in passing (and in parentheses), was '(now free of Jews)'.[3] The same applied to Lublin, where a central area of the city '*was* largely inhabited by Jews'. And on the subject of the mass evacuations in the area around Zamosc the guidebook notes that 'an area heavily colonized by Germans from the Palatinate in about 1800' was 'currently being consolidated by an influx of new settlers'.

'Called up for service in the East'

The passages below are taken from the diary entries of a Dr Dietrich Troschke, then a 34-year-old economist who was 'called up for service in the East'.[4] The entries begin on 22 April 1940, and the extracts quoted here cover the period up until October of that year:

> While still working in Germany I received a despatch summoning me to take charge of the economic management of an area in the newly created Government General of Poland. The matter had been discussed in a series of brief telephone conversations

prior to my receipt of the call-up order. The company for which I had been working up until then was virtually under contract to the Wehrmacht. Now, thanks to the war, I had been offered a unique opportunity to extend the scope of my activity overnight, and furthermore to escape from the monotonous daily grind of work. Everyone embarking on a career probably sets out with very specific ideas and dreams. My ultimate dream was to get to a point in my life where I could put my own ideas into practice in a larger economic context.

Now I am to take charge of the Office of Economic Affairs in the administrative district of Reichshof [= Rzeszów]. The office was previously run by the 26-year-old officer cadet, who of course had no experience in economic matters; consequently nothing of any significance has been done to develop the economy of the region. I am at something of a disadvantage in that I am not a Party comrade, and have no intention of joining the Party.

The working day in the offices of the administrative district begins – with German punctuality – at 7.30 a.m. The offices are located in a spacious castle built by a Count Lubomirski, a member of the old Polish aristocracy. The castle is constructed in the form of a rectangle around a central courtyard, and is surrounded by a high stone wall with a deep ditch in front of it. I walked in at the main gate full of expectation.

As I went round the various departments I discovered that a relatively small proportion of the staff are Germans, and that only the managerial posts are staffed by Germans. This seems to me the right approach when one is ruling a foreign country. Only a limited number of the German personnel are professional administrators. Most of the Germans here are quite young. Out here everyone is expected to be extremely active and mobile, which comes more easily to younger limbs than it does to older ones.

Those who are on service in the East find themselves in a unique situation. Every individual is confronted with extraordinary opportunities. Nobody could ever have imagined a posting that offers so much more in the way of challenges, responsibility and scope for initiative than anything else they have done in their entire lives. Out here, someone who was just a small cog in the administrative machine back home, dutifully performing his daily tasks in return for a modest salary, suddenly found himself in charge of a whole department or government agency, far better off financially, and with ten times the responsibility.

When we spend time together in the evenings the talk is hardly ever of private matters. Everyone talks about what has been going on in the office that day. The district administrator gets asked questions on all kinds of subjects, and is happy to give us his views on many of them. There is a tremendous sense of commitment and dedication. Out here people tackle things with all the energy and zeal they can muster.

Towards evening I felt a desire to wander through the town and take a closer look at the townspeople. Once again the town commissioner was my valued companion, conducting me through his domain like a tourist guide. In the course of our walk I noticed that the proportion of Jews in the population is extraordinarily high, and that most of the shops are owned by Jews. In fact Jews account for 40 per cent of the population of 32,000. This is particularly noticeable in the main street of the town.

So writes Dr Dietrich Troschke. In the coming months he acted 'with energy and zeal' to change the things that had so discomfited him. In October 1940 his superior reported on the changes in the economic life of Rzeszów for which Troschke, among others, had been responsible:

As I have already pointed out, on the basis of several months' experience I have furnished proof that even in a town as riddled with Jews as Reichshof the process of Aryanization can be carried out without crippling the local economy. (...) Aryanization has now reached the point where nearly all the main streets are free from Jewish businesses. Before long the main streets of my district capital will be completely free of Jews. (...) It was not possible to establish a ghetto as such. But we have been able to arrange things so that separate Aryan and Jewish streets could be created, where both the businesses and the homes are now exclusively in Aryan or Jewish hands. I have also made a start on the Aryanization of the countryside. (...) In two towns we have already set up substantial Aryan ironmongery businesses to replace Jewish businesses in that line which have been liquidated.[5]

Tabula rasa

'An intellectual bulwark of German nationhood in the East' was how the *Kasseler Neueste Nachrichten* described the Institute for German

Development Work in the East in Cracow. Another newspaper spoke of an 'armourer of the mind and spirit'. Such verbal breast-beating by the Nazi propaganda machine disguises the fact that this was in reality a very modern and flexibly organized research establishment. The Institute had been founded on 20 April 1940 by the Governor-General in person. The reporter on the *Frankfurter Zeitung* was struck by two aspects in particular: the 'deliberate combination of scientific method and practical, applied aims' and the 'youthfulness of the governing board'. Most of the Institute's departments were said to be 'fully involved in the tasks of the day', and gave 'pointers for the German administration'. Performing this function were the departments of law, racial and ethnic studies, forestry and agriculture, and not least the department of economics.[6]

Working here since 6 January 1941 was Helmut Meinhold, an economist trained at the Kiel Institute of World Economic Studies.[7] At his new post in Cracow, Meinhold set about 'establishing an effective apparatus for carrying out scientific work', demanding from his staff 'a capacity for hard work and personal dedication' and 'finesse' when it came to 'supervising the Polish ancillary staff'.[8] But as the volume of 'highly confidential material' increased, it was not long before the ancillary staff were phased out as a security risk.[9]

The department of economics was set up to advise the German occupation executive, and its role was both reactive and proactive – giving advice in response to specific requests, and dispensing advice on its own initiative. Needless to say, the nature of the work demanded discretion rather than publicity-seeking. But it did give the Institute's staff access to the centres of power:

> I. The department of economics exists primarily to provide a service to the directorate of economic affairs and other government agencies, which from time to time will ask the Institute to carry out detailed preliminary studies of practical policy proposals. In particular the department will be involved in drawing up economic plans and studying the economic effectiveness of transport infrastructure projects, cultivation measures, industrialization plans, pricing and work creation schemes, etc. (...) This work creates opportunities for putting forward suggestions and ideas to government agencies for the planning of practical measures.[10]

The scientists and academics at the Institute for German Development Work in the East led a privileged and comfortable existence. They were housed in palatial offices, had assistants at their beck and call, exerted influence over political decision-making, led a free-and-easy life and felt themselves to be part of a metropolitan cultural scene. The so-called 'eastern supplement' doubled their salary, and it was much easier to get hold of everyday household goods – and indeed luxury items – than it was back home in Germany. It was considered good form to maintain a certain critical distance from the ordinary Party Nazis.

The apartments and furniture used by the Germans had previously belonged to wealthy Jewish families or 'enemies of the state'. The better pieces went to German officials, officers and businessmen, those of inferior quality went to needy – non-Jewish – Poles. The city administration set up its own furniture collection point for this purpose. And so the members of the German master race lined their pockets with the property left behind by those who were soon to be murdered in their millions. From 1942 onwards a special trust company set up for the purpose of turning looted precious metals into cash sold 'valuables such as pearls, gold cigarette cases, diamonds, gold, etc.' to privileged Germans 'at discounted peace-time prices'. The same state-owned company subsequently complained that 'a large number of these Germans then sold these items on to Polish jewellers a few days later for 80 to 100 times their peace-time value', with gold fetching up to 150 times its purchase price. An official whose job it was to scrutinize the transfer of valuables noted that 'various Germans' soon amassed 'a small fortune'. The official was powerless to act, since 'most of the figures in authority [had] received substantial valuables from the company'.[11]

The Governor-General, Hans Frank, repeatedly urged the members of his scientific planning staffs to conduct their research 'quite freely' and independently of all political agencies.[12] He expected them to present him with alternative options, properly grounded in theory and supported by statistical evidence, that would form the basis for practical decision-making: he did not want political pamphlets. Helmut Meinhold was the man to meet these expectations. In a review of a book on the restructuring of regional economic activity he indicated what his own position was. He had approached the book 'from a practical angle, as it were (...) from the point of view of establishing the new regional economic order in the East'. 'If we are not to capitulate from the outset before the challenges confronting us in the East,' so he and his kind believed, 'idea and method [are] absolutely indispensable.'

Only three years previously Meinhold had been struggling with the problems of pig-farming in Schleswig-Holstein and the expansion of the harbour at Büsum, where he was faced with the prospect of seeing his proposal to scrap thirty unprofitable and obsolete crabbers founder on the obstinacy and cussedness of the fishermen and lack of finance. Now, in the Government General, he encountered a situation that seemed to offer complete carte blanche for the planner by comparison with what he could expect in Germany. The only givens here were the economy of the country that served as the major point of reference – the German Reich – the people, the land, a few transport routes and a handful of industrial sites: 'The deployment of the people within the economy, however, needs to be completely rethought for the long-term future. (...) Here the economic planner is confronted by a totally new set of circumstances. It is not a matter of where to site an individual industrial plant or how to develop the best transport infrastructure for a country when other economic factors are a known quantity. In economic terms what one has here is pretty much a tabula rasa situation.'[13]

Emancipation

Among those working in the department of racial and ethnic studies at the Institute for German Development Work in the East was Dr Elfriede ('Fritzi') Fliethmann. She hailed from Vienna, and kept in close touch with the Institute of Anthropology at the university there, where she had studied. She was particularly close to Dr Dorothea ('Dora') Maria Kahlich, who had obtained her doctorate in 1940 under her maiden name of Koenner, with a study of the Jewish inmates of a charitable institution in the Viennese suburbs. Her 'Preliminary report on ethnological photographs of Jews' can be found in the tenth volume of the *Proceedings of the German Society for Racial Research*. Thus prepared, in July 1941 she gave a 'brief course of lectures in genetic methods' at the Institute for Genetic and Racial Hygiene at the University of Prague.[14] Fliethmann had also obtained her doctorate in 1940 with an ethnological study of an Austrian border region, considered by her examiners to be 'of particular importance for the implementation of racial and population policies in the frontier zone'.

The department in Cracow where Fliethmann subsequently worked was engaged in the study of racial types. Body measurements and full-length photographs of prisoners of war, ethnic Germans and in particular of Jewish women and men constituted the 'research material'. But time was running out. 'We do not know,' wrote departmental head and fellow Viennese Anton Plügel to Kahlich on 22 October 1941, 'what action has been planned regarding the resettlement of the Jewish population over the coming months. By waiting too long we may lose valuable research material, and there is a particular danger that our material could be taken out of the natural family context and its familiar environment, which would mean not only that the photographs themselves would have to be taken under much more difficult conditions, but that the opportunities for taking photographs would be greatly curtailed.'[15]

Fliethmann and Kahlich immediately prepared to travel to Tarnów, in order to take the measurements of '100 [Jewish] families in the meantime (…) so that we will at least have saved something of the material in the event that action of some sort is planned'.[16] This was not achieved without difficulty, for as Fliethmann complained: 'The resistance among the population was once again very strong, so we were forced to call upon the police and border guards to help us.'[17] This official assistance was 'most kindly' arranged by 'SS Obersturmbannführer Bernhardt and SS Sturmmann Sach from the security service in Tarnów and Cracow'. For 'each person documented in the family unit 18 head measurements and 13 body measurements were taken', in addition to which '4 photographs of the head (Contax 18 cm Sonnar) and 3 nude photographs of the whole body (Contax 13.5 cm Sonnar) were taken'. The subjects used for the study were the largest families from the town of Tarnów, chosen 'as the most characteristic representatives of the original Galician Jewish stock'. And large families would soon be a thing of the past, given that 'there will be no population growth worth speaking of from now on'.[18] Fliethmann's 'material' was analysed by Maria Kahlich in Vienna, and she wrote back to the 'dear doctor' in Cracow:

> First of all there's something I need to put right. My own finding was simply that the Jews in Tarnów can be classified as of mixed Middle Eastern-Oriental race, but that is not to say that they don't exhibit other racial characteristics. I also think that the pictures are going to contain many more surprises (…) So far we have prepared the list for cataloguing the data. As you can see from the enclosed slip, we don't have details of many people's ages. So I'd be grateful if you could let me have this information soon. I would also like to know something about the possibility

of kinship ties between the families recorded. I don't have the
colour of the eyes for subject No. 424, and would ask you to send
that information on to me as well. Otherwise it all seems to be in
order. I'm curious to know if that is also the case with the
measurements. Now begins the tedious business of counting the
dermal ridges, and more than half the specimens have already
been catalogued. But I haven't checked through them yet, so I
don't have an overall picture as yet. What's happened to the pho-
tocopies? Our little pictures are ready, but I haven't had time to
stick them on yet.[19]

Fliethmann immediately asked for the missing data to be forwarded
via the appropriate department of the security police and the SD.[20]

Since the Tarnów study had 'yielded material of extraordinary
interest',[21] the head of department inquired of the SS 'whether it
might still be possible, perhaps in June or July of this year [1942], to
have a rural Jewish village community (peasants and artisans) in the
eastern part of the Galicia district, preferably complete and intact, in
order to carry out a racial and ethnological study, or whether it might
be possible to leave a particularly interesting example of such a
community in place, and more or less undisturbed, until that time'.[22]

Fliethmann and Kahlich set to work with a will. Personal friend-
ship evidently lent added impetus to their ambition and commitment. Kahlich wrote: 'I am full of admiration for your enthusiasm
and energy. (...) If things work out this time, then perhaps we can set
up something nice for the summer – and keep everyone happy. But it
needn't be something that requires such complicated preparation.
My colleagues are already looking forward to processing the material.
So I think it won't be too long before my part is ready.'[23]

The 'successful' study in Tarnów led on to further joint projects.
Fliethmann was quite carried away by the possibilities:

> We could easily go back to Tarnów for a few days and fill in the
> gaps in the material. (...) I do think that if the opportunity is
> there one should record the material in as much detail as possi-
> ble. Forget about your classes and other things for a week, let
> your husband fend for himself – and come with me. Surely you
> too are tempted by the fleshpots of Tarnów. (...) I've got a great
> plan for the summer, by the way. You remember I told you about
> the ethnic German settlements near Kielce. (...) I'm fascinated by
> these places because they are said to be in an advanced state of

degeneration as a result of intense inbreeding, so I think they may yield some useful information, particularly on the subject of heredity. (...) Hopefully we can meet during my vacation to discuss our future work in more detail.[24]

Shortly before this, Kahlich had hinted at the possibility of excursions that went rather further afield: '...saving the best until last, I was about to write you a nice long letter when Professor Eickstedt suddenly turned up, stopping off on his way back from Budapest. So my plans for work went out of the window and I was promptly monopolized for a five-hour "session", at the end of which, not surprisingly, I felt pretty drained. But I learned some very interesting things, which made me think of you, and I wondered what you would say if I were to suggest a little trip to China or the South Seas. But I suppose we should stick to the GG for the time being.'[25]

Fliethmann's big moment came when her superior, 'Plügel', and other 'gentlemen from the Institute' were drafted into the Wehrmacht ('All I can say is that it will do them good'),[26] leaving her 'to run the show here' on her own without constantly having to contend with irritable and domineering male colleagues.[27] Her friend from Vienna was very much on the same wavelength: 'I've gradually come to understand how you must be thoroughly fed up with certain things and certain gentlemen, because things have reached a similar pitch here. These men! Dreadful! Ours is as moody as an old maid.'[28] And: 'You know where I stand: we need to show them what women are made of.'[29]

As in Kahlich's case, many women became war widows, remarried, changed their names, and were less likely to make a career for themselves after the war. This makes it more difficult to investigate them. But the archives of the University of Vienna did yield one small file for the years 1946–7. After Kahlich had completed her 'practical ethnological training' at the Institute of Anthropology in the summer semester of 1944, she was dismissed in 1945 – illegally, so she believed. At her denazification hearing, a defence witness stated on 3 January 1946 that the accused had 'always declared herself politically and ideologically opposed to National Socialism' and had 'seriously expressed her intention of leaving the NSDAP', a course of action that third parties had advised against 'in order not to jeopardize her livelihood'. Speaking of the time she spent in Tarnów, the accused claimed that she had 'been on friendly terms with the Jews', had 'helped them out with gifts of food, discussed all kinds of political issues with them and given them advice on how to get to Hungary if they found themselves in danger'.

Men, inevitably, had rather different ideas about their ideal working conditions and about combining a professional career with private interests. We have not found any similar documents relating to the scientists working at the Institute for German Development Work in the East. So we cite another example instead which seems to us representative. This is the story of Lothar Stengel von Rutkowsky, who was still a medical student in 1933, but who by 1943 was in Prague working on a plan for the development of the research and teaching department within the SS Central Office of Race and Resettlement. This department was supposed to train 'Sippenpfleger' (racial monitors), welfare officers, registrars and aptitude testers in the SS for the task of classifying people according to 'racial' criteria. In his report Rutkowsky stipulated a number of non-negotiable conditions for his work:

'The experiment can only succeed if I enjoy the kind of confidence that is not going to be shaken by constant sniping from the sidelines, and if I can decide on all important matters with a completely free hand, according to my own lights.' He demanded a personal secretary, typists, one senior and two ordinary assistants, a suite of six offices, a photographic laboratory, a large and a small lecture room. And furthermore: 'If we are to compete successfully with the scientific achievements of the other side, we won't get very far if we are bogged down in petty bureaucracy. We must model ourselves on the Kaiser-Wilhelm Institutes. If I have to fight for months for every typist and every box of paper clips, the amount of real work I can get done will be correspondingly slight.' Naturally Rutkowsky also insisted on the right to hire his own staff and 'to dismiss employees who seem to me unsuitable and who disrupt the work of the department'. On top of this he wanted a 'full professorship' with suitable living accommodation: 'My ambition is to have a house in the country by the time the war is over.' Rutkowsky's working hours would be dictated 'not by the stopwatch' but 'by the academic workload'. With that in mind he needed an additional sitting room at home that he could use as a study: 'Somewhere I can work through into the night if necessary without being bothered by house rules or the noise of colleagues – which of course presupposes that the room in question is comfortably furnished.' And all these demands are made – naturally – not out of 'self-indulgence or egoism, but in order to maximize the energies I can bring to the great task before me'.[30]

An appetite for destruction

The university-educated members of the German occupying administration in Eastern Europe quickly developed a virulent desire to
destroy and exterminate. This seems to have been motivated by a
variety of – frequently interlinked – psychological responses. These
included disgust at the sight of poverty and dirt, and contempt for
the people, particularly Jews, who lived in such conditions; fear and a
residual guilty conscience, which were sublimated into an aggression
all the more intense; outrage at the pointless waste of labour
resources; and the satisfaction of 'intervening' to bring order into this
chaotic situation and turn it completely around. Their appetite for
destruction paved the way for the work of the practical policy-
makers. Below we cite three examples in chronological order.

Eduard Könekamp, as we saw earlier, had been sent by the German
Foreign Institute to observe the resettlement operations in occupied
Poland. In December 1939 he reported back to his colleagues in
Stuttgart:

> For many Germans this is probably the first time in their lives
> that they have seen so many Jews en masse. [The ghettos] are just
> about the filthiest places you can imagine. Here the Jews just veg-
> etate, some of them in basements that go down four stories below
> the ground. The hygienic and moral conditions are simply
> appalling. (...) Exterminating these subhumans would be in the
> best interests of the whole world. But exterminating them poses
> incredibly difficult problems. There are too many of them to
> shoot. And one can't simply shoot women and children. They
> reckon on some losses here and there on the evacuation trans-
> ports, and on a transport of 1,000 Jews that started out from
> Lublin 450 are said to have died en route. (...) All the agencies
> involved with the Jewish question are in no doubt about the
> inadequacy of all these measures. But an effective solution to this
> complicated problem has yet to be found.[31]

In the diaries of Dietrich Troschke for January 1941 we read:

> We embarked on the journey with mixed feelings. The warnings
> that everyone kept giving us were not unfounded. The driver had
> to maintain a good speed, otherwise we were sure to get stuck in
> the snowdrifts. At such times it is extremely dangerous to leave

the car and go off on foot through the snow, which lies a metre deep. It's easy to sink down into the snow, and it's nothing unusual in Poland for people to get trapped in the snow and die. Suddenly we spotted a farm cart up ahead of us, travelling in the same direction. We had to keep pretty much to the middle of the road to avoid getting stuck in the snow. The farmer didn't react at first when we sounded our horn. Coming up fast behind him, we hooted again. The farmer obstinately refused to give way. Only at the last moment did he grasp the situation and pull his horse hard round to the right: but it was too late. Our right mudguard caught his rear axle with considerable force. The impact was such that the cart literally fell apart: all four wheels dropped off, the central plank of the cart crashed down on the ground together with the shafts, and the farmer landed with a bump on the road, still sitting on his plank like a garden gnome. Although those of us in the car hadn't recovered from our shock yet, we had to laugh; the whole scene was just too grotesque.

The driver jumped out of the car, inspected the bent mudguard and hammered it more or less back into shape. Leaving the man to his fate, on which he could now reflect at leisure as he slowly carried the pieces of his cart back to his farm one by one – no joke, certainly, in that weather! – we went on our way.

Hermann Voss, an anatomist at the 'Reich University' of Posen since April 1941, noted in his diary:

23.6.1935: The Polish people are reproducing twice as fast as the Germans – and that's the crux of the matter! The far more primitive Slavic peoples will simply gobble up the German nation, which is not reproducing in anything like sufficient numbers.

18.5.1941: Köhler got back on Friday and has taken a room in my Institute. Now I have some company on Sundays, which is very agreeable. The Sundays here have been so awfully lonely, it's been absolutely dreadful. Yesterday afternoon we went out to Kundorf. (…) The people we met there were almost all Poles from the suburbs, and it made us realize how many of these wretched people are still around. If you normally only go into the city centre, you just don't notice them in the same way.

24.5.1941: In the basement here there's an incinerator for disposing of corpses. It's kept now for the exclusive use of the Gestapo.

The Poles shot by them are brought here at night and incinerated. If only the whole of Polish society could be eliminated in this way! The Polish people must be exterminated, otherwise there'll be no peace here in the East.

2.6.1941: I think one must look at the Polish question with complete emotional detachment, as a purely biological issue. We must destroy them, otherwise they will destroy us. And for this reason I take pleasure in every Pole who ceases to live.

15.6.1941: Almost daily now the grey truck with the grey men, i.e. SS men from the Gestapo, turn up with material for the oven. As it wasn't working yesterday we were able to take a look inside. It contained the ashes of four Poles. How little is left of a human being when all the organic matter has burned away! There's something very comforting about looking into one of these ovens. What was it Marshal Ney said before his execution: 'ou bientôt un peu de poudre'? The Poles have become very insolent again just now, and our oven is working hard in consequence. How wonderful it would be if we could herd the whole lot of them through such ovens.[32]

CHAPTER 6

THE GOVERNMENT GENERAL: AN EXERCISE IN GERMAN REDEVELOPMENT

'Population management and welfare'

A matter of weeks after the German invasion of Poland the occupation authorities in the newly constituted Government General set up a special department to direct and coordinate selection and resettlement policy. It was given the ambiguous title 'department of population management and welfare', and operated under the control of the interior ministry. The new agency was run by Dr Fritz Arlt until the beginning of September 1940, when the 27-year-old administrator was despatched to Upper Silesia, as we have seen, to reorganize the work of the Reich Commissioner for the Strengthening of German Nationhood. Having taken part in the invasion as a serving soldier, Arlt was asked to set up the department of population management and welfare by the Governor-General, Hans Frank, in late October 1939. In effect this made Arlt responsible for reorganizing state welfare provision for 12 million people under wartime conditions and under the dispensation of German 'ethnic policy'. This involved organizing public soup kitchens, negotiating with the International Red Cross and above all taking charge of population policy, which included the supervision of religious communities and all resettlement operations. He was responsible for the mental hospitals and nursing homes where elderly and seriously ill patients were murdered shortly after the occupation began.[1] According to a report in the *Krakauer Zeitung*, Arlt's agency had 'a separate section for processing each ethnic group'. The various sections responsible for the Polish, German, Ukrainian and Jewish 'ethnic groups' (the report went on), together with the sections in charge of 'emigrant groups' and 'statistics', provided the 'material needed by the "resettlement" section'. Arlt's activities were determined by two factors: 'On the one hand by overpopulation, and on the other by the fact that the tide of war, with its attendant population movements, has swept across the territories. The work of welfare distribution had to be completely reorganized to take account of German administrative needs, while also being integrated into a rigorous system of monitoring and surveillance.'[2]

In the first progress report prepared by the department of population management and welfare in June 1940 we read: 'An essential element in the German National Socialist administration of territories populated by dependent minority races is an agency that concerns itself specifically with the ethnopolitical structure of said territory; for ethnopolitical data of all kinds – historical, ethnological, racial, statistical, etc. – form the basis of any practical work of administration, from the calculation of projected tax revenues to the distribution and deployment of police forces.'[3]

Arlt gave more concrete shape to this programme in the second issue of the confidential journal *Volkspolitische Informationen* edited by him: 'If the entire population of the Government General were to look after its own needs, this would inevitably foster a solidarity among all sections of the population that is plainly not in our best interests. (...) The guiding principles of our welfare work in the GG are therefore political in character. All welfare issues must be handled in accordance with German racial and population policy. This will safeguard us against allowing our welfare work to be influenced solely by charitable and humanitarian considerations, when instead we should be guided constantly by the national and ethnopolitical interests of the German Reich.' The aim was to develop a 'planning strategy [for the Government General] based largely on the purely numerical ratio of its inhabitants', in order 'to be able to rule more easily'.[4]

Arlt and his staff sought to combine racial, population and social policy in their administrative practice. This led them to conclude that 'social stratification in the population of the Government General is simultaneously a racial stratification'.[5] As Arlt's successor, Lothar Weirauch, later wrote, it was a matter of 'shaking the mass of the Polish workers and peasants out of their idle stupor and keeping them to some form of productive activity'.[6]

Arlt followed Himmler's principle of 'breaking up' the population of the East 'into countless small fragments and particles'. The policy of divide and rule was to be furthered by 'fomenting strife between the different ethnic groups', as Himmler put it.[7]

By introducing racial criteria into the 'practical work of welfare' Arlt's intention was 'to exert influence indirectly on the ethnopolitical situation'[8] through a deliberate policy of selection and discrimination.

This included a graduated system of welfare benefits and exclusions, from food rations for resettled ethnic Germans to hunger, expropriation and forced labour for Jews. Arlt cited overpopulation as the reason behind the policy, pointing out that 'population numbers' in the Government General were 'quite incommensurate with the available capacity for meeting their basic needs'.[9] Arlt lost no opportunity of announcing publicly that population density was 'the critical factor for the success of welfare work'.[10] And of course he always emphasized what a 'drain on resources' the Jewish population was. As one means of redressing the imbalance between population numbers and resources he recommended an 'enlargement of feeding capacity' in the form of soil improvement programmes and increased agricultural yields – but also a 'reduction in population size'. A start had already been made: 'The thousands of war casualties have already made inroads into population numbers,' noted Arlt. Furthermore, 'due to the effects of the war the mortality rate is higher than heretofore', with young children, old people, the sick, weak and infirm being 'especially subject to the process of dying off'.[11]

At the same time Arlt's department was in no small measure responsible for aggravating the 'overpopulation problem'. For it acted in partnership with the RKF to expedite the enforced resettlement of hundreds of thousands of people from annexed western Poland to the Government General. In June 1940 Arlt reports: 'We were involved in the implementation of plans for evacuating and resettling people from the German eastern territories, the implementation of the 1st immediate-action plan (40,000 Poles and Jews), the 2nd immediate-action plan (120,000 Poles and Jews) and the processing of a portion of the 35,000 gypsies we have been asked to take. The resettlement quotas have been fixed for each district in consultation with the district commanders, and arrangements have been made for the necessary feeding and transportation.' In addition Arlt expected another '450,000 Jews to be deported to the GG' from 'Greater Germany', and in particular from the newly annexed provinces of western Poland.[12] And not even the department of population management and welfare disputed the fact that the victims of enforced resettlement were subjected to 'exceeding hardships' as a result.[13]

As Arlt recognized, the strain placed on the economy by the deported persons was all the greater because everything they owned had been taken away from them beforehand. From this it followed 'that the number of those who cannot support themselves or who must depend on society for a living is constantly increasing'.[14] But

Arlt also saw a positive side to all this. He pointed out that the 'accelerating process of sociological restructuring' – i.e. the increasing social, economic and legal discrimination – was affecting the 'fertility of Jewry' and having a 'negative impact on the birth rate'.[15] In September 1940 Arlt publicly proposed the wholesale deportation of the Jewish minority. This 'would reduce the pressure on living space [*Lebensraum*] in the Government General by something like 1,500,000 Jews'. The population density would then fall from 126 persons per square kilometre to 110, a figure that opened up the prospect of a 'successful, constructive solution', given 'the continued existence of opportunities for seasonal emigration into the German labour market':

> Initially there would be a large number of work opportunities for the local non-Jewish population, i.e. the unemployed or under-employed section of the Polish population would benefit considerably. (...) Through a process of sociological restructuring some of these people could then take over those jobs in industry, commerce and the skilled trades that were previously held by Jews. This would be a major contribution towards the social regeneration of the Polish rural proletariat. At the same time it would reduce overemployment in the agricultural sector and thus create a further opportunity for dealing constructively with the problem of overpopulation.[16]

To illustrate his arguments the writer published a map showing the geographical distribution of the 'Jewish encumbrance' on the Government General. Once the Jewish minority was 'removed from the living space', Arlt believed, 'the influx of the peasant class to the towns and cities' would follow. Only in this way could 'the social structure' of the population 'be gradually altered'.[17] The department of population management and welfare pressed for a 'total solution' early on: 'The Jewish problem has a great bearing on questions of population policy (...). It goes without saying that the Jews must be ousted from commercial and economic life, and gradually got rid of altogether. This can only be done one step at a time, of course, but comprehensive plans for a total solution are being drawn up.'[18]

In line with this thinking, Arlt's department had been pressing since June 1940 at the latest for 'the entire Jewish population to be concentrated within a specific area'.[19] Since this would be an opportunity to deport as many people as possible from the Government

General, Arlt's staff made every possible effort to increase the number of persons earmarked for compulsory resettlement. They suggested amending the Nuremberg Laws in such a way that 'half-Jews' in the Government General could be persecuted in the same way as 'full Jews'. The department's Jewish specialist Heinrich Gottong, a particular protégé of Arlt's, argued that the non-Jewish partners of 'mixed marriages' should be subject to the same anti-Jewish laws and discriminatory measures as their spouses, and should be deported accordingly.[20]

The deportation plans for 1939–40 centred first of all on the 'Lublin Jewish reservation', which was also destined to become a 'gypsy reservation',[21] and then on the so-called 'Madagascar plan'. Both schemes – which will be discussed in more detail in the next chapter – had been abandoned for different reasons by the autumn of 1940. With their demise the central project of Arlt's department – to reduce the population density in the Government General – also suffered an initial setback. While the leadership of the German occupation government prepared itself for the influx of another million deportees in the spring of 1941, the population experts continued to insist on the need for reducing the population in the Government General.

When Arlt himself suddenly took a completely different view of the problem in September 1940, this only made the situation more critical. As stated earlier, in the section on the Reich Commissioner for the Strengthening of German Nationhood, he now took on the task of selecting persons from Upper Silesia for deportation to the Government General – to the very region, in other words, where he had only just noted a desperate 'overpopulation problem'.

The department of population management and welfare continued to be involved in the organization of every resettlement operation that took place within the Government General. This is revealed by Arlt's service testimonial ('establishment of a central resettlement agency (…) that helped to look after incoming colonists and organize the resettlement and evacuation of hundreds of thousands of persons …'[22]) and by the fact that the 'department of resettlement' in the Warsaw district was closed down in March 1941, when its functions were taken over by the department of population management and welfare. In Warsaw it was headed by Heinz Auerswald, who shortly afterwards was appointed 'commissioner for the Jewish residential district'.[23] Arlt's successor, Lothar Weirauch, described the department he took over in these terms: 'Since my office is responsible for all ethnic policy issues that affect the administration of the Government General, including matters relating to resettlement, I have been kept constantly informed in broad outline about every evacuation and resettlement operation.'[24]

From the very outset the department of population management and welfare collaborated closely with the security police and the SD.[25] And later it was directly involved in the administrative preparations for the mass murder of Jewish men, women and children. When Frank announced on 16 December 1941 that 'the Jews must be dealt with one way or another', his undersecretary Josef Bühler issued an order on the same day to the effect that every resettlement operation in the Government General involving more than fifty persons required the approval of the department of population management and welfare. [26] In March 1942 this department worked in close conjunction with the SS to arrange the mass deportation of Jews from the Lublin district to the newly completed extermination camp at Belzec.[27] The day-to-day work of the department is documented in a private letter written by the deputy head of the department of population management and welfare, Walter Föhl. The letter is dated 21 June 1942, and the language used contains clear echoes of the minutes of the Wannsee Conference:

'Every day we have trains coming in with more than 1,000 Jews a time from all over Europe. The medics patch them up, and we either house them here temporarily or mostly ship them on into the Ukrainian marshes, in the general direction of the Arctic Ocean, where – assuming they survive (which the Jews from the Kurfürstendamm or Vienna and Bratislava certainly won't!) – they are all being collected together to await the end of the war, though not without having built a few autobahns in the meantime. (But we're not supposed to talk about that!)'[28]

On 27 October 1942 Föhl's superior, Weirauch, attended the third officially recorded follow-up discussion to the Wannsee conference.[29] In November 1942 the department of population management and welfare and the Reich Commissioner for the Strengthening of German Nationhood held a joint meeting in Cracow. One of the items on the agenda was the rapid spread of tuberculosis throughout the region. Among those present at the meeting was the chief medical officer of Warsaw and public health specialist Wilhelm Hagen, who was responsible for the control of tuberculosis in the Government General. He called for a comprehensive programme of measures to combat this dangerous infectious disease. Five minutes

into his presentation Hagen was interrupted by a question: did he
'propose to provide the same standard of tuberculosis care for all
Poles alike and for the entire population'? Hagen's reply was 'Yes'. 'At
this point,' Hagen recalled on the witness stand in 1962, 'Weirauch
leant towards the SS commander and whispered something to him. I
couldn't hear what was said. But the SS commander nodded to
Weirauch in approval. Weirauch then said to me that I had got hold
of completely the wrong end of the stick, and in order to make the
situation clear he was going to tell me something in strict confidence
that would show me how totally misguided my plans were. He
pledged me to secrecy with a handshake.'[30] What Weirauch now
divulged Hagen subsequently wrote down – in a letter to Hitler,
urging him to block the plans of the department of population management and welfare. In the planned resettlement of 200,000 Poles
'to make room for incoming German militia farmers', wrote Hagen, it
was intended 'to deal with a third of the Poles – 70,000 old people
and children under the age of 10 – in the same way as the Jews, i.e. to
kill them'.[31]

This letter cost Hagen his job. He had broken a fundamental taboo
by his explicit use of the word 'kill'.

Collaboration

In July 1940, alongside his work as population policy supremo, Arlt
took on the job of head of education and training for the NSDAP in
the Government General. He founded the journal *Das Vorfeld*,[32] and
collaborated closely with Theodor Oberländer,[33] formerly an officer
in the military intelligence service in Cracow. At the same time Arlt
found time and energy to build up the 'department of racial and
ethnic studies' at the Institute for German Development Work in the
East in Cracow,[34] which under his regime was initially named the
'department of population science and racial studies'[35] and had a
special section for 'Jewish research' from the very beginning. Arlt's
Jewish specialist in the department of population management and
welfare, Heinrich Gottong,[36] moved to the Institute for German
Development Work in the East in the spring of 1941, where he continued his career in racial research. Here he worked under Josef
Sommerfeldt, who in 1943 made an entirely unambiguous and public
declaration to the effect that there were 'only two possible options'
for 'solving the Jewish question': 'evacuation or physical annihilation'.[37] There was close collaboration between the Institute's

department of racial and ethnic studies and its department of economics.[38] The German Foreign Institute in Stuttgart, which was involved in all issues relating to resettlement, had a spokesman in the department of population management and welfare in the person of Hans Hopf. In February 1943 the director of the Institute in Cracow and the representative of the Reich Commissioner for the Strengthening of German Nationhood (Dr Hans Weibgen) agreed to work together closely, and both institutions organized at least one conference conjointly with the department of population management and welfare.[39] This collaboration gave a 'big boost' to the racial research department. The racial research staff at the Institute for German Development Work in the East were to 'provide documentary material for the requirements and measures of practical ethnic policy' and for 'political purposes of immediate practical relevance'.[40]

As a population policy-maker and a leading functionary of the RKF Arlt was also on good terms with the Frankfurt Institute for the Study of the Jewish Question. He was one of a select group of guests invited to the opening ceremony in March 1941.[41] At this gathering the head of the Racial Policy Office of the NSDAP, Professor Gross, spoke about the future of the Jews: 'The only way to eliminate the pernicious effects of their presence in Europe is to remove them as a physical presence altogether.'[42] The Institute for German Development Work in the East and the new Frankfurt Institute agreed to 'collaborate very closely' on the 'handling' of the 'East European Jewish question'. The purpose of this collaboration is explained in a report: 'A thorough scientific treatment of this problem is essential in preparation for a definitive pan-European solution to this question by the Führer after the war.'[43] The director of the Institute in Cracow – Wilhelm Coblitz, an old confidant of Hans Frank – became a corresponding member of the Frankfurt Institute[44] and observed not without pride: 'The Jewish research at the Institute is carried out in close collaboration with the central agencies of the NSDAP in the interests of resolving the whole European Jewish problem.'[45]

Peter-Heinz Seraphim, who has already figured in this study at several points, served as war administration officer for the 'Upper East Armaments Inspectorate' from the beginning of the war against Poland to the end of 1940. This meant that he was based in Cracow – like Oberländer and Arlt – and was responsible for 'observing economic policy in the GG'.[46] During this time he also appeared as a guest lecturer at the Institute for German Development Work in the East, where he addressed audiences on his favourite theme: the poverty of the Polish Jews and their annual population growth of nearly 9 per cent. Seraphim lamented that 23 per cent of Polish families had not been able to feed themselves by their own efforts even before the war: 'We need to focus on the basic fact that confining the Jews [he is referring to the start of the ghettoization process] is not enough in itself. Instead of just isolating the Jews, a constructive solution has to be found. (...) The action that has been taken to date suggests that a solution to this problem is being sought in a very specific direction. There can be no doubt that Germany will one day find a constructive solution based on the principles of National Socialism.'[47]

In March 1941 Seraphim published a book under the house imprint of the Institute for German Development Work in the East. The book was called *Die Wirtschaftsstruktur des Generalgouvernements* [The Economic Structure of the Government General], and in it he called for 'a radical restructuring of the region, its pacification, a revival and intensification of economic activity, (...) social and economic recovery'.[48] Nor did Seraphim spare his readers the by now commonplace arguments that Oberländer and he had developed in the preceding years. From the 'total fragmentation of the retail sector' and the 'packed' towns and cities to the 'fragmentation of land ownership and rural overpopulation', which were 'agriculture's greatest structural problem', he did not fail to mention virtually every standard argument in the demographic and economic repertoire. Depending on the region in question, and using the calculations devised by Oberländer, he classed between 41 per cent and 63 per cent of the rural population as surplus to requirement.[49] He called for the industrialization of occupied Poland and the development of a 'middle-class ethos'. At the same time he demanded the 'suppression or exclusion of the Jewish population element'. At the inaugural conference of the Frankfurt Institute for the Study of the Jewish Question Seraphim read a paper on 'the demographic and economic problems associated with a comprehensive European solution of the Jewish question'. Seraphim, whose book *Das Judentum im osteuropäischen Raum* [The Jews in Eastern Europe] was praised by Arlt as 'an outstanding major work',[50] and whom Arlt brought into negotiations in 1940 as a consultant on Jewish questions,[51] was appointed in March 1941 to the editorship of the anti-Semitic journal *Weltkampf*, which was published by the Frankfurt Institute for the Study of the Jewish Question.

Economic redevelopment

The idea of radically restructuring the Government General at the expense of the Jewish minority, as championed by Arlt for sociological, demographic and racist reasons, accorded well with the strategies of the economic experts. They embarked on their programme of 'economic redevelopment' in occupied Poland in January 1940. On 13 June 1940 Hans Frank appointed a new director to the Central Department of Economic Affairs in the shape of the Hamburg legal expert Walter Emmerich, who (as we saw in an earlier chapter) had gained his first experience of this kind of work in Vienna and learned there how to 'rationalize' a comparatively backward economy with the aid of 'Entjudung' – the systematic elimination of Jews from economic life. Before Emmerich took up his new post he had already been working for two months as Frank's personal adviser on economic policy matters. In this capacity he initially bore the grand title of 'general adviser to the office of the Governor–General on economic relations between the Reich and the Government General'.[52]

He began his work in Frank's administration with clearly defined aims. This was not Austria, where the aim had been to increase economic productivity to German levels. The plan instead was to maintain the existing gap in wages and prices in the Government General and to exploit it to the benefit of the German economy. The frontier, and in particular the customs frontier, remained in place. Emmerich's efforts in Cracow were directed towards turning the Government General into a low-wage country that depended on the economy of the German Reich. This was not without its problems. Wages were certainly much lower than in the Reich, but it could not be said that labour was 'cheap in real terms', as one of Emmerich's closest associates wrote at the time. The 'output per man and per shift' was unsatisfactory for various reasons, the means of production were 'in all-too-short supply'. This led to the formulation of the following 'core objective': 'To ensure the genuine cheapness of labour in the Government General, without which the region must be continually plagued by the old problem of "invisible unemployment" on the land, is one of the core policy objectives of the German administration.'[53]

A few days after his appointment Emmerich explained 'the principles of his proposed economic policy' to his boss Hans Frank. His remarks sounded like an economic supplement to Fritz Arlt's plans for reshaping the population profile: 'The prerequisite for thriving economic activity' was 'a fundamental change in the whole structure of the economy', involving first of all 'a significant rationalization of the Jewish sector'. In place of the 'multiplicity of small businesses more viable medium-sized businesses needed to be established', using the methods tried and tested in Vienna: 'By compressing the Jewish sector opportunities would be created for the Polish sector to catch up. (...) Naturally this commercial migration had to be properly organized, so that it didn't take place in an anarchic, undisciplined way.' What Emmerich meant by this, quite simply, was the organized plunder and officially authorized social disadvantaging of the Jews, using a combination of legislation, trustees and a state monopoly on the use of force. In the locally confined Jewish business community, made up of small and very small businesses, Emmerich saw an obstacle to the economic restructuring of the recently conquered 'territorial region'. The 'commercial migration' envisaged by him, on the other hand, was intended to open up the markets of the East. The new, artificially created Polish 'medium-sized businesses' would be easier to monitor and control. 'The Poles could do their share of the work, but they could not share in the decision-making process.' Frank assured his new economics minister of his 'unstinting support'.[54]

This marked a fundamental change in the economic policy of the Government General. Only in September 1939 Frank had received orders from Hitler 'to exploit this territory ruthlessly as a war zone and a source of plunder, (...) to turn it effectively into a heap of rubble'. This plan was very quickly changed by the Four-Year Plan Authority. Even though Hitler remained wedded to the idea, Frank came to an understanding with Göring which he formulated in January 1940 in these terms: 'This view has been completely transformed as a result of our efforts to inform and educate over the past few months. (...) The principle of total destruction has given way to the concept of actively promoting and assisting the region in so far as it can be of benefit to the Reich in its present situation. An important consequence of this new concept is the introduction of the Four-Year Plan to the region, which will thus be geared to serving Germany's overall aims.'[55]

The fact that Frank appointed the highly qualified economist Emmerich to be minister of economics in his Cracow government, which was just then getting established, testifies to an overall strategy that placed professional expertise above loyal adherence to the Party line. Emmerich had not joined the NSDAP until 1937, and then only in order to further his career. His relations with the Party remained cool. He regarded their officers as incompetent, and in Cracow he made it absolutely clear to them that they should leave economic policy to the experts.[56] At the same time there was a good deal of common ground between the goals formulated in the Party programme and those of an economic management strategy that placed efficiency first. In so far as racial policy could be accommodated to their social and economic policy aims, it was just one economic instrument among others as far as Emmerich and his colleagues were concerned.

Six weeks after taking up the reins of office, Emmerich was talking about the 'imminent evacuation of the Jews'. Like Fritz Arlt, he placed his hopes at this time in the plan for deporting all Jews living in the German-occupied territories to Madagascar. On 12 July 1940 Frank had informed the heads of his 'central departments' in the Government General – his ministers, in effect – that he had received Hitler's approval for the plan. He believed it would bring a 'huge relief of pressure' before very long.[57] And although this 'evacuation', which seemed a very immediate prospect in the summer of 1940, would, in Emmerich's words, produce 'a certain amount of turbulence' in the economy, he thought it a price worth paying. Indeed, in the short term he could see a definite advantage: it would now be possible to acquire 'household items for our officials from the property left behind by the Jews', and thus make good the present 'great deficiency of domestic furnishings'.[58]

Emmerich and his 'trust administration' – the institution set up to confiscate property owned by the Jews, the Polish state and Polish 'enemies of the state' and sell it off at a profit – now took the whole process a stage further, placed public finances on an entirely new footing and created new 'constraints' that supplied additional reasons for the 'evacuation' of the Jews. On 30 October 1940 the head of Emmerich's trust administration, Oskar Plodeck, reported that 'with regard to the exclusion of Jews from economic life there is still some way to go' and that 'the department of economics has been applying itself energetically to the solution of this problem in recent weeks'. They had now embarked on the expropriation of Jewish real estate, the value of which was put at 'around two thousand million zlotys in Warsaw alone' – the equivalent of a thousand million Reichsmarks. The economics department – formally concerned, always, to safeguard property rights – added a compensation clause to the expropriation order, albeit one that was, on its own admission, 'very carefully worded'. This stipulated that all payments to the dispossessed Jews were to be deferred until 1 January 1945.[59]

The point on which all these plans still officially hinged was the proposal for deporting the Jewish minority to Madagascar. By October 1940 it had already become apparent that this was no longer a practical possibility. But the German economic administration continued to use the Madagascar plan, however fanciful it might be, as a pretext to legitimize and press ahead with their own plans for eliminating the Jews from economic life. As the political situation changed, the talk within a few months was no longer of 'evacuation to Madagascar', but simply of 'evacuation'.

Emmerich was soon airing his plans for economic redevelopment in print, in a column entitled 'Government General – Outpost of Empire' that appeared in the *Berliner Börsenzeitung*. In essence, the idea was to take the Viennese model of economic restructuring pursued in parallel with 'Entjudung' and to develop it further. But now the plans took a far more radical form, and one that reflected the poverty of the country. The Germans had contributed in no small measure to that poverty: by war, by their annexation of the corn-growing regions of western Poland, the hard-coal basins and heavy industry, by the enforced resettlement of people who had been utterly pauperized, by the dismantling and destruction of the infrastructure. Through the 'elimination of the Jews from economic life' Emmerich planned 'to counter the effects of overmanning in commerce and the skilled trades (...) and thereby also to give the densely populated country an internal structure through the creation of a broad middle class of indigenous composition. The redevelopment of the economy of the Government General (...) will be directed towards productive participation in the new European community under the leadership of the Reich.'[60]

Such plans, it must be said, had little in common with the official policy line that still held sway in Hitler's inner circle. There the intention for the present was to carry on using the Government General as a dumping ground and a pool of labour, to be ruthlessly exploited without a second thought. Emmerich and most of the other professionals and experts on the ground paid scant regard to such directives. Undeterred, they applied themselves to the task of turning their model of an efficiently organized economy into a practical reality.

Frank was quick to adopt the plans of his senior officials for combining the deportation of the Jews with the social and economic mobilization of the conquered country, and in this he received the support of Göring's Four-Year Plan Authority.[61] Hitler, on the other hand, never once talked at this stage about economic parity or even about raising the standard of living in occupied Poland – even if he was prepared to make occasional concessions to Frank and called a temporary halt, at a number of points, to deportations to the Government General. In October 1940 Hitler still looked upon Poland as a territory for absorbing deportees from the Reich – a buffer zone of strategic rather than economic importance. Theories about overpopulation, rationalization of agriculture, the accumulation of capital for the development of industry – these things were of no interest to him as far as Poland was concerned. Hitler categorically rejected plans for the economic regeneration of Poland, and continued to see in the Government General a region that he needed – as he had observed back in 1939 – in order to 'cleanse the old and the new Reich territories of Jews, Polacks and riff-raff'.[62]

On 2 October 1940 Hans Frank unveiled his grand economic design to Hitler, which he had modified months before, and pointed out that overpopulation threatened to undermine all their constructive efforts. With this argument Frank hoped to head off further mass deportations to 'his' territory.[63] But to no avail: Hitler took him to task, as can be seen from a memorandum Martin Bormann made of this meeting:

'The Führer expressed his views on the whole problem in forthright terms. He said he did not care how high the population density in the Government General was, that the population density in Saxony was 347 persons to the square kilometre, in the Rhine province it was 324 and in the Saarland it was as high as 449 persons per square kilometre. He could not see any reason why the population density in the Government General had to be lower. (...) The standard of living in Poland *should* be low – and/or kept low.' The reason being that it brought down the cost of labour, which was 'good news for every German, and good news for every German worker. The Government General, he said, was on no account to become a separate and self-contained economic region, supplying some or all of its own need for industrial products. Instead the Government General was our reservoir of labour for low-grade manual work (brickworks, highway construction, etc., etc.) (...) The hiring centre for unskilled labour (...), a vast Polish work camp.'[64]

The subject of the meeting was the dispute about further deportations to the Government General – and in particular plans for the imminent shipment of 60,000 Viennese Jews to the region. Typically, Hitler deferred a decision, requesting a report from the Reich Governor of Vienna, Baldur von Schirach. When this had been submitted, Hans Lammers, the head of the Reich Chancellery, wrote to

Schirach that the 60,000 Jewish men and women 'still resident in Vienna' – thrown out of work, dispossessed and left behind despite the programme of enforced emigration – were to be deported to the Government General as a matter of priority 'owing to the present housing shortage in Vienna'.[65] Schirach had been promised this arrangement nine months earlier, yet nothing happened until the gas chambers were completed in 1942. In late February/early March 1941 5,000 Viennese Jews were deported to ghettos and labour camps in the Government General. However, further deportations were thwarted by the opposition of the German administration in the Government General, and more particularly by the transport ban imposed by the Wehrmacht on 15 March 1941 as part of its preparations for war against the Soviet Union. It was not until the autumn of 1941 that Hitler reverted to the plan for creating additional housing capacity by deporting the rightful tenants or property owners. On 2 November 1941 Bormann wrote to Schirach in Vienna: 'The Führer emphasizes that you should make it your task not to build new housing stock in Vienna, but to reorganize the existing housing arrangements.' With that in mind 'all Jews are to be deported as soon as possible in collaboration with SS Reichsführer Himmler, followed by all Czechs and other dependent minority races'.[66] The extent to which Himmler and Heydrich concerned themselves with these matters can also be seen from the minutes of the Wannsee conference of 20 January 1942, where we read: 'When it comes to the practical implementation of the final solution (...) the territory of the Reich, including the Protectorate of Bohemia and Moravia, will have to be dealt with first (...) if only for reasons relating to the housing shortage and other social-political necessities.'

The future that Hitler was still mapping out for the Government General in October 1940 had already been overtaken by a different reality in April of that year, in terms of the economic changes being made on the ground by German economic experts, agronomists, Wehrmacht and SS officers. While Hitler was still speaking of the 'homeland of the Poles', Frank was already using the term 'satellite of the Reich' in his exchanges with him.[67] Where Hitler, speaking of Poland's future, had in mind a region populated by exiles and outcasts, which had to be kept under control by police terror tactics and whose population was to be used as a pool of industrial labour, Frank was already formulating the concept of a well-ordered, colonial-style state associated with the Greater German Reich and on a fast track to modernization. In occupied Poland the policy of simply dismantling factories had been long since abandoned, work on the construction of dams had long since been resumed, the flow of the Vistula regulated, and the abortive programme of land reallocation initiated by the Poles had been taken up and carried forward with characteristic German energy and German instruments of power. At the latest by the time the campaign against France was being planned, the occupation authorities in Poland had settled in for the duration. Up until then Germany's military strategists had counted on limiting the scope of the war and 'only' annexing the western parts of Poland. The portion that was left, spared from German and Soviet annexation, could then have been used as a bargaining counter in peace negotiations. Scarcely had this idea been rejected, however, when a rapid shift in policy took place within the Government General. Now there was a move towards constructive development of an alarming kind – development on German terms and entirely subordinated to German interests. The new policy was geared to the 'principles of the Four-Year Plan', and came increasingly to mirror the concept that had been developed in Austria, the Sudetenland and the annexed provinces of western Poland, namely a development policy that discriminated against minorities, dispossessed them and drove them from their homes, in order to reshape the entire social and economic fabric of the country.

Raiding parties from Hamburg

In Cracow, Walter Emmerich saw himself as 'a Hamburger serving in a forward outpost', as one of those 'who have the courage to offer themselves for the work in the East', and who made sure that the 'ties with Hamburg' were not broken.[68] From Vienna he had brought with him Rudolf Gater, the rationalization expert who was mentioned in an earlier chapter. To head the economic policy unit of his department he appointed Max Biehl, who had previously been editor of the Hamburg business journal *Wirtschaftsdienst*. As head of the department of economics at the Institute for German Development Work in the East – which was also under Emmerich's overall control – he appointed Helmut Meinhold. He had obtained a first degree in economics from Hamburg in 1935, studied for his doctorate in Kiel and subsequently won his spurs at the Kiel Institute of World Economic Studies. Meinhold's two assistants, Hans-Kraft Nonnenmacher and Erika Bochdam-Löptien, also hailed from Hamburg – as did Dr Helmut Seifert, lawyer and manager of the so-called 'trust administration' in

Warsaw, set up to administer the stolen assets of the Polish population. At the age of thirty Seifert had already weathered a number of
corruption scandals and now administered 4,000 businesses and
50,000 pieces of real estate – 'assets to the value of several thousand
millions'. At the same time he acted as German commissioner for the
Polish national bank.[69] Emmerich himself had studied economics in
Hamburg from 1922 to 1930, worked at the university for four years,
then moved to the city's Board of Trade in 1934.

The appointment of Emmerich was a political coup for the
Hamburg business community, backed by the city's representatives at
the Reich Ministry of Economic Affairs.[70] Since the war had left
Hamburg firms largely cut off from their old trading partners around
the world, they looked to the East for financial recompense. Goods
had been piling up in their warehouses since September 1939 – goods
that could no longer be exported because of the war, but for which
there were no buyers in Germany either. These products now flooded
the new market offered by the Government General, favoured by a
zloty exchange rate that was kept artificially high. The official
purpose of this trade was to 'supply the essential needs of the
Government General', but in practice things often looked very
different, as the following letters reveal:

> Wolfers & Pontt, Hamburg 8, Fischmarkt 11, to the German
> Chamber of Commerce in Warsaw
> Ref.: Cancelled export orders.
> We have a large consignment of hair grips in various colours,
> card-mounted, which are not saleable in Germany and which we
> believe may therefore be suitable for export to the Government
> General...
> We await your response with interest.
> Heil Hitler. [71]

Or:

> We also have a large consignment of pocket mirrors with
> embossed backs and portraits of saints, which were originally des-
> tined for South America. To date we have been unable to find a
> buyer on the domestic market.[72]

The Reich Ministry of Economic Affairs initially authorized such
firms to export goods to the value of 10 million Reichsmarks to the

Government General,[73] and Emmerich arranged for solvent Jewish firms to be handed over to them as local operating bases.[74] In order to make this possible 'Jewish wholesalers naturally [had to be] put out of business'.[75]

Within three months the spoils had been divided. The *Ostdeutscher Beobachter* reported that 'a number of reliable German wholesale firms' had been 'commissioned to establish a trading company in each of the 40 districts'. They carved up the territory by mutual agreement, operated without any commercial competition and seized Jewish firms and their stocks as start-up capital.[76] In order to 'achieve a satisfactory position vis-à-vis manufacturers and suppliers in the Government General and also in our dealings with the authorities', these firms set up their own trading company, the Handelsgesellschaft deutscher Kaufleute m.b.H.[77] The term 'satisfactory' reflected a Hanseatic penchant for understatement, for as Emmerich himself implied, the German wholesalers – many of them based in Hamburg or Bremen – turned out to be a particularly rapacious and effective business combine. At a gathering to celebrate his birthday, their representatives regaled him with a performance of 'Ali Baba and the Forty Thieves' – a song they had composed in his honour. The reference was to the forty district wholesalers and their leader, Walter Emmerich, who took the 'firms on the ground' under his protective wing – just as in Vienna, where he had pushed open the 'gateway to south-east Europe' for Hamburg-based import and export firms. He described their role in these terms: 'They have been a dependable institution for a number of key functions, such as the collection of harvested produce, and have furthermore taken a very active role in getting small local businesses back on their feet; and by setting up proper shops they have introduced an element of German order and organization into totally run-down country backwaters.'[78]

The activities of the wholesale firms were to be directed towards 'supplying the needs of the population in the Government General' and 'making available certain surpluses for the German economy'. In other words their job was to squeeze goods out of the Government General, and in particular food for the German Reich. They were now 'in the business of buying up goods of every kind in bulk from the producer'.[79] Farmers were encouraged to deliver their produce to the collection points through a system of premiums introduced in the summer of 1940, and shortly afterwards draconian penalties were imposed as an additional incentive. The district wholesalers issued vouchers for the agricultural produce brought into their depots.

During the harvest period these could then be exchanged for textiles and ironmongery, paraffin, schnapps and tobacco.[80] Farmers who 'wilfully and maliciously' delivered nothing or too little risked the death penalty.[81]

The activities of these German businessmen were recalled in a memoir published in 1944 under the title 'Overseas Firms Supplying the Needs of Europe'. Under the heading 'German firms in the Government General' we read:

> It turned out that the firms most particularly suited to this task [i.e. the collecting of agricultural produce] were the ones that had previously run their own plantations and been engaged in the production and harvesting of agricultural produce in large quantities. (...) The special aptitude of overseas firms for this type of development work lay in the fact that their past activities had accustomed them to dealing with unusual situations in a foreign country with foreign people. (...) Now that the region has been freed up in economic terms and civilized once again, we shall be confronted with new tasks and problems in the future. (...) But the fact remains that these firms carried out their work of civilizing the region despite the burden imposed on them by the ravages of war – and that at a tragic moment in their history.[82]

The article goes on to describe how much the 'civilizing of the region' left to be desired prior to the arrival of the Hanseatic wholesale companies. Trade and commerce, we are told, had been severely handicapped by the 'countless small and very small businesses', many of which were simply not viable. Furthermore, two-thirds of all trade and commerce had been in Jewish hands. That was now a thing of the past, and the author of this retrospective was pleased with the outcome – even now, in 1944, when the end of the 'firms on the ground' was already in sight:

> The redevelopment work carried out by the firms on the ground in the Government General was the continuation by economic means of the conquest of the country by military force. Without the development of its economic life the region would have been nothing but a burden on Germany for the rest of the war. At the same time the work of these businessmen helped to advance the reconstruction of the region for those who had conquered it by force of arms.[83]

'Entjudung' and the new middle class

The 'reconstruction of the region' called for a fundamental change of structural policy in the Government General. Responsibility for implementing change rested with a number of different institutions, but they all agreed on the need to apply modern economic principles to the problem. The RKW (Reich Board for Industrial Rationalization) and the Institute for German Development Work in the East set about tackling the task. But they were not alone: the department of population management and welfare, the RKF (Himmler's resettlement authority), the ministries of agriculture and economic affairs and the office of regional planning all lent their active support.

In July 1940 the RKW had set up an 'Office for the Government General', headed by Rudolf Gater. In December of that year Gater completed his first report, entitled 'The economic foundations of the Government General'. Starting, like most other German economists, from the premise of massive overpopulation, Gater feared that the population would continue to grow by 120,000 a year: 'While the Government General as such has very little industry, so that there is definitely scope for enlarging the industrial sector, there is no possibility of providing enough jobs in industry to absorb the large population surplus. Simply in order to absorb the year-on-year population growth the economy would have to grow by around 11 per cent a year – and that is *after* it has recovered to the level of 1939.'[84] This growth target was never remotely attained under German occupation, and Gater never thought that it could be, given that it would have required 'American growth rates'.

Helmut Meinhold, the executive head of the department of economics at the Institute for German Development Work in the East, put the 'surplus population' in the Government General at 2.56 million or 3.75 million, depending on the yardstick of comparison adopted.[85] Summing up the situation in the Government General as a whole, he writes: 'While approximately one quarter of the population in pre-war Poland was surplus to requirement in its present employment, the figure in the territory of today's Government General was closer to 30 per cent.'[86] Meinhold too was of the opinion that industrialization alone would not suffice to absorb this surplus. On paper he reallocated the jobs done by the Jewish population, in so far as they seemed to him economically essential, to non-Jewish Poles. At the beginning of 1942, he estimated the population of the

Government General at two million less than it actually was. He calculated that in the wake of the 1931 census '17.6 million people – 15.6 million excluding practising Jews' – were living in the Government General, and then took the last (lower) number as the basis for his subsequent analysis.[87]

Around the same time Meinhold's assistant, Erika Bochdam-Löptien, carried out a survey of 'businesses in pre-war Poland'.[88] Trade and commerce were stagnating, she claimed, with a retail sector involving large numbers of middlemen. The effect of this was to 'stifle any ambition among the commercial population to rise higher and work harder'. Bochdam-Löptien shared the view that the Jews were responsible for the 'overcrowding' in trade and commerce. In 1942 she noted with satisfaction: 'But of course in the two years of German administration the Jews have largely been eliminated from commercial life.'[89]

This marked the end of a process that had been pushed through without undue haste, but none the less speedily and systematically – in line with the wishes of German economic experts.

Back in December 1940 Gater had warned against the economic disadvantages that would result from the precipitate and ill-prepared elimination of Jews from trade and commerce, and had mapped out the route that would be systematically followed up until the end of 1943: 'The elimination of Jewish merchants and tradesmen is best carried out in stages, so that they can be replaced by others in the meantime.'

One such stage was taken up with 'the retraining of Poles to replace the Jews', another with the closing-down of businesses in those branches of the economy where 'overmanning' had been identified as a problem. In this way Gater planned to achieve 'the broad aim for the immediate future', which was 'to progressively eliminate the Jews from commercial life altogether' and 'to achieve a much more balanced population structure through the creation of a sustainable Polish middle class'.[90]

According to Bochdam-Löptien, 65 per cent of those working in trade and commerce were Jews, and 84 per cent of these were self-employed. By contrast, over 50 per cent of the non-Jews working in trade and commerce were wage and salary earners. So the expropriation and liquidation of Jewish firms also produced a surge in new business concentrations, an easing of competitive pressure on Polish-Aryan retailers and more opportunities for non-Jewish Poles to set up in business on their own. In the majority of cases it also meant that dependent Polish wage-earners were 'freed' from their Jewish bosses. Cutting out some of the middlemen from the supply chain led to a reduction in trading margins and hence to a strengthening of the purchasing power of the impoverished rural population – but without adversely affecting the earnings of primary producers.[91]

The Germans failed in their attempt to create a Polish petite bourgeoisie at the expense of the Jewish population that was both willing to collaborate and imbued with 'middle-class values'. They failed not least because of Polish resistance, the frequently indiscriminate use of violence against all sections of the indigenous population, and above all because of the changing fortunes of war. But the occupation authorities were able to point to some initial successes. The newspaper reports below, while largely propagandistic in nature, nevertheless serve to document this middle-class policy at the expense of the Jewish minority:

> The head of the department of resettlement in the office of the Warsaw district commander, Reich Bureau Chief Schön, emphasized that the elimination of the Jews from economic life will lead to the emergence of a healthier economic structure within the Polish population. In the past there has never been a Polish middle class as such, because the sources of income for this class of society have always lain in Jewish hands. But the fact that in Warsaw, for example, 4,000–5,000 shops and workshops have already been handed over to Poles marks a significant step forward in the creation of a Polish middle class. (*Krakauer Zeitung*, 13 March 1941)

> In Nowy Sacz some 70 shops that were formerly owned by Jews have been taken over by Aryans. The municipal authorities have seen to it that these shops not only have new owners, but also a new face and character. In many cases two or even three of the filthy holes that the Jews called shops have been knocked through to form attractive, spacious salesrooms which let in the daylight and fresh air. (*Krakauer Zeitung*, 28 June 1941)

> When the German authorities announced their intention two years ago of eliminating the Jews from Polish economic life completely within a short space of time, it was initially feared by all sections of the Polish business community that this drastic step would deal an enormous blow to the economy, which had already largely collapsed as a result of the failed military

adventure against the Reich. Great was the astonishment, therefore, when this massive operation on the Polish 'body economic'
was performed almost painlessly, thanks to carefully planned
measures aimed at cushioning the initial shock and managing
the transition. That astonishment soon turned to pleasant sur-
prise when many Poles who had been able to salvage assets from
the great debacle found that they could become a partner in a
company in place of a Jew. Suddenly there were any number of
job openings for young skilled tradesmen. The German authorities had to act quickly to organize vocational training facilities
and the retraining of unemployed workers in order to maintain
the necessary supply of skilled labour for the future. (*Die Deutsche
Stimme*, 10 December 1941)

One example of this is the 'capital of ready-made tailoring',
Tarnów, which in Polish times was a Jewish town through and
through. The skilled trades, industry, commerce – in a word, the
entire economic life of the town – was in the hands of the Jews.
Until very recently there were still Jewish workers of both sexes
employed in the internationally renowned tailoring workshops
of Tarnów. Through a combination of special measures introduced by the German education authorities in the Government
General, the establishment of an ongoing programme of intensive training courses in tailoring and the use of final-year students from the vocational schools, Jewish workers have now
disappeared altogether from the tailoring industry in Tarnów. In
short, Tarnów is now a Jew-free zone. (...) On the back of the
drive to eliminate Jews from economic life a general restructuring
of trade and commerce in the Government General is taking
place. The smaller Jewish firms are being closed down, and some
that are of vital economic importance have been taken over by
Poles. Larger Jewish firms are being handed over to war-disabled
Germans. (*Government General Press Service*, Issue 212, 20 October
1942)

Because of the Jewish stranglehold on economic life, salary
earners in industry and commerce have been systematically
excluded from senior management positions and denied the
opportunities to broaden their experience or establish the necessary relationships with buyers, suppliers and local government
departments. Now that the Jews have been weeded out, the population of the Government General has more scope for career

advancement, although those applying to take over Jewish businesses will need to be both open-minded and prepared to acquire a working knowledge of the trade or business concerned. (*Die wirtschaftliche Leistung* I (1942), No. 5, 15 December 1942)

So the expulsion of Poland's Jews from commercial life was used as an instrument for creating a 'sustainable Polish middle class' in the medium-term future. At the same time it paved the way for a radical programme of economic rationalization. But the Germans who ran the economy of the Government General had no intention of transferring the whole of trade and commerce to Polish ownership. The really profitable businesses were reserved for German entrepreneurs – even in the ghettos.

'Population numbers to be reduced'

The 'elimination of the Jews from economic life' in the Government General, as called for by Rudolf Gater and others, opened up the possibility of applying German standards of productivity. Dr Karl Kuchenbäcker developed models for the rationalization of agriculture in the Government General which need not be discussed in detail here. What is important, however, is the position occupied by Kuchenbäcker within the power structure of the Government General. He was one of the leading functionaries of the Reich Commissioner for the Strengthening of German Nationhood, which extended its activities into the Government General as from the spring of 1940. Prior to that he had headed the section responsible for racial policy and resettlement in the office of the senior SS and police commander in Cracow. And throughout this time he continued to run the department known as 'New Land Order' in the agricultural ministry of Frank's government.[92] As a trained agronomist, an official in the civilian administration and a high-ranking SS functionary, Kuchenbäcker moved freely between the various power centres within the Government General and passed on information of a general kind about planning and policy between the government and the SS. Like so many of his colleagues, Kuchenbäcker believed the main problem was overpopulation: '…the villages are overflowing with people, and…many of them just have no idea what to do to pass the time'. The reasons for this state of affairs were so obvious to him that he was able to reduce the problem to a succinct formula: 'Cause of present sorry predicament: wrong agrarian structure!'[93] As a result of the 'new land order' tens of thousands of peasant families were to be 'released' each year. The more the merrier, in fact. As Kuchenbäcker himself put it: 'The bigger the changes we can make, the more successful and enduring will be the outcome.'[94]

These measures only added to the 'population pressure'. Yet this, according to Meinhold, who was himself a consistent champion of rationalization, undermined the 'internal stability of the whole region'. For him the 'ideal national solution' was a situation where 'all the available labour resources in the Government General are absorbed there'. But that would have meant creating several million new jobs in industry – a proposal that Gater had already dismissed as completely impracticable in his first report of 1940. So a conflict of aims arose: on the one hand the rationalization programme was to be pushed through in an incredibly short space of time; on the other hand it was impossible to create a sufficient number of new jobs for those made redundant. Meinhold proposed four measures aimed at resolving this conflict 'which may be applied singly or in combination':

1. Labour in the Reich, in particular migrant labour, is to be regulated by law in terms of its character and scope so that it cannot become a threat to the essence of German national identity.
2. The number of jobs in the Government General is to be increased as far as possible.
3. The density of the population in the Government General is to be reduced.
4. The scale and pace of labour redeployment within the Government General are to be adapted as far as possible to the changing situation as the other three measures take effect.[95]

The second and fourth of these proposals could only be implemented to a limited extent and in the longer term. The third of the measures called for by Meinhold – 'the density of the population in the Government General is to be reduced' – was subject to no such restrictions.

The proposal regarding 'migrant labour' – deportation to the Reich for forced labour, in other words – had likewise been made with some reservations. Meinhold feared the 'many political, ethnopolitical, biological and economic dangers' associated with the 'mixing of nationalities'.[96] He saw it as a problem that 'employment will have to be found for the families of the migrant workers who stay behind at home, partly in order to utilize all the labour resources in the GG to the maximum, partly in order to keep the wages of the migrant workers at a relatively low level – and also to prevent their families from becoming a socially destabilized and therefore politically volatile element as a consequence of their idleness.'[97]

Rudolf Gater took a more dispassionate view of the 'migrant labour' problem. But in his report he too came to the conclusion that the forced labour option was not sufficient in itself to 'absorb' the huge population surpluses of the Government General. By the end of 1940 a total of 340,000 persons had already been deported to the Reich. Gater estimated – very realistically – that the number of forced labourers could 'perhaps be pushed up to 2 million persons of working age'.[98] Even if the 'population pressure' could be alleviated to some extent through an extended programme of public works in the Government General, Gater viewed the situation as 'extraordinarily difficult'. He believed that it was not possible to solve the overpopulation problem in this way. It was therefore necessary 'to look for other ways of accommodating these people and the surplus population of the GG (less the Jews who are due to be deported)'.[99]

By December 1940, then, there was no doubt in Gater's mind that the Jewish minority would be deported – and deported *from* the Government General, which was supposed to be, and indeed still was, a dumping ground for precisely these people. At the same time the Jewish specialist Heinrich Gottong from the Government General's department of population management and welfare, whom we have already encountered, was also arguing for the need to 'relieve the pressure' created by the Jewish minority. His arguments are worth repeating here: 'The events of the war and their consequences have placed tight constraints on the lives and living conditions of the Jews. Jewish workers have been replaced by Aryans in many businesses, so that as well as being physically confined they are now subject to economic and social restrictions that will become increasingly acute. The mounting pressure of these restrictions will have to be relieved somehow, and a solution found.'[100]

In the January 1941 issue of the Hamburg journal *Wirtschaftsdienst*, Emmerich's colleague Max Biehl outlined the new 'starting points for the German work of redevelopment in the Government General', announcing that in future people would be deported *from* the Government General, which was originally intended to receive deportees: 'However, it would be beyond the scope of the present article to list all the individual categories of persons who might be considered in due course for deportation on the one hand or for repatriation or admission to the Government General on the other.'[101]

The calls for action from Gater, Biehl and Gottong were formulated during a phase that we shall be examining in some detail below. Following the abandonment of the Madagascar project in September 1940, concrete plans for deportations from the Government General were not on the agenda. On the contrary: both Hitler and Himmler were insisting on more and more deportations of people *to* the Government General, even though, from the winter of 1940–41 onwards, they looked upon such measures as merely temporary. After all, once the Soviet Union had been defeated there would be no shortage of new territories to which these deportees could then be transferred. Frank had no alternative but to agree to these plans, contrary to the advice of his experts.

The annexation of Galicia – predicated on extermination

Meinhold's proposal – 'the population in the Government General is to be reduced' – dates from the period prior to the beginning of the systematic extermination of the Jews in occupied Poland. In the summer of 1941, just a few days after the attack on the Soviet Union was launched, he discussed the 'possibilities of extending the Government General to the east'. This would open up entirely new perspectives for the economists and regional planners: instead of occupying a rather marginal position, the Government General would move centre stage and become a 'key element within the regional sphere'. It was to be a 'transit territory', with its own modern industrial base of light industry. From now on the railway authorities used a new advertising slogan: 'The Ostbahn [Eastern Railway] – linking the Reich to Eastern and South-East Europe'. For Meinhold – and for others besides – the time had come to make big plans. He first of all considered 'moving some of the Poles, or maybe all of them, much further east'. The deportation of 13 million people from the Government General was nothing unthinkable for the young regional planner. He had evidently been rehearsing such plans on paper, for he noted that this option 'has already been examined briefly in a report prepared by the Institute for German Development Work in the East'. There is a passing footnote reference to a memorandum, which has not been found: 'Cf. the report on the evacuation of the Poles, Cracow, June 1941.'[102] In the section entitled 'General principles of population policy' Meinhold then went on to explain that every 'new territorial addition to the Government General (...), if it is to be of economic benefit to the region, must obviously be accompanied by the resettlement of population groups'. In the event he confined himself to the suggestion that 'only' a portion of the 'Poles destined for resettlement way out to the East' should be expelled from the Government General, possibly for relocation in the Pripet Marshes. He then looked at different variants of his expansion plan, based on the 'annexation' of various regions. Each variant involved the resettlement of several million people; and in each case it was taken as read that 'the Jews would be deported along with the others'.[103]

Forty years later Meinhold excused himself with this argument: 'We thought they would be sent to the Rokitno Marshes in order to drain them and settle there.'[104] But in the contemporary study just referred to, he raised an environmental objection to this very plan: 'The deployment of a large labour force to drain the marshes (or a similar scheme for the Rokitno Marshes) is conceivable, but only after the climatic effects have been very carefully studied first.'[105] Three months later Hitler voiced similar concerns: 'We shall leave the marshes as they are, not only because we need to use them for military exercises, but also because of the weather conditions, to prevent them turning into a barren steppe.'[106]

Meinhold can never seriously have believed that Poland's Jewish minority would be relocated to the Rokitno Marshes – quite apart from the fact that even these marshy regions had been identified by him as 'overpopulated' already.[107] It is safe to assume that all this talk of relocating the Jews to the Marshes would have meant an early death for many of them, if not for the majority. That this was the intention may also be inferred from the comments of Walter Föhl, the executive cited earlier in this chapter, who named the 'Ukrainian marshes' (i.e. the Pripet and Rokitno Marshes) as the final destination of the Jews deported from Bratislava, Berlin and Vienna, and assured his SS colleagues that they 'certainly won't' survive the experience.

Instead of the marsh regions, however, it was eastern Galicia that was incorporated into the Government General in mid-July 1941, following a decision of Hitler's.[108] This region played a key role in the German redevelopment plans, partly on account of its oil deposits, partly on account of its geo-economic and strategic importance within the German grand design for eastern Europe. At the same time, however, Galicia was regarded as particularly backward and overpopulated. The decision to enlarge the Government General by the incorporation of this territory could only aggravate the existing situation. And this decision was taken against the background of the fact that the imminent 'evacuation' of the Jewish minority was already agreed policy. In the draft notes for an initial administrative report on the new territory dated 26 August 1941, under the subheading 'The region and its population', we read: 'The territory is 48,081 square kilometres in area. The population density of 95 persons per square kilometre is one of the highest of any agricultural area in Europe.' The area was overpopulated to a degree 'not to be found anywhere else in Europe'.[109] Furthermore, Galicia was known to the department of food and agriculture as 'the land of tiny agricultural enterprises'. The fragmentation of land ownership had accelerated under Soviet rule (1939–41), since 'the Russians [have] with few exceptions distributed all farms over 5 hectares to agricultural labourers and smallholders, leaving only a few state-owned farms (sovkhozy) or collective farms (kolkhozy) in existence, plus a handful of newly formed ones, with the aim in the first instance of satisfying the hunger for land among farm workers and smallholders'.[110]

But in Galicia as elsewhere, the German administrators and government advisers saw the Jewish population as the real economic problem. Helmut Meinhold moved into Lvov a few days after the Wehrmacht,[111] and reported in the following terms: 'The overpopulation of the rural areas, and the fact that Jews flooded into Galicia and Congress Poland without regard for the available opportunities for productive work, put constant pressure on the development of commercial life. A constantly growing population had to share a national product that was not increasing at the same rate, with the result that purchasing power and capital formation both suffered in equal measure.'[112]

Galicia was viewed as the gateway 'that connects central Europe with eastern and south-east Europe'. It was to be 'integrated as quickly as possible into the overall fabric of the Government General'.[113] Meinhold's assistant, Hans-Kraft Nonnenmacher, put the 'excess population' of eastern Galicia immediately after its annexation at 800,000 to 900,000 people – and that out of a total population of around four million. Just as Meinhold had already done for the Government General as a whole, Nonnenmacher now proposed a three-point strategy aimed at solving a 'whole series of major population problems': 'Creation of additional employment opportunities through the development of local industry, emigration of the population into regions that are not yet overpopulated, or their deployment as migrant workers in the industry or agriculture of other regions.'[114] 'Emigration into regions that are not yet overpopulated' was Nonnenmacher's way of referring to the necessary – as he believed – deportation of Galicia's Jewish population. Since German demographic experts – as we shall show below – had already calculated that there was a 'population surplus' of 30–50 million people in eastern and south-east Europe as a whole, Nonnenmacher knew full well that no such regions existed anywhere in Europe.

CHAPTER 7

1940: PLANS, EXPERIMENTS AND LESSONS LEARNED

The Madagascar project

From the very outset the German administration in occupied Poland viewed the ghettoization of the Jewish population as a 'transitional measure'. Guarding and feeding all these people once they were shut in presented, in the words of Peter-Heinz Seraphim, 'problems of a difficult nature'. At the same time the ghettos were 'an inhibiting factor for the development of the towns and cities in the East in terms of municipal policy, town planning and public health'. Seraphim went on: 'Since the Jewish problem in these territories is not just an economic issue but also a demographic issue on a vast scale, finding a definitive solution is extremely difficult. The only definitive solution to this and the whole Jewish question in eastern Europe, which would be in the interests of the non-Jewish population and in the interests of the Jews themselves, who have no economic foundation where they live now, is to undertake a programme of mass resettlement, transferring the East European Jews now living in the German sphere of influence to a new overseas homeland.'[1]

The deportations to the Government General had barely got under way in earnest before they ground to a halt in March 1940. The scheme to set up a 'Jewish reservation' in the vicinity of Lublin, close to the German–Soviet line of demarcation, was abandoned after abortive beginnings. Eichmann himself had toured the area and inspected the proposed site, and in October 1939 he ordered the deportation of several thousand Jews from Vienna, Ostrava (the capital of northern Moravia), Prague and Katowice.[2]

This initial attempt at deportation failed because of various organizational difficulties, and because of the opposition it encountered from the German occupation authorities in Cracow. In the wake of this debacle the central government agencies in Berlin – the Foreign Office, the Central Office for the Security of the Reich, the Four-Year

Plan Authority and the Ministry of Propaganda – devised the so-called Madagascar project in the summer of 1940. With reference to this plan Heydrich informed the Reich Foreign Minister on 24 June 1940 that 'the problem of the 3¼ million Jews in the territories under German control could no longer be solved by emigration; a territorial solution was now necessary.'[3] Palestine was no longer an option for mass emigration: Germany's political and economic strategists now regarded North Africa and the Near East as 'satellite regions' and had therefore summarily proclaimed Palestine to be 'Arabian living space'. In the light of German interests in oil, cotton and other raw materials the Foreign Office warned of the risks posed by an independent Jewish state, however small, which could be just as influential in foreign-policy terms, and could become just as much of a political thorn in Germany's side, as (say) the Vatican.[4]

The basic idea behind the new project – which in fact had clear historical antecedents[5] – was summed up by the Central Office for the Security of the Reich in terms of population numbers and the faltering resettlement projects in the East: 'Now that the masses in the East have to be included in the total, any prospect of settling the Jewish problem by emigration has become impossible.'[6] Of the four million Jews that the Germans wanted to deport, nearly three million were to come from a crushed and defeated Poland. On 11 July 1940 Hans Frank reported triumphantly on the outcome of a recent discussion with Hitler:

> Very important too is the Führer's decision – which he took in response to my submission – that no more Jewish transports are to be sent to the Government General. On a more general note I would point out that there are plans to transport all the Jews in the German Reich, the Government General and the Protectorate – the whole pack of them – to some African or American colony as soon as peace is concluded. One possibility is Madagascar, which France will be required to cede for this purpose. With a land area of 500,000 sq. km. there should be plenty of room here for a few million Jews. I have been at pains to ensure that the Jews in the Government General are also allowed to benefit from this opportunity to make a new life for themselves in a new land. My point has been taken, so we can expect to see a huge relief of pressure here in the very near future.[7]

Although the Madagascar project was found to be impracticable only ten weeks later, the population planners and economists took it as read from now on that the Jewish population would be 'disappearing' from Europe. And for the first time they linked the 'final solution of the Jewish question' with the vision of a Greater European trading area.[8]

The new resettlement plan envisaged the deportation to Madagascar of the four million European Jews then living under German rule. In the bureaucratic jargon of Eichmann's relocation organization, it was 'an overseas solution of an insular character'. In constitutional terms the idea was to 'establish a Jewish homeland under German sovereignty'. In overall charge of the project would be the head of the security police and the SD, who would thereby be continuing the work that Göring had entrusted to him on 24 January 1939 as 'special commissioner for Jewish emigration'. The plan envisaged two ships a day docking in Madagascar for the next four years, each one carrying 1,500 deportees. The new arrivals would be put to work reclaiming the land, constructing highways and draining swamps. On the model of the abortive 'Jewish reservation' in Lublin, an advance party of younger Jews with a good grounding in the skilled trades and agriculture would be sent out ahead of time to make basic arrangements for 'housing the masses that were to follow'. On the island the deportees would remain under German police supervision, living in the shadow of large German air force and naval bases, and of course subject to a German monopoly on foreign trade. The project was to be financed by English and American Jews as 'restitution for Versailles'.[9] According to a memorandum of the Foreign Office, the following 'practical division of labour' was proposed:

1. Conduct of negotiations with the hostile powers on the basis of the peace treaty and with the other European powers on the basis of special treaties – Foreign Office.

2. Registration of Jews in Europe, transportation to Madagascar, resettlement there and future administration of the island ghetto – Central Office for the Security of the Reich.

3. Registration of Jewish assets held in Europe, establishment of an inter-European bank to act as trustee in administering and realizing these assets and to undertake the financing of the resettlement enterprise – Four-Year Plan Office, Councillor Wohltat.

4. Propaganda measures designed to prepare public opinion for the plan and forestall a possible smear campaign from the USA:

(a) for the domestic audience: the Ministry of Propaganda, senior executive officer Dr Taubert with his 'Anti-Semitic Campaign';

(b) for foreign audiences: the public information department of the Foreign Office.

As far as the Jews of western Europe were concerned, the Four-Year Plan Authority and the Foreign Office spelled out their particular priorities in relation to the Madagascar plan: 'The aim is to replace Jewish economic influence in Europe at a single stroke, so to speak, with German economic influence, but without disrupting the economies of the countries concerned by the closure of large Jewish-owned firms.'[10]

In the course of the exploratory discussions that took place between the Foreign Office and the Chancellery of the Führer, a certain 'head of section Brake proposed that the transport organization he had built up on the special orders of the Führer for wartime needs be pressed into service for the shipment of the Jews to Madagascar'.[11] It is clear that the memorandum in question did not refer to anyone called 'Brake', but to Viktor Brack and the 'Public-Sector Patient Transport Company' that he had helped to build up. As a member organization of the so-called 'Aktion T4' ('T4 Programme') it was currently transporting tens of thousands of German psychiatric patients to the extermination clinics. It was a 'well-oiled organization with a wealth of experience', as the Foreign Office noted with gushing approval. The connection between the Foreign Office and the 'well-oiled organization' had doubtless come about through the fact that the head of the Chancellery of the Führer, and Brack's immediate superior, Philipp Bouhler, had ambitions to become Governor-General of East Africa. On 23 June 1940 he asked Hitler for 'the colonial commission'. Hitler initially refused.[12] But Bouhler and Karl Brandt were the two men whom Hitler had authorized in 1939 to organize the murder of German mental patients.

While non-Jewish patients of both sexes were singled out for killing in the mental hospitals on the basis of diagnoses and prognoses (however superficial) of their illnesses, Jewish mental patients were simply murdered indiscriminately from the middle of July 1940 onwards without any kind of medical examination procedure. It is quite conceivable that this was connected with the planned deportation of the Jewish population to Madagascar: doubtless there were fears that the mentally ill could easily panic if they were put onto ships and deported, and under certain conditions their panic might spread to the other deportees on board.

In the event, the 'Public-Sector Patient Transport Company' was not able to deploy its 'wealth of experience' on the Berlin to Madagascar route via Genoa and Suez, but the contact between Brack and Bouhler, who directed the programme of mass murder in the 'euthanasia' clinics, and the authorities who were seeking a 'final solution of the Jewish question', remained in place. A year later the Aktion T4 organization offered the services not of its transport operation, but of its 'well-oiled' killing machine – personnel who were suitably versed in the operation of gas chambers and the incineration of corpses. More than a hundred employees of Aktion T4 were posted in 1941–2 to the extermination camps established under 'Aktion Reinhard': Belzec, Sobibor and Treblinka. They set up the camps and ensured that the whole operation ran smoothly thereafter. They also supplied the camp commandants and the inspector for all three camps.

The German Foreign Office was in overall charge of the Madagascar project. It commissioned two reports to evaluate the project paper drafted by the Central Office for the Security of the Reich. One of these reports was prepared by Friedrich Schumacher, professor of geology at the Freiberg Mining Academy in Saxony; the other was drawn up by the president of the Bavarian Office of Statistics, the demographer Professor Friedrich Burgdörfer. Schumacher presented his report on 1 August 1940;[13] Burgdörfer had submitted his two weeks earlier.[14] Responding to the brief he had been given, Schumacher concluded that Madagascar possessed little in the way of valuable mineral resources – thus dismissing fears that the island might be too good for the Jews, so to speak.[15] Burgdörfer wholeheartedly endorsed the plan for 'resettling' 6.5 million Jews on the island. But his report went far beyond the terms of the brief. Not only did he quote numbers for 'world Jewry' as a whole, he also calculated that it would be possible to resettle other Jewish populations on Madagascar too: not just the nearly four million who were then living under German rule, but also another million Jews from Palestine and 1.6 million 'from other parts of the world' (excluding the Soviet Union and the USA). Burgdörfer summarized his findings:

> At the last census (1.7.1936) Madagascar had a population of 3.8 million, which, on a total land area of 616,000 sq. km., is equivalent to 6.2 persons per sq. km. The total number of Jews being considered for resettlement is thus only 2.7 million greater than

the present population of the island. If the island were to be given over exclusively to the Jews, the presence of 6.5 million Jews on the island would increase the population density to just 10 persons per sq. km. If the intention is to resettle the 6.5 million Jews there in addition to the existing indigenous population, the mean population density would rise to around 16 per sq. km., which is the average figure for the earth's surface as a whole – and slightly more than one tenth of the population density of the German Reich. Even this figure should be well within the natural capacity of the island.[16]

The Madagascar plan proved impossible to implement. It was closely associated with another plan, the subject of serious discussion between the Wehrmacht, Hitler and the Foreign Office: namely the proposal for creating a German 'colonial empire in Central Africa' following the defeat of France. This was to serve as a 'colonial satellite region', with the 'ultimate aim' of safeguarding 'supplies of food and other essentials for 150 million people' living in the 'Greater European trading area'.[17] The Madagascar plan was not an isolated project, therefore, but an integral part of German expansion plans. And it was a condition of those plans that the Jews of Europe and Palestine should be relocated to the margins of the new German empire. As it became obvious, however, that British naval power could not be broken, the Madagascar and Central African projects were abandoned in the autumn of 1940 in favour of the 'eastern solution', i.e. preparations for war against the Soviet Union.

Although rejected as such, the 'Madagascar project' lived on as a code term for deportation and mass murder. The Foreign Office did not officially close the file on the scheme until three weeks after the Wannsee conference, when 'the war against the Soviet Union [had] opened up the possibility of making other territories available for the final solution'.[18]

The murder of the mentally ill in Germany

In retrospect, the Madagascar project was nothing more than a logistical exercise, a dry run, in propaganda terms, for the campaign of mass murder that was shortly to follow. The willingness of German ministerial officials to accept as a matter of course the deportation of millions of people to inhospitable marshland areas was significantly increased in consequence. The German leadership had learned something else, too. They now knew for certain that mass murder would not be significantly detrimental to 'public morale'. The so-called 'euthanasia programme' showed government and Party leaders just what they could get away with behind the mask of 'official secrecy'.

Preparations began at the end of 1938, at the time when anti-Semitic measures were being stepped up. Meanwhile the German police were just embarking on the 'settlement of the gypsy question on the basis of racial principles',[19] and the Reich Department of Criminal Investigation was given the task of 'drawing up a list of all gypsies and gypsy half-breeds living in the Reich (...) and preparing legal measures aimed at solving the gypsy question'.[20] A whole year previously the head of the Thuringian Regional Office of Racial Affairs, a Professor Karl Astel, had secured Himmler's support for a rather unusual piece of fieldwork in the social sciences. Astel applied for a grant to 'undertake an extensive study of criminals'. One of the aims of this study in criminal sociology was to evolve 'a yardstick for the use of preventive detention and possibly also for the elimination, i.e. execution, of criminals, even in cases where they have not yet killed another person themselves'. Himmler wrote back: 'I very much welcome the clarification of [these] issues.'[21]

From the outset the Blitzkrieg campaigns against other nations were accompanied by equally violent assaults on 'undesirable' sections of the German population. On the domestic front, as in the international arena, the status quo was to be altered by the use of brute force. One day – 1 September 1939 – symbolizes this combined intent. On this day Germany embarked on its military expansion to the East – and the preparations for the first wave of systematic mass murder took concrete shape. Although it was actually drafted somewhat later, Hitler's written 'authorization' for the killing of mental patients in hospitals and nursing homes under certain circumstances was backdated to this day.

An 'authorization' or 'authority' is not the same as an order. It was formulated in vague terms and set no specific limits to the projects on which various groups of experts had been working for the previous year. On the contrary: this authorization unleashed the energies of the planners, liberated their imaginations and awakened in them a determination to exploit to the full the resources of a highly organized administrative machinery.

The organizers moved quickly, and at a meeting on 9 October 1939 they established a formula that would determine the number of future victims. In the minutes we read: 'The number is calculated on the basis of the ratio 1,000:10:5:1. This means that for every 1,000 members of the population, ten require psychiatric treatment. Of these, five receive treatment as in-patients, and one patient out of these five falls within the scope of the programme. In other words, one in every 1,000 persons will be covered by the programme. Applying this ratio to the population of Germany and Austria as a whole, we arrive at an aggregate figure of 65–70,000 cases. It should be clear enough from this at whom the programme is targeted.'[22]

No sooner had the essential bureaucratic and logistical arrangements been put in place, a list of the sick drawn up, a small quasi-governmental organization created and the technology of killing tried out, than all the agencies affected by this 'programme' were informed and involved. As a rule, information was given out orally by the personnel of Aktion T4, whose cover name derived from the organization's office address at Tiergartenstrasse 4 in Berlin. Their favoured line of argument was economic pressure – the need to save on costs, hospital beds, nursing staff and food in time of war. At a meeting of German local authority representatives on 3 April 1940 – organized 'at the instigation of a senior government agency (...) the subject for discussion will be announced at the meeting' – the mayor of the city of Plauen noted what was said by Viktor Brack from the Chancellery of the Führer:

> In the many hospitals and nursing homes of the Reich there are countless people with incurable diseases of every kind, people who are of no use at all to the rest of humanity, who are only a burden on society, incurring endless costs for their maintenance, and there is absolutely no prospect of these people ever recovering and becoming useful members of society again. They sit and vegetate like animals, they are social misfits undeserving of life – and yet physically they are perfectly healthy human beings who may well live on for many more years. They eat the food that could be given to others, and in many cases they need twice or three times as much nursing care. The rest of society needs to be protected against these people. Given that we need to make provision now for keeping healthy people alive, it is all the more necessary to get rid of these creatures first, even if only to take better care for now of the *curable* patients in our hospitals and nursing homes. The space thus freed up is needed for all kinds of things essential to the war effort: military hospitals, civilian hospitals and auxiliary hospitals.

The mayor's notes ended: 'The cost to local authorities will be minimal, since the expense of the cremations will be borne by the Reich. For the rest the programme will greatly ease the financial burden on local authorities, as no future costs will be incurred for maintenance and nursing care in any of these cases.'[23]

This utilitarian line of argument recurs in numerous documents and witness statements. The first systematic National Socialist programme of mass murder turned upon the definition of a person's economic 'usefulness'. This is why the questionnaire – on the basis of which a decision about life or death was then made – asked for detailed information about the subject's fitness for work. Doctors were required to identify patients 'who were unlikely ever to be discharged and who furthermore do not do enough work for this to be offset against the cost of keeping and feeding them'.[24]

With the bottom line in mind, it was only logical that a meticulous record should be kept of the progress of the mass murder programme, and the resulting economies precisely calculated. In 1942 the statistician Edmund Brandt, who was later employed by the postwar Federal Ministry of the Interior, drew up a statistical report on the first phase of the murder programme under the title 'What has so far been accomplished by the various institutions in terms of disinfection?' The 'institutions' were the six death centres: Grafeneck, Brandenburg, Bernburg, Hadamar, Hartheim and Pirna. 'Disinfection' referred to the murder of patients by gassing. According to Brandt's reckoning, the total number of patients killed between January 1940 and August 1941 came to exactly 70,273. While the murderers subsequently defended their actions with the argument that they had 'granted death as a blessed release' to 'seriously ill patients' who were 'at death's door' anyway, Brandt sat down in 1942 to work out the projected savings – in food, accommodation, coats, shirts – over a ten-year period (to 1951 inclusive). Based on the average daily needs of an institutional inmate, this calculation indicated that the killing of sick persons unfit for work – the 'accomplishment' referred to by Brandt – would yield more than 880 million Reichsmarks in savings by 1951.[25]

Institutionally, Aktion T4 had especially close ties with Section IV 3a in the Reich Ministry of the Interior. Headed by Herbert Linden, this unit was responsible for 'population policy (basic principles), criminal biology, cultivation of the genetic and racial heritage, the mentally ill'.[26] And it was this unit that drafted the guidelines referred to earlier, under which the German population was to be classified as 'antisocial' or 'socially undesirable', 'passable', 'average' or 'genetically high-grade'. The Aktion T4 organization was also able to cooperate without appreciable difficulties with the Ministry of Justice and the multiplicity of institutions involved at the local and regional level, including the medical councils, health insurance institutions, companies providing insurance cover for funeral expenses and cemetery inspectors.

A question of key importance for our inquiry has not been posed in any of the published literature on these crimes. Here we can only formulate the question: any answers must remain purely speculative for the present. The question is this: to what extent were Göring's Four-Year Plan Authority and the Ministry of Food involved – perhaps even crucially involved – in planning and actively promoting this first large-scale, systematic programme of mass murder? There are clues that point to their involvement, but no proof as such.

The government wanted to cut back on welfare expenditure and food consumption. This is confirmed by countless documents. We have already cited one such source. The point of the 'euthanasia programme', as of the campaign to drive the Jews out of Vienna and Berlin, was to maintain or even improve the social status quo for the broad majority by murdering, or at least expelling, a minority defined as 'useless'. If the Aryanization and liquidation of Jewish businesses brought economic and personal benefits, the murder of the incurably ill resulted in a somewhat better standard of care for those who were curable. The selective dividing-up of people into different categories that were variously favoured or disadvantaged – to the point of mass murder – was a central component of National Socialist social policy in general. It was one of the principles on which the Four-Year Plan Authority operated – and likewise the Ministry of Food, as will be shown. The kind of thinking and forward planning that went on in these institutions before the outbreak of war can be seen from a report by hospital director Ludwig Schaich:

> When it became increasingly apparent, in the final years before 1939, that war was imminent, we learned that there had been discussion in the Reich Ministry of the Interior about putting the inmates of hospitals and nursing homes for the mentally ill, the mentally deficient and epileptics on drastically reduced rations in the event of war. When we objected that this would mean condemning our patients to a slow but certain death by starvation,

they carefully began to sound out how the Home Mission would react if the state were to contemplate the elimination of certain categories of sick persons in wartime, given that food supplies, once imports dried up, would no longer suffice to feed the entire population.[27]

The rationale for the 'euthanasia programme' outlined here, which is documented in many written records and witness statements, points precisely to the possibility that the Four-Year Plan Authority and the 'Working Party on Food and Nutrition' attached to it may have been a driving force behind this organized campaign of murder. The transfer of the sick was carried out 'on orders from the Reich defence commissioners'. Historians of the period have generally interpreted this as a cover: by declaring this to be a matter for the Reich defence commissioners, the authorities (so the argument goes) were seeking to conceal the identity of those who were really responsible behind the claim that the euthanasia programme was a matter of national defence. But in actual fact it is not improbable that Göring chose to assert his authority precisely through this particular channel. Göring was not only head of the Four-Year Plan Authority, he was also president of the Reich Defence Council, so that the Reich defence commissioners were directly under his jurisdiction.

Meanwhile, the German medical establishment was undoubtedly devising its own justifications for the murder of handicapped patients. But it is open to question whether these arguments played such a critical role in the decision as historians have assumed. As far as the medical profession was concerned, it was a matter of establishing very precise distinctions between individual diseases, of drawing a clear line between the 'curable' and the 'incurable', of improving the 'active' therapeutic possibilities. Physicians drew up a comprehensive legal code governing 'the termination of life in the case of the incurably sick and the medically non-viable'. They discussed this draft code with Reinhard Heydrich. As a long-term proposition, questionnaires, remote assessment and finally the mass murder of people in gas chambers were not their preferred methods. They looked upon this indiscriminate and semi-covert procedure as a necessary expedient for the initial phase. In the future of the 'thousand-year Reich', however, 'death by euthanasia' would 'differ hardly at all from a natural death'. They formulated their goal thus: 'No nursing homes for hopeless cases, but hospitals with a highly proactive therapy programme, scientific research – and the option of euthanasia.'[28] What they were talking about was clinical execution as an accepted part of everyday hospital life – to be enshrined in standard medical practice, medical training and legislation.

There are many points of contact between the Aktion T4 programme and the extermination camps that were later built in occupied Poland. The organization based at Tiergartenstrasse 4 supplied both know-how and personnel. Viktor Brack, Philipp Bouhler and Herbert Linden, who oversaw the murder programme from their positions in the Chancellery of the Führer and the Ministry of the Interior, were regular participants in discussions and decisions relating to the murder of the European Jews. But the fact that such decisions could be taken at all was due in no small measure to a lesson that had been learned in the course of the euthanasia programme: namely that the murder of tens of thousands of defenceless people could be carried out at any time by the German authorities, and that the German population – the fathers, mothers, children and spouses of the victims – would accept it without serious indignation or collective protest.

Other factors played an important part, of course: the accompanying propaganda, the semi-secret nature of the Aktion T4 programme, the compartmentalized, bureaucratic procedures, the semblance of scientific objectivity. But at the heart of it all was the one question of how best to go about anaesthetizing the human conscience.

In the summer of 1939 Hitler's personal physician, Theo Morell, wrote a small report on the subject for his powerful patient. He cited a survey of parents of severely handicapped children that had been carried out in Saxony in the early 1920s. The parents had been asked the 'purely hypothetical' question whether they would 'consent to a painless procedure that would cut short the life of their child', and the vast majority had answered 'yes'. But Morell did not conclude from this that one could therefore embark with impunity on the proposed course of criminal action. Instead he focused on the views of a minority among the respondents who seemed to him particularly significant. They had said that they did not want to decide the fate of their own children, but would be quite happy for the doctors to take such a decision – without consulting the parents – and then carry it out.[29] In his report for Hitler, Morell wrote: 'A number of parents expressed the view: "If only you had done it and then told us that our child had died from an illness." There is a lesson for us there. We need not suppose that we cannot carry out any salutary measure without the consent of the sovereign people.'[30]

On this basis it was decided to carry out the murder of German mental patients in secrecy. However, the information blackout was deliberately not so complete that news of the murders did not leak out very quickly. In truth the official policy of secrecy was an expedient that allowed the population to assent tacitly to measures taken by the state. If the relatives did not flatly decline the government's offer of 'release' for their severely handicapped children or their mentally ill wives or husbands, the inference was that they did not care to know the precise circumstances of death. It mattered little what had brought them to this state of emotional denial – indifference, despair or the effects of eugenic propaganda. A similar attitude is encountered among the medical practitioners responsible for the bureaucratic processing of the victims. As one woman doctor, working in a mental hospital in the Rhineland, confided to her diary in the winter of 1940–41: 'Officially we knew nothing of the programme, unofficially it was assumed that everyone somehow knew the score.'[31] This form of 'official secrecy', which was in fact quite open and public, offered the people an escape from personal responsibility by entering into an unacknowledged passive complicity designed to ease the conscience.

On 23 April 1941 the organizers of the murder programme were able to report figures for public acceptance to a gathering of higher court judges and chief public prosecutors: 'In 80 per cent of cases the relatives are in agreement, 10 per cent speak out against, and 10 per cent are indifferent.'[32] Apart from a handful of easily manageable exceptions, there was no opposition or resistance from anyone within the German bureaucratic establishment.

This was a lesson of fundamental importance for the organizers of the 'final solution of the Jewish question'. It convinced them that cover names would not be questioned, but would on the contrary be gratefully accepted, indeed expected, as an invitation to denial and moral indifference.

This unspoken consensus was a fragile affair, of course. It was put at risk the moment somebody like the Bishop of Münster, Clemens August Graf von Galen, said in public what was supposed to remain unsaid – and all the more so when the loyalty of the population began to waver under the impact of the changing fortunes of war. But the euthanasia programme effectively remained on track until the spring of 1945, albeit with a period of interruption and thereafter in a modified form.[33]

It is always very dangerous to speculate on what 'might have been' in history. But we believe that even a limited protest against the 'euthanasia' murders in 1940 would have averted the development of the strategy of systematic genocide in 1941.

To put it another way: if people made little protest when their own relatives were murdered, it was hardly to be expected that they would protest against the murder of Jews, 'gypsies', Russians and 'Polacks'.

CHAPTER 8

INTERIM REFLECTION

Following the annexation of Austria, German economic experts had developed an anti-Jewish policy for that country which combined discrimination with a far-reaching programme of economic reconstruction. Unprofitable businesses were shut down and the concentration of capital was increased as a result. In principle Germany's economic planners continued to pursue this line in all the occupied countries up until 1941, combining – more especially in western Europe – the policy of 'Entjudung' with that of German inward investment into foreign industry. The programme had its most prominent proponents in Göring's Four-Year Plan Authority. It was designed to underpin economic modernization, preparations for war, and ultimately Germany's economic war aims.

After some initial toing and froing the Viennese model of economic reform was also adopted for occupied Poland. The careers of Emmerich, Gater, Globocnik and others encouraged the transfer of the Viennese experience to occupied Poland. But in addition to this the German occupation officials and theorists in Poland, and more especially in the Government General, refined the 'theory of overpopulation' in ways that brought it into line with the policy of racial discrimination. In the annexed provinces of western Poland, the so-called 'annexed eastern territories', the Reich Commissioner for the Strengthening of German Nationhood laboured to establish a completely new and meticulously planned social and economic order. The basis of that order was a population that could be exchanged and selected at will. It was no part of a planner's job to take any thought for the people who lived in these geographical 'spaces' or for their traditional way of life. In fact people as such scarcely featured in most of the proposals for redevelopment. The Reich Commissioner for the Strengthening of German Nationhood combined executive resettlement and structural policy with state-of-the-art regional planning based on scientific principles. He collaborated closely on this with the Four-Year Plan Authority, and in particular with its regional offshoot, the Central Trust Agency for the East. The phrase 'regional planning' [*Raumordnung*] may sound harmless enough, but it has programmatic significance here: countries, broken up into 'territories', continents, subdivided into 'regional spheres', were 'restructured' initially on the drawing-board and on the basis of columns of statistics. Scientists and academics determined where the political instruments of power could be most simply and effectively deployed.

The 'restructuring' process presupposed sufficient freedom of movement to be able to alter historically established structures within a short space of time and in line with predetermined criteria, to replan the transport system and population centres and to enforce social mobility not through economic necessity but through preventive structural change. To that end the population planners and economic planners, whose institutions were closely linked, via the RKF, with the whole apparatus of repression of the SS and police, called for a section of the Polish population and the whole of the Jewish population in the annexed provinces of western Poland to be deported at short notice to the Government General.

Here another group of experts, who came from the same academic background, had very similar histories and experiences and were essentially pursuing the same goals, had been working since the spring of 1940 on the construction of a new economic order. They were intent on making the Government General into a productive 'satellite of the Reich'. In this they were acting under the aegis of the Four-Year Plan Authority in open defiance of Hitler's wishes and instructions. On 17 October 1939 Hitler had insisted: 'It is not the task of the administration to turn Poland into a model province or a model state along German lines, or to restore the country's economy and finances. (...) Any beginnings of a consolidation of conditions in Poland must be eradicated. A state of economic chaos must be allowed to prevail. We must rule the place in a way that allows us to purge the Reich too of Jews and Polacks.'[1]

This declaration of Hitler's provided the RKF in annexed western Poland with backing for its resettlement plans. But since January 1940 the government of Hans Frank in Cracow was no longer content with the role assigned to it. The special feature of its 'reconstruction model' for the Government General was not the model as such – which essentially corresponded to the procedure adopted in

Austria and in annexed western Poland – but the region for which it was designed, namely the rest of Poland – the Government General – a poor and impoverished land. As already stated, this region was originally intended to absorb persons from the rest of the territory under German rule who were earmarked for 'resettlement'. But now the occupation government pursued a diametrically opposed course of action. It called for the 'deportation' *from* the Government General of 'population surpluses' – and on an unprecedented scale for the areas under German control, amounting to many millions of people.

The Germans themselves were responsible for aggravating the social conflicts that they had defined long before the occupation as a 'population question'. Military invasion and annexation, deportation and economic rationalization all contributed to this process. The same experts whose proposals and actions were making the situation so much worse pointed to the consequences of their policy as 'objective imperatives' in order to force an early and definitive 'settlement of the Jewish question' as a first step towards 'solving' the 'population question' in general. In October 1940, when Hans Frank was trying to convince Hitler that further resettlement operations must be halted, Peter-Heinz Seraphim published an article in the quarterly journal of the Institute for German Development Work in the East that may well have furnished Frank with many of the arguments he used in his discussion with Hitler.

In his article, Seraphim notes that in 1939–40 the Government General has already absorbed 350,000 resettled Poles and Jews from the so-called 'annexed eastern territories'. Into an area that was

> already over-saturated with Jews (...) new Jewish population elements have consequently been flooding in who (...) almost without exception are without means of subsistence and impose a heavy economic and social burden on the Government General. In consequence the Jewish question (...) has become a demographic problem of the first order and on a massive scale. It compounds the immensely difficult demographic issue of rural overpopulation in this region, and sooner or later a solution will have to be found. This mass of Jews, who, without productive employment for the most part and without means of subsistence, are currently clogging up the towns and cities and thereby hindering not only their own healthy development but also the solution or alleviation of the rural overpopulation problem, are an enormous obstacle to progress and development within the Government General. It

follows from this that our long-term aim – which need only be touched upon here – must be the ethnic cleansing of this region. But until that task can be undertaken in earnest, any further aggravation of the underlying demographic and economic tensions in the Government General must be avoided, and a halt must be called to further influxes of Jewish population elements into the territory of the Government General.[2]

Seraphim was here putting forward the consensus view on matters of population policy that emerged in the late autumn of 1940 between Cracow, Katowice and Berlin. His arguments are identical to those voiced by Gater, Emmerich, Arlt, Meyer, Oberländer, Streckenbach, Kuchenbäcker and Gottong. Seraphim was calling for two things: firstly, that the resettlement of population groups from the annexed territories of western Poland and the German Reich must cease forthwith, and secondly that the Government General itself must be 'ethnically cleansed' in the interests of the region's economic development. Like all these other writers, he saw anti-Jewish policy as part of a broad plan to solve the problem of rural overpopulation. The deportation of the Jews from the cities and small market towns was intended to create an urban vacuum that would 'suck in' the 'underemployed' rural masses.

By the time Seraphim's article was published, the Lublin and Madagascar projects for the so-called 'territorial solution of the Jewish question' had both been abandoned. Both projects had, however, given a massive boost to the continuing marginalization of the Jewish population. And their very failure made the need for new 'solutions' seem all the more urgent.

The grand design for combining economic restructuring with the relocation of population groups in the Government General and in the annexed eastern territories led to a new stalemate following the failure of the Madagascar plan. In Vienna, Lódź, Berlin, Prague, Paris and Amsterdam, German officials regarded it as necessary to deport the dispossessed Jewish population, the 'gypsies' and other 'undesirable elements' to the Government General. Yet from the early months of 1940 the drive to restructure the economy of the Government General was predicated, precisely, on the removal from this territory of several million people. The German occupation authorities in the Government General therefore employed every possible means to prevent further deportations from the Reich that might have hindered their endeavours.

Himmler and Hitler, too, were at least aware of the 'population question' in the Government General. In January 1940 Himmler had remarked of the people in the Government General: 'They're all living on top of each other there anyway.' He would be 'ecstatic', he confessed, if the Russians would 'take half a million of them'.[3] In March 1940 Hitler declared that 'shortage of space' prevented him from proceeding with the project for a 'Jewish reservation in Lublin'. This project could 'never constitute a solution, since the Jews would be living too closely together there as well'. 'Wherever people are living together at a density of more than 70 per square kilometre, life becomes cramped and difficult. And the world crisis that we face today has been brought about by the rush of nations to escape from the overpopulated regions of the earth into the unpopulated regions.'[4]

In the summer of 1940 a solution to the population problems in occupied Poland appeared in sight. The planned mass deportations of Jewish persons to Madagascar would – so the population planners hoped – not only avert further shipments of deportees to the Government General from the Reich and the annexed eastern territories, but would also provide an opportunity for getting rid of their 'own' Jewish minority. Ten per cent of the population were to be offloaded in this way. At the same time the 'population pressure' in the Government General was to be further reduced by deporting another 20 per cent for forced labour. In the light of the Madagascar project Hitler had promised Frank at the beginning of July 1940 to halt all further shipments of deportees to the Government General. But only three months later he was forced to abandon his colonial plans in Central Africa for military reasons – and with them the Madagascar project. He now sought to back-pedal on the absolute commitment he had given. Hans Frank was present when Hitler assured the Gauleiter of Vienna, Baldur von Schirach – in vague terms at first, more specifically a few weeks later – that he could deport the Jews of Vienna to the Government General because of the acute housing shortage in the city.[5] In the two months that followed, Hitler furthermore made it clear to the Governor-General – in direct defiance of the views of the German 'demographic experts' in Cracow – that 'the organized transfer of Poles to the Government General was part of his policy and that the measures necessary to effect that transfer must be put in place before the end of the war'.[6] All of which brought things back to the stalemate position of March–May 1940, when plans for economic redevelopment in the Government General were totally at odds with its function as a dumping ground for unwanted population groups. Once again the experts in Cracow, absorbed in their ambitious visions for the future, found themselves confronted with a problem they had thought resolved, namely the 'influx' of hundreds of thousands of impoverished people. Their demands for the 'population pressure' to be removed, or at least significantly alleviated, once again became strident – not that they had any concrete suggestions of their own to make at this time, beyond calls for 'relief' and 'solutions'.

In January 1941 hundreds of thousands more people were due to be shipped off to the Government General. The deportations had hardly begun when they had to be halted because the Wehrmacht imposed a transport ban in advance of its deployment for the attack on the Soviet Union. Against the background of these events Frank and Hitler met once more to discuss the situation. On 16 March 1941, when plans for the 'solution in the East' – meaning the war against the Soviet Union and the concomitant expansion of the German 'sphere of colonization' – were already far advanced, Hitler promised that the Government General would become 'a purely German country within the space of 15 to 20 years'.[7] Looking ahead, this meant that the Government General would be subject to the same principles of regional planning and population selection as the annexed eastern territories. The Government General, hitherto on the periphery of empire, would now become part of the centre – a 'transit zone', as the economists termed it. Logic dictated that the evacuation of all persons regarded as superfluous to the new periphery further to the east – to the marshes of the Ukraine, the Arctic Ocean or Siberia – would inevitably follow.

With this, and after much vacillation, Hitler had finally accepted the programme of German redevelopment in the Government General – and definitively abandoned the option of turning it into a heap of ruins and a dumping ground for undesirables. The record documents his remark to the head of the German High Command, Wilhelm Keitel, in the summer of 1943: 'It's perfectly obvious, of course. They say there is no properly organized economy in the Government General. But how can there be a properly organized economy in a country with 120 people to the square kilometre (...), where they send all the dregs from the Reich, and where anything of any value is shipped out?'[8]

The stop–start approach to deportations, and the quarrels between Frank on the one hand and the Gauleiters of the annexed eastern territories and Vienna on the other, demonstrate that there was no consensus on the question of the enforced resettlement of millions of people at the highest levels of the National Socialist political leadership. Uncertainty and unsatisfactory compromises were the order of the day. The professionals and experts, however – whether it was the economists in the Government General or the experts on population policy in the annexed eastern territories – had very clear ideas about what should happen. They had prepared detailed plans, worked out to a precise timetable, with clearly defined goals for the short, medium and long term. The plans for the two German-occupied parts of Poland were so similar that between March 1940 and March 1941 each one effectively blocked and cancelled out the other. Hitler failed to resolve this conflict with a clear political decision. Instead he manoeuvred – a course of action that only increased the power and influence of the expertocracy and encouraged them to create a *fait accompli* and come up with ever more far-reaching solutions.

In their underlying philosophy the German plans for dealing with occupied Poland that have been discussed in earlier chapters pick up on ideas that enjoyed general international currency before the war. The 'exchange of populations' was regarded – not just in Germany – as an effective instrument of modern structural policy, and 'solving the overpopulation problem' was seen as an essential and obvious prerequisite for improving poor productivity more quickly and skimming off the capital that was needed.

The conflict between plans for economic redevelopment and calculations of 'overpopulation' was not only on the agenda for occupied Poland, but also, as the next chapters will show, for the occupied territories of the Soviet Union and for south-east Europe. The calls from the population experts to make the people they had marginalized 'disappear' altogether predated the taking of the decision on the 'final solution', as we have already shown with reference to a number of examples. By the beginning of March 1941 the rationalization expert Rudolf Gater was already looking at ghettoization as a possible option for the 'liquidation of the Jewish population'. To avoid having to support the totally dispossessed Jewish minority out of public funds, he proposed a possible alternative, as will be seen in the next chapter: 'Conditions of undernourishment could be allowed to develop without regard for the consequences.'

Even though the more ambitious programmes for economic restructuring and the long-term consolidation of German power could not be realized because the war developed in ways which the economic experts had not expected, the prerequisite (as they saw it) for the economic revival they wanted to bring about, namely the annihilation of millions of people, was in fact largely achieved (albeit, as these same experts noted in 1942–3, 'not on a big enough scale'). And when, following the defeat at Stalingrad, they occasionally recommended that the non-Jewish population of Poland and the Ukraine be terrorized a little less, this signified only that they wanted the principle of 'divide, rule and destroy' to be applied with more discrimination in a critical military situation. But even at this juncture the economists made no secret of the fact that they agreed in principle with the murder of the large Jewish minority.

The peculiar combination of development policy, colonial policy and resettlement policy is doubtless what Meinhold meant when he spoke of the 'very important research project' undertaken by the department of economics at the Institute for German Development Work in the East, namely 'the creation of a special theoretical political economy for the Government General'.[9] The new theory was closely linked with the German policy of expansion and land-grabbing of those years, whose aims were jointly formulated by Emmerich and Meinhold in these terms:

> The political events of recent years have posed challenges for economic science in Germany that not only break new ground in scientific terms, but also afford this branch of knowledge a unique opportunity to participate in the building of the new continental order, and thus to prove itself as a genuine political science. In all areas of economic life, whether it be monetary and foreign trade policy or policy relating to agriculture, trade and industry, the political reorganization of Europe brings with it the need for planning on a grand scale, which frequently makes it necessary to emancipate oneself from the economic thinking of the past, even the most recent past. Economic science must play its part in this work of planning by helping to prepare and systematically organize the facts and figures required by the political leadership, and also by assisting the leadership in the task of drawing up the planning guidelines.[10]

What was new about this kind of national economy was the marriage of demographic theory and ideology with practical economic policy – an approach that Meinhold had also wanted to adopt for the industrialization of the Government General and its expansion to the east.

Meinhold also formulated this theory for publication, albeit only after 8 May 1945. A few months after the German defeat Helmut Meinhold was already back in business as an economic adviser. This time he was writing a report for the British military government on the industrial regeneration of Hamburg and its hinterland.[11] In this document he also assessed the opportunities created by the massive devastation. Meinhold now saw in Germany the economic chaos he had previously seen in Poland: severe overpopulation due to the influx of refugees, destruction of production facilities and lack of capital. In his terms, the erosion of manpower due to the war had not kept pace with the erosion of capital, at least not as far as the Germans were concerned. Consequently there were too many people living in Germany in 1945 for their combined labour resources to be exploited to the full with the capital that remained.

For Meinhold, there were two possible ways out of this dilemma: either through the extension of foreign credit – which is what subsequently happened under the terms of the Marshall Plan – or through the supply of production facilities from abroad in exchange for agricultural exports from a starving Germany. With the second option Meinhold was thus effectively speculating with the starvation of the German population in order to restore economic equilibrium. This was the very same road the German economic administration had gone down in the Government General. And in the summer of 1945 it still appeared a reasonable proposition to Meinhold. Privately revisiting the past, he wrote: 'So a section of the population would have to starve or at least succumb to deficiency diseases.'[12] In such conditions of deprivation – assuming that no foreign credits were forthcoming – either the available capital would be completely used up in providing for the bare essentials of life, or people would 'go under' while capital was allowed to accumulate. 'Even in the interests of creating employment Germany cannot afford to carry out work requiring an input of material resources where such work would reduce the country's stocks of essential materials.'[13] This means (he continues) that even the most necessary work, even if it 'requires almost no material input', such as the clearing of rubble in war-damaged cities, 'should logically be left undone'. When he wrote these words Meinhold may well have had in mind the columns of Jewish slave labourers, men and women, who in 1940, 1941 and 1942, equipped at best with a shovel, and 'requiring almost no material input', carried out such relief works – until they were eventually murdered. But in the economic reckoning of a Helmut Meinhold, Germany 'could not afford' such works.

Where commodity and exchange value are all, work that produces no surpluses but serves only to keep people alive constitutes an ongoing drain on capital resources, because the investment of capital can only yield a return if labour is put to efficient use. In occupied Poland, such a return on investment was not achievable through relief works or mass labour programmes, either inside or outside the ghettos. And so Meinhold was logically able to conclude that 'over-population effectively constitutes an erosion of capital'.[14] Reversing the train of thought: the murder of people for whom no productive employment can be found is an indirect way of getting a return of sorts on capital investment. And when, as in wartime, productive investment virtually disappears, murder serves to minimize the erosion of capital. Meinhold used his Hamburg study to elaborate this theory, which might be termed 'mass murder as an instrument of economic development':

> We have assumed up until this point (and will continue to assume hereinafter) that the present economic objective must be rather to sustain the whole population, however meagrely, than to provide more plentifully for one part while another part is allowed to perish. In this sense it is better to employ only 50 out of 100 workers, who can carry the other 50 through until such time as the situation improves, than to have 75 working and allow the other 25 to starve. However, this assumes that there is a real possibility of the situation improving later on – and the prospects for that will be discussed in a moment. One could of course choose to look at things from a different point of view, particularly if one is doubtful about things getting better. One could argue that in the struggle for survival it is better for the 75 to remain alive and for the other 25 to die immediately, than to have all 100 effectively perish in the end. Such a view would be defensible if it were really a matter of selecting the fittest candidates for survival.[15]

This theory of the selective annihilation of people for economic reasons, which Meinhold formulated openly in the autumn of 1945, is that 'special theoretical political economy for the Government General' which he developed in 1941.[16]

In Poland, 'one' had indeed chosen to 'look at things from [this] different point of view', and had selected people accordingly. It might be asked why the Germans, having robbed the Jewish population of its rights and its property, did not simply set them to work building roads, instead of killing them at some cost in terms of transport capacity, labour and materials. The hard economics of German population policy in Poland supply the answer. For to Meinhold's way of thinking, in which human beings are viewed as an economic commodity, it is perfectly obvious that keeping a person alive, even at the most basic subsistence level, necessitates the production and transportation of many tonnes of material and food each year. All these materials bring no productive gains whatsoever if they are used to feed people who – for whatever reason – are either not working or not working productively enough. They simply 'devour' capital. The transportation and killing of a human being, on the other hand, requires a far smaller economic outlay. To put it another way: the railway system in the East, already overstretched by the war in the Soviet Union, was placed under increasing strain with every day that the Warsaw ghetto remained in existence. Even under a policy of total starvation, several hundred wagon-loads of goods had to be shipped in every day to keep the ghetto supplied, whereas the carriage costs involved in transporting those people to their death were much lower – and they were incurred only once.

In the present-day debate about the Holocaust the fact that millions of people were shipped to the death camps by rail, despite the limited carrying capacity of the rail network in wartime, is still seen as an indication that the policy of annihilation had no basis in rational thinking. We believe that it indicates the precise contrary – which is why we have chosen to explore the arguments here. For Meinhold, Gater, Emmerich and their like, there was nothing to discuss. They took it as read that the 'resettlement' of millions of people would facilitate and accelerate the accumulation of capital. The ratio between manpower and capital input per employee would shift, swiftly and unequivocally, in favour of capital. A massive short-term drive for business concentration and investment would yield a decisive increase in productivity. From this point of view the policy of mass murder was not primarily motivated by racist or terrorist ideology, but was an instrument designed to speed up the industrialization and agrarian rationalization of the Government General as an 'emerging country'. 'Solving' the 'overpopulation problem' by brute force – within the framework of the racist and anti-Semitic precepts of Nazi ideology – broke the alleged vicious circle of population growth and 'underproductivity'. And with that the way was clear to turn the Government General – upgraded to a 'transit zone' through the war with the Soviet Union – as quickly as possible into a productive province of German-controlled Europe, generating economic surpluses and profits.

In the chapters that follow, we shall seek to show what other factors and concerns came together with the theory and practice of population policy to create, in the summer of 1941, the patchwork of restructuring plans and wartime economic 'constraints' already referred to, in which an aggressive, anti-Jewish ideology was transformed into a programme for the 'final solution of the Jewish question' founded on rational economic and political calculation in the interests of German imperialism. These factors included the study of the business and financial management of the ghettos that was carried out in January, February and March 1941; the countless studies that portrayed the 'overpopulation problem' in eastern and south-east Europe as a fundamental obstacle to the creation of a single European economy; and the plans for letting 30 million people starve to death beyond the front line in the Soviet Union in order to make central Europe independent of overseas imports. And finally there was the 'General Plan for the East', under which more than 40 million people behind the front – from Poland and from the western and southern parts of the Soviet Union – were to be murdered or driven out into the yet-to-be-created starvation belt beyond Germany's new eastern frontier. By such methods was room to be made for German colonists and their families, for German productivity and economic interests.

CHAPTER 9

THE ECONOMIC EXPLOITATION OF THE GHETTOS

The effect of 'German redevelopment' in the annexed provinces of western Poland, and shortly thereafter in the Government General, was that neither region was now able to contemplate 'shunting off' its unwanted population to the other. And when plans for the mass transportation of European Jews to Madagascar fell through, the ghettos, initially established for a transitional period, became a permanent institution. The original plan was to shut people up in the ghettos pending their deportation and leave them to their own devices, without employment opportunities or adequate provisioning. But when the situation changed, German economic analysts moved in to study the ghettos in terms of their business and economic potential. They considered how they could prevent 'Jewish residential districts' that were becoming a 'permanent fixture' from also becoming a drain on the public purse. In January 1941 the Reich Audit Office looked at the economic viability of the Lódź ghetto; in February the Reich Board for Industrial Rationalization prepared a cost-benefit analysis for the Warsaw ghetto. The findings were devastating in more senses than one. The calculations of profitability led in the spring of 1941 to the conclusion that for every additional month that the new ghettos remained in existence they would cost the state millions of Reichsmarks, even if the occupants were kept on starvation rations. Forced labour was thought to be difficult to organize, and of doubtful productive value.

Lódź – the problem of the 'productive use of labour'

The Lódź ghetto, together with the one later established in Warsaw, was the largest in occupied Europe. The German authorities had begun preparing the ground as early as December 1939. Then on 8

April 1940 a police order 'on the rights of residence and domicile of the Jews' created a so-called legal basis for permanently sealing off the ghetto from the outside world on the night of 30 April–1 May 1940. Its internal administration was placed in the hands of the 'Eldest of the Jews'. He acted on behalf of the German authorities and under their strict control. The 'Jewish self-governing body' was directly subordinate to the 'Food supply and provisioning agency for the ghetto', which changed its name to 'Ghetto administration' in October 1940 when it had ceased to view itself as a merely transitional institution. For four and a half years, the entire period of the ghetto's existence, it was headed by the Bremen business entrepreneur Hans Biebow.[1] Estimates indicate that at the beginning of August 1940 more than 160,000 people were living in this 'section of the city completely sealed off by a wooden fence and barbed wire'.[2] Hand in hand with ghettoization went the 'elimination of Jewish elements' from the life of this industrial city. German economic experts viewed the structural consequences for Lódź's famous textile industry, which was still languishing in the aftermath of the world depression, as no less salutary than they had previously proved to be in Austria and the Government General: '...excluding the Jews made it possible to streamline the production process by getting rid of most of the very small workshops, which were poorly organized and poorly equipped...'[3]

At local authority level and among those who were concerned with the daily problems of production and provisioning, the ghetto looked like an incalculable risk, a cost factor and a financial loss. Initially the German authorities in the Warthegau assumed they would be closing it down again in October 1940 and deporting the people interned there to the Government General. But by March it was already becoming clear that this would meet with resistance from the administration there, which saw such plans as a threat to its own plans for economic regeneration, and which was indeed working towards a *reduction* in population numbers in the Government General. In July the Gauleiter of the Warthegau, Arthur Greiser, was forced to admit that 'a new decision [had] been taken' in Berlin.[4] This new situation brought the city administration and the Reich Ministry of Finance on to the scene. They feared that the ghetto, whose future now suddenly appeared open-ended, would 'be a drain on [their] resources': after all, it was they who had robbed the people living there of their property and their means of production, thus depriving them of any real possibility of earning their own living and effectively turning them into a 'surplus population'. It could not be very long, they argued, before those shut up inside the ghetto ran out of cash and goods to barter. The time was approaching 'when the maintenance costs for the Jews will become a burden on the public purse'.[5] And indeed the Lódź ghetto had already reached this point in September, when the Eldest of the Jews informed the authorities that they were 'no longer able to raise sufficient funds to pay for the food that had been supplied to the ghetto'. When the suspension of food deliveries for several days produced no 'positive result', Biebow was forced to raise an initial loan of three million Reichsmarks. He fixed the term of the loan at six months, but the creditors were 'very sceptical about repayment' and assumed from the outset 'that repayment of the principal and interest must be seen as a purely *pro forma* arrangement'.[6]

The Reich Minister of Finance recommended the placing of work contracts in the ghetto, so that the 'Jews [would] be earning their own living and contributing to the public purse'.[7] However, the data available to the Ministry of Finance appeared to rule out any such possibility. Here it was stated that 'the value of the work done [in the ghetto] would only amount to an estimated 20 per cent of the value of the goods to be supplied.' The monthly maintenance costs had been worked out at approximately two and a half million Reichsmarks. In the light of these figures the Central Trust Agency for the East, which acted on behalf of the Four-Year Plan Authority and administered the expropriated assets of the internees, was asked to provide the city of Lódź with 'the provisional sum of 25 million Reichsmarks to maintain the Jewish quarter until it is closed down again'.[8] In other words, monies that the German government had previously stolen from the Jewish population were now to be made available to the ghetto – albeit with extreme reluctance and in fractional quantities – in the form of a 'credit'. And made available 'until it closed down again'. Implicit in the figures was the intention to prolong the life of the ghetto for exactly ten months – until June/July 1941 at the outside. Since the Reich Minister of Finance regarded the whole ghetto project as a big financial unknown, whose long-term fiscal consequences had not been properly thought through, he asked the Reich Audit Office on 31 December 1940 to conduct a review of the entire ghetto administration. The review was carried out between 23 January and 5 February 1941.[9]

The Reich Audit Office began by commending Biebow's office for 'basing its entire work on the principle … that the maintenance of the Jews in the ghetto should be funded out of assets that the individual occupants of the ghetto still have in their possession, and that the idle workforce should be made to work for a living wherever possible'.[10]

Between May and December the ghetto had received goods to the value of 10 million Reichsmarks. Biebow's office had levied a 15 per cent 'administration charge' on these deliveries. From July the Reich Minister of Finance demanded an additional 3 per cent to cover lost tax revenues. By issuing a special 'ghetto currency' the administration quickly extracted the remaining holdings of Reichsmarks from those on the inside, while debts owed by the non-Jewish population to Jewish creditors in the ghetto and donations from family and relatives in Germany and Poland (amounting to 7,800 RM a day in January 1941) were credited to the ghetto account by Biebow, as were the proceeds from the sale of furs, shoes, clothing and furniture. On the debit side Biebow included the cost of food, gas, water and electricity, as well as the bribes paid by the Gestapo to Jewish spies.[11]

The Reich Audit Office estimated that by January 1941 there were no significant stocks of cash and valuables remaining in the ghetto, 'so that the decisive factor for the continuation of the ghetto's self-financing status is now the productive use of Jewish labour'. But none of the conditions were in place to make that possible. For one thing the ghetto had next to nothing in the way of means of production, so there were few jobs to be had. For another the occupants of the ghetto were in such a poor state of health that their productivity was bound to be very low. To make the ghetto more economically viable the auditors proposed first that the number of jobs be increased wherever possible, thus increasing also the proportion of 'genuinely productive persons' in the population at large. Secondly they recommended increasing the food allowance in the ghetto to prison ration levels, 'so that working Jews receive the prime ration and non-working Jews the basic ration'. The report noted further: 'The value of prison rations is between 0.40 and 0.50 RM. This is double the sum of 0.23 RM that has previously been spent on the ghetto occupants, which covered the cost not only of food, but also of the other daily necessities of life.'[12]

In other words, the Reich Audit Office was calling for expenditure on food to be doubled in order to have any prospect of harnessing the available manpower in the ghetto. This would automatically increase the deficit on the ghetto's balance sheet by around one million Reichsmarks each month, which would have to be secured by some sort of start-up funding.

In line with its brief, the report focused primarily on the specifics of 'creating employment for the Jews': 'The first requirement for making the Jewish community self-supporting is to find employment for the skilled tradesmen and unskilled labourers in the ghetto.' The number of people fit for work was put at 50,221. At the end of January 1941 only 12,000 of these were working, mainly in tailoring shops, which were making greatcoats and fatigues for the Luftwaffe. Their wages were transferred directly into the ghetto account. But of course these payments were not enough to cover even the bare subsistence needs of all the ghetto's occupants. Textile production also had limited scope for expansion, since the procurement of 'raw materials, work premises, machinery, etc.' was difficult, according to the report – and doubtless in Biebow's judgement as well. So the Reich Audit Office suggested putting Jewish labourers to work in their tens of thousands outside the ghetto, on 'road-building works for the future urban redevelopment programme', on the 'construction of new housing projects' and on the 'demolition of old housing stock'.[13] Since the end of December 1940 '1,300 Jews and Jewish women' had been working on the construction of the autobahn between Frankfurt/Oder and Posen. They lived in hut camps, and the ghetto received – in theory at least – 80 per cent of their wages 'for the needs of the Jews who remained behind'.[14]

However, the economic analysts were in some doubt themselves about the extent to which their recommendations regarding food supplies and employment were based on realistic assumptions. They had to listen to complaints from Biebow about how he was fighting 'a constant battle over the release of the most basic food requirements', while requests for materials and equipment needed 'in order to put more Jews to work' were 'regularly refused on the grounds that there was nothing there for the Jews'.[15]

Whether or not productivity in the ghetto could be increased, the officials from the Reich Audit Office charged with assessing its economic potential continued to assume that it would be closed down sooner or later – even if not quite so soon as originally intended. Summarizing their findings they wrote:

> As is generally known, Lódź had the largest Jewish population of any large European city. With a population in its day of over 700,000, the city housed no fewer than 340,000 Jews within its walls. (...) The attempt to create order in Lódź was doomed to failure so long as the very large Jewish component of the

population enjoyed unrestricted freedom of movement and activity. (...) The German authorities in charge recognized that the problem of pacifying and Germanizing the city and developing its economic life could only be solved in conjunction with the complete evacuation of the Jews, or, as a temporary expedient, their isolation from the rest of the population. (...) How the situation will develop in the future it is impossible to say with any certainty.

Although no firm date could be put on the closing-down of the ghetto, there was another possibility that presented itself in the meantime, and that was to 'improve' the economic viability of the ghetto. 'According to information received from government vice-president Dr Moser,' the report continued, 'it is safe to assume that a substantial number of ghetto occupants who are unfit for work will be evacuated to the Government General in the spring of 1941, and their place may well be taken by able-bodied Jews from the Gau territory. If permanent employment can be found for at least 20,000 skilled tradesmen in the workshops and for a larger number of unskilled labourers on excavation works outside the ghetto, then it should be possible to defray a substantial portion of the maintenance costs for the Jewish community out of their wages.' But on condition, of course, that 'a substantial number of ghetto occupants who are unfit for work will be evacuated'. This comment evidently refers to Heydrich's approach to Hitler aimed at resuming evacuations to the Government General in 1941.[16] The officials on the ground were already looking forward to this as an opportunity to get rid of people who were unfit for work. Meanwhile, however, the authorities in charge of labour and economic affairs in the Government General were pursuing a similar strategy for the ghettos there. They were keeping a very close eye on the situation in Lódź in order to learn the lessons of that experience and forearm themselves against further deportations that would threaten the work of 'German economic redevelopment' in the Government General.

The 'evacuations' to the Government General that the economic analysts in Lódź were expecting failed to materialize, for the reasons we have already indicated. So the most important precondition for the economic viability of the ghetto was not met. On 4 July 1941, however, Biebow was able to report some progress in his attempts to create more employment inside the ghetto with a view to financing the upkeep of the occupants from their own earnings. He had started by extracting the valuables of the ghetto occupants to pay for their upkeep, having been given a 'firm assurance' that 'the Jews from the Lódź ghetto would be removed completely' by 1 October 1940. He continued: 'When it became apparent that the ghetto was not going to be closed down at the appointed time, concerted efforts were made to develop and organize employment inside the ghetto. As a result of these efforts the ghetto can no longer be viewed as a kind of "holding or concentration camp", but has become an integral part of the city's economy – a large business concern in its own right, so to speak. At present some 40,000 of the 160,000 ghetto occupants are in work, a ratio that corresponds with the general employment quota in the Reich, and one that will shortly be increased.'[17]

This formulation leaves open the question of whether Biebow was planning to create more jobs in the ghetto, or whether he was thinking of 'improving' the employment ratio by deporting 'unproductive' persons. For as the report of the Reich Audit Office had already shown, the economic experts intended to create more jobs inside the ghetto, but at the same time they wanted to deport people who were not working – for whatever reason. The 'credit' extended by the Central Trust Agency for the East must have been used up by the time Biebow was cataloguing his successes in the area of employment creation. So there was no capital available anyway for the creation of new jobs. A complete ban had been placed on evacuations to the Government General in March 1941. It was therefore necessary to cast around for new 'solutions'. What options were specifically discussed, we do not know. What is clear, however, is that at this time, with deportations halted and pressure from the Reich Audit Office to make the ghetto more productive, the possibility of mass murder was contemplated among the lower echelons.

Twelve days after Biebow had been turning over in his mind how to make the ghetto pay its way, Adolf Eichmann received the notorious memorandum sent by SS Sturmbannführer Höppner from Posen, the administrative capital of the Gau in which Lódź was located. In this document Höppner summarized 'various discussions' that had taken place in the Warthegau on the 'Jewish question', and divulged 'things' that sounded 'fanciful', but which in his view were 'entirely feasible'. What he then wrote, in reference to those Jewish men, women and children who could not be put to work, was this: 'This winter there is a risk that there will not be enough food to feed all the Jews. Serious consideration should be given to the possibility that the most humane solution might be to despatch the Jews who are unfit for work by some fast-acting agent. This would certainly be more pleasant than allowing them to starve to death.'[18] These 'fanciful' thoughts seemed to offer an escape from the impasse of a ghetto policy trapped between the pressure to produce and the ban on further deportations. They echoed the view put forward by Reich Minister of Finance Schwerin von Krosigk, the instigator of the Audit Office report on the Lódź ghetto, when he endorsed Heydrich's position at the historic meeting on 11 November 1938: 'What we really need to make sure of is that we don't end up keeping the social proletariat here. Looking after them will always be a terrible burden.'

From December 1941 onwards, in line with the proposal communicated by Höppner, the 'unproductive elements' in the Lódź ghetto were selected on an ongoing basis, taken to the camp at Chelmno and gassed in specially converted vans. And it was not the SS who informed the German administrative authorities in the annexed eastern territories of this 'solution': the information was divulged, significantly enough, in the course of a discussion on the use of Jewish labour which took place on 28 November 1941 in the Reich Ministry of Labour. One of the officials present told the others around the table that the 300,000 Jews in the Warthegau would 'all be out of the picture by the end of March – all except the Jews who are fit for work'.[19]

The 'selections' in the Lódź ghetto were carried out in December 1941 and in January, February and March 1942 on the basis that the unproductive ghetto occupants were to be deported first. According to reports from survivors, the deportees were 'with very few exceptions the poorest and most socially disadvantaged section of the ghetto population'. Schlomo Frank writes about the transport of 17 January 1942 in his diary: 'This morning the first batch of evacuees was shipped out, consisting of 780 men, 853 women and 154 children. Poor wretches for the most part, broken, naked and starving.' In due course, on 29 April 1942, all occupants of the ghetto above the age of ten who did not possess an employment permit had to submit to a 'selection' carried out by German doctors.[20]

Warsaw – 'The value of a Jew'

When the German occupation authorities gave orders in October 1940 for the establishment of the Warsaw ghetto, and finally sealed it off from the outside world on 15 November, they too had been dithering for more than a year. The decision to ghettoize the Jewish population had been repeatedly postponed in favour of so-called 'territorial solutions' which appeared in prospect – beginning with the 'Jewish reservation' in Lublin and ending with the plan for mass deportations to Madagascar. The ghettoization of the Jewish community in Warsaw was a direct consequence of the abandonment of these projects. The economic experts in the Government General had been forewarned by the experience of Łódź. In the course of December the head of the Central Department of Economic Affairs, Emmerich, asked the Reich Board for Industrial Rationalization – i.e. Gater – to prepare a preliminary report on the economic consequences of ghettoization.[21] According to this very general survey, the hastily implemented measures for resettling and sealing off Warsaw's Jewish population had for the most part proved damaging to the city's urban and economic structure. (Admittedly the city's economic administration and the RKW had been counting all summer on a rapid 'evacuation' of Polish Jews, and had successfully sought to delay their ghettoization for economic reasons.)

Three months later the Office for the Government General at the RKW submitted another report, far more detailed this time and marked 'Secret', on the 'economic potential of the Jewish quarter in Warsaw'.[22] Its authors made explicit reference to the report on the Łódź ghetto prepared by the Reich Audit Office. Once again, it was Emmerich who had commissioned the report. In order to gather the necessary data, Gater and his deputy Meder had held discussions with over thirty different agencies. Contrary to the optimistic projections of the Warsaw city and district authorities, who were directly responsible for ghettoization, the RKW came to completely different, and very sobering, conclusions 'regarding the Jewish quarter' ('jüdischer Wohnbezirk' – invariably abbreviated in the German original to 'j.W.'). The Warsaw department of resettlement assumed that of the 'Jews initially made redundant by the establishment of the ghetto', 200,000 could soon 'be put to work in supervised working parties' outside the ghetto. Moreover the same officials felt able to guarantee 'a 100 per cent utilization of this manpower' in workshops – workshops which did not exist at the time.[23] Gater countered these rosy prospects with his own assessment of the situation. When all reserves were exhausted – and he was thinking mainly of the valuables belonging to the ghetto occupants, which were used for bartering purposes – rent receipts would largely dry up. Tax revenues would decline sharply, and at least 55 million Reichsmarks a year would be needed in food subsidies – 'if', as was pointed out in the summary that appeared at the head of the report, 'the intention is to keep the occupants of the Jewish quarter alive'.[24]

On the other hand, Gater wrote, the 'elimination' of the Jewish population from the skilled trades and the retail trade would bring substantial benefits for the 'Aryan' section of the population, once the initial difficulties had been overcome. That also meant taking action to prevent Jewish black-marketeering on the side. Here Gater was revisiting his earlier proposals for rationalizing the economy in the Government General. The 'Aryans', he noted – meaning non-Jewish Poles – would be able to take over Jewish jobs or other money-making opportunities previously open to the Jews.[25] Having already worked on the projects to dispossess and marginalize the Jewish population in Vienna and Cracow, Gater now set about analysing the misery and destitution he had helped to create as if they were an unalterable fact of life and he himself a dispassionate observer. His aim, he writes, is to 'paint a picture of economic conditions as they really are, uninfluenced by political considerations, and [to] assess their probable future development'.[26] With a few casual remarks Gater dismissed the received thinking on the subject. He was particularly critical of the so-called 'transfer agency', which at this time exercised much the same function as Biebow's 'ghetto administration' in Lódź. By controlling and regulating the entire traffic in goods and supplies between the ghetto and the outside world, the Warsaw transfer agency, in Gater's words, had 'largely removed from the individual Jew the responsibility for supporting himself and his family'.[27] He greeted with scepticism the plans of the Warsaw politicians to employ 200,000 people from the ghetto on forced labour programmes, and to organize them centrally via the transfer agency. As he commented drily: 'If it works out as planned this scheme will be the largest manufacturing enterprise in the Government General, and indeed one of the largest in the entire German Reich.'[28]

The Warsaw ghetto, like its counterpart in Lódź, possessed virtually no resources that would have allowed the people confined within its walls to produce the means of supporting themselves in the longer term. Before the ghetto was sealed off, the Jewish population had been largely dispossessed. There were also rules specifying exactly which kinds of valuables and household items had to be surrendered by the ghetto occupants. Within the ghetto itself, formerly an impoverished residential area, there were very few factories or workshops. The transfer of production facilities into the ghetto from outside had been forbidden by the Germans. Raw materials for the production of goods of any kind had already been taken away from those shut up inside – in so far as this was possible. Everything they needed in this regard had to be purchased via the transfer agency, along with their day-to-day food supplies. Furthermore, the Jewish community had to pay the construction costs for the ghetto wall, erected to seal them off from the outside world. On the debit side of the 'Jewish quarter's' account Gater also listed unpaid rent and depreciation on the housing stock inside the ghetto – in effect, the loss of income suffered by the 'Aryan' property owners. Yet Jewish-owned land and property outside the ghetto was not included on the credit side of the Jewish community's account. While the ghetto population was not expected to settle its accounts in cash, these 'debts' were nevertheless factored into the arithmetic of economic viability – and for Gater it was this, ultimately, that determined the right to life of the imprisoned occupants.

Gater proceeded on the assumption that the ghetto would remain in existence for some time to come. The Madagascar plan had long since been abandoned for military reasons, but on economic grounds, too, Gater believed it was off the agenda for the next five years: 'For the duration of the war, and probably also for some considerable time after the war, the Government General will remain the final rear area for the cleansing of the German-occupied East from the Jews. When the war is won the available shipping capacity will have to be used in the first instance for importing raw materials and resuming our overseas exports, before we can contemplate using it for the mass deportation of Jews. With all this in mind we should reckon on a life-span of five years for the Jewish quarter in Warsaw.'[29]

The authors of the report anticipated difficulties in finding employment for the Jews outside the ghetto. They pointed out that there was no shortage of manpower already in the Government General, and furthermore the use of Jews for forced labour would be a particularly cost-intensive exercise, since they would need to be kept under guard and housed in secure camps. So it was likely, surmised Gater, that employers would prefer to use non-Jewish labour.[30] At the time the German civilian administration in the Government General was running forced labour camps for Jews between the ages of twelve and sixty. On the subject of forced labour, euphemistically termed 'employment on public works' by Gater, Chaim A. Kaplan confided the following thoughts to his diary on 29 August 1940:

It's not just a matter of fetching and carrying, moving building materials around, loading furniture. It involves hard physical labour – draining marshes, building dykes and embankments, building roads, constructing flood barriers. Only Jews are obliged to do this work. The Jews will be unskilled labourers, working without pay, and they will work under the supervision of paid Aryan overseers. Camps of this kind are run with military discipline, and the workers are treated like prisoners and criminals, forced to sleep in field tents and receiving a daily food ration of half a pound of bread. (...) It's safe to assume that anyone entering a camp of this kind will not leave it again. Or if he does, then only as a completely broken man.[31]

In the face of this reality Gater could see absolutely no economic rationale for the use of Jewish labour on public works contracts: 'It would take three Jews employed on public works to create sufficient value to balance the cost of maintaining one Jew living in the Jewish quarter.'[32]

Only two months earlier the calculations prepared by the Reich Audit Office for the Lódź ghetto had looked very different. According to these, one Jew on forced labour outside the ghetto could support two to three persons inside the ghetto, depending on his qualifications. The RKW turned this calculation on its head, claiming that three men working outside the ghetto could at most finance one person on the inside who was out of work or unfit for work. On this reckoning, outside work details could not be regarded as a viable option either for the ghetto or for the public-sector employer, and in June 1941 the scheme was abandoned.

The second argument advanced against 'employment on public works' is especially noteworthy. Gater, and therefore the RKW and the Central Department of Economic Affairs, knew as early as March that the war against the Soviet Union would be beginning later that year. Long-term infrastructure projects, for which Jewish slave labour had generally been used in the past, would then be deferred, and the jobs associated with them would disappear. The report puts it in coded language, but the meaning is clear enough: 'Due to the special circumstances that are expected to arise in 1941, the transport system and traffic operations will be placed under very great strain. (...) Consequently a number of projects that were originally scheduled for 1941 will probably not now come to fruition.'[33]

On a more general note the RKW warned that it was hard enough

as it was to provide work for all the able-bodied persons in the
Government General, and that the Jews inside the ghetto should not
be accorded 'preferential treatment':

> In its present form the Jewish quarter is like a fortress under siege.
> The present purpose of that siege is to force the Jews to surrender
> their supplies of goods, gold and foreign exchange. When this
> has been accomplished, the first economic priority will be to
> exploit the manpower available in the Jewish quarter. The
> problem is that apart from a lack of skilled workers the
> Government General, unlike the Reich, currently has no shortage
> of manpower – quite the reverse, in fact. In finding work for
> people, therefore, there must be no positive discrimination in
> favour of the Jewish quarter, and any measures undertaken for
> the Jewish quarter must have regard to the overall economic situ-
> ation of the Government General. If it is not possible to provide
> work for the existing labour force in the Government General,
> then clearly it will be that much harder to find work for the
> Jewish quarter.[34]

In this context Gater also reminded his readers of 'the inferiority of
the Jewish populace'.[35] He saw a further problem in the fact that
nearly half the workforce inside the ghetto were 'clerical and administrative workers' or were classed as 'workers with no fixed occupation'. As such they were 'eminently unsuitable for heavy or
moderately demanding physical labour', and would be the cause of
'considerable lost working time and additional expense'.[36]

The organization of work inside the ghetto, which was Gater's
clearly preferred option, being both easier to administer and more
lucrative, would no longer, under these proposals, be the responsibility of government agencies, as it had been hitherto in Łódź and
Warsaw, but would be entrusted to private German firms. These firms
would have 'to be given a kind of concession or licence to exploit
Jewish manpower in specific areas'.[37] But that still left unresolved the
problem of feeding the Jews. According to Gater, one could 'adopt
one of two basic positions' on this issue:

> 1. One can try to turn the Jewish quarter into a productive
> section of the population. This presupposes that the capacity for
> work of the occupants, or of specially favoured groups among
> them, is maintained by a reasonably adequate supply of food.

2. One can view the Jewish quarter as a means of liquidating the Jewish people.[38]

In actual fact these two 'positions' contained within them three different options: (1) all the ghetto occupants would be fed; (2) only those who did productive work would be fed; (3) all would be left to starve. In Gater's view, these three options could be implemented as alternatives, in parallel or in succession. It is interesting to note how openly, even at this stage, Gater could speak of 'liquidating the Jewish people', and how this possibility could be discussed as a real option.

Gater calculated the quantities of food that were available to meet the ghetto's needs – deliveries by the German occupation forces, food parcels from abroad and black-market produce. Then he worked out the total daily food requirement, before calculating 'the productive yield of one Jew'.[39] These calculations showed that at least 60,000 people in the ghetto would have to be in productive work in order to fund the daily per capita food allowance of around one zloty (50 pfennigs) for the total ghetto population of 450,000: 'So with a workforce of approximately 60,000 in regular full-time employment the Jewish quarter would not require any financial subsidies,' whereas if only 20,000 people were in work 'the Jewish quarter would require a daily subsidy of around 300,000 zlotys, or something like 110,000,000 zlotys a year'. In other words, the ghetto would need to be subsidized to the tune of 55 million Reichsmarks a year.[40] An employment quota of 20,000 seemed a realistic target figure to Gater – but also the maximum that was attainable.[41] Getting production up and running on this scale and financing the purchase of the necessary raw materials and machinery would require a credit of 30–40 million zlotys. Gater left open the question of where this money was to come from: 'It has already been shown that no substantial funds can be raised from the sale of existing Jewish assets. And there seems absolutely no prospect of finding these sums from Warsaw's municipal budget, not least because the city of Warsaw is already receiving a kind of state subsidy in the form of an increased share of the indirect tax take. So the shortfall will have to be made up from the funds of the Government General.'[42]

On the basis of these economic considerations Gater finally recommended that those in the ghetto who could not be productively employed should be left to starve, and that new work opportunities should be created at the same time:

In order to avoid the need for a subsidy, or at least to reduce it in size, the following options are available:

1. Conditions of undernourishment could be allowed to develop without regard for the consequences.

2. The preparation and resourcing of organizations for the exploitation of Jewish labour in the Jewish quarter could be brought forward to ensure that a large-scale deployment of Jews for these purposes really does take place.

3. The tight seal on the Jewish quarter in Warsaw could be relaxed to some degree, provided this is acceptable to the health department. This would give Jewish tradesmen in certain lines of work the opportunity to do business directly with the outside world again, albeit on a modest scale.[43]

At two government meetings chaired by Hans Frank on 3 and 19 April 1941, the governors and economic experts of the Government General looked in detail at the possibilities for developing an efficient ghetto economy and arriving at a positive 'balance of trade' – in contrast to Lódź. At the first of these meetings Emmerich presented the report prepared by the Reich Board for Industrial Rationalization; he had also brought along its author, Rudolf Gater. Unlike the ghetto in Lódź, which was completely isolated economically from the rest of the city, Gater took the view that the Warsaw ghetto, while existing as 'a separate business district', must nevertheless 'stand in relationship to the surrounding world', i.e. it should maintain certain economic ties with 'Aryan' Warsaw.

Gater went through his figures, which, as he himself observed, were based not on the 'system for calculating subsistence level needs (...) but on a system of calculation that takes into account only the bottom line'. In other words, Gater was proposing that they 'import' into the ghetto only those goods which the Jewish community was able to pay for, regardless of whether these were sufficient to meet the needs of the people living there or not. Emmerich supplemented Gater's analysis with the suggestion that German wholesalers be encouraged to place their contracts with firms in the ghetto in future. Naturally they would then 'be granted a certain influence' on the organization of Jewish labour 'to ensure that producers in the Jewish quarter met all the requirements with regard to quality, delivery times, etc.'[44]

The assembled governors and heads of government central departments quickly agreed that 'the whole ghetto issue' must be 'handled in total accordance with the guidelines laid down by the Central Department of Economic Affairs', as district governor Ludwig Fischer put it: the licensed firms must be allowed to extract the maximum profit from the Jewish workforce. At the same time the maintenance costs for the ghetto population should be passed on as far as possible to the Jewish community itself, the aim being 'to run the ghetto in such a way that it costs the state virtually nothing'.[45] With this, the cost-benefit principle espoused by the economic experts received the stamp of official approval. They continued to view the ghettos at this time as a 'temporary arrangement', albeit one that 'could not be wound up in a year'.[46] Implicit in this projection is the clear desire to begin the winding-up process as soon as possible.

The new policy for the Warsaw ghetto had already been in operation for a number of weeks in another city. The ghettoization of the Jewish population in Cracow clearly bore the signature of Gater and Emmerich. In the order 'for the establishment of a Jewish quarter' in Cracow issued by the city commandant Rudolf Pavlu on 3 March 1941 the new principles are clearly enshrined:

> The district commander's economic commissioner for the city of Cracow will determine which and how many firms within a given sector of the economy will be licensed to operate in the Jewish quarter. [...He will determine] whether, and if so which, Jewish businesses are to be amalgamated or wound up when they are transferred to the Jewish quarter. [...He] will order the liquidation of businesses whose continuation is not in the public interest. (...) Tools and machine tools of the kind normally used in workshop enterprises may be removed to the Jewish quarter. (...) Jewish firms engaged in mass production outside the Jewish quarter may not be transferred to the Jewish quarter.[47]

In contrast to the situation in Warsaw, the workers were allowed to carry on going to their normal places of work.[48] The policy of 'Entjudung' – the elimination of Jews from economic life – was proceeding smoothly along the lines envisaged by the economic experts.

One of the consequences of the economic exploitation of the ghetto was the recall of the head of the Warsaw transfer agency, Alexander Palfinger, who remained firmly wedded to his conception – already tried out in Lódź – of a purely state-run ghetto organization. He regarded a radical reorganization of the 'ghetto economy' as a mistake, and in a rejoinder to Gater he insisted that 'the running of a ghetto – something that has not been tried for centuries – must be based on purely political principles...'[49] At the beginning of May Palfinger was replaced as head of the transfer agency by Max Bischof, a Viennese bank manager.

At the same time a new post was created, that of 'Commissioner for the Jewish quarter'. The first incumbent was the lawyer Heinz Auerswald, who had previously been in charge of the department of population management and welfare in the Warsaw district. At the induction of Bischof and Auerswald the officiating representative of the Warsaw district governor described 'the establishment of work-shops in the Jewish quarter as the most important measure for the future'.[50] Bischof, who now assumed overall responsibility for the economic relations of the ghetto, had aligned himself completely with Gater's position. [51]

Another success chalked up by Gater was the closing-down in June 1941 of the Jewish forced labour camps, which he regarded as ineffi-cient. In the winter of 1940 and the spring of 1941 these camps housed several thousand Jewish men. Productivity in the camps was low, and the projects for which they were set up, such as the regula-tion of streams and rivers, had to be shelved anyway on the outbreak of war with the Soviet Union. The closure of the forced labour camps had an immediate adverse impact on the employment situation in the Warsaw ghetto. The economists, however, saw the closure of the camps as a success. For months past they had been studying reports on 'Jewish labour deployment' and shaking their heads at the lack of efficiency they uncovered at every point. On 25 October 1940, for example, the Central Department of Labour reported as follows:

> The deployment of Jews on labour duties continues to create sub-stantial difficulties. Productivity, in particular, is generally very low; this is compounded by problems with pay, accommodation and food. Many man-hours are lost through illness, brought on by the completely inadequate clothing they wear. Local employ-ment offices also complain that lack of cooperation from other agencies is constantly hindering their efforts to deploy Jewish work parties on a regular, organized basis.[52]

In March 1941 the Central Department of Labour reported that the situation had not improved: 'The deployment of Jews in work camps has produced very little in the way of economic gain. The evidence suggests that this is due to their poor physical condition, months of undernourishment and in large part also to the Jews' lack of willingness to work.' Within a short time, we read, 20 per cent of inmates from the ten labour camps then in existence had been signed off as sick and returned to the ghettos.[53] The closure of these camps, in which many people were worked to death, was not a humanitarian decision but a purely economic one.

The appointment of Bischof also signalled victory for the Gater–Emmerich policy line. Their proposal for issuing licences to – mainly German – private firms for the exploitation of Jewish labour was accepted and implemented. The simultaneous appointment of Heinz Auerswald as Commissioner for the Jewish quarter meant that the administration of the ghetto was now entirely separate from the various offices and departments of the Warsaw city administration. The resulting centralization of decision-making made it easier to change ghetto policy at short notice.

In point of fact, the 'jobs for the ghetto' project was probably planned from the outset as an experiment of limited duration. In the weeks that followed, the new masters paved the way for an import and export business in the ghetto regulated in accordance with Gater's principles. At the same time, however, they implemented the other option put forward by the RKW: 'Conditions of undernourishment could be allowed to develop without regard for the consequences.' As a result of this policy, the number of deaths in the ghetto during the second half of 1941 was much higher than in any previous six-month period. Meanwhile Bischof was also pursuing the second and third proposed options, which called for the creation of new jobs, the relaxation, within limits, of economic restrictions on the ghetto and the establishment of an 'outside trade' that was no longer prescribed in every last detail by the Warsaw transfer agency, but merely regulated in its operation. While Bischof wrote to German businessmen urging them to place their future contracts with suppliers in the ghetto,[54] Gater kept a close and suspicious eye on the progress of the experiment. To this end he made use of the statistical department of the Jewish Mutual Aid Society in Warsaw.[55] Although no further reports of the RKW on the economic viability of the Warsaw ghetto have survived, we can be certain that they existed. On 15 August 1941 the department of regional planning, which was responsible for important planning decisions that disadvantaged the Jewish minority, noted the receipt of a confidential document from the RKW entitled 'Economic performance of the Jewish quarter in Warsaw'.[56] Staff from the Central Department of Economic Affairs in Cracow came to Warsaw on a fact-finding visit to see how this new form of ghetto economy was working out. They cut the administration charges imposed by the transfer agency from the original 10 per cent on the sale of all goods to 5 per cent on goods coming into the ghetto and 2 per cent on goods going out, they removed legal obstacles to trade, opened up the ghetto to goods traffic, had telephone lines installed and revived the system of cashless payments. Emmerich, Bischof, Gater and Meder got together with the Jewish Mutual Aid Society and the business affairs representative on the Jewish Council in an effort to simplify and fine-tune the mechanisms of production and exploitation.[57]

Bischof, Auerswald and Gater also arranged for soup to be distributed to the workers in the newly established ghetto 'shops' twice a day, together with a supplementary ration of bread from time to time, in order to raise the general level of productivity. While they 'opened up' the ghetto to trade, they simultaneously sealed it off from the outside world far more tightly than ever before with draconian police measures and death penalties, designed to prevent the people inside from circumventing the economic system and obtaining extra food from the 'Aryan' parts of the city by black-marketeering. These further restrictions caused black-market prices to soar by more than 100 per cent overnight. The cost of the publicly distributed soup rations increased by 80 per cent. And all the social benefits which the Jewish Council had introduced for the poorest of the poor were immediately abolished.[58] In other words, one of the most important features of the new ghetto economy was that the finite quantity of food brought into the ghetto was not increased in any way, the available food being distributed unequally between 'productive' and 'unproductive' persons. The terrible consequences of this policy soon became apparent. The number of dead rose in leaps and bounds. Although the incidence of epidemics in the ghetto was not unusually high, and the summer had brought relief from the scourge of the winter cold, the number of people who died under the new regime, where profitability was all, was initially double, then three, then five times greater than the number who had died in the preceding winter months. In January 1941 there were 818 deaths, in February 1,023, in March 1,608, in April 2,061, in May 3,821, in June 4,290, in July 5,550 and in August 5,560.[59] This rapid increase in the number of deaths from starvation, equivalent to 11 per cent of the entire ghetto population when projected over a twelve-month period, was directly attributable to the reorganization and redirection of the transfer agency by Gater and Emmerich. According to paragraph 2.1 of its new charter, it was responsible for 'supplying the needs' of the ghetto.[60]

'Offloading them by next year'

With the attack on the Soviet Union it became clear that the days of the ghettos in the Government General were numbered. It was doubt-less no coincidence that the reasons for this were expounded by Hans Frank at the Government General's economic conference, which took place exactly one month after the new war in the East had begun. Frank made it clear that this programme was related to the food shortages and the ongoing work of 'German redevelopment':

> As we prepare to draw up a plan for food supply and reconstruc-tion, it is clear that certain issues with which we have had to wrestle constantly over a period of nearly two years will no longer trouble us to the same extent in the future. I believe too that conditions in Warsaw and the other big cities will now start to ease. (...) In a discussion I was able to have with the Führer in the Reich Chancellery three days before the invasion [of the Soviet Union], he told me amongst other things that the Jews will be the first to leave the Government General. In the next few days I will be giving the order for the clearance of the Warsaw ghetto. We must ensure at all costs that we get the Jews out of the Government General as soon as possible.

In the light of this plan, which accorded with the long-standing wishes of the German civilian administration in the Government General and the annexed eastern territories, even the Central Department of Food and Agriculture was optimistic about the future: the harvest had been a good one, and 'furthermore the pressures on the territory will hopefully be somewhat eased by the deportation of Jews and other antisocial elements to the East'.[61]

At the meeting of the occupation government on 15 October 1941 in Warsaw there was only one item on the agenda – the ghetto. Both the Commissioner for the Jewish quarter, Heinz Auerswald, and the head of the transfer agency, Max Bischof, had to make their reports. Bischof revealed that the ghetto's fixed capital assets, in the form of machinery and the like, were 'extremely limited as a result of the transfer or sale of such assets and the closure of hundreds of small businesses on police orders'. The utilization of manpower (he continued) was therefore confined almost entirely to manual work processes that required no machines. But this was precisely the kind of work which, according to Gater and Meinhold, served only to erode capital: it consumed materials and necessitated the feeding, clothing and equipping, albeit to very basic standards, of a workforce that would have been far more productively employed in other jobs with better tools and equipment. Orders farmed out by suppliers in the Reich, said Bischof, could obviously not be priced on the basis of conditions there. Despite the low wages, production costs were higher. So if goods were to be supplied at dumping prices, 'increased productivity from the Jews on piecework terms' would be required. Moreover the Jewish Council was responsible for ensuring that the workers in question received 'preferential' food rations, i.e. at the expense of those who were not working. Banking expert Bischof's final conclusion was as follows: 'The economic disaster area that is today's Jewish quarter is clearly in no position long-term to cover both its day-to-day running costs and its extensive arrears in government taxes, community charges, social security contributions, pre-war business liabilities, etc.'

By the end of August 1941 there were 36,000 people working in the ghetto, according to the Warsaw employment office. On the basis of Gater's costings that still meant a daily subsidy of 75,000 Reichsmarks out of the Government General's budget just to maintain the status quo. Bischof too, believed that the number in work was 'insignificant compared with the overall mass of 500,000 people'. A campaign to explore the possibilities of 'transferring work to the Jewish quarter' was conducted among the seventy chambers of commerce in the Reich, and the response was said to be encouraging; but Bischof ended his report on a somewhat sceptical note: 'If it can be done at all, then this may conceivably be the way to deploy Warsaw's Jewish workforce in sufficient numbers to serve the needs of the Reich in the final struggle for the future.'

After Bischof, it was Auerswald's turn to present his report. He spoke not about the rather dubious economic prospects, but about the political perspectives. This suggested another possibility for 'serving the needs of the Reich': 'If it is definite that the Jews are going to be deported from the Government General next year, then it would make sense, in order to avoid unnecessary work and expense, to leave things pretty much as they are.'[62] The Warsaw district governor Fischer proposed that efforts to boost productivity in the ghetto, of doubtful value as they were, should be abandoned. Immediately following this meeting the project for transferring work to the Jewish ghetto was cancelled.[63]

During the meeting Fischer also announced that 'more closures of larger businesses' were likely, due to energy shortages,[64] that the forthcoming winter in Warsaw would be the hardest since the German occupation began,[65] and that the supply of potatoes and bread-cereals for the population amounted to only a third of the officially prescribed starvation rations:[66] 'Compared with the two main issues – the economy and the food supply – all other problems fade into the background.'[67]

The next day Emmerich spelled it out in plain language. He announced a verdict: it turned out (as the record of his remarks states) 'that the ghetto was not financially self-supporting, that it could not survive without subsidies – assuming the object was to maintain the viability of the Jewish community. In itself this was not a justification for the continuing existence of the ghetto. But it did serve as a temporary concentration camp until the time when the Jews could be deported.'[68] So the practical result of the government meeting of 15–16 October was that all the measures designed to make the ghetto pay its way (and thereby 'maintain the viability of the Jewish community') – measures that appeared to have little prospect of success anyway – were finally abandoned in the light of the impending deportations.

In Lvov, which was annexed to the Government General in July 1941, the principle of drawing a distinction between Jews who were fit for work and those who were not, a principle developed in the early months of 1941 with the economic exploitation of the ghetto, was embraced almost from the outset. Albeit with one significant difference: those who were deemed fit for work were either carted off to camps or housed in a special 'skilled workers' enclave' inside the ghetto, where facilities of a marginally better standard were provided for so-called indispensable Jews.[69] Unlike their colleagues in Warsaw and Lódź six months previously, the German authorities in Lvov made no attempt to evaluate the ghetto's long-term economic viability. Instead they used the ghetto occupants as a kind of buffer to soften the impact of any shortages or 'supply bottlenecks': they took people from the ghetto if extra manpower was needed anywhere, or had others shot if they came under pressure to 'release' housing accommodation or save on welfare costs.

On 20 January 1942, the day of the Wannsee conference, clear instructions were issued to all municipal undertakings in Lvov: '...in so far as there are still Jewish employees working in your organization (...) you are to start looking for replacements immediately'. This applied particularly to 'indoor establishments (workshops, etc.)'. An exception was made only for 'special types of work (excavation works, etc.)', where 'Jewish workers [could] remain employed until further notice'.[70] These Jews were not deported in the first instance, and were to be 'resettled' later as and when they could be replaced by other workers or when their work was no longer considered vital to the war effort.[71]

In the raids and mass shootings of the early months the Germans primarily targeted for killing those who were 'surplus to requirement' ['Ballastexistenzen'], the 'particularly tiresome Jews', as Heydrich put it – in other words, the old and the sick. When the mass killings began in Belzec new categories of victims were defined, and preference was given to the deportation of women and children. Towards the end of the first systematic 'resettlement operation' in Lvov, on 25 March 1942, town commandant Egon Höller gave orders regarding the domestic arrangements of 'working Jews who remain here': in the case of married men the wife 'would suffice' to look after them; in the case of single workers he decreed that 'one housekeeper per household of five or six persons' was sufficient.[72] In practice this meant some agonizing decisions: 'A man could choose whether to protect his wife or his mother. Male members of the family could not be saved by a work permit.'[73]

The department of population management and welfare – or as it was tellingly known in Galicia for a while: 'population management, welfare and resettlement'[74] – set about establishing a corresponding hierarchy of victims within the normal daily life of the ghetto. Its 'welfare policy' was based on the same criteria that were applied to the deportations, discriminating first of all against those who were 'unproductive'. So the director of the internal administration, in his parallel capacity as head of the department of population management and welfare, argued that the first candidates for deportation should be those people who might otherwise be a financial 'burden' on the community. His proposal was to prioritize the murder of Jewish families who were dependent on welfare because their breadwinners had been locked up in labour camps.[75]

On 25 March 1942 Höller issued an order requiring all public and private employers to draw up 'lists of Jewish skilled workers who are not thought to be dispensable at the present time' – these lists to be submitted to the employment office within two days. The latter organization would then decide – in consultation 'with other interested agencies' – on the granting of 'working Jew' status and on the issue of appropriate armbands and permits.[76] In other words, the employment office exercised centralized power of decision over whether a person would keep or lose his job – and therefore whether he would live or die.[77]

Adolf Folkmann, a Jewish survivor from Galicia, describes the sequence of events: 'Every mass murder began (...) with an order requiring all Jews to re-register. Working Jews were to be given new work permits. Those who were not doing "strategically important" work were killed over the next few months in three organized mass murder operations.'[78] So the announcement of a new issue of work permits soon unleashed a wave of panic and desperation in the ghettos and stimulated the trade in these documents, putting money in the pockets of German entrepreneurs and company administrators. Jews threatened with deportation and death would pay large sums for a "strategically important" job. The wages they received – if they were paid at all – were below subsistence level. To earn enough to survive – and enough to pay the bribes – they had to barter and deal on the black market.[79] The steadily increasing amounts that the Jewish population of Lvov now had to pay in bribes to secure their survival were one of the reasons why German factory owners in October 1942 'had a genuine interest in preventing the closing-down of the ghetto'.[80]

While from 1 August 1941 onwards Jewish women, children, welfare recipients, the old and the sick became the priority victims of the German policy of annihilation, the plans were in fact targeted from the outset against all Jews; it was just that the Germans could not and would not proceed against the working population as speedily as they had against the 'unproductive elements'. In his report of 30 June 1943 on 'The solution of the Jewish question in Galicia', SS and police chief Friedrich Katzmann writes: 'Due to the peculiar circumstance that nearly 90 per cent of the skilled tradesmen in Galicia were Jews, it was necessary to stagger the implementation of the solution, since their immediate removal would not have been in the interests of the war economy.'[81] In this way the Jewish minority was 'removed' from the economy of Galicia over a period of two and a half years – in part by the expedient of issuing fewer and fewer work permits from one 'operation' to the next and filling more and more jobs with 'Aryans' or doing away with the jobs altogether.

While the ghettos in the Government General were progressively reduced in size as the people living there were deported – despite the complaints of the factory owners that they were short of manpower – we need to bear in mind that the ghettos were not producing cost-effectively by the standards of the German war economy. The jobs had become a refuge for the ghetto occupants. To a large extent they were fictitious jobs. Where people were actually producing something, productivity was way below the level that might have been achieved because the workforce was undernourished and sick, and often lacked the most basic machines to do the job. In many cases Jewish forced labourers were employed on marginal economic activities that were shut down anyway in the 'total war'.

In his report, Rudolf Gater had already shown that the ghettos as they were then constituted were bound to remain 'subsidized enterprises'. The German occupation authorities were financing a production sector from which others – such as German factory owners – could make money, but which in straight economic terms had no chance of ever getting out of the red. Moreover, production based on the use of cheap forced labour in the ghetto was in direct competition with firms in the Aryan sector, where wages and the cost of living were higher. Products from the ghetto were sold at dumping prices, which only served to prop up outdated structures of production and prevent the speedy rationalization of industry that the war economy planners regarded as essential. But the decisive factor for the early closure of businesses in the ghetto was the shortage of raw materials. In April 1941, in the discussion of the RKW report on the Warsaw ghetto, Emmerich himself had raised the issue of 'whether businesses in the ghetto should receive priority allocations of raw materials, even at the risk of putting workers in non-Jewish Polish firms out of work'.[82] At the time the question remained unanswered, but in the months that followed it became increasingly clear which way the decision would go. As the continuation of German rule in occupied Poland and the outcome of the war became increasingly dependent on maintaining adequate food supplies, the Germans were less and less able to afford the 'erosion of capital' that a backward ghetto economy represented.

It is frequently claimed that the systematic murder of the Polish Jews from the spring of 1942 onwards damaged the German war economy, which was short of manpower at the time. The economists who were then in charge in the Government General saw things very differently, and for sound economic reasons. In 1942 and 1943 the civilian and military economic administration closed down hundreds of unprofitable firms in the Government General in a bid to make industry 'leaner and meaner', concentrating resources in a 'limited number of highly efficient' firms.[83] The Office of Price Formation, for example, was one agency in the Government General that pushed very hard for rationalization. For here it was understood that the theoretical labour cost advantage over the Reich, which derived from the low standard of living, was effectively cancelled out by the supply shortages, high absenteeism due to sickness and the obsolete equipment and organization of existing firms. In fact unit wage costs in the Government General were generally quite a bit higher than in the Reich – even though wages and employers' contributions were substantially lower. A study undertaken in September 1942 demonstrated that firms were producing at only 10–60 per cent of their available capacity. And up to a third of their workforce would be missing, partly for the simple reason that hunger forced workers to shop for food on the black market instead of working.[84] At the first meeting of the Armaments Commission of the Government General on 24 October 1942 the head of the Office of War Economy and Armaments, Lieutenant-General Max Schindler, highlighted the problem: 'The general level of absenteeism at present is running at 25 per cent, and in the summer months the figure in some factories is as high as 70 per cent.' Consequently, he complained, firms had to take on an average of 30 per cent more staff than they actually needed.[85] Schindler asked Emmerich to set the political and administrative machinery in motion to bring about the necessary rationalization, and at the same time he engaged an adviser in the person of Dr Rudolf Gater.

Under Gater's supervision, all firms were now required to introduce a comprehensive bookkeeping regime, and in 1942 he published a textbook on the subject in German and Polish.[86] He introduced the Refa system for calculating working times,[87] and brought in the German DIN system of industrial norms ('Higher productivity through standardization!') by government order. Together with Max Biehl he founded the journal *Die wirtschaftliche Leistung*, likewise published in German and Polish.

But Gater's main achievement was to employ all the resources at his command, including the leadership of the war economy, to force through a second wave of rationalization in the Government General that went beyond the policy of 'Entjudung' he had himself promoted.[88] Even in 1942 the results achieved thus far were by no means satisfactory, according to a report by August Heinrichsbauer: 'The labour-intensive nature of the economy in the Government General is already giving cause for concern. There can be no doubt that the bustle of commercial activity we now see in the GG is largely illusory. The sheer number of people in work creates the appearance of a boom: but by the standards of a modern economy there is excessive overmanning. (...) The productivity of the individual, and of the economy as a whole, is correspondingly low.'[89]

Clearly the idea had become established that the economic problems of the rump of Poland – squeezed and compressed by conquest, plundered and packed tight with evacuees – could be alleviated, but not actually solved, by the 'exclusion' of the Jewish minority.[90] An unsigned article entitled 'The eradication of non-viable economic activity' appeared in the January 1943 issue of *Die wirtschaftliche Leistung*, probably written by its editor, Max Biehl: 'The streamlining of business and industry must start by getting rid of firms that not only do non-essential work, but also do unacceptable damage to the economy as a whole by their persistent inefficient use of labour, energy and raw materials. (...) Nobody can deny that there is a great deal of dead wood to be cleared away here.'[91] In April 1943 the Office for the Government General at the Reich Board for Industrial Rationalization formulated the following goal: 'The closure of 20–25 per cent of existing businesses and the restructuring of those that remain should create a sound basis for the regeneration of industry in the Government General.'[92]

In 1944 the results of this rolling programme of rationalization were summarized as follows:

> In 1939 there were some 195,000 businesses within the Government General as at present constituted. This number has been reduced as follows:
>
> | | |
> |---|---:|
> | 1. by progressive exclusion of the Jews | 112,000 [93] |
> | 2. by destruction at the hands of the Bolshevists in Galicia | 18,500 |
> | 3. by business closures following the departure of the owners to take up other jobs – to the end of 1941 | 3,100 |
> | 4. by business closures in 1942–3 | 10,500 |
> | Total | 144,100 |

This means that approximately 26 per cent of the industrial base that existed in 1939 now remains, or some 50,000 businesses. (...) In contrast to the Reich, where business closures and amalgamations are seen as temporary measures for the duration of the war only, the restructuring of business and industry in the GG was undertaken as a genuine exercise in rationalization and concentration, with the aim of ensuring the long-term viability of every remaining business. That aim has been achieved.[94]

Himmler argued along basically similar lines in October 1943 when he addressed a meeting of senior Party functionaries and Gauleiters in Posen:

I can tell you that I have had great difficulties with many economic institutions. In the rear areas I have cleared large Jewish ghettos. In Warsaw we had four weeks of street-fighting in a Jewish ghetto. Four weeks! We took out something like 700 bunkers there. This entire ghetto was making fur coats, dresses and the like. In the past, if we wanted to go after them, we were told: Hands off! You're disrupting the war economy! Hands off! This is an armaments factory! (...) It is these so-called armaments factories that Party comrade Speer and myself intend to clear out in the coming weeks and months. And we will do our work without sentimentality, just as everything in the fifth year of the war must be done without sentimentality, but with a full heart for Germany.[95]

Himmler also used this speech to announce 'Operation Harvest Festival'. This was the cynical code name for the events that took place on 3 November 1943, when all the Jewish prisoners in the camps at Majdanek, Travniki and Poniatova, most of whom had been used as forced labourers, were summarily shot: a total of 42,000 people.

The process of rationalization that had begun with the 'elimination of Jewish elements from economic life' was continued in the following years, even when the businesses in the ghettos had been liquidated and the great majority of the Jewish population had already been murdered. The armaments industry also underwent rationalization, which for the Jewish forced labourers employed there, who had previously hoped to be saved because of their 'strategically important' work, now meant death.

In November 1942 Meinhold calculated as follows: 'If we assume that of the 3 million workers who are surplus to requirement some 1.5 million can be found jobs in trade, transport and the small business sector – especially when the Jews are out of the picture – that still leaves a surplus workforce of 1.5 million for whom work needs to be found.' At the time these words were written, 835,000 people had already been deported from the Government General to Germany for forced labour, and most of the Polish Jews had been murdered. So the 'total mobilization' of the remaining 600,000 workers remained for Meinhold 'one of the most important prerequisites for the redevelopment of the territory'. Only in this way, he wrote, could the 'overpopulation pressure' be relieved to the extent that was necessary; only in this way could the necessary shrinking of the labour force be achieved. This would 'force firms in the Government General to adopt rationalization measures, however crude these might at first appear'.[96]

Even in January 1943 an interim report published by the department of agriculture at the Institute for German Development Work in the East still assumed the existence of a 'surplus' of 1.5 million people, equivalent to 20 per cent of the able-bodied population of working age. And that assumption remained intact despite the author's acknowledgement that 'the Jews have now been eliminated'.[97]

CHAPTER 10

'POPULATION SURPLUSES' IN THE EUROPEAN TRADING AREA

The German claim to leadership of the 'European economic community'[1]

On 22 June 1940 Göring officially charged the Reich Ministry of Economic Affairs with the task of preparing for the new European economic order. The Hamburg economist Gustav Schlotterer was appointed to head the department that would oversee these preparations. According to Heinrich Bechtel, president of the Association of German Economists, the priority now was to reposition economics 'as a militant science' and, while the war was still on, '(to) help forge the tools that will prepare the ground for the completion of the European continental economy'.[2] Economic reports on all European countries that were important for the German economy were greatly in demand.

In 1979 the economist Hermann Gross wrote: 'The studies carried out by the Central European Economic Conference, as well as those commissioned by I.G. Farbenindustrie, were planned and conducted in close collaboration with German and south-east European scientists, institutes and ministries, and were generally available to all interested parties in scientific, economic and administrative circles. Concerned as they were with issues of an essentially practical nature, they formed a very valuable supplement and addition to the more academic economic research carried out at colleges and universities.'[3]

How this worked in practice can be seen from the 'committee of twelve' of the South-East Europe Society. This association, based in Vienna, had been founded at the beginning of 1940 with the aim of coordinating economic policy vis-à-vis south-east Europe. The committee of twelve, set up in the winter of 1941–2 at the instigation of very senior Reich officials, was also known officially as 'the planning committee of the South-East Europe Society'. Its chairman was Walter

Rafelsberger, who as head of the Property Transaction Agency had formerly been in charge of 'eliminating the Jewish element' from the Austrian economy. The other members of the committee were leading figures from industry, public administration and the scientific community.[4] No limits – figurative or literal – were set to their planning fantasies: national frontiers, forms of government and economic structures could be altered at will, under the committee's remit, as it saw fit. In the summer of 1942, for example, the committee members discussed 'whether or to what extent the countries that make up south-east Europe should remain as separate national entities in the future', and 'what arrangement of frontiers' was 'most practical in terms of carrying out a restructuring of the industrial economy of south-east Europe that accords as far as possible with German interests'. From this point of view it would be all to the good if national sovereignties in south-east Europe were 'curtailed or eliminated', since then 'the German agencies concerned with industrial planning (...) can have a completely free hand (to set up industries, close them down, expand them or limit their growth)'.[5]

The basic outlines of a continental economy and the division of Europe into a series of more or less interdependent economic zones, whose functions would be assigned to them by the German Reich and whose economic activities would be coordinated in the interests of German capital, had been worked out by the Central European Economic Conference back in the late 1920s. This international economic association, in which, according to its chairman, German industry exercised 'a decisive influence',[6] had 'identified' south-east Europe as an 'area of special interest', and had sought to secure economic control over the Danubian countries with the usual instruments of capitalist penetration – trade agreements, the export of capital, direct investments, etc.

The policy of economic intervention was directed in the first instance at the agricultural industry in the countries of south-east Europe, which was to be exploited as a market for German products and a supplier of raw materials. German firms would either export chemical fertilizers and agricultural machinery at cut prices or build their own production facilities on the spot in order to dominate the local market. The countries of south-east Europe would pay for German industrial goods not with hard currency, of which they had very little, but with agricultural products – preferably excluding any that were already being produced in Germany. Otherwise they would be competing with German agriculture, and thereby damaging not just the interests of big German landowners: given the possibility of a new war, any decline in German food production was to be avoided at all costs. For all these reasons German economic advisers worked intensively to restructure the agrarian economy of south-east Europe. Production there was to concentrate not on foodstuffs, which in times of famine and general shortage would be consumed by the local population, but on industrial plants for export to Germany: tobacco, cotton, soya, animal feedstuffs, flax, hemp, linseed, sunflowers, rape, etc. In Romania and Bulgaria the company set up by I.G. Farbenindustrie to grow and export soya, Soja A.G., successfully took the area under cultivation from nothing to 120,000 hectares in a few years.[7] At the same time, the parent concern induced farmers in Bulgaria and neighbouring countries to use artificial fertilizers – not at all their normal practice – with the aid of economic incentives, low prices and tax concessions.[8] As in the 'emerging nations' of today – Brazil, for example, where sugar cane and coffee are grown for export in large plantations, while the families of the plantation workers go hungry – the production of food in south-east Europe in the 1930s was restricted in the interests of German big business, despite food shortages in the countries concerned.[9]

However, the economic offensive in south-east Europe did not produce the desired results. It served the short-term commercial interests of the companies involved rather than the goal of long-term economic restructuring – let alone the needs of the rural population in south-east Europe. So for example it was not long before 'machine graveyards' began to appear. The agricultural machines imported from Germany often proved useless in south-east Europe; they could not be properly utilized in the villages, nor could they be repaired when they broke down. So they just sat there and rusted away.[10] The big concerns were able to grab a significant share of the market, and Germany was one of the most important trading partners for the countries of south-east Europe: but crucially it was not their only trading partner. Until 1939 these countries avoided any one-sided economic bias, exporting a proportion of their domestic production to England and France, among other countries.[11] The outbreak of war changed all that. Germany blocked all exports to the countries it was fighting. The German-dominated European trading area, which had proved politically impossible to establish by the normal instruments of economic imperialism, was now dragged into being by military force.

Immediately before the outbreak of war the Four-Year Plan Authority also became actively involved in these matters. A study labelled 'Top Secret' explored 'the possibilities of a continental war economy under German leadership'.[12] The economic experts calculated the maximum possible 'deliveries' of raw materials that could be extracted from each country, as for example: 'Poland under occupation would provide substantial supplies of coal (22 per cent), zinc (18 per cent), mineral oil and iron ore. Unless the Polish coal-mining industry remains fully operational at its peacetime level, the war economy in the German-controlled European trading area will not be in a position to meet all the demands placed upon it.' The study concluded: 'In the absence of economic union with Russia the European trading area consisting of Greater Germany, Slovakia, Hungary, Italy, Spain and the Balkan countries (excluding Greece) can achieve only limited self-sufficiency for its war economy in the event of a blockade, even if we exert ourselves to the utmost and assume the very best that can be hoped for regarding the willingness of the northern region [meaning Scandinavia] to supply our needs.' In order to realize this grand design 'a peaceful fusion and integration of national economies' was necessary 'where possible', including the 'closest possible customs union', if not 'a full currency union'. An appropriate system of alliances was to 'make south-east Europe and the northern region subservient to the coalition' and 'facilitate an acceptable relationship with Russia'.[13] In terms of military action, that might mean the subjection of Poland from the outset in order to secure the land bridge to the Soviet Union and Romania, and the occupation of Denmark and Norway to 'secure the northern region'. Implicit in the plan, if diplomatic and economic pressure failed of their purpose, was war against at least some countries of south-east Europe, and eventually against the Soviet Union – if 'economic union with Russia' could not be achieved in any other way.

While the Four-Year Plan Authority was primarily concerned with the relatively short-term economic aims of a war economy, officials at the Reich Ministry of Economic Affairs were working on the longer-term aspects of the plan for a European trading area, which were aimed at securing market domination. Gustav Schlotterer explained in July 1940 how this would work:

The essential goods that we need must be produced as far as possible in Germany and in the German-controlled European economic area. (...) Since 1932 south-east Europe has aligned itself strongly with Germany. Our aim is to focus the region's trade and exports more and more on Germany. All goods must be traded on the German market. This will enable us to keep a close check on the movement of goods. At the same time the private-sector economies of our trading partners must be so tightly bound up with German interests that these countries cannot extricate themselves from these ties and commitments even if they wish to. We must secure economic positions in these countries and be able to influence their organization and political life. (...) More specifically, we must establish a presence in the following sectors: cereals in south-east Europe, metals in Norway and Yugoslavia, oil in Romania. (...) Central commodity markets must be set up in Germany for overseas goods. We don't want every small country conducting its own overseas trade and forcing prices down.[14]

In the years from 1933 to 1945 Gustav Schlotterer was extraordinarily influential as an economic policy-maker. From 1931 onwards he worked as economics editor, and later as managing editor, of the *Hamburger Tageblatt*, the newspaper whose masthead had carried the traditional Hanseatic cog sail with swastika since its foundation in 1928. From 1933 to 1935 Schlotterer served as president of the Hamburg Board of Trade, until he was drafted into the Reich Ministry of Economic Affairs as a leading expert on foreign trade and the 'new economic order'. Here he headed up the 'special department for preparation and organization', and liaised between the Ministry and the Four-Year Plan Authority. In 1939–40 Schlotterer coordinated the interlocking of capital relationships between German industry and industrial companies in the occupied countries of western Europe. Appointed a chief of division in 1941, he became – at the high point of German expansion to the East – head of the East European department in the Ministry of Economic Affairs and *ipso facto* head of the economics department in the Reich Ministry for the Occupied Eastern Territories, as well as head of the trade and industry section in the Economic Policy Unit for the East and a board member of the South-East Europe Society. In all these capacities he shared responsibility for the economic 'restructuring' of Europe, and for coordinating 'the exigencies of war' with the aims of the restructuring programme.

In October 1940 Schlotterer gave a speech before the senior

advisory board of the Reich Federation of Industrialists. As a representative of the National Socialist state apparatus, an experienced
economist and a 'veteran' of the NSDAP, he warned the assembled
representatives of large industrial concerns against taking an excessively dictatorial approach in the pursuit of their interests within the
European economic community. He argued that it was not possible
to do business with subjugated peoples. Instead of descending upon
the occupied countries of Europe in raiding parties protected by military force, and either violently appropriating the businesses they
found there or crushing them as unwelcome competition, Schlotterer
urged German firms to pursue their interests by economic pressure in
order to 'achieve the right solutions in Europe' by this means. It was,
he maintained, a matter of striking a 'healthy balance' between
German interests and those of other countries: 'These countries are
dependent on cooperation with us, and that will drive them into our
arms. (...) We must attempt to arrive at a sensible system of industrial
cooperation and division of labour within Europe.' Companies that
were founded on 'sound principles of profitability' were to be integrated into the German economic strategy through a system of interlocking capital relationships, market regulations and economic
agreements. 'Worthless' production facilities, on the other hand,
were to be shut down. Schlotterer also pointed out to the assembled
industrialists that the 'Jewish question' would be settled in the occupied territories too in the foreseeable future. The important thing was
to 'take over the good Jewish positions with as little loss of business
as possible'.[15]

In foreign-policy terms, the German model for Europe envisaged that
Germany would lead and the other European states would follow
faithfully where Germany led. It was therefore necessary to establish
a 'good understanding on foreign-policy matters' with the governments of the countries of south-east Europe. If diplomatic pressure
was not enough, the internal administration was to be 'purged'.

Inside these countries 'checks on domestic consumption' would be
imposed and an 'intensive education drive' would be carried out that
would 'extend to the last peasant and schoolboy'.[16] In their 'social
blueprint for the future' the German experts sought to inculcate 'the
ethos of a new work culture' that would 'shed its light across the
whole of Europe': 'The prospects that this opens up for the growth
and prosperity of peoples and nations in a pacified Europe are
promising indeed. It will be no land of milk and honey, but those

who work hard – individuals and nations alike – will find the path to advancement and to the application of their creative powers.'[17] 'As far as the creation of a properly planned economy is concerned,' observed Hitler in August 1941, 'we are still in the very early stages, and I imagine it is something really quite wonderful to be building a new economic order for the whole of Germany and Europe.'[18]

South-east Europe

Since the dying days of the Weimar Republic, German eyes had traditionally turned towards the countries of south-east Europe in the search for a dependent 'satellite economy'. And here, once again, the architects of a continental economic strategy found themselves confronted by the old familiar problems. 'Overpopulation' – according to their analysis – resulted in lack of capital, 'backwardness', inefficiency, poverty and barely suppressed social conflicts. All this hindered the development of modern economies capable of playing their part in a 'European economic community' under German leadership. But it was clear to the Germans that their regional policy would aggravate these problems, at least in the short term. Gustav Schlotterer pointed out that the new European division of labour would result in far-reaching rationalization and cause the overpopulation problem to become acute. As he wrote in the journal *Die Deutsche Volkswirtschaft* in 1940: 'The problem of housing and feeding a growing population surplus right across Europe is crying out for a solution.'[19]

In Bulgaria, Romania and Yugoslavia some 80 per cent of the population made their living from agriculture. In all three countries there had been agrarian reforms in the 1920s – attempts to satisfy the hunger for land of the discontented and rebellious peasant farmers, and thus prevent the spread of socialist revolution on the Russian model that was every government's nightmare.

As a consequence of these agrarian reforms the number of peasant smallholdings increased substantially in all three countries and property became increasingly 'fragmented',[20] divided up among the heirs from one generation to the next. Agricultural productivity declined. However, the rural population in Romania, which was considered 'unimaginably frugal' by German standards, had no sooner cast off the fetters of feudalism than it began to raise its standard of living and use a larger proportion of its food production to meet its own growing needs.[21] In other words, it did the reverse of what was needed to accumulate capital. On balance, therefore, according to a 1938 study by the Labour Science Institute of the German Labour Front, 'the agrarian reform, which was aimed in part at eradicating overpopulation on the land (...)' had 'served only to increase over-population in some areas'.[22] The economics department of I.G. Farben reached essentially the same conclusion, not only about Romania[23] but also about Bulgaria. Here the 'surplus agricultural labour force' was estimated at '720,000 men at least', who could 'be otherwise employed'.[24] The East European Institute in Breslau put the percentage of unused labour in Bulgarian agriculture in 1943 at 63 per cent.[25]

The same applied in principle to the newly created satellite state of Slovakia, where the rural economy was likewise dominated by tiny farms and smallholdings that were 'essentially geared to supplying their own needs'.[26] At the same time the German experts identified an 'excessive population pressure' there which had not yet been successfully channelled into manufacturing industry.[27]

The 'insufficient utilization of the available manpower' was seen as 'economically and socially dangerous in equal measure'.[28] Just like Theodor Oberländer before them,[29] the experts at the Labour Science Institute of the German Labour Front lamented the 'disproportion between the number of workers and the number of idle mouths to be fed',[30] which was manifested in the fact that 'barely half the members of each family are actively involved in the production process'.

Himmler's planning and resettlement authority, the Reich Commissioner for the Strengthening of German Nationhood, also subscribed to this analysis:

> Taking a broad regional view, nearly all the territories in the Danubian-Carpathian area are characterized by varying degrees of rural overpopulation relative to the present state of agricultural production methods and yields. Previous attempts to tackle the problem through social legislation and agrarian reform aimed at redistributing land from large publicly or privately owned estates (including an increasing number now owned by Jews) have failed to improve the situation because they were ill-conceived. And in many ways, with the retention of old agricultural methods and forms of 'farm organization', they have only made things worse.[31]

Hungary occupied a kind of in-between position in the thinking of German regional planners. The country's industries were in a more advanced state of development, and most of its agricultural land remained in the hands of large landowners. But even industrialization had not served to defuse the socio-political situation – quite the reverse. The Labour Science Institute of the German Labour Front wrote: 'The social stability of Hungary [is] constantly threatened by the disproportionate poverty of the masses and the failure to construct a balanced and natural economic and social order.' The Institute viewed 'the mass of very small landowners and the rural proletariat' as a special problem of its own. 'The impoverishment of these masses, their physical degeneration, their apathy, combined with the danger of Communist agitation, place an enormous strain on Hungarian society and present the country's social policy-makers with their most urgent task. (…) It has been calculated that the rural proletariat and their families number approximately 4 million, or nearly half the total population of Hungary.'[32] In other words: unless the Germans took action to prevent it, the fragmentation of land ownership was likely to happen here too – with all the attendant manifestations of rural overpopulation.

As in Poland, so in the countries of south-east Europe, the German economists and social scientists lamented the absence of an indigenous middle class which they believed would collaborate with the occupation forces. In Hungary they detected a 'decline of the urban middle class' attributable mainly to the fact that since the middle of the nineteenth century the Jews had taken over the key positions of economic power and influence.[33] History, they claimed, had denied the Romanians 'an organically evolved middle class capable of sustaining the cultural heritage of the nation'. [34] This was seen as dangerous for other reasons too: '…following the recent economic crisis, which has created an unemployed intellectual class, the Balkan-Slavic peasant class is exposed to an increased risk of Bolshevization.' Furthermore: 'The peasant class in the agrarian countries is scarcely capable of revolution without a guiding "intelligence" to give it leadership: but with such leadership it could easily pose a threat to the internal structure of the state, particularly in the absence of a conservative middle class.'[35] The radical restructuring of this social system was one of the most important prerequisites for the realization of German plans for a European trading area – putting in place the infrastructure, as it were, to make development of these countries possible. In order to extract supplies of agricultural produce from south-east Europe it was necessary to rationalize and increase agricultural production there and get rid of the 'surplus mouths' – either by exploiting their 'idle' labour or, if that proved impossible, by 'resettling' the people concerned.

Even before the war all attempts to increase agricultural productivity while simultaneously finding employment in industry for 'family members who merely consume resources' had met with little success. In Romania the planners had even found that many of the peasant farmers turned their back on factory work after a short period, preferring a return to their 'wretched rural conditions'.[36] Not that the Germans were interested in developing an industrial base in south-east Europe that might have ended up competing with German industry. Instead the most that they were prepared to allow, in the words of the director of the Kiel Institute of World Economic Studies, Andreas Predöhl, was a 'labour-intensive production of low-quality goods (...) principally the more basic branches of the textile industry'; for 'these are to be found all over the world in areas of rural overpopulation'.[37]

Under Otto Donner's leadership the research bureau for the war economy at the Four-Year Plan Authority focused from the very outset on the population policy aspects of Germany's economic development plans for south-east Europe. In January 1941 it presented a discussion paper in which it was concluded that 'the ability of the South-East to supply agricultural produce is predicated on an unusually low standard of living'. The aim must be to increase agricultural production in these countries by appropriate development policies, but on no account to raise living standards there, since this would lead to 'a shortfall in supplies of food and raw materials at a European level that could not possibly be made up'. So there could be no question of export surpluses in south-east Europe. For the research bureau, famine and malnutrition were part of the price that had to be paid when a country made the transition from an agrarian economy to a modern industrial economy. 'Germany,' the authors of the paper continued, 'along with a large number of today's other "developed" countries, was able to progress in the last century mainly through the hard work and intelligence of its population and through the systematic reinvestment of the fruits of its labour in new projects (thrift). There is no reason why the South-East should be spared this "collective famine", nor is such a thing economically possible.'[38] The experts at the research bureau for the war economy therefore advised against long-term measures for developing the economy and stimulating consumption. Similarly 'job creation measures and the like', aimed at 'eliminating the oppressive burden of agrarian overpopulation', were not a priority in their estimation. Although the countries of south-east Europe had attempted to develop manufacturing industries in the 1930s in an effort to create employment for their 'surplus' rural populations, the German experts on south-east Europe concluded after the outbreak of war that these attempts had failed, and therefore proposed a different strategy for German economic policy vis-à-vis these countries. A proportion of these 'masses', they argued, could play 'a more important role as migrant workers in the trade between Germany and south-east Europe'. 'In many respects these migrant workers could become agents for change and economic development in the South-East. They would acquire discipline from us and accustom themselves to a faster pace of work.' Furthermore they would become acquainted with superior production methods and by sending their savings home they would be contributing to the economic growth of their native lands.

But there were drawbacks to the migrant labour proposal. The German economists were worried about possible social and political consequences, and voiced 'the strongest reservations on ethnic policy grounds'. They warned of a 'Slavic infiltration', and spoke of 'the German rural working class being swamped by foreigners'. Then there was the danger that the 'migrant workers' would compare the German standard of living with the 'primitive conditions in the East', which, 'if one wishes to prevent the development of agricultural processing industries [in the countries of south-east Europe], must inevitably give rise in the long term to serious social and political unrest'.[39]

So the German planners of the new European economic order viewed 'migrant labour' as a possible option only for a limited number of people labelled as 'excess population'. As for what was to be done with the remaining 'surplus mouths', they had nothing to say on this subject for the moment. What they were clear about, however, was that these countries should not be industrialized. Since the start of the war the experts had reckoned on the starvation of the population in south-east Europe, referring to it as the German 'war reserve'.[40] They called for 'restrictions on consumption' for the rural population in the south-east European countries. But such a policy was unenforceable, given the food-supply situation there and the pattern of land ownership. 'Public information initiatives' of one sort and another had already been tried to little effect in peacetime; under wartime conditions they proved a total waste of time. When the peasant farmers of Romania and Yugoslavia found their country under German occupation and themselves under orders to limit their own consumption and produce more for export, they responded by producing only for their own immediate needs – a traditional ploy to prevent the state from robbing them of the fruits of their labour.

In a highly confidential 'report on conditions in the South-East' ('Not to be given to third parties. This report must be kept in a safe place or destroyed!'), Karl Janowsky described his impressions of the Danubian countries in September 1942: 'Passive resistance is the primary weapon of the peasant farmer, who now produces only enough for the immediate needs of himself and his family. If this attitude cannot be changed by the use of appropriate means, Serbia will soon cease to be a viable source of arable and animal products for us.' In Romania, which was not under German occupation, the peasant population was no more cooperative: 'If farmers in Moldavia and Walachia are no longer able to buy what they want with their surpluses, they will simply produce only what they require for their own consumption.'[41] Janowsky reported falling yields in Romania for virtually all important categories of agricultural produce.[42]

German policy against minorities in the European trading area

It was therefore proving difficult to achieve the two primary goals of long-term economic restructuring and the extraction of 'surpluses' in the short term. The first step, however, was to get a grip on the rebellious peasant farmers and the problem of overpopulation. The elimination of the Jews from economic life in the countries of south-east Europe created some room for manoeuvre to begin with, although this varied from country to country.[43] 'Entjudung' accordingly became the lever used by the German economic planners to open the door to the economy of south-east Europe. The deportation of the Jewish minority – in south-east Europe this amounted to some 2.5 million people – simultaneously signalled the beginning of the 'solution of the population question'.

As well as giving socio-political 'guidance' to their populations and 'inculcating the work ethic and a right understanding', the governments of south-east Europe were pressed by the German Foreign Office to find a 'solution to the Jewish question'. The case was argued in part on economic and socio-political grounds, based on scientific studies prepared in Germany on the economic significance of the

Jews in the countries concerned. The German ambassadors to Hungary and Romania impressed upon their host governments the virtues of the Vienna project for the economic marginalization and expulsion of Jewish minorities, and dispensed 'advice' on how to implement similar measures in their own countries.[44]

In 1939 Hungary had passed a 'law on the legal status of the Jews', under which they were to be driven from all public offices within four years, while their representation in the liberal and academic professions and in business was to be limited by quota 'commensurate with their 5 per cent share of the country's population'.[45] This social discrimination against the Jewish minority was to be combined with a 'Magyarization' of business and commerce, to the benefit of non-Jewish Hungarian entrepreneurs and businessmen. The opportunities for Germans to make money from these transactions and so establish a German presence in the Hungarian economy were limited. To the regret of the German economic experts, 'German takeovers [of Hungarian businesses] will be considered only in exceptional instances', namely 'where we can make a convincing economic case for Germanization'.[46] 'The exclusion of the Jews,' observed the German Labour Front apropos of the new law, 'is also designed to give a new impetus to land reform. In the light of the situation in Hungary the law against the Jews (...) undoubtedly means a major upheaval, whose economic and socio-political consequences can scarcely be gauged at the present time. Compared with German legislation, however, it must be seen as only a beginning.'[47] At the urging of the German ambassador in Budapest, Dietrich von Jagow, the Hungarian government announced in December 1942 that it was ready to embrace a far-reaching anti-Jewish policy, but pointed out how difficult it would be to force the Jewish minority out of trade and industry quickly. 'Whole sections of Hungarian society' would have to be 'retrained to perform new tasks', and a 'radical restructuring' would have to be undertaken.[48]

These delaying tactics are also mirrored in the proceedings of the Wannsee conference. Heydrich deemed it necessary to impose an 'adviser on Jewish affairs' on the Hungarian government – although there had been no difficulties at all about despatching similar 'advisers' to other countries. It was only after German troops had occupied Hungary on 19 March 1944 that the Hungarian government initiated the 'radical restructuring measures' which the German Foreign Office had long been calling for – while at the same time mass arrests were carried out among the country's Jewish population. On 22 April the senior SS and police commander reported that the 'special operation' in the Carpathian region of north-east Hungary was proceeding 'according to plan and without a hitch', and that the 'concentration of the Jews continues to meet with the approval of the population at large'. Most Jewish businesses were closed down in compliance with a government order. An exception was made for those businesses that were deemed essential for supplying the needs of the non-Jewish population. These enterprises were to be managed in future by 'trustees'. 'For the rest,' reported the SS general in charge, 'some Jewish shops are to be transferred to Aryan ownership while others are shut down for good, since Budapest has too many shops anyway, which is very unhealthy for the city's commercial life.'[49]

German scientists also made detailed calculations for Slovakia to determine the percentage of Jews working in all the different branches of business – and these data were used to justify the 'exclusion of the Jews from economic life' and their deportation. In 1941 the Institute for Economic Research was engaged in 'gathering together reliable documentary material on the profitability of agricultural enterprises'. A total of 340,000 hectares of agricultural land had already been expropriated and added to the holdings of other farm units, 'including 100,000 formerly owned by Jews'.[50] While Jews accounted for only 5 per cent of the total population, according to a highly confidential report prepared by the 'Hamburg-Bremen Business Information Committee', 37.1 per cent of all persons employed in commerce were Jews and 20.3 per cent of all persons employed in trade and industry – which also accounted for the 'large concentrations of Jews in the towns and cities'.[51] In an article on Slovakia Max Biehl wrote that the 'starting point for the reorganization of trade', for a 'restructuring of the banking industry' and the intensification of agriculture was 'the solution of the Jewish question' together with 'the general expropriation of Jewish real estate'.[52] In order to marginalize and exclude the Jewish minority from economic life a 'Central Jewish Office' was set up in association with the Central Office of Economics, which was responsible for 'Aryanization'. The activities of the new agency were described in an article in the *Berliner Börsenzeitung*: 'The rather half-hearted and ineffectual measures initially undertaken against the Jews acquired a new vigour and purpose with the creation of the Central Jewish Office. Having segregated the Jews rigorously from the rest of the population, the new agency took action in a planned and systematic way to implement the programme of Aryanization and eject the Jews everywhere without disrupting the economic life of the country.'[53]

The German Labour Front had calculated that approximately half the national income of Romania (63 out of 122 billion lei) was earned from 'financial transactions and trade', the bulk of this – 57 billion lei – by the country's Jewish population. By listing the Jewish share of the Romanian national income separately and punctuating the entries with exclamation marks,[54] the Berlin economists were sending a clear message: there was a tried and tested way to create room for manoeuvre for an 'overhaul' of the Romanian economy, and that was through the expulsion and dispossession of the Jewish minority.

In the autumn of 1940 the government imposed tougher anti-Semitic measures and laws. According to the *Frankfurter Zeitung*, 'new measures directed against the business interests of the Jews followed thick and fast. On 5 October 1940 the state was declared the legal owner and beneficiary of all rural property belonging to the Jews; most of the expropriated farms and estates were to be handed over to refugees from the ceded territories [i.e. ceded to Hungary and the Soviet Union in 1940]. (...) In March of the following year Jewish-owned real estate in the towns and cities went the same way.'[55] In March and April 1941 the Romanian government arranged a census. Professor Friedrich Burgdörfer, one of Germany's most celebrated demographers, was invited to sit in as an observer and adviser. Burgdörfer was the expert who in 1939 had organized the cataloguing by name of the entire Jewish population of the German Reich for the SD, and in 1940 had prepared a report on the proposed Madagascar project. The census in Romania recorded 'Jews' and 'gypsies' under separate headings. Burgdörfer was impressed by what he saw: 'Overall a remarkably comprehensive survey, in which questions of ethnicity, and above all the Jewish question, received very detailed consideration.'[56]

The problem in Romania, as in Hungary, was that economic 'restructuring' could only be brought about gradually. In March 1941, speaking at the inaugural meeting of the Frankfurt Institute for the Study of the Jewish Question, Peter-Heinz Seraphim had pointed out that one could not 'make a third or a half of the towns and cities disappear overnight'. Apart from anything else,

> this third or half has hitherto accounted for ⅘ or even ⁹⁄₁₀ of all urban commercial and business life. (...) In other words, the removal of the Jewish population element from the towns and

cities in the East where they are particularly numerous can only proceed as fast as the Jews can be replaced by others – by other small traders and shopkeepers, who can take over the economic functions previously exercised by the Jews. This possibility undoubtedly exists, for among the peasant population of the Romanians, Magyars, Ukrainians, Slovaks and Poles the pressure of excessive numbers is such that the Jewish petite bourgeoisie could easily be replaced by native population elements. For years each new generation of peasant sons born to the indigenous peoples has been prevented by the Jewish element (...) from making its way in the towns and cities. The towns and cities were effectively 'blocked' by the Jews. The time now seems right to break that monopoly![57]

With calls on every side for the surplus rural population to be 'siphoned off' into the towns, the arguments used by Seraphim gave an indication as to how this might be achieved, given the general consensus that industry and commerce were not to be expanded in the medium term: namely, by adopting a racist structural policy based on the expulsion of the Jewish minority. How else was it possible to deliver what the Four-Year Plan Authority called for in May 1941 – namely the 'solution' of the 'most urgent problem facing the countries of south-east Europe' by 'the transplanting of the surplus rural population into the towns and cities'?[58]

Two years later Hitler urged the Hungarian government to 'take tougher action against the Jews', repeating almost word for word the socio-political arguments quoted above. On 18 April 1943 he told the Hungarian head of government, Admiral Horthy, that 'Hungary could put the Jews into concentration camps, just like Slovakia. In doing so it would be creating many new opportunities for its own citizens by freeing up the positions previously occupied by the Jews and providing career openings for its talented young nationals that have previously been closed to them by the Jews'.[59]

The same line of thought reappears in the situation report of the SS Central Office of May 1944. Here we read: 'In Hungary the Jewish question has become extremely pressing. (...) A significant proportion of the land is in Jewish hands, 60 per cent of the big tenant farmers at any rate are Jews.' The same SS report goes on to quote statistics for the number of Jews working in trade and commerce, in the textile and footwear industry, in banking and joint stock companies, together with the percentage of Jewish lawyers and doctors,

concluding with the following argument: 'The Hungarian state is suffering in its national make-up from the absence of a broad-based and
healthy middle class. There is nothing between the ruling upper class
and the broad mass of the people, peasants for the most part, who
grow up and live under a totally oppressive regime.'[60] In the summer
of 1944 the journal *Deutsche Aussenwirtschaft*, recently founded by
Otto Ohlendorf and Gustav Schlotterer, announced the deportation
of Hungary's Jewish minority to its readership in the German export
and import trade under the headline: 'Goods trade disrupted
following restructuring of Hungarian economy'.[61]

At the end of 1942 the Berlin economic adviser Alfred Maelicke,
writing in the journal *Die Deutsche Volkswirtschaft* ('Special feature:
Setting up the European economic community'), discussed the
advantages of a new demographic order imposed by force against the
background of the murder of the European Jews:

> The complete elimination of the Jews from the continental
> European trading area is based on clear principles, moving ahead
> speedily and proceeding relatively easily and according to plan.
> (...) Only the total removal of all Jews from economic life can
> solve the problems that still face many countries today – prob-
> lems such as overpopulation and other social issues in south-east
> Europe and elsewhere. The eradication of the Jewish shopkeeper
> mentality and greed for profit and the elimination of the Jews are
> creating space and security ('full employment') for many workers
> and peasants, skilled craftsmen and other traders who have previ-
> ously led rootless and impoverished lives. (...) If the principles
> and procedures adopted in Germany for getting rid of the Jews
> are observed elsewhere, the necessary profound shifts in the
> pattern of property ownership, and even major structural
> changes, can take place without serious disruption to the
> economy of the country concerned. Workers will not need to be
> laid off, and supply problems should not arise. We can even
> expect sales figures to be maintained.[62]

The same Maelicke was executive secretary of the German Industry
Advertising Standards Council, in which capacity he had campaigned
for the expropriation of Jewish businessmen in Berlin back in
1938–9.[63] From 1942 onwards the Council was attached to the
Ministry of Propaganda, and Maelicke became responsible for
'business propaganda' and 'special assignments'.

Neither Seraphim nor Maelicke nor any of the other German population experts really supposed that the deportation of the Jews would create enough space in the towns and cities of south-east Europe to provide adequate employment for all the people who were to be drafted out of agriculture in the name of economic rationalization. But they did see it as a first step towards providing new economic opportunities for a section at least of the 'surplus' rural population at the expense of the Jewish minority. They assumed that this would serve to instil hopes of a secure livelihood and advancement in the majority as well, thus preventing social unrest or at least cushioning its impact. But beyond all this, German regional planners believed that further resettlement operations, conscriptions of forced labour and campaigns of genocide were also necessary.

The repressive laws and measures passed against the Jewish minority in the countries of south-east Europe also applied in many instances to those labelled as 'gypsies'. They too were conscripted for forced labour, subject to police controls, sent to concentration camps and finally deported to the extermination camps. In the years of German rule in Europe at least 105,000 gypsies were murdered in Hungary, Romania, Slovakia, Serbia and Croatia alone.[64] In August 1942 Harald Turner, the German head of the civilian administration in Serbia, sent a telegram in which he reported, not without pride: 'Serbia only country where Jewish question and gypsy question solved.' In the same telegram Turner made reference to a further genocide – the murder of hundreds of thousands of Serbs in neighbouring Croatia: 'Daily atrocities, butchery of the Serbs. (...) By October 41 approx. 200,000 Serbs murdered; figure much higher in months following.'[65] The economic research department of I.G. Farben viewed this massacre of many hundreds of thousands of Serbian men, women and children by the Croatian Ustase government, Germany's ally, as a constructive contribution to solving the local 'overpopulation problem'. In its report on the economic structure of Croatia, it speaks in the usual veiled language of 'evacuation' and 'resettlement': 'In conjunction with the evacuation of large numbers of Serbian peasant farmers it is also hoped that the problem of severe rural overpopulation in certain areas such as Zagoria, Dalmatia and the Lika can be solved by large-scale internal colonization. At the same time the yields per hectare, which are well below the European average, are to be increased by more intensive cultivation.'[66]

When in August 1940 southern Dobrudja was detached from

Romania and handed over to Bulgaria as a result of German 'arbitra-tion', 110,000 Romanians were forced to leave their country, while only about half as many Bulgarians were forcibly resettled in Romania. The I.G. Farben concern, keenly interested in the economic exploitation of Bulgaria,[67] welcomed the deportations as an opportu-nity: 'The resettlement operation presents great challenges and new opportunities for Bulgaria's economic and social policy-makers', most notably the chance 'to relocate a certain proportion of the excess rural population, estimated to number 800,000 workers'.[68] As part of a 'demographic strategy' the 110,000 displaced Romanians were relo-cated to northern Dobrudja and southern Bukovina, where space had been created by the Romanian government's seizure of Jewish-owned land and the evacuation, by the Reich Commissioner for the Strengthening of German Nationhood, of German nationals to the annexed territory of western Poland. A published report by the Reich Office of Regional Planning on the 'resettlement operation in Romania' gives some actual figures: 'The material element consists for the present of 260,000 hectares of agricultural land that have passed into state ownership following the relocation of ethnic Germans living there and the expropriation of the Jews.'[69] So the deportation of the indigenous Jewish and Polish population from western Poland, to which the ethnic Germans of south-east Europe were relocated, was also directly connected with the redrawing of frontiers in, and the demographic restructuring of, south-east Europe.[70]

CHAPTER 11

THE WAR AGAINST THE SOVIET UNION AND THE ANNIHILATION OF 'X MILLIONS' OF PEOPLE

'This year 20 to 30 million people will starve in Russia. Perhaps this is for the best, since certain nations must be decimated.'

(Hermann Göring, 25 November 1941)[1]

With the war against Yugoslavia and Greece, Germany and Italy secured a position of supremacy in south-east Europe. The military conquests were an integral part of the grand economic design for Europe, and were intended to safeguard vital supplies of raw materials both for Germany's conduct of the war and for German industrial production in the post-war period. However, the shortfalls in the food supply could not be overcome by this means. By 1941 there were food shortages even within the Reich. As a result of the war, agricultural production in Germany had fallen. But adequate food rations were absolutely critical for maintaining the loyalty of the masses to the regime, and for guaranteeing the continuation of that consensus between the nation and its leaders that was without parallel in German history. The food-supply experts therefore regarded their efforts to maintain a constant level of food intake for the Germans as another kind of war, and themselves as 'warriors on the home front'.

Since the end of the First World War the German war planners had been busily analysing the causes of their defeat. And the failure of their first attempt to seize world power they attributed in very large measure to the food supply situation, which in 1917–18 had become sufficiently critical to lose the war for Germany.

They were haunted by fears of the consequences of a naval blockade and the destabilizing effects of food shortages. However victorious the Blitzkrieg campaigns might be, continental Europe at that time still needed to import 12–13 million tonnes of grain a year from overseas. That equated to the food requirements of more than 25 million people. And that was just the peacetime deficit: in wartime things were bound to get worse,[2] with shortages of labour, vehicles, horses, diesel oil. Nitrogen was needed to make gunpowder, so it was no longer made into artificial fertilizer. One bad harvest could trigger a famine – or at least, defeatist memories of 1917–18. Goebbels spoke of 'a slump in morale'. The European continent was by no means immune to the effects of a blockade – far from it. It lacked what the war economy strategists referred to as 'spare feeding capacity'.

Planned famines

Long before the war this very problem was exercising the undersecretary in the Reich Ministry of Food and Agriculture, Herbert Backe.[3] He had grown up as the child of German parents in pre-revolutionary Russia, and had been interned there during the First World War. Later he studied agricultural science in Göttingen. In 1933 – now a 'veteran from the early days' of the NSDAP and an expert in his chosen field – he was appointed to his post of undersecretary at the Reich Ministry of Food. In marked contrast to the overblown 'blood and soil' rhetoric of his minister and boss, Walther Darré, Backe campaigned single-mindedly for the mechanization and rationalization of German agriculture. He succeeded in gradually manoeuvring his minister into a political siding. His position as a member of the general council of the Four-Year Plan Authority had already enhanced his power considerably: in fact it meant that he now effectively outranked his own minister.[4] From 1939 onwards Backe was in charge of the entire wartime food-supply programme. He was Germany's 'food czar'. It was his job to hold the home front steady. And that could not be achieved by propaganda alone. It was essential to maintain supplies of bacon, butter and meat. In 1942 the long-since sidelined Darré retired 'for health reasons'; in 1944 Backe was formally appointed as Reich Minister.

Herbert Backe belonged to the intellectual elite of the Third Reich. He was the senior vice-president of the Kaiser Wilhelm Society [a prestigious scientific society, forerunner of the Max Planck Society]. With his ruthless energy and his sovereign expertise he was not unlike people such as Konrad Meyer, Otto Ohlendorf, Heinrich Himmler and above all Reinhard Heydrich, all of whom he counted among his friends.

Backe's first response to a food-supply situation that was precarious from the very first day of the war – in 1939 the German Reich was still importing 17 per cent of its food needs – was to introduce a tightly controlled and carefully targeted system of rationing. This was very soon followed, particularly in the occupied countries, by the systematic slaughter of livestock on a large scale, on the grounds that meat production is a highly inefficient way of producing food. The animals are fed on grain, potatoes and root crops, and it took six kilograms of grain to produce one kilogram of meat. So Germany's stock of pigs was reduced from 29 million to 18 million. In Holland 30 million of the country's 33 million chickens were slaughtered as soon as the occupation was complete, in accordance with a prearranged plan. In the occupied areas of the Soviet Union even draught animals were in short supply by 1943. The resulting meat mountains were canned and hoarded to feed the population of Germany.

But another part of Backe's strategy was to allow whole peoples and population groups to go hungry. After the occupation of Norway, for example, which was reliant to a very large extent on foreign food imports and consequently now had to be fed by Germany, Backe travelled to the Government General on 24 April 1940 and told Hans Frank that he must start shipping grain, sugar and meat to Germany, despite the local food shortages. Frank explained the difficulties they were having in maintaining supplies, and intimated a possible solution that clearly met with Backe's approval: 'I am not interested in the Jews; whether they have anything to eat or not is absolutely no concern of mine.'[5]

However, Backe felt that his elaborate rationing arrangements and the lowering of meat consumption were not enough in themselves to maintain the undying loyalty of the German nation to their Führer. So he developed more far-reaching plans for overcoming the shortfall in food supplies. These were based on the premise that the food-supply problems in Germany and occupied Europe could only be solved by waging a war against the Soviet Union designed to achieve precisely defined economic goals. But before Germany, Italy and the occupied countries of central and northern Europe could benefit from the agricultural and raw material resources of the Soviet Union, Backe believed that one essential condition had to be met: to make central Europe proof against the effects of a blockade, millions of Soviet citizens would have to be murdered, deported or starved to death. So the attack on the Soviet Union was driven not just by long-term economic considerations, which called for a 'decimation of the population' as part of Germany's strategy of domination, but also by a more immediate motive for mass murder, namely the attempt to solve Germany's food-supply problems in the short term at the expense of millions of other people. To put it another way: in order to guarantee that German food intake, and more particularly the consumption of meat, would remain steady, and with them the morale of the nation, the undersecretaries who formed the general council of the Four-Year Plan Authority, Herbert Backe among them, drew up a plan for mass extermination. This plan was formulated prior to the 'final solution of the Jewish question', and it envisaged the killing of people in far greater numbers. The members of the general council, their officials and researchers were reckoning on a death toll of around 30 million.[6] On the eve of the campaign against the Soviet Union, Himmler mentioned the same figure: 'The purpose of the Russian campaign [is] to decimate the Slavic population by 30 millions.'[7]

The managers of the German war economy and Göring's undersecretary Erich Neumann were also justifying policy in terms of the need to maintain food supplies. In a speech to the Berlin Academy of Public Administration in April 1941, Neumann stated: 'Since the agricultural production of the countries that have recently been added to the German supply zone was largely dependent on overseas imports of animal feedstuffs which are no longer coming in, these countries now have no choice but to move over to a more extensive system of agriculture. This means that they are no longer in a position to make further significant deliveries to us. Only Denmark will perhaps be able to go on exporting certain agricultural surpluses to us in the future. But if the war continues for some time the remaining countries, far from having surpluses for export, will gradually become dependent on imports for their survival.'[8] The text of this speech had been written by Neumann's personal assistant, Professor Otto Donner.[9] Neumann made the speech three weeks into the campaign against Yugoslavia and Greece. He and his staff had been helping to plan the attack on the Soviet Union for some considerable time – not least for the reasons outlined in his speech.

At the beginning of June 1941, the weekly meat ration for the German 'normal consumer' was cut from 500 to 400 grams, a move that Backe had considered 'unacceptable' only nine months previously.[10] It certainly didn't mean that the German population went hungry: but for the reasons of morale stated above it was undesirable. Just to restore this cut in the meat ration – which was the government's declared intention – 300,000 tonnes of meat a year would be needed, requiring 1.8 million tonnes of grain to produce. This represented the annual subsistence-level food intake of four to six million people – depending on how the figures are calculated.[11]

On 1 May 1941 Goebbels noted in his diary: 'Backe reported to me on the state of our food supply. The meat ration will have to be cut by 100 grams a week from 2 June. (...) Bread supplies should hold out, provided we don't have a bad harvest. We are all right for fats. If the war goes into a third year we'll be using up our last reserves of bread. (...) I must say Backe has really mastered his brief.'[12]

A day later, on 2 May, a key meeting took place at which the economic management of the war against the Soviet Union was discussed further. The minutes of that meeting are quoted here for the second time:

> (1) The war can only be continued if Russia supplies the food for the entire German armed forces in the third year of the war.
> (2) Millions of people will undoubtedly starve if the food supplies necessary to meet our needs are extracted from the country.[13]

Four days after this meeting, on 6 May, Backe reported back to Goebbels once again: 'Backe outlined the food supply situation. As he reported it to me a few days ago. With a few additional statistics that give grounds for optimism. If only this year's harvest is a good one. And then we'll do very nicely for ourselves in the East.'[14]

On 23 May the Economic Policy Unit for the East – an institution created specially for the war against the Soviet Union, and dominated by Göring and the Four-Year Plan Authority – approved the 'economic policy guidelines for the organization of the economy in the East, workgroup "agriculture"'. These had been drafted by the experts in the Reich Ministry of Food under Backe in collaboration with the government ministries represented in the Four-Year Plan Authority and the leadership of the Wehrmacht.[15] These guidelines spell out how the German Reich planned to 'do nicely for itself' in the occupied Soviet Union:

> Many tens of millions of people in these territories (i.e. the forest belt and the northern industrial towns) will be surplus to need, and will either die or have to emigrate to Siberia. Any attempts to save the population there from starvation by drawing on surpluses from the black earth country [i.e. the Ukraine] would be at the expense of maintaining food supplies to Europe. Such attempts would cripple Germany's ability to keep going in the war, and

they would cripple Germany's – and Europe's – capacity to survive a blockade. This needs to be made absolutely clear.[16]

These guidelines, which justified and sanctioned the death by starvation of 'many tens of millions of people', had 'met with approval at the very highest level'. So Hitler, Göring, Himmler and Goebbels had agreed to the plan. In a toned-down form the guidelines were reprinted in the so-called 'Green Dossier', published for the information of the entire German military and economic leadership. They furnished a detailed justification for the programme of extermination – without a single reference to racial ideology.

The authors of the guidelines argued their case on straightforward economic and geopolitical grounds. Before the First World War Russia had been the world's biggest exporter of wheat. That had all changed since the October Revolution. For one thing, the Soviet population simply consumed more – even though the anti-Bolshevist propaganda denied it. And for another, the size of the population had increased significantly, from 140 million to at least 170 million. The social structure had also undergone a radical shift: now one in three of the population lived in towns and cities, not one in ten as in 1914. In practice Russia was no longer producing grain surpluses. Consequently, as the guidelines pointed out, 'consumption must be reduced', 'ruthlessly cut back'. And all the more so as the impending 'military events' would send agricultural production into decline, possibly for a period of years. The general remarks in the Green Dossier were followed by '12 commandments' for the occupation regime, signed by Herbert Backe. Here he writes: 'Poverty, hunger and thrift have been the lot of the Russians for centuries. Their stomachs are elastic – so let us have no misplaced pity.'[17]

In terms of prosecuting the war the problem for the German conquerors was how to reduce the food consumption of the indigenous population without having to put a guard on every peasant farmer in Russia. Backe and his ministerial officials duly came up with a proposal for policing consumption that made both the economic exploitation of the country and the act of genocide appear feasible. In contrast to other occupied countries, there was a very clear geographical separation in the Soviet Union between the areas given over to intensive agriculture and the industrial zones, which had to be supplied with grain from outside. So the plan was simply to seal off, by military force, those areas inside the country which relied on food imports from the agricultural areas of the Ukraine that produced the agricultural surpluses: 'All of this surplus production has to be made available for Europe's needs. In other words, it is a matter of getting back to the way things were in 1909–13, or even 1900–1902.' The consequences for the people living in the 'food-importing areas' were spelled out: 'We shall have to redirect the population into the Siberian outback. Since there is no question of laying on rail transport, this will also pose very serious problems.'

'For special economic reasons' only one of the industrial 'food-importing areas' was to be conquered rather than destroyed or cut off by the line of the German front, and that was the oilfields of Transcaucasia. The fate of the Soviet urban population in the other major industrial centres was anticipated in the guidelines: they 'must expect conditions of severe famine'. This being the case (the guidelines continued), Germany must make 'a single early foray' into these regions, which 'will in future be famine areas', and bring out all the meat and industrial products it could lay its hands on. Any factories taken by conquest in the industrial zone were to be destroyed – 'an absolute necessity', 'not least for the long-term future peace of Germany'. The guidelines concluded by reiterating 'the fundamental point': 'Russia under the Bolshevist system has withdrawn from Europe purely for reasons of power politics, and in so doing it has upset the economic equilibrium of Europe based on a proper division of labour.' That was about to change, and the 'inevitable consequence' would be the 'destruction of the current economic equilibrium within the USSR'. 'So there can be no question at all of trying to preserve the status quo. The ways of the past must be consciously rejected, and the Russian food-producing economy integrated into a European framework. This will inevitably lead to the demise of industry and of a large section of the population.'

Two years later – after the defeat at Stalingrad – Göring's official in charge of 'Eastern questions' wrote in a self-critical review: 'From this situation the Backe thesis emerged, which argued that the key food-producing areas of western and southern Russia must be cut off from their markets in central Russia and reintegrated into the European system of food supply. A realistic enough proposition, provided one has the long-term military capability to keep the central Russians away from their fields.' This view (the writer continues) had 'led many men of influence to support the campaign on economic grounds'.[18] Göring put the whole concept very succinctly: 'If someone has to go hungry, it won't be the Germans but someone else...'[19]

'Sparing the German taxpayer'

This murderous plan for maintaining food supplies to the German population during the war and securing the lasting independence of German-dominated continental Europe from overseas food imports was already associated with a scheme for financing the war debt. In the 'General principles of economic policy in the newly-occupied eastern territories', approved at a meeting chaired by Göring on 8 November 1941, we read:

> By using cheap [agricultural] production methods and maintaining the present low living standards of the indigenous population, the maximum possible production surpluses will be generated to feed the Reich and the other European countries. In addition to supplying as much of Europe's needs in food and raw materials as possible, this will also open up a source of income for the Reich that will enable us to repay in a few years a substantial proportion of the debt incurred to finance the war while sparing the German taxpayer as far as possible.

When the experts from the Four-Year Plan Authority and the Ministry of Food declared that 'in future (...) southern Russia' would have to 'turn its face towards Europe', they meant not only that 'food surpluses' were to be squeezed out of it, but also that the country would 'obtain its industrial consumer goods from Germany or Europe'.[20] They therefore concluded that Russian manufacturing industry must be destroyed. An expert's report on the subject envisaged terms of trade hugely favourable to Germany, based on expensive exports of industrially produced consumer goods and cheap imports of raw materials, which would allow Germany to pay off its war debts as quickly as possible. This thinking too was promptly crystallized in the form of guidelines: 'Russian prices and wages must be kept as low as possible. Any disruption of this prices and wages policy, which will be geared exclusively to serving the interests of the Reich, will be severely punished.'[21]

These aims were clearly reflected in Hitler's 'monologues': 'The Ukraine and then the Volga basin will one day be the granary of Europe', and 'Belgian industry' – for example – 'will be able to exchange its products – cheap consumer goods – for corn from these regions'.[22] Likewise the notion of paying off war debts at the expense of the Soviet population, as developed by the Four-Year Plan

Authority think-tank, is also echoed by Hitler: 'We shall be a grain-exporting country for all in Europe who are dependent on grain imports. (...) We'll supply the Ukrainians with headscarves, glass bead necklaces and whatever else tickles the fancy of colonial peoples.'[23]

So the planned (and later partially implemented) mass murder of the Soviet civilian population was intended not just to secure supplies of food for the Reich for the duration of the war. Genocide was also designed to bring the German Reich long-term economic gains and trading advantages. Here, it seemed, was a solution to the problem of financing the war debt without burdening the German taxpayer. Through a one-off military-economic incursion the Soviet Union was to be relegated overnight to the status of a dependent agrarian state and a supplier of raw materials. This plan also accorded with the overall interests of German industry, which had stated that it had no interest in the continued existence of Russian manufacturing capacities.

Mass murder by common consent

The German leadership was largely in agreement on this plan. How broad that consensus was may be judged from the speech that Alfred Rosenberg gave on 20 June 1941 before the assembled staff of what would later become the Ministry for the Occupied Eastern Territories:

> Feeding the German people undoubtedly heads the list of demands that Germany will make upon the East in the coming years, and here the southern territories and northern Caucasia will have to make up the deficit in food supplies for the German people. We do not accept that we have any responsibility for feeding the Russian population as well from these surplus-producing regions. We know that this is a harsh necessity, which has no truck with pity or sentiment. A massive evacuation of the population will undoubtedly be necessary, and the Russians will certainly have some very hard years ahead of them.

Rosenberg then went on to reflect on 'the harsh necessity of evacuation', which called for 'strength of character' on the part of the perpetrators. While the Ukraine 'looked to the West', 'Muscovy' must 'turn its face to the East again' – to the 'Siberian outback'.[24]

Backe had put the same arguments to Hitler, who had signalled his approval. He demanded that the cut in the weekly meat ration be restored. But this proved to be a problem. At the eleventh meeting of the general council of the Four-Year Plan Authority on 24 June Backe spoke on the subject of meat: 'The reduction in the ration as from 2 June [1941], which also applied to the armed forces, was the only way of stretching our current stocks. A projection of our requirements for next year indicates a shortfall of 207,000 tonnes – based on the present ration of 400 grams – which drops to 67,000 tonnes if the ration is further cut to 350 grams. Increasing the ration again for the winter, which the Führer would like to do, is possible if several million cattle and pigs are slaughtered in Russia and shipped back to Germany.'[25]

On 28 June Goebbels made a further reference in his diary to Germany's food-supply problems: 'Food situation in Berlin is very bad. No potatoes, few vegetables. But Backe tells me things will be much better in a few weeks. (…) It's even worse in the occupied territories. There's real famine in some areas.'[26]

On 16 July Hitler, Rosenberg, Lammers, Keitel, Göring and Bormann discussed how they could best combine an offensive war with mass annihilation and the procurement of food supplies. Bormann kept a written record of the meeting, in which Hitler is quoted as saying: 'The motivation of our action must therefore be guided by tactical considerations.' And: 'None the less we can and shall take all the necessary measures – shootings, evacuations, etc.' During the meeting Göring observed that the first priority was to safeguard food supplies – 'all the rest could come much later'.[27] In the course of this meeting it was also confirmed that Backe's representative, Hans-Joachim Riecke, would be directly responsible for plundering Soviet food supplies.

On 27 July Göring approved the establishment of the 'Central Trading Company (East) for Agricultural Sales and Supplies', with the object of 'ensuring that all agricultural produce in the occupied eastern territories is collected by a central agency' and used exclusively for German interests. Working under Riecke's direction in the Trading Company was a team of import specialists from the German Corn Exchange in Hamburg.[28]

On 31 July the experts at the Economic Policy Unit for the East had a discussion chaired by Göring's deputy, undersecretary Körner. Regarding the Soviet Union, Backe said: 'Only very small quantities of food are available for feeding the non-agricultural population, since the bulk of the produce collected will be kept for feeding the troops and shipping off to the Reich.' In actual fact the plundering of corn and meat in the Soviet Union was largely carried out for the benefit of the three-million-strong German army, which resulted in severe famine among the indigenous population in large areas of the country. Körner added that Göring had issued 'clear instructions (...) that the interests of the German food economy must be given absolute precedence over all other food supply considerations in the newly occupied territories.'[29]

On 15 September the situation was discussed at a meeting attended by Göring, Backe, Riecke and the leadership of the armed forces. Göring's remarks are recorded in the minutes kept by a government official: '1. The Reichsmarschall gave orders that rations on the home front were not to be cut under any circumstances. 2. He said that he would never permit this to happen, since morale on the home front was a very significant factor for the defence of the Reich in wartime. (...) If any economies have to be made because of the present food-supply situation, they must be borne without exception by the nations we have conquered.' Göring continued: 'Even if one wanted to feed all the other inhabitants, it could not be done in the newly occupied eastern territories.'[30] He concluded with a statement of strategy that was soon to be applied to Leningrad: 'For economic reasons it is not advisable to take large cities by storm. It is better to encircle and besiege them.'[31]

This strategy of annihilation had clearly been discussed with Hitler. Sidestepping the fact that the offensive in the Soviet Union had ground to a halt, Hitler boasted about this selfsame strategy of encirclement and starvation in a speech he gave before the 'old guard' on 8 November 1941: 'I don't need to tell you that considerations of prestige have absolutely nothing to do with it. So if somebody today says that we are on the defensive in Leningrad... We were on the offensive before Leningrad for exactly the amount of time needed to encircle Leningrad. Now we are on the defensive, and it is up to the enemy to break out; he will either starve in Leningrad, or he will surrender!'[32]

In Göring's 'Guidelines for the occupied Soviet territories' – issued on the same day, 8 November – we read: 'For the present nothing at all can be done for the large cities (Moscow, Leningrad, Kiev). The resulting consequences are harsh but unavoidable.'[33] What he meant by that was spelled out quite clearly by Göring in a conversation with the Italian Foreign Minister two weeks later: 'This year 20 to 30 million people will starve in Russia...'

The fate that awaited the besieged populations of Leningrad and other Soviet cities was an open secret. On 27 November 1941, for example, the mayor of Hamburg, Carl V. Krogmann, noted in his diary: 'Glade from the central administration office, who is travelling on official business, reported on Leningrad and the conditions there. He believes the siege will last another 2–3 months. The food-supply situation in Petersburg is extremely bad, and the troops are getting just 150 g of bread a day and 400 g of meat a month; the civilian population is getting considerably less, of course. They reckon that most of the people in Leningrad, around 5½ millions, will starve.'[34]

Contrary to all assumptions and informed scientific projections, the blockade of Leningrad lasted 900 days. The calculations on which these projections were based were made by Professor Wilhelm Ziegelmayer, the resident nutrition expert at the Armed Forces High Command. On 10 September 1941 he wrote in his diary: 'In future we shall not burden ourselves with calls for the surrender of Leningrad. It must be destroyed by a scientifically proven method.' To that end, Ziegelmayer calculated the stocks of food remaining in the city and the number of people living there, including those who had taken refuge there. He even underestimated their number. Based on these calculations, Ziegelmayer concluded 'that people cannot physically live on such a ration', and that it was therefore unnecessary to risk the lives of German soldiers by attempting to take the city by force. Ziegelmayer could not understand how the population of Leningrad was able to hold out against the blockade for two and a half years until the besieging German troops were finally forced to retreat. Shortly after the end of the war he became the senior nutrition expert for the Soviet-occupied zone, where his standard work – *Rohstoff-Fragen der deutschen Volksernährung* [Sourcing Raw Materials to Feed the German Nation] – was immediately reprinted, albeit with the omission of the chapter 'Looking ahead to the new continental economy' which had been included in the 1941 edition. In his new post Ziegelmayer was naturally in contact with Russian colleagues. On the subject of Leningrad he said to one of them: 'I'm just an old-fashioned nutritionist. It's a mystery to me how you managed to pull off such a miracle.'[35]

As incorrect as Ziegelmayer's calculations turned out to be, the hunger blockade nevertheless claimed more than 600,000 victims. Documentary evidence is available to show that the German war strategists looked upon the starvation of millions of people in the Soviet Union not only as a 'necessary' concomitant of their war, but also as a population control measure that supplemented other methods of annihilation.[36] In a teletype message sent on 6 November 1941 Martin Sandberger, head of the security police and the SD in Estonia, suggested to Ohlendorf and Müller in the Central Office for the Security of the Reich that the 'racially superior' Estonians should be evacuated from the area around Leningrad 'because the mortality rate in the whole area is going to be very high in the coming months for reasons relating to the food supply and for other reasons'.[37] By 'other reasons' Sandberger meant mass shootings.

On 1 December 1942 Göring reaffirmed the starvation policy line: 'The food-supply situation in Europe as a whole makes it necessary to procure the largest possible agricultural surpluses from the occupied eastern territories to feed the troops and the population of the Reich for the foreseeable future. In order to achieve this the local food consumption of the indigenous population must be kept as low as possible.'[38]

The provisional results of this policy were summarized by Hans-Joachim Riecke on 3 February 1942 in a confidential briefing for journalists:

> We are getting deeper and deeper into the forest zone, an area that relies heavily on imports of agricultural produce. (...) Now let me say a word or two about the problem of feeding the civilian population in the towns and cities of Russia, since word of this has got back to Germany in one way and another, even though it is not exactly intended for public consumption. I pointed out from the very beginning, two months before the start of operations, that the problem of supplying Leningrad with food simply could not be solved if the city was to fall into our hands. For political reasons I think this is impractical. We must not give the enemy any opportunity to make us look responsible for the famine conditions. The whole of the Leningrad area relies on supplies being brought in from outside. (...) So it is not surprising that we are now seeing signs of severe famine in the countryside up in the north too. The same applies more or less to all the large cities.[39]

Hans-Joachim Riecke (1899–1987) volunteered for military service in the First World War in 1914, at the age of fifteen, and later joined a Freikorps unit of volunteer marauders fighting the 'red peril' in the Baltic states. He subsequently studied agriculture, joined the NSDAP in 1925 and became an official in the Westphalian Chamber of

Agriculture. He rose rapidly through the ranks of the Third Reich hierarchy. From 1936 onwards he became the closest collaborator of Herbert Backe, who made him an undersecretary in 1944.

In his person Riecke united key functions of the Reich Ministry of Food, the Four-Year Plan Authority, the Ministry for the Occupied Eastern Territories and the Economic Policy Unit for the East. In this accumulation of offices he was following in the footsteps of Gustav Schlotterer. In 1944 the Economic Policy Unit for the East recommended him for the award of the 'Knight's Cross with swords', in recognition of his contribution to the war effort: in just three years the organization he headed had plundered 6.9 million tonnes of grain, 763,000 tonnes of oil-seeds, 664,000 tonnes of meat and 150,000 tonnes of fats from the Soviet Union, thus ensuring that 'food supplies to the German people could be maintained at their previous level'.[40] Over and above this, the Wehrmacht had requisitioned several times these quantities for its own needs.

In accordance with the policy line of starving out the enemy, the plundering of grain took priority over maintaining the availability of labour resources and improving food supplies to the subjugated peoples of eastern Europe as part of a strategy of pacification. Theoretical arguments were adduced to support this position. Thus Riecke declared even the Ukraine – which was not part of the forest zone, and where millions of people had already died as a result of Stalinist enforced collectivization, deportation and starvation – to be an overpopulated region still. In March 1942 he found himself 'faced with the question (...) of whether it will be necessary to carry out major resettlements of the indigenous population under the terms of the [new, reprivatizing] agrarian order'. Riecke explained why: 'There are very densely populated rural areas there, with extraordinarily large numbers working on the individual collective farms. (...) There is no possibility of allocating land to all these people. That would lead to fragmentation, with large numbers of small farms that are no longer economically viable. It would also be a waste of manpower.'[41] The head of the central department of politics in the Reich Ministry for the Occupied Eastern Territories, Otto Bräutigam, wrote in 1942:

> With 78 households and 484 hectares of cultivable land to one collective farm in 1937, when mechanization was already well advanced, the amount of usable land available to one farm unit was no more than 6.8 hectares. Under these conditions there was virtually no possibility of utilizing all the available labour

resources. No doubt the extermination of the kulak class during collectivization, the migration of many rural dwellers into the towns and cities and the rise in mortality as a consequence of collectivist famine had done something to reduce the numbers of agricultural workers, but to the last there were excessively large reserves of them still on the collective farms. In 1937, for example, 11.4 per cent of men and 56 per cent of women, including private smallholdings and households, were out of work.[42]

And in 1943 the 'Publications for the Ideological Education of the NSDAP' noted: '…the Ukraine, White Russia and major portions of the Baltic states are regions characterized by rural overpopulation.'[43]

Six thousand dead prisoners of war every day

The strategy of annihilation by famine found its clearest expression in the 900-day siege of Leningrad, and in the systematic practice of allowing Soviet prisoners of war to starve to death. From the start of the war against the Soviet Union an average of six thousand POWs died each day for the next seven months. Many died of hunger and other privations, others were systematically shot en masse. When the Blitzkrieg ground to a halt before Moscow, and the representatives of the Four-Year Plan Authority thought about putting the Russian POWs to work, the head of the 'labour deployment unit' summarized the situation on 19 February 1942 in these terms: 'There were 3.9 million Russians available, of whom only 1.1 million are still left. Between November 41 and January 42 alone 500,000 Russians have died.'[44] Within a period of a little over six months some two million Soviet prisoners had starved, and tens of thousands more had been shot in captivity. Neither the onset of winter nor actual difficulties over supplies can plausibly be blamed for the death rate in the camps. In fact rather fewer Soviet troops entered German captivity than had been projected by the Armed Forces High Command. From the outset the Wehrmacht propaganda machine had been claiming that the food-supply problems were the result of Soviet policy. This propaganda line was in complete accord with Hitler's insistence that their real motives must be concealed from the world, but that they must none the less carry out all the 'necessary measures – shootings, evacuations, etc.' In reality the responsibility for the starvation of Soviet prisoners of war lay fairly and squarely with the Germans.

As early as August 1941 the German military intelligence officer

Helmuth James Count von Moltke wrote to his wife: 'The news from the East is again dreadful. We have obviously suffered very great losses. That would be bearable, but for the hecatombs of corpses that lie upon our shoulders. We are constantly hearing reports that transports of POWs or Jews are arriving with only 20 per cent of the people alive, that famine is rife in the prison camps, that typhus and every other kind of deficiency disease have broken out.'[45] Between June 1941 and 15 April 1942 a total of 309,816 Soviet prisoners of war, the vast majority of them healthy young men, died in the prison camps in the Government General – more than 85 per cent of the prison population in these camps.[46] By the end of the winter of 1941–2 the prison camp at Bergen-Belsen was 'almost completely dead and deserted'. And out of all the Russian POWs who had survived the marches and transports to the German camps, nearly half had 'died from hunger and typhus' by April 1942, according to the Wehrmacht's quartermaster-general.[47] From the very beginning, the political and military leadership were at one with Backe and his nutrition experts in their determination to allow the Soviet prisoners only 'the bare minimum food ration', in order to avoid 'putting pressure on German food supplies'. What the agencies responsible for the prisoners of war understood by the 'bare minimum food ration' was 700 to 1,000 calories a day, a ration that must inevitably lead to death by starvation within a matter of weeks. Up until 31 October 1941 the officially prescribed rations – and those actually dispensed were considerably smaller – were progressively cut, and the officers responsible for feeding the POWs were repeatedly reminded that they must 'apply very strict standards (...) as every portion of food too many which is given to the POWs must be taken from the mouths of our families back home or from the German troops'.[48]

On 15 September 1941 Göring and Backe again sought to justify this planned and premeditated policy of annihilation to those in the Wehrmacht who were responsible for carrying it out: 'In feeding the Bolshevist prisoners we are not bound by any international obligations, as we are when feeding other prisoners. Their rations must therefore be based solely on the value of their labour for us.'[49] Food supplies that could not be shipped out of the occupied areas of the Soviet Union immediately were to be 'stockpiled at certain secure points as reserve stores for the Reich', and were on no account to be issued to prisoners of war or 'devoured by the local population roaming at large'.[50] Officially this policy changed after 31 October 1941, when it was decided that Soviet prisoners should now be put to work for the Germans. But initially this made little difference in practice: while the prisoners of war represented 'a necessary addition to manpower', they could not be used for that purpose 'in their present condition' and would 'succumb to exhaustion in large numbers'. What *that* meant was spelled out by the army's quartermaster-general, General Eduard Wagner, at the same meeting of 13 November 1941: 'Non-working prisoners of war in the camps will be left to starve.' And Wagner put this in the context of the overall German strategy for depopulation, based on famine and starvation: the problem of feeding the cities was, he said, 'insoluble...it is absolutely clear that Leningrad in particular must be starved out'.[51]

'Lack of space – decimation of the population'

In June 1941 Hitler had demanded 'that the cut in the meat ration be restored in the autumn'. And after the start of the war against the Soviet Union Göring said: 'The home front is standing firm for two reasons that make this war different from the [First] World War: (1) losses are light, and (2) living standards are being maintained.'[52] In the preface to Backe's book *Um die Nahrungsfreiheit Europas*, published in 1941, we read: 'The defining characteristic of a "granary" as such has always been its low population density.'[53] In a 'Draft for a presentation to the Führer' dated 19 August 1943 Backe included the note: 'Lack of space – decimation of the population'.[54] Göring's analysts in the Four-Year Plan Authority had already reviewed the outcome of this policy in October 1942: 'Since the population in the occupied (Soviet) territories has fallen by a quarter to two-thirds, and on average by a third, and the (wheat) rations will no longer be 250 kg as in peacetime, and assuming that peacetime harvest yields are more or less maintained, we can reckon on a surplus of more than a quarter, so that not only the German shortfall in bread cereals but also the European shortfall can be made up just from southern Russia alone.'[55] By this time the people at whose expense these 'surpluses' were being requisitioned had already been driven into the planned starvation zones beyond the German front; and many had died as a result of this policy of starvation and terror.

In the light of Backe's plans for maintaining food supplies to central and western Europe by the genocide in the Soviet Union, one has to ask whether the deportation and murder of large numbers of Hungarian Jews in 1944 was not connected in some way with these plans. On the face of it the deportation seems peculiarly pointless at a time when defeat was staring Germany in the face – and it was carried out in great haste. This is generally interpreted as an attempt by Hitler, Himmler and Eichmann to complete the annihilation of the European Jews at the last minute without regard for the exigencies of war or their own interests. While we cannot adduce proof for our alternative hypothesis, we nevertheless believe that the existence of a connection between these deportations and German food-supply policy is entirely plausible and deserving of further examination.

The Jewish minority in Hungary accounted for 10–14 per cent of the total population, depending on how the figure is calculated. In 1943, when it was becoming clear that the Ukraine would be lost, the German food-supply experts demanded that Hungary should supply five times more bread cereals to Germany than it had in 1942. In all they called for 450,000 tonnes, even though there was already 'a significant shortage of bread, flour, fat and meat' in Hungary itself.[56] Nevertheless an extra 360,000 tonnes of bread cereals were to be shipped to the Reich. This corresponds fairly closely to the quantity of food needed to provide a subsistence-level diet for a million people – approximately the size of the Jewish minority in Hungary, according to German estimates. We therefore think it conceivable that in the wake of the Wehrmacht's defeats in the Soviet Union the dubious distinction of being the 'most important granary' for the German Reich now passed to south-east Europe, and that this function was to be safeguarded by 'measures for decimating the population' of the kind already used in the Soviet Union.

Whether the decision taken in 1941 to murder the European Jews was also determined in part by the desire to reduce the total population of Europe for food-policy reasons is a question that at least deserves serious consideration.[57] The existence of such a linkage is suggested by the simultaneous pursuit of projects to annihilate the Soviet civilian population and the whole of the Jewish minority in Europe. It is also suggested by a number of statements made by Backe. And it is made abundantly clear in a report written by Peter-Heinz Seraphim. In the autumn of 1941 Seraphim was working as a war administration officer in the Ukraine, and here the man who had constantly pushed for a 'definitive solution of the Jewish question' now witnessed mass shootings in person. These were 'dreadful', he wrote, and his report went on: 'The type of solution to the Jewish question practised in the Ukraine', while it had many adverse consequences, including economic ones, did at least have the merit of 'removing some of the unwanted extra mouths from the towns and cities'. Seraphim then described the conflicting aims of this policy from his perspective:

> A skimming-off of agricultural surpluses from the Ukraine for purposes of feeding the Reich is therefore only feasible if inland traffic within the Ukraine is reduced to a minimum. Efforts will be made to achieve this:
>
> 1. by exterminating the unwanted extra mouths to feed (Jews, population of the larger Ukrainian cities, which, like Kiev, will receive no food rations at all);
> 2. by reducing to an absolute minimum the rations available to the Ukrainians in the remaining towns and cities;
> 3. by cutting the food consumption of the rural population.[58]

Here, then, the murder of the Jewish minority in the Soviet Union is seen as one part of a general strategy of annihilation developed by the German food-supply specialists. It is quite likely that Backe also argued along these lines. He was guided by two maxims. One stated that the struggle in which the German nation was engaged must not be made more difficult 'by food shortages in any shape or form'.[59] The other was his implacable anti-Semitism.

When confronted with his murderous plans by Robert Kempner, one of the prosecutors at the Nuremberg trials, Backe hanged himself, fearing that he would be handed over to the Russians. In the words of a memorandum prepared for Heinrich Himmler, Herbert Backe was 'a frank, indeed a brutally frank character'.[60]

CHAPTER 12

THE 'GENERAL PLAN FOR THE EAST'

Planning for expansion all the way to the Crimea

With the start of the war against the Soviet Union the German territorial and economic planners believed they now had virtually unlimited freedom of action. Victory appeared to be within Germany's grasp, and suddenly all things seemed possible. In June 1941 the Institute for German Development Work in the East in Cracow prepared a memorandum on the subject of 'The evacuation of the Poles'.[1] A professor was commissioned by the Armed Forces High Command to carry out anthropological studies on Soviet prisoners of war, and one of the options he proposed was 'the liquidation of the Russian people'.[2] On 12 July 1939 a Wehrmacht general in occupied Prague had declared that in order to 'destroy the Czech national community as a geographical and spiritual presence ... the radical recourse to physical extermination is not possible under normal circumstances'.[3] But there too the time now appeared ripe for 'an immediate ethnic cleansing of the body politic and a fundamental restructuring of the economy'.[4] On 8 August 1941 a speaker for the German Labour Front announced, to the horror of the SD in occupied Czechoslovakia: 'The "Wenzels" [meaning the Czechs] are only guests in this country. If they are not prepared to change their attitude in the course of this war, they could end up in a country on the far side of the Urals with plenty of time to reflect.'[5]

But above all, the start of the war against the Soviet Union enabled the planners at the RKF to extend their radius of action. Building on their work in the annexed western provinces of Poland, they devised the so-called 'General Plan for the East', aimed at changing the demographic and economic structure of eastern Europe from the Crimea in the south-east to the Leningrad approaches in the north-east. Once again these far-reaching proposals were predicated on colonization by resettled Germans, the expulsion of 'alien ethnic groups' and the

Germanization of a select portion of the indigenous populations. Writing in 1941, Konrad Meyer, head of planning at the RKF, was exultant: 'The victory of our arms and the expansion of our frontiers have burst old bounds.'[6]

In his reflections Meyer set great store by the new 'possibilities for solutions' that had presented themselves through the 'opening-up of the East'. The 'mighty tasks' that had 'arisen' for the German nation were not confined to the Germanization and 'reconstruction of the conquered territories'. Rather the visionaries of 'reconstruction' were intent on 'overhauling' the entire social fabric of the Reich, which they saw as obsolete and broken-down. The social engineering that had begun in the frontier regions would now carry over into the Reich homeland, and they looked upon the population movements and restructuring processes in the East 'as a first and necessary step towards a fundamental reordering of the nation and its territorial sphere'.

Expanding on this, Meyer wrote that the great 'process of reordering' would begin 'with the restructuring of the economy, the elimination of overmanning in the trades and professions, the planning and ordered management of production, markets and prices, and the organization of purchasing power'. Ultimately this would lead 'to the complete reshaping of the pattern of settlement'. In this man's fevered imagination, just about anything was possible following the military victory in the East. With the new freedom of action thus acquired, the shortage of labour in Germany could be overcome, new markets could be created for industry and agricultural manpower could be fully utilized. In sum, the aim was to achieve a 'systematic loosening-up and restoration to health of our entire social and economic order'.[7] And when the 'primitive and low-spending' indigenous population in eastern Europe had been supplanted by 'a German population with high levels of consumption', then the process of industrial expansion in the newly conquered territories would 'be able to enter its full development'.[8]

But all this was contingent upon changing the population structure. As with the annexed eastern territories, the German planners saw this as a first and necessary measure that had to be put in place before they could set about the task of 'developing' and 'reshaping'. A close collaborator of Meyer wrote: 'The various regions and zones can only fulfil their particular roles and function as autonomous entities if the following factors have been correctly constituted: population density, population distribution, occupational and social breakdown, gradation of incomes and wealth. The population density must be no higher than is required for the full development of the biological force.'[9] In plain language this meant that the population density was judged to be too high, and therefore had to be reduced. The composition and structure of the population was to be changed at the same time.

Just one day before the German attack on the Soviet Union was launched, Himmler officially charged Meyer's planning department at the RKF with the task of drawing up a 'General Plan for the East'. This was intended as a blueprint for colonization and restructuring – not only for the whole of occupied Poland, but also for large expanses of the Soviet Union, which the Germans hoped to occupy soon. In fact Meyer had been working on this project for some considerable time, with Himmler's knowledge and agreement. Hence the fact that he was able to present a first draft of his plan only three weeks later, on 15 July. This draft has been lost, but it is possible to reconstruct it in broad outline from various reports,[10] preliminary sketches, partial plans and a surviving later draft from July 1942.[11]

The people destined to be deported or murdered on the planners' drawing-boards – and soon enough in reality too – were no longer counted, as they had been in the annexed eastern territories, in hundreds of thousands or even a few millions, as later. Now the planners were making strategic policy decisions that affected the entire populations of Poland and Russia, and the only question was whether the number of people to be 'resettled' was 31 million, or whether the figure was closer to 45 or 51 million. Expulsion, enforced Germanization, slave labour and social restructuring, the razing of entire cities and industrial centres, the murder of millions: in the thinking of the population experts these were self-evident necessities, on a par with modern propaganda for birth control. Common to all the plans for a new demographic and economic order in the East was the intention to expel large parts of the population of Poland and Russia, to kill many of these people, and to 'Germanize' the land on which they had hitherto lived with the aid of an imported German elite. Nor was it just a matter of making room for 'German colonists'.

Like occupied Poland before it, the western Soviet Union was seen as a region still afflicted by agricultural overpopulation – despite collectivization and the policy of starvation practised by Stalin between 1930 and 1933. In one scheme submitted in connection with the General Plan for the East we read: 'The land that lies between Vilna,

Kazan, Saratov and Odessa [the region in which most of the Soviet Jews were living] is already suffering from agricultural overpopulation.' The remaining areas of the Soviet Union were looked upon as 'fully settled or well populated', or else as 'agriculturally unsuitable'.[12] In a report prepared for those in charge of Germany's war economy the Berlin agronomist Wladimir von Poletika wrote in 1941: 'Despite its low overall population density Russia suffers from serious rural overpopulation, even by comparison with the countries of western Europe.' Worst affected, according to this writer, was the Ukraine, the most important region for Germany's purposes.[13]

As we have already seen, the purpose of the general planning initiative was not simply to bring about a reduction in population numbers and the reorganization of social structures and the system of production 'in the East'. It was also an attempt to head off foreseeable structural crises within the German Reich itself. Or as Konrad Meyer put it (here writing in 1940, when his horizons were limited to the annexed eastern territories):

> What is about to take shape and form at the new frontiers of the Reich is an expression of the national interest, which by its example will affect conditions back in the Reich homeland. It will bring about a loosening-up of social and national structures, and – with proper planning and direction of the great process of population migration now beginning – it will lead to a reform of the agrarian economy and indeed of the entire social order throughout the Reich. For in the Reich homeland we not only have an agricultural population living in part on too little land with poor-quality soil, who need to be given more space: we also have much 'redrawing of boundaries' to do in the commercial and skilled trade sectors as well.[14]

Herbert Backe argued along the same lines: 'In parallel with the colonization of the newly acquired territories (...) it will also be possible to convert many non-viable small farms and smallholdings back home into going agricultural concerns, which will support the use of modern machinery.'[15] Hitler too was enthusiastic about the idea of expelling and annihilating Soviet peasant and worker families as a means of solving problems in the Reich: 'We can take our poor working-class families from Thuringia or the mountains of Bohemia, say, and give them plenty of space.'[16] The German Labour Front – as we learn from their report on the opportunities for colonization in the conquered eastern territories – was hopeful that in Germany 'at least 700,000 small and struggling farms will disappear' and that 'a one-off transfer of German nationals to the East [should] take place, in order to improve the economic and social structure in the Reich homeland'.[17] The German Labour Front was a civilian mass organization, but its estimates went far beyond those of Himmler's planning office, which reckoned on only '220,000 farming families' becoming available for resettlement in the East 'following a restructuring of the overpopulated agricultural regions in the Reich'.[18] But by the end of 1942, it seems, someone had actually done the sums. In a secret draft regional plan for the occupied Baltic states, and more specifically in the section examining the role of 'the Ostland [the occupied Baltic states] in the Greater European trading area', we learn that an audit of the German agricultural industry had been carried out to 'determine the number of farms that qualify for relocation to the East'. The audit revealed that 500,000–600,000 farms had to be classed as 'in need of repair and improvement'. 'Of these some 250,000–300,000 can be considered for relocation to the East, which amounts to approximately one million of the agricultural population.'[19]

In the later draft of the General Plan for the East, Konrad Meyer distinguishes between 'settlement areas' and three 'forward settlement zones' and 'base settlements'. He wanted the 'settlement areas' (which included the annexed portions of western Poland) to be Germanized as quickly as possible. The 'forward settlement zones' were to be partially Germanized over a period of twenty-five years: this would affect up to 50 per cent of the population in rural regions and up to 25 per cent in the towns, which were also to be reduced in size. The regions in question were the Crimea and the area around Kherson (the 'Gotengau'), the area around Leningrad (Ingria) and West Lithuania/Bialystok (the 'Memel and Narev' region). Meanwhile the Transylvanian Germans, instead of being repatriated to the Reich, were apparently to form a further 'forward settlement zone' under the terms of the General Plan for the East. In between, at intervals of approximately 100 kilometres 'along the mainline railway and autobahn routes', thirty-six German 'base settlements' were to be established. To that end, a corresponding number of Soviet towns were singled out for Germanization, extending to 25 per cent of the population in the first instance. The new German occupants were to turn these towns into forward bases from which to conduct further colonization operations in the future. The necessary space had been created in the towns concerned in 1941–2: 'Germanization' was made possible by mass shootings and deportations of the towns' original inhabitants, particularly the Jewish population. In the proposed 'Germanic base' of Vilna, 28 per cent of the population had been Jewish prior to that, in Tarnów 43 per cent, in Rovno 56 per cent…

The General Plan earmarked the following towns and cities to serve as German bases: Vilnius, Daugavpils, Rezekne, Pytalovo, Pskov, Luga, Narva, Siauliai, Riga, Valga, Tartu, Paide, Tallinn, Rakvere (Estonia), Cracow, Tarnów, Jaslo, Zamosc, Przemysl, Lvov, Czestochowa, Kielce, Sandomierz, Radom, Lublin, Siedlce, Warsaw, Tomaszów, Rovno, Shepetovka, Berdichev, Belaya Tserkov, Bobrinsk, Pyatikhatki, Krivoy Rog, Nikolayev. This concept was the equivalent, in colonization policy terms, of Backe's plans. It also complemented the strategies of the military and of the war economy planners. It meant, quite simply, that the Ukraine and the Baltic states were to be encircled from their furthest extremities – from Leningrad to the Crimea – by German 'forward settlement zones', while the bases in between were designed to split up the indigenous peoples, isolate them from their neighbours and paralyse them politically. The head of racial affairs at the Ministry for the Occupied Eastern Territories, Erhard Wetzel, wrote: 'There is no doubt that this administrative fragmentation of Russian territory, allied to the systematic development of the individual regions along separate and divergent lines, is one way to prevent the growth of Russian nationalism.'[20]

Thus the General Plan for the East combined the concept for making continental Europe self-sufficient in food supplies with strategies aimed at achieving permanent German hegemony. While Germany's agricultural experts were intent on cutting off the western parts of the Soviet Union from the rest of the country and redirecting grain supplies from the southern regions of the USSR to central Europe – in the full knowledge that millions of people would starve as a result – the General Plan for the East also envisaged the destruction of Leningrad and its population. This merits no more than an oblique passing mention: 'The future urban population of Ingria was put at 200,000 (1939: 3,200,000).'[21] In the aforementioned draft regional plan for eastern Europe of November 1942 it was assumed that this region would be 'relatively depopulated following the cessation of hostilities'.[22] In an older version of the General Plan for the East an additional 'forward settlement zone' was planned for the Middle Dnieper basin – so the intention had clearly been to obliterate the city of Kiev as well.[23]

12,400 million man-hours for 'development'

The July 1942 version of the General Plan for the East has survived in a six-page summary and an extended document of about forty pages. It is subtitled 'The legal, economic and territorial foundations of Eastern development'. While the legal underpinnings of land seizure and land settlement are of no further interest in the present context, it is important for our understanding of population policy to discover exactly *how* it was proposed to create 'forward outposts of the Reich' and 'bases against Russian and Asiatic elements' in selected 'front-line' regions.[24]

The plan called for these regions to be placed not under the general German military or civilian administration, but under Himmler and his organization. Alfred Rosenberg and the leadership team at his newly created Ministry for the Occupied Eastern Territories opposed this as an unwarranted interference in their jurisdiction.[25] In the colonization of the East the importance of 'shared regional origins' was very much to the fore. Each 'base' was to be colonized by Germans from one particular area or region, and these home regions would then 'act as sponsors to at least one district in the East'.[26]

Meyer and his deputy Felix Boesler, a professor of public finance from Jena, believed that only a very small part of the funding for the General Plan for the East should come from the Reich budget and from private investment. The whole enterprise was to be funded from stolen assets (or 'newly accumulated special assets of the RKF', as they were termed) and the ruthless exploitation of foreign labour ('Savings could be achieved by the use of cheap labour put to work in large gangs.'[27]). What level of savings the architects of the General Plan had in mind can be seen from the fact that they had estimated the total labour input for their 'development measures' at 12,400 million man-hours. The financing proposals of Boesler and Meyer were summed up by Himmler thus: 'If we do not make the bricks here [in the East], if we do not fill our camps with slaves – and in present company I prefer to call a spade a spade – with slave labourers who will build our towns, our villages and our farms regardless of losses, then we shall not have the money, even after one year of war, to furnish and equip the settlements to a standard such that true Germans can actually live there and put down roots in the first generation.'[28] This view undoubtedly formed part of the first version of the

General Plan, because on 20 October 1941 those in charge of directing the war economy judged it necessary to take 'measures aimed at maintaining the capacity for work' of those Soviet prisoners of war who would be needed 'for intensive post-war labour duties in the eastern territories'. Skilled construction workers and stonemasons were especially in demand.[29]

But the idea was to cover all expenditure, whether defined as private or public, from the proceeds of robbing and plundering. So even in areas where it was not possible to exploit local labour directly, the massive programme of investment had to be financed by the occupied countries themselves. The possibility of development loans was ruled out by implication: 'The means to develop the settlements will have to be provided largely from local resources.'[30] But under the conditions then prevailing in Poland and the Soviet Union this meant that a section of the population had to be deprived of the means of subsistence. It was not as if the Germans were planning to invest in higher productivity, in order to facilitate the accumulation of capital for the 'development of the settlements': their only concern at this stage was to upgrade the infrastructure so that they could dominate and plunder the country more effectively. A rough estimate put the required investment – not counting cheap forced labour – at 65,000 million Reichsmarks over a period of twenty-five years. In addition, the Four-Year Plan Authority planned to use the profits from Soviet grain to pay off Germany's war debts and to exact 'tribute payments' to meet the costs of occupation.

Mass murder and birth control

The concept of Germanization was modified in July 1942 in favour of a three-tier society graded according to racist criteria. By this time the authors of the General Plan for the East no longer took 'Germanization' to mean the expulsion of all non-Germans, but instead regarded the process as 'completed once all the land has been transferred into German ownership and the professional classes, civil servants, salaried employees, skilled workers and their families are all Germans'.[31] These new criteria were adopted not least because the 'nation without a land' ['Volk ohne Raum'] simply did not have enough people to carry through the 1942 colonization plans for eastern Europe. Although the German authorities did their utmost, through propaganda and financial incentives, to encourage families to have more children, the 'population surplus' in the Reich was nowhere near sufficient. So to supplement the numbers they planned to bring in Germans living overseas and involve other nationals 'of kindred stock' – meaning Dutchmen, Flemings, Danes and Norwegians – in the enterprise of colonization and subjugation. In line with these plans Hitler wanted to 'channel them into the eastern territories' so that they could become 'members of the German Reich'.[32] And it was even proposed to integrate the 'valuable' sections of the Polish and Soviet populations into this scheme. The precise quotas were fiercely debated, but the ultimate intention of the planners was to isolate 'desirable' categories of persons from the 'eastern peoples' and to subject them to long-term Germanization. In other words, they were to be torn from their cultural roots and forcibly made into Germans. But the concept of 'race' as such played a notably subordinate role in the summer of 1942. The first criterion for the Germanization of 'non-Germanic ethnic stock' was defined by the General Plan for the East as 'whether or not the persons concerned can be brought up to German levels of productivity and achievement'.[33]

In 1940 the German population planners were still demanding that the annexed eastern territories – western Poland, in other words – should be completely colonized by Germans. But in the 1942 version of the General Plan for the East this had changed: two-fifths of the rural population in these provinces were to remain as 'alien minority' labourers with limited rights, while in the towns and cities they were to make up almost half the population.[34] So the 'adjustment of ethnic borders' that had previously been the aim, with separate and distinct German and Polish settlements clearly demarcated, had now been dropped. In line with the new policy thinking, the 'settler requirement' for the annexed provinces of western Poland in 1942 was revised sharply downwards: instead of the five to six million people from the Reich who were originally to have been relocated there, the number was now put at just one and a half million.

The broader aim of 'permeating the expanses of the East with German life' remained intact. But since there was not sufficient 'German life' available to accomplish this task, the pursuit of this programme against the Polish and Soviet population made it necessary 'to match the area of land to the number of German persons available at any given time'.[35] These 'German persons' were now cast in the role of a managerial elite, while the 'remaining alien minority population' would make up 'the lower classes of society'.[36] Or, in the analogy favoured by the participants in a discussion on the General

Plan at the Ministry for the Occupied Eastern Territories: 'The Germans will be the Spartans, the middle class, consisting of Letts, Estonians, etc., will be the *perioikoi*, while the Russians will be the helots.'[37]

According to Meyer's calculations, 4.9 million people would become available over a period of twenty-five years to meet the demand for German 'Spartans' – although this total also included 750,000 Estonians and Letts, persons of 'non-Germanic ethnic origin' who 'can be recruited by systematic selection and grooming for achievement' to become 'Spartans' instead of 'perioikoi'.[38]

The 'achievement principle' is likewise the only criterion mentioned in the concluding remarks on how to proceed with the indigenous population. Here the word 'evacuation' features prominently. The 'evacuations' that had previously been carried out were now to be abandoned in favour of 'selections'. Persons who were to have been deported under the original plan were to be 'pacified' in the summer of 1942 by 'relocation' and the 'social advancement of positive elements' – the 'perioikoi' paradigm, in other words. 'Race' does not figure at all in this discussion, whose agenda is set instead by political expediency and the demands of demographic economics. The policy of 'evacuation' – the extermination of the Jews in eastern Europe, the killing and deportation of millions of Polish and Soviet men, women and children and the murder of prisoners of war – is here discussed as an integral part of the population policy concept underlying the General Plan for the East. Under the subheading 'Relationship with contiguous peoples' we read:

> Since the collaboration of the present [!] native population cannot be dispensed with, the new ethnic and demographic order to be created in the East must aim at the pacification of the existing inhabitants. This will be achieved by making available the land needed for incoming German settlers not, as hitherto, by means of evacuations, but by transferring the previous occupants to land formerly belonging to collective or state-owned farms and simultaneously giving them rights of land ownership. This transfer must be conditional upon a proper selection process based on the achievement principle, and must go hand in hand with the social advancement of positive elements within the alien ethnic stock.[39]

This passage (it comes from the July 1942 draft of the General Plan) must be seen as a response to criticism of the radical resettlement plans outlined in the earlier drafts that had been voiced by the Ministry for the Occupied Eastern Territories (amongst others). On the mass murder of the Jewish minority, however, there was complete agreement. In eastern Europe the so-called 'half-Jews' were also included, on the grounds that the latter were 'a mixture of Jews and other racially undesirables of alien ethnic stock'.[40]

The original – or a later – draft of the General Plan for the East had called for 31 million people to be deported, leaving 14 million in the colonization areas as labourers and candidates for Germanization. This is revealed in a document that bears the title 'Observations and thoughts on the General Plan for the East of the SS Reichsführer'. This position paper was presented on 27 April 1942 by Erhard Wetzel, the aforementioned head of racial affairs at the Ministry for the Occupied Eastern Territories.[41] Here the writer explains why he is sceptical about the forcible evacuation of undesirable persons from the Baltic states: 'The fact is that those of alien ethnic stock who are acceptable to us would be pretty clear in their own minds that such an enforced evacuation would mean the end of their brothers and sisters.' So Wetzel himself, at least, was evidently 'pretty clear in his own mind' what 'evacuation' – a word he uses in quotation marks – really meant. And while it did not necessarily always mean immediate physical extermination, it was plain enough that most of the deportees would not survive hunger, cold and hard labour in Siberia – if indeed they survived the journey there.

Wetzel's criticism of the draft General Plan and the proposals for 'Germanization' and 'evacuation' outlined therein was that the planners had got their numbers wrong by some 15–20 million people. The figure of 45 million persons from 'dependent minority races' 'in the East' quoted in the draft General Plan was far too low in Wetzel's estimation, because it failed to take account of natural population growth. In addition he pointed out: 'The only way we can arrive at the figure of 45 million is to assume that the 5 to 6 million Jews living in this area will be eliminated prior to evacuation. Yet it is clear from the discussion in the Plan that the Jews are still included in that total of 45 million.' So the sums did not add up. Realistically one would have to work on the basis of 60 to 65 million people, subject to one condition: 'A resettlement of the Jews referred to throughout the Plan will not be necessary once the Jewish question has been resolved.' The work of 'resolving' this 'question' had just then got under way in earnest, as Wetzel knew full well. He it was, after all, who had sat down together with specialists from the Chancellery of the Führer six months earlier to discuss the production and installation of the 'accommodation and gassing equipment necessary for the solution of the Jewish question'.

'If one assumes,' continues Wetzel in his position paper, 'that 14 million persons of foreign ethnic origin will remain in the areas concerned, as the Plan envisages, this means that 46–51 million people will have to be evacuated' – so not 'just' the 31 million referred to in the Plan. In the process, the Polish population was to be almost completely exterminated: 'The Plan envisages the evacuation of 80–85 per cent of the Polish population,' summarizes Wetzel, 'i.e. 16 to 20.4 million Poles – depending on whether we start from an overall figure of 20 or 24 million Poles – would be evacuated, leaving something between 3 and 4.8 million Poles in the German area of colonization.' Wetzel was not opposed to this procedure in principle, he just thought it 'went too far'.[42]

Leaving aside these arguments about numbers, by the summer of 1942 the architects of annihilation had already accomplished many of the aims that their policy of mass murder was designed to achieve in terms of eradicating 'undesirable' and 'superfluous' population groups. Those aims included the total annihilation of the Jews in eastern Europe – about five million people – under the terms of the General Plan for the East. They also included the systematic starving to death of Soviet prisoners of war, who now numbered more than two millions. The annihilation of Leningrad's three million inhabitants was imminent, in Meyer's view, and remained – as we have already seen – part of the revised draft of the General Plan for the East. In addition the number of Soviet troops and civilians killed in the course of the war was estimated at around five millions. Back home in the Reich, meanwhile, under the pressures of war, the last 'reservations on racial policy grounds' about the employment of foreign workers had been put aside. By the summer of 1942 more than three million Polish and Soviet men and women had been deported to Germany for forced labour, and everything indicated that their numbers would rapidly grow. So when the author of the General Plan, Konrad Meyer, added up these figures in the summer of 1942, he could assume that 20 million people were either going to be killed in the foreseeable future or deported – in smaller numbers – as 'helots'. He regarded the 'loosening-up of the population structure' as largely achieved, and was forced to put back a series of more ambitious objectives in the light of the now-precarious military situation.

In fact, as we saw earlier, the Four-Year Plan Authority estimated in October 1942 that the population in the occupied parts of the Soviet Union had 'fallen by a quarter to two-thirds, and on average by a third', as Göring's economic analysts put it.[43]

Meanwhile Himmler, in his capacity as Reich Commissioner for the Strengthening of German Nationhood, had people working on an alternative instrument of population policy, namely state-directed birth control. The necessary medical techniques were already being tried out in Auschwitz. And no sooner had the experiments on humans begun in an effort to develop new methods of mass sterilization than people like Wetzel, Eichmann and Meyer knew all about them. In his paper Wetzel dwelt at some length on the possibilities of birth control and the need for an accompanying propaganda campaign:

> We must pursue a deliberately negative population policy in the territories concerned. Through various forms of propaganda – press, radio, cinema, handbills, leaflets, public information talks and the like – we must constantly hammer home to the population the idea that having lots of children is a bad thing. We must remind people that children cost a lot of money – and then point out all the other things they could buy with the money. We could emphasize the great health risks that women run when they give birth, and that kind of thing. In conjunction with this propaganda we need to run a high-profile campaign promoting contraception. An industry must be set up specially for the manufacture of contraceptive devices. The advertising and sale of contraceptive devices must be legalized, as must abortion. We should actively promote the establishment of abortion clinics. We could train midwives and female medical orderlies to perform abortions. (...) There is no doubt that by the systematic application of the methods outlined above we shall be able to achieve considerable success in terms of weakening the Russian ethnic stock. At the same time, should the continuing existence of the Russian nation be threatened by too steep a decline in the birth rate, we would be able to take corrective action at any time by suspending this or that birth-control measure. The complete biological destruction of the Russian people would not be in our interest, certainly not until such time as we are in a position to populate the land with our own people. Otherwise other peoples would

move into these territories – which would likewise not be in our interest. Our aim in carrying out this programme is simply to weaken the Russian nation to the point where it can no longer overwhelm us by sheer weight of numbers. Once we have converted the mass of the Russian people to the idea of having only one or two children per family, then we will have accomplished our aim.[44]

These thoughts also met with Hitler's explicit approval. His remarks on the subject of birth control on 22 July 1942 are recorded: 'He said he had recently come across a suggestion in some essay that the sale and use of abortion aids in the occupied eastern territories should be banned. If some idiot were actually to try and impose such a ban in the occupied eastern territories, he [Hitler] would personally riddle him with bullets. Given the high birth rate among the indigenous population, we should be delighted if the girls and women go in for abortion as much as possible. A lively trade in contraceptives in the eastern territories should not only be allowed, it should be positively encouraged...'[45] While the suggestion put forward by undersecretary Wilhelm Stuckart at the Wannsee conference – that they should 'proceed with the compulsory sterilization of German Jewish half-castes' – proved initially impracticable because of a shortage of doctors and hospital capacity,[46] Eichmann was able to tell a meeting of Jewish specialists from the various government ministries in October 1942 'that new advances in the science of sterilization will probably make it possible for us to carry out a simplified programme of sterilization based on a quicker procedure during the course of the war.'[47]

Here Eichmann was alluding to the experiments in mass sterilization that had been started in Auschwitz by Carl Clauberg, a professor of gynaecology, and his colleague Horst Schumann, who had previously murdered his patients as a participant in the Aktion T4 programme. The new procedures had to be cheap and quick, and capable of being carried out 'without those concerned noticing anything'. In Clauberg's words, what was needed was a 'non-operative procedure for the sterilization' of people who were 'not fit to reproduce' or for whom 'reproduction was not desirable'.[48]

On 29 May 1941 Himmler's health policy adviser Ernst Grawitz had also spoken out strongly in support of Clauberg's plans for the 'non-operative sterilization of inferior women' on account of the 'huge significance (...) that such a procedure would have for the conduct of a negative population policy'. A year later, on 30 May 1942, Carl Clauberg turned again to Himmler, having first discussed the matter with Fritz Arlt, head of the RKF in Upper Silesia: 'As you may recall, Herr Reichsführer, I was unable to carry my work forward at that time [i.e. in June 1941] because of unresolved difficulties over the supply of female concentration camp inmates. In the course of a conversation on scientific matters with the chief of staff in your local office, SS Obersturmbannführer Dr Arlt, I got onto the subject of my research work in reproductive biology. Dr Arlt told me that the one man in Germany who had a special interest in such matters now and who was best placed to help me was none other than yourself, sir...'[49] So in effect Himmler was being approached through the Katowice office of the RKF, not in his capacity as SS Reichsführer, but as Reich Commissioner for the Strengthening of German Nationhood.

After some delays Himmler gave formal approval for the project on 7 July 1942. For the victims in Auschwitz and Ravensbrück these human experiments entailed terrible suffering, often ending in death. The experiments were carried out on those camp inmates – predominantly women – 'for whom reproduction was least desirable', namely Jews and 'gypsies'.[50] The experiments were designed to further the population policy objectives of the General Plan for the East. In October 1941 medical practitioner Adolf Pokorny had put a proposal to Himmler – specifically in his capacity as planning supremo for the eastern territories – for a sterilization procedure based on medication. 'I feel it my duty,' wrote Pokorny, 'to submit the following to you as Reich Commissioner for the Strengthening of German Nationhood: Dr Madaus has published the results of his research into sterilization by medicinal means. (...) On reading this article I was struck by the enormous significance of this medical drug for the struggle in which our nation is currently engaged. If it were possible, on the basis of this research, to produce a medical drug as soon as possible that had the effect of sterilizing people within a relatively short space of time without their being aware of it, we should have a new and powerful weapon in our hands. Just the thought that the three million Bolshevists now in German captivity could be sterilized, so that they could work for us but not reproduce, opens up the most far-reaching possibilities.'[51]

Himmler's interest was excited by this appeal to the broader demographic perspective and by the prospect of new ways and means of conducting a 'negative population policy'. He was particularly keen to find out from Clauberg 'how much time would be needed for the sterilization of, say, 1,000 Jewish women'.[52] The development of procedures for a simple, low-cost programme of birth control that could be directed by the state was expedited with all available means in parallel with the plans for mass murder and forcible resettlement. After the war, when German medical professionals were put on trial at Nuremberg, Pokorny stated that he had written the letter because he 'knew about Himmler's intentions to sterilize all the Jews and the indigenous populations of the eastern territories'.[53] Those intentions are also apparent from a letter written by Clauberg. On 7 July 1943 he reported to Himmler that his method was now 'as good as ready'. Which meant – in answer to the question put by Himmler a year earlier, about the possibilities of mass sterilization – that 'in all probability several hundreds, if not indeed thousands' could be sterilized 'in a single day by a suitably trained doctor at a suitably equipped facility, aided by a staff of perhaps ten assistants (the number of assistants depending on the desired speed of processing)'.[54]

Although in the event it was not put into practice, the possibility of a new form of birth control in the service of economic imperialism was seen as a modern complement to the bloody extermination of whole peoples. It allowed a more finely nuanced, economically and politically more flexible approach, while still producing the same end result. In keeping with the Nazi doctrines of productivity and achievement, the German population experts proposed to use this new method first and foremost on those 'inferior persons' who were fit for work. This thinking finds its clearest expression in a letter written by Viktor Brack, who as a high-ranking official in the Chancellery of the Führer even considered the possibility, in June 1942, of modifying the 'final solution' by the systematic mass sterilization of those Jews who were 'quite capable of working':

> Among the 10 million European Jews I imagine there are at least 2–3 million men and women who are quite capable of working. In view of the extraordinary difficulties we are facing in terms of manpower, I believe that we should pull out these 2–3 million and keep them alive. Of course, this will only work if at the same time we make them incapable of reproducing.[55]

How high were the hopes placed in new medical procedures as an instrument of population policy right up to the last days of the National Socialist state, and how extensively they were to be applied, can be seen from a remark by Ernst Kaltenbrunner in the spring of

1944 (Kaltenbrunner had succeeded the assassinated Heydrich as head of the Gestapo, SS and SD – indeed the entire Nazi security apparatus – in 1943). 'Germany must see to it,' he said, 'that the populations of eastern Europe and most of the Balkan and Danubian countries are forced to die out as a result of sterilization and the destruction of the ruling class in these countries.'[56] At the Nuremberg trials of German medical professionals Himmler's personal assistant, Rudolf Brandt, stated: 'Himmler was extremely keen on devising a cheap and quick method of sterilization that could be used against the enemies of the German Reich such as the Russians, Poles and Jews. The hope was that the enemy would not only be defeated in this way, but would actually be wiped out. The labour of the sterilized persons could be used for Germany's benefit, while they themselves would be unable to reproduce. Mass sterilization was an integral part of Himmler's racial theory. This is why so much time and effort were devoted to sterilization experiments.'[57]

'Ethnic conversion' and selection

Following the annexation of western Poland the Germans in the occupied eastern territories expelled two or three, in some areas as many as five, Poles to make way for every one expatriate German resettled there. In the occupied 'Russian lands' the standard ratio was eight to ten persons driven out for every one incoming German colonist. So to make way for four million German colonists some 36 million indigenous people would have to be expelled. The intention was to proceed here in the same systematic way as in the occupied eastern territories. To that end Wetzel not only addressed 'the Jewish question', which he regarded as already settled, but also the 'Polish, Czech and Ukrainian questions'. Inspired by the plan before him, he reflected on how the 'White Ruthenian problem' and the 'question of the future treatment of the Russians' were to be 'solved'. And it is clear that in the discussion about the General Plan for the East the possibility of murdering all those men and women from Poland and the Soviet Union who were destined neither for Germanization nor for 'helot' status was actively considered. Wetzel, however, rejected the suggestion with this memorable argument: 'It should be obvious that the Polish question cannot be solved by liquidating all the Poles in the same way as the Jews. Any such solution of the Polish question would blacken the reputation of the German people for many years to come, and we should forfeit sympathy on all sides, particularly as the other peoples on our borders would anticipate being treated in the same way at some point in time.'[58]

Instead Wetzel proposed that these various 'questions' be 'resolved' in other ways: by a combination of calculated extermination, 'more or less voluntary emigration' and social restructuring. Thus those Balts who were 'incapable of Germanization' would be relocated in the East, where they would constitute a new middle class that would help to keep the remaining Russian population under control. Those inhabitants of the Baltic states who were deemed 'capable of Germanization' were earmarked for menial agricultural and industrial work in the German Reich, where they would become Germans in the course of two or three generations. Meanwhile German smallholders and their families, along with low-income labourers, would be given new lands in the East, and would not only be members of the master race, but would actually be masters. The principal short-term consequence of this social 'restructuring programme' – designed to give new opportunities for German workers and smallholders in the East, while foreign workers were absorbed into the Reich – was that the last remaining Jewish men and women working in the armaments factories in the Reich now became 'surplus to requirement'. This is confirmed by Wetzel, albeit indirectly. While he does not specifically refer to the Jews being replaced by 'Nordic stock' drafted in from the Baltic states, he does mention other 'undesirables' who ranked well above the Jewish population in the Nazi hierarchy of values. The Balts who qualify for Germanization, writes Wetzel, will 'be able to replace the millions of undesirable workers of foreign extraction from southern and south-eastern Europe'.[59] In his eyes this would make it easier to circumvent the danger of a European 'racial morass' – and with the advent of immigrant families from eastern Europe, relocated to the Reich as 'capable of Germanization', the 'racially inferior sections' of German society were to be placed under social pressure – or simply deported in exchange:[60] 'When a district leader in Germany says that the best racial specimens are the Poles relocated to his district for Germanization, it says something about our situation.'[61]

That Wetzel was not alone in his thinking is shown by the minutes of a meeting that took place at the Ministry for the Occupied Eastern Territories on 4 February 1942. Here various experts had discussed how the conquered eastern territories could be controlled with the help of an appropriate colonization strategy. The meeting was attended by representatives of the Central Office for the Security of the

Reich (Obersturmbannführer Heinz Gummitsch and the architect Theodor Girgensohn) and the central staff office of the RKF (Hauptsturmführer H.H. Schubert), while Professor Bruno K. Schultz spoke for the SS Central Office of Race and Resettlement. Also present were Professor Eugen Fischer, director of the Kaiser Wilhelm Institute for Anthropology, Human Genetics and Eugenics in Berlin-Dahlem, who was there as an expert on averting the dangers associated with racial adulteration; and Dr Gerhard Teich of the Institute for Border and Foreign Studies, who was also a section head in the Ministry for the Occupied Eastern Territories with responsibility for 'the political control and direction of the foreign ethnic groups in the East – Russians, Poles, Ukrainians, Swedes, Crimean Tartars and other ethnic offshoots'.[62]

The participants at the meeting discussed how they were to proceed with the racially undesirable population of the Baltic states. They rejected the option of 'turning them to scrap through the industrialization of the Baltic region', as Hitler had already planned to deport them. However, deportation carried with it the risk that even the racially desirable elements would be less willing to undergo Germanization. For this reason, the racially undesirables were to be persuaded by suitable job offers to 'emigrate of their own free will into Russian territory proper'. Experience had shown 'that it was not possible to develop an administrative apparatus for these territories based on Russian personnel'. So it seemed 'very appropriate' to the German general planners 'to draft in the racially undesirable elements of the Baltic peoples to serve as a middle class'. This would be dependent on a 'thorough examination of the population (...), which must not be presented as a process of racial vetting, but rather disguised as a medical examination or something, in order not to excite popular unrest'.[63] (This procedure – which probably went back to Heydrich – was followed in many occupied countries.)

Prior to this conference, lengthy studies examining 'the Balts' capacity for Germanization' had been carried out in the German-occupied Baltic states; further studies were to follow. In experts' reports and conference presentations the professionals on the ground sought to hammer out the practical specifics of the General Plan for the East, to which they were clearly party. As soon as German troops had marched into Estonia, Latvia and Lithuania, racial experts, regional planners, ministerial officials and Wehrmacht officers[64] had toured the conquered territories and reported their observations and conclusions to the Reich Commissioner for Eastern Europe, Hinrich

Lohse, who was based in Riga. He passed these reports on to the Reich Ministry for the Occupied Eastern Territories, headed by Alfred Rosenberg. Among them was the report prepared by senior civil servant Friedrich Trampedach on 16 August 1941, which dealt with the political situation in Latvia and Kaunas.[65] Trampedach had identified the Latvian intelligentsia as the 'standard-bearer for Latvian aspirations to independence', and had largely written it off, therefore, as a prop for German interests. Yet even here, among the country's intellectuals, he found some 'deserving of Germanization'; the only thing standing in the way of this was their present political attitude. 'These elements,' he proposed, 'could be assigned a "European cultural role" in Russia, where, finding themselves in an alien environment, they would be forced into loyal collaboration. Here they would help to fill the huge gaps in intellectual leadership within the Russian people, and thus make our job of administering the country much easier.' The same thought is reiterated in the later version of Meyer's General Plan for the East.

All the experts concerned with 'ethnic conversion' and Germanization in the Baltic states were in broad agreement that the people living there were relatively 'valuable ethnic stock', even if opinions differed as to the percentage of those who were 'capable of Germanization'.[66] The only population group they classified as generally 'inferior' – and therefore undesirable – were the Latgallians. These were the inhabitants of a province in south-east Latvia, in the area around Daugavpils. According to German analysts, the region was overpopulated and 'especially backward' and the people there 'quite unsuitable', having been 'extensively corrupted by Polish and Russian elements'.[67] They would either have to make way for their 'racially valuable' compatriots, who had been displaced by incoming German colonists, or else be relocated to 'the Russian interior' in order to permit the establishment of a 'continuous expansive zone of German settlement extending outwards from a number of central points'. In any event it would be necessary to undertake a 'large-scale expulsion of the racially inferior indigenous population' from eastern Latvia,[68] along with a programme of land and agrarian reform aimed at 'smashing the smallholder system of agriculture'.[69] As for the rest of the Baltic population, here too Germanization would only be considered 'on an *ad hoc* basis. It may take place in conjunction with social advancement, if such advancement is associated with relocation to the Reich.'[70] 'The racial selection of Letts for assimilation,' we read in a report on the issue of 'ethnic conversion', 'must not be based on one-sided anthropological considerations.'[71] Instead, a 'selection based on the achievement principle' must be carried out.[72]

The avowed aim of these selection procedures in the German-occupied areas of the Soviet Union was to underpin German rule by the 'destruction of the mammoth state edifice of the Soviet Union (...) and the construction of a new order of peoples mutually protected by well-defined borders and security arrangements, which are to be incorporated into Europe, according to their state of development, under the aegis of a three-tiered Reich consisting of the German heartland, its dependencies and outlying territories'. Instead of 'levelling down and proletarianization', the creation of 'national homelands' would serve to erect artificial barriers between people and strengthen existing barriers. The German occupiers hoped to bring about the 'purging of Bolshevism, internationalism and Russification ...by affirming, and where necessary fostering, separate national identities'.[73] These various papers, reports and conferences, all of them concerned with the 'practical work of Germanization' in the occupied Baltic states, were later incorporated into the General Plan for the East. This can be seen from the fact that various 'proposals for ethnic conversion' are repeated almost word for word in the discussion papers of the Ministry for the Occupied Eastern Territories, while for their part the ethnic policy experts in the Reich Commissariat for Eastern Europe took it for granted that they were supplying 'the building blocks for a solution to the great problems of the East'.[74]

A similarly selective population policy like the one developed for the Baltic states was proposed by Friedrich Gollert for the Government General. Here too the proposal was put forward in the context of the General Plan for the East. Gollert was personal assistant to the district governor of Warsaw and ran the district's regional planning department. In a working paper that he drafted in March 1943, in which he examined 'the future fate of the population of the Government General', he wrote: 'There are currently some 15 million Poles living in the territory of the Government General. Although the earlier population surplus has declined sharply as a result of the war and war-related conditions, so that in some parts of the Government General today the birth rate among the Polish population is actually falling, this trend should not be seen as permanent.' Based on his assessment of the situation, Gollert developed four alternative strategies for 'radically transforming the population structure of the Government General'. This he viewed as 'absolutely essential' and – in common with others involved in planning the future of eastern Europe – a condition of further progress: 'a decision must be taken on the fate of the 15 million Poles currently living in the Government General'.

The first possibility, only hypothetically considered and immediately rejected, was to Germanize all 15 million Poles. 'A second solution,' writes Gollert, 'would be to exterminate these 15 millions by drastic measures (...), as has been necessary with the Jews, for example.' (Note the words 'for example', implying that the Jews were simply a case in point.) 'But,' he continues, 'to eliminate a foreign people in *this* way alone [Gollert's emphasis] is unworthy of a civilized nation.' The third option contemplated by Gollert was to 'remove' the entire Polish population 'from the Vistula region by a process of organized migration'. But Gollert rejected this possibility too, with arguments similar to those used by Wetzel: he feared the political dangers that a 'concentration' of Polish deportees would bring with it.

Gollert then formulated a fourth option for putting the General Plan for the East into practice:

> If none of the above solutions is viable, the last option available to us is to divide the Polish population into various segments and then to treat each of these segments differently. The Poles would have to be split up into three categories:
> (1) Those who can be Germanized over a period of time.
> (2) Those who constitute a potentially valuable labour resource, and who can therefore remain in the Vistula region.
> (3) Those who do not serve German interests in any way, and who must therefore be removed from the Vistula region.

Gollert went on to estimate the number of persons who could be Germanized at around half of the Polish population of the Government General (seven to eight millions). That corresponded to the order of magnitude that had already been discussed for the Baltic population. The Poles in their turn were not to be judged according to external racial characteristics, but on the fact that Prussian stock was a 'very favourable blend of Germanic and Slavic elements'. Another five million Poles were to be excluded from Germanization, but constituted a 'very welcome labour resource' in Gollert's estimation. He planned to use them for the 'development' of the Government General. He then writes: 'The remaining third category of some 2–3 millions comprises all those who are of absolutely no value to us Germans. They include not only the fanatical Polish nationalists, who must obviously be exterminated root and branch, but also all the socially undesirable elements, the sick and any other persons who are of no use to us, not even as labourers.'[75]

The proposals put forward by Gollert in March 1943 for dividing the Polish population into three groups and killing those who fell into the third category had already been discussed in wider circles and cleared with the SS. The following report had reached the Berlin Ministry of Propaganda on 15 February 1943: 'Among the Poles (...) rumours spread about an alleged plan to divide the Polish population into three classes. The first class was said to be destined for labour duties in the Reich; the second class was the grass-roots Polish working population, which would be left in place; the third class was destined for extermination. The Polish flysheets have taken this up and are calling on the Poles to offer active resistance, since they have nothing to lose anyway under the circumstances.'[76] Gollert is also the author of the memorandum issued by district governor Ludwig Fischer in February 1944, entitled 'Basic observations on the development of Warsaw during and after the war'. Here Gollert boasts that he has laboured tirelessly for four years to see that 'Warsaw is diminished in size'; the population has already been reduced by a third and the built-up area of the city has been reduced by a fifth 'through the destruction of the ghetto'. To bring about 'a definitive solution of the Warsaw problem' he planned to reduce the city's population from 1.5 million to 300,000.[77]

The Zamosc project

When Himmler was presented with the latest version of the General Plan for the East in the summer of 1942, he reacted with indignation. 'I have looked at the General Plan for the East,' he wrote to Ulrich Greifelt, 'and on the whole I like it well enough.' But: 'on one point I have been misunderstood'. Everything was going too slowly for Himmler. 'This twenty-year plan must provide for the total Germanization of Estonia and Latvia as well as the entire Government General. We need to accomplish all that in twenty years if at all possible.'[78] It is in this context that we need to see the order issued by Himmler in Cracow on 3 October 1942 for the immediate construction of the 'base' at Zamosc, a little to the east of Lublin, as envisaged in the General Plan. All the resettlement operations planned in conjunction with this project were likewise to be set in motion immediately.

Himmler had set his sights on this project back in the summer of 1941, when he had ordered an SS and police district to be established in Lublin and linked this with a first step towards the implementation of the General Plan for the East. 'Starting from a small area (...) the German colonization of the entire district' was to be put in hand, and 'over and above that (ideally!) the formation of a bridging link between the Nordic/German-colonized Baltic countries and German-colonized Transylvania via the Lublin district'. In the General Plan for the East, Lublin lay at the intersection of the south-east axis and one of the two north-east axes. The city was a strategic jumping-off point for further colonization projects in the future. The SS experts responsible for implementing the policy planned to 'bottle up' the Polish population living in the region 'and suppress their biological development'.[79]

The events of the war had put a temporary hold on the Zamosc pilot project. When Himmler decided to push it through in the autumn of 1942, the agency in charge was Section IV B 4 in the Central Office for the Security of the Reich, which was not in fact responsible solely for 'Jewish affairs', but whose remit, according to the internal schedule of departmental functions, extended to all resettlement operations. Instructions went out from here to the Emigration Bureau (UWZ) in Lódź 'to prepare for the operation (...) so that the first transports to Berlin and Auschwitz can be processed on 15 November 1942'.[80] Why Berlin and Auschwitz? The reason behind this choice of destination was the need to 'select' the population of Zamosc for forced labour, Germanization or murder, as provided for in the General Plan for the East. Himmler treated this 'resettlement operation' as a kind of test case or trial run, partly in order to learn practical lessons for the implementation of population policy in the future. On 31 October 1942 Eichmann's superior, Heinrich Müller, wrote a paper on the 'evacuation of Poles from the Lublin district (Zamosc) in order to make room for the relocation of ethnic Germans'. This sets out in great detail how men, women and children were to be shipped off to a transit camp and 'selected' there according to 'category':

1. The Polish families in categories I and II will be picked out and sent to Lódź for Germanization or closer scrutiny (...).
2. The children of the families in categories III and IV will be picked out along with Poles over the age of 60 and sent off together – i.e. basically children plus grandparents – to so-called

'retirement villages'. Sick and infirm Poles under the age of 60 who are unfit for work will also be sent to 'retirement villages'. (...)

4. Able-bodied family members in category III aged between 14 and 60 will be sent to the Reich – without family attachments who are unfit for work – for labour service. In consultation with the General Commissioner for labour service they will be assigned as replacements for the Jews who are still employed in work vital to the war effort.

5. Family members in category IV between the ages of 14 and 60 will be shipped off to the Auschwitz concentration camp.[81]

So children and old people were to starve in 'retirement villages', cut off from those who could have fed them or fought for them with the partisans. They would, as Arlt had once put it, 'be subject to an accelerated process of dying off'.[82] Some of the adults, but mostly the children, were to be 'won back for the German nation', others – 'without family attachments who are unfit for work' and at the younger end of the age spectrum – were to replace the Jewish forced labourers in the Reich, who would then be put to death, along with their non-working dependents. A fourth group was to be taken straight to Auschwitz, where they would either be worked to death or sent to the gas chambers.

And this is exactly what happened in the weeks that followed. Between the end of November 1942 and the early days of March 1943, over 100,000 people from nearly three hundred villages were 'evacuated'. The winter was seen as the ideal time for this, since the spring is taken up with sowing and the summer and autumn months with harvesting. The selection criteria were refined, and from 13 December 1942 onwards[83] the first transports with deportees from the Zamosc region began to arrive in Auschwitz. Other transports arrived shortly afterwards from Berlin, carrying Jews who had once been forced to work in the armaments industry and who had now been replaced by category III Poles from Zamosc ('without family attachments who are unfit for work'). The so-called 'arms factory Jews' from Berlin were shipped off together with their families – the 'attachments' deemed 'unfit for work' – and murdered.[84]

This programme of exchange and extermination reached its climax on 27 February 1943 with the so-called 'factory operation', when 1,500 Jewish men, women and children were deported to Auschwitz from Berlin in a single day. The men had previously been employed as

labourers in the armaments industry. The deportation of the 'arms
factory Jews' is seen as a particularly cruel and senseless instance of
blind racial hatred: the clear documentary evidence linking it with the
resettlement experiments in the East has gone largely unremarked.[85]
The 'factory operation' was part of a 'population exchange', as it was
termed in the demographic jargon, aimed at establishing a highly productive German agricultural industry in Zamosc, Germanizing those
Poles who appeared willing to work and assimilate, and organizing
forced labour in such a way that only the youngest and most productive workers – but not their dependents – would need to be fed. The
deportation of the younger age groups to forced labour camps was
also designed to have a useful side effect – very important from the
RKF's point of view: they would not be able to have children and start
families. In so far as pregnancies and births could not be entirely prevented, abortions were compulsory and newborn children were placed
in special 'baby camps' – as the district labour office in Munich termed
them – where they were killed by undernourishment, cold and lack of
nursing care. These crimes too take their place within the overall
concept of the General Plan for the East.

The Zamosc project was to be a kind of model exercise in economic
and social rationalization, where more would be produced by fewer
workers. The intention was that a portion of the people living there –
those who were not capable of sustained hard work – should die
sooner rather than later. The German population planners saw
obvious advantages in substituting young workers of both sexes for
others who needed more in the way of support for themselves and
their families. In this particular case it was the Berlin 'arms factory
Jews' with their wives and children. They could not be so intensively
exploited as the young deportees from Zamosc – and they were at the
bottom of the racist hierarchy.

This programme was also accommodated by the special timetables
of the national rail network, the Reichsbahn. On 25 January 1943 a
goods train travelled from Zamosc in eastern Poland to Berlin carrying 1,000 young forced labourers of both sexes 'without unproductive dependents', as the expression went. In Berlin they were to take
over the jobs of 'arms factory Jews', who were now deported to
Auschwitz on the same train, together with their 'unproductive'
dependents. There the train was loaded up with the luggage of settlers of German origin from south-east Europe, including a large
number of Bosnian Germans, before making the return journey to

Zamosc. Here the incoming Germans were received by the SS resettlement unit and relocated in the surrounding area, now 'cleared' of
Poles – and of Jews before them. The German colonists were given
farm units of 20 hectares, each one made up by amalgamating five
'unproductive' Polish smallholdings. From Zamosc the train returned
to Auschwitz, carrying 1,000 Poles who had been classed as especially
'undesirable' by the security police and the SS racial scrutineers.[86]

Although separate groups of 1,000 Jews and 1,000 Poles were both
despatched to Auschwitz under the terms of this particular 'train circulation plan', the fate that awaited them there was very different.
This does not need to be specifically documented, but the comments
made by one of the men in charge of a similar transport about the
conversation he had with his SS colleague in Auschwitz are revealing:
'On the subject of incapacity for work SS Hauptsturmführer Haumeier
stated that only able-bodied Poles should be brought in, to avoid
putting unnecessary strain on the camp facilities and the transport
system. The mentally retarded, idiots, cripples and the sick should be
liquidated in short order so as to ease the strain on the camp.
However, matters are complicated by the fact that the Central Office
for the Security of the Reich has given instructions that Poles must
die a natural death, as opposed to the procedure adopted in the case
of the Jews.'[87]

This particular 'train circulation plan' was by no means the only
one of its kind. It documents the interlocking machinery of resettlement, deportation and genocide, the crazed logic of systematic population exchange, the integration, in planning and organizational
terms, of so-called positive and negative population policy. The cycle
of population redistribution and annihilation ended in Auschwitz
with the murder of those deemed to be 'inferior' – but also in Zamosc
with the resettlement of ethnic Germans, who, although they were to
benefit directly from these crimes, were likewise displaced unasked.
But for those at least who framed the General Plan 'the villages awoke
to new life and to a hard-working but sunny future'. With this in
mind they had taken care to 'reorganize and open up' the new
German settlements by 'combining four or five former smallholdings
into one farm enterprise'.[88]

Postscript

While the Zamosc scheme was very much a pet project of Heinrich
Himmler's, pushed through at his personal insistence, his planning

experts had been preparing the ground for the previous eighteen months. The whole undertaking foundered in the shadow of Stalingrad and in the face of well-organized partisan activity. Consequently it encountered massive resistance from other German agencies, who raised all kinds of tactical objections. But the Zamosc project shows very clearly what the planners of 'manpower deployment' and the new territorial order had in mind, and what they were capable of. Through their colonization projects in the East they hoped to blaze a trail for the modernization of Europe along Nazi lines, involving a huge programme of social restructuring on the one hand and the murder of millions of 'useless' and 'surplus' people on the other. These resettlement programmes were an attempt to improve social and economic conditions through 'state-directed migration'.

The demographic and statistical data used by the architects of the General Plan were supplied for the most part by the Berlin-Dahlem Publications Office, a branch of the Secret Prussian State Archive. It collaborated closely with the SD and with the Reich Commissioner for the Strengthening of German Nationhood, drawing on Soviet census records and statistics to prepare data and reports on specific regions within the Soviet Union, or simply having Russian and Polish studies translated into German. Nearly all the specialized studies prepared for the RKF in general, and in aid of the General Plan for the East in particular, were funded by the German Society for the Promotion of Research (DFG). While a man like Mengele received something in the order of 10,000–20,000 Reichsmarks for his 'research' in Auschwitz, the DFG invested well over half a million Reichsmarks in the General Plan for the East. Konrad Meyer requested a budget of 150,000 Reichsmarks for 1942, supporting his claim with the following argument: 'As a result of the new responsibilities assumed by the Reich Commissioner for the Strengthening of German Nationhood (Government General and occupied eastern territories), the quantity of research needed in connection with our planning studies has increased.'[89] His claim was successful.

Meyer's colleague, Professor Herbert Morgen, received an additional 100,000 RM between 1942 and 1945 for the purpose of 'laying the foundations for the creation of a new ethnic and demographic order based on the principle of strengthening German nationhood in the colonized territories of the Reich'.[90] The financial expert Professor Felix Boesler from Jena was given 40,000 RM by the DFG for 'studies on the problems of reconstruction in the East – ongoing research commissioned by the RKF',[91] and on Meyer's recommendation he received additional funding on top of that. Boesler acted as Meyer's representative in dealings with the DFG. Boesler had been advising the RKF on all financial and fiscal matters in the annexed eastern territories since 1940; his particular area of expertise was the relationship between finance and population questions. In 1943, even though work on the General Plan for the East was ostensibly suspended after Stalingrad, the DFG paid out another 130,000 RM for this purpose, followed by the same amount again in 1944. In a letter of 22 March 1945 Meyer applied for 100,000 RM in funding for the financial year 1945/46 – 'for carrying out planning studies on behalf of the Reich Commissioner for the Strengthening of German Nationhood'.[92] The resettlement operations themselves had been halted by Himmler on 18 May 1943 'in the light of the overall political situation'.[93]

Students and historians of the crimes perpetrated by Germany in the years between 1939 and 1945 often fail to accord the General Plan for the East the attention it deserves, and they seriously underestimate its practical impact on social and population policy. The General Plan belongs in the context of other policies and initiatives aimed at bringing about a 'final solution'. The experiments in mass sterilization carried out at Auschwitz by Carl Clauberg and Horst Schumann cannot simply be written off as an inhuman perversion of medicine, for they were designed from the very beginning to extend the range of instruments available for the conduct of 'negative population policy'. Clauberg's research was likewise funded by the DFG. Both doctors were working to find an answer to the question posed by Himmler: how can 1,000 compulsory sterilizations be carried out by one sterilization team in one day with the least possible cost and effort? The techniques were never fully developed, but the intention undoubtedly was to use them as weapons of population policy against the 'Slavic masses' and against 'half-castes' and 'inferior beings'. The sterilization experiments, the millions of murders carried out by various means and the carefully planned programmes for exploiting and controlling the populations of the conquered regions as effectively as possible – these were not separate, isolated crimes. Instead they all emerged from the same climate of thinking, and must therefore be considered as parts of a single whole. The General Plan for the East formulated the concept of a development policy that combined programmes of economic reconstruction and exploitation with mass murder and measures designed to limit population growth. If we look at the relationship between development policy and the limiting of population growth, leaving aside the actual methods used, then what we have here, in essence, is a modern procedure that is now pretty much standard practice vis-à-vis the poor and impoverished countries of the world, and which also exhibits similarities with Stalin's policy of enforced resettlement.

Even though the General Plan for the East was only implemented in part, there is no reason to suppose that this project – seemingly so insane – would have been the victim of its own megalomania if Germany had won the war. The criminal acts of displacement and the murders that had already been perpetrated suggest otherwise, as does the remarkable popularity of the Plan. Although discussions about the General Plan for the East were carried on in secret, a whole string of regional research institutes and individual experts were involved in the elaboration of its component parts: and although they may not have known all the details of the Plan, they understood the context in which their research was being conducted. Among broad sections of the population at large there was also an awareness of the resettlement programmes, even if the term 'General Plan for the East' was not used to describe them.

At the beginning of the 1940s hopes of a 'country estate in the East' and of a future life as 'militia farmers in the black-earth country' were cherished not only by high-ranking officers in the Wehrmacht, but also by perfectly normal families. The connection between these enticing prospects for Germans and the reality of genocide was quietly glossed over.

CHAPTER 13

CONCLUSIONS

When we began, back in 1985, to examine German economic policy and planning in occupied Poland, we discovered two phenomena that have come to influence our analysis of National Socialism far more than we initially anticipated. First of all there was the activity – hardly touched upon in the secondary literature – of those intellectual experts who acted as advisers both to the civilian administration and to the SS in occupied Poland: young academics who did not match the stereotype of the zealous, narrow-minded Nazi ideologue, and who argued their case objectively and dispassionately – aside from the occasional racist remark. And as we read their reports and reviews we noted a recurrent paradigm: time and time again the argument came back to the 'overpopulation problem'. Whatever their area of expertise – be it agricultural policy, the 'Jewish question', specific branches of trade and commerce or the way ahead for colonization and resettlement policy – and whatever their territorial focus – the Government General, south-east Europe or the occupied portions of the Soviet Union – the assumption that there is an underlying 'overpopulation problem' or 'population pressure' runs like a red thread through the secret reports and published works alike of these political advisers. And in nearly every case the exposition of this 'problem' was followed by calls for an early 'solution', in the shape of a fundamental change in the population structure.

The post-war critical literature about National Socialist policy in eastern and south-east Europe, however, contains virtually no references to this line of argument. Yet the belief that the central problem in eastern and south-east Europe was massive overpopulation was just as much taken for granted in the 1930s as the well-known eugenic and racial-biological positions. While the link between eugenic theories and eugenic practice, in the form of compulsory sterilization leading on eventually to the 'euthanasia' killing programmes, is not disputed, the link between the theory of overpopulation and the policy of mass murder as a radical form of demographic engineering is not even up for discussion.

We found only one exception: a completely unknown dissertation by Tadeusz Kudyba. Kudyba was deported to Mauthausen-Gusen from the area around Zamosc in 1943. In 1950 he obtained a doctorate in economics in Bonn. In the abstract of his dissertation we read: 'Within the wider context of the German body politic the economic structure of the Polish territories was to be rationalized not by an increase in the factor that was lacking – i.e. jobs – but by a reduction in the factor that was available in abundance, namely human lives: that is to say, by a process of annihilation.'[1]

It is true that Hannah Arendt identifies the mass murder programmes as a form of population policy, but she does not pursue this idea any further. She writes: 'The commandment "Thou shalt not kill" is powerless in the face of a population policy that embarks on the systematic, industrialized annihilation of "inferior races and individuals who are unfit to live", the "dying classes" – and this not as a one-off operation, but as part of a process that was plainly seen as ongoing. The death penalty [for the perpetrators put on trial at Nuremberg] becomes an absurdity if one is not dealing with murderers who know what murder is, but with population policy-makers who organize the murder of millions in such a way that all those involved are subjectively innocent.'[2]

Just as contemporary anthropologists, medical professionals and biologists viewed the marginalization and annihilation of 'inferior persons' on the basis of racial criteria and standards of achievement as a scientific method for improving humanity, or 'renewing the body of the nation', so economists, agrarian and regional planners believed they had a duty to work at the 'renewal of social structures' in the underdeveloped regions of Germany and of all Europe. They imagined that by summarily 'relieving' the 'population pressure' in broad areas of eastern and south-east Europe they could create the conditions for a speedy and all-encompassing modernization, and that this would have positive repercussions on Germany's 'social renewal'.

Demography is an interdisciplinary undertaking. Sociologists, anthropologists and political scientists all have their contribution to make, along with public health experts, economists, statisticians, agrarian planners and regional planners. The deliberate and systematic sorting of people, based on 'qualitative' criteria as well as quantitative ones, was one of the cornerstones of the 'new order'. Against the background of these plans the German policy of measuring human worth in terms of ethnicity – at first sight driven only by blind Nazi fanaticism – and the policy of mass murder appear in a different light.

In their drafts and plans for a modernized and 'realigned' Europe the German technocrats concerned indicated that the quickest and cheapest way to attain their goals was to 'adjust' the 'population factor' in order to 'optimize' the population. Population policy was not conducted for its own sake, but was seen as an instrument of economic rationalization: it was a matter of minimizing the 'dead costs' and increasing the productivity of society as a whole. The planners were absolutely convinced that massive population shifts throughout Europe were the prime prerequisite for the conduct of an effective continental policy. That inevitably entailed a process of selection. And relocation or resettlement was only the first recourse of this so-called 'negative population policy'. Other methods followed: deportation for forced labour, ghettoization, the displacement of people into artificially created famine regions, attempts at birth control – and mass murder.

There was nothing taboo about the forcible resettlement of population groups and entire peoples in the first half of the twentieth century. Indeed, it was widely practised – in Greece and Romania, for example, and on a very large scale in the Soviet Union. Scientists from different nations developed a theory of 'optimum population size'. Resettlement programmes were routinely justified by reference to economic and ideological arguments. For the power to define which people are 'surplus to requirement' lay – as it still lies today – in the hands of the state.

Selection and 'population shifts' destroyed the traditional ties that bound people together – and in so doing gave the lie to Nazi ideology, which claimed to safeguard existing traditional orientations and allegiances. The blood-and-soil ideology merely masked the fact that in reality something quite different was going on: the fragmentation not only of foreign peoples, but of the German nation too, the placing of people at the disposal of any and every purpose. Zygmunt Baumann, writing from the very different perspective of a social philosopher, comes to similar conclusions in his 1989 study of the Holocaust. He sees the 'Nazi revolution' as a large-scale experiment in social engineering, an attempt to create social structures by artificial means that would meet predetermined criteria of excellence.[3]

In their visions for the future the planners saw road and rail links, raw material deposits, expanses of territory and human beings as 'factors' of equal importance. From their point of view, transport problems, 'food-supply shortages' and the eradication of 'overpopulation' were all practical constraints that had to be overcome by the application of modern, rational methods of planning and administration. The bureaucratic and scientific objectification of mass murder did not allow moral scruples to surface. And the language in which 'Top Secret' documents were couched, at once reified and nebulous, reinforced this ethos.

Reading the text of the lecture given in Kiel in 1935 by the director of the Warsaw Institute for Economic and Price Research, Edward Lipinski, on the subject of industrialization, overpopulation and emigration, one realizes that Meinhold and his like were in part simply reproducing what others had analysed and quantified before them.[4] So it seems only natural that Meinhold should have tried to recruit Lipinski as a collaborator in 1941, offering him a post as a scientist at the Institute for German Development Work in the East. He refused[5] – and with good reason. For between his scientific method and that of Meinhold there was a fundamental difference. Where Lipinski recommended a policy designed to encourage emigration, Meinhold spoke of the 'necessity for resettlement'; where one called for long-term foreign credits to develop industry and create jobs, the other insisted that the *first* step must be 'to siphon off the surplus population'; and where Lipinski spoke of an unfavourable trade structure, Meinhold welcomed the 'elimination of the Jews' and called for more of the same. While the proposals of the one foundered on bureaucracy, the multi-party system and political quarrels, the other was an academic in the employ of an executive that was ready to commit almost any crime, taking proposals from expert advisers like him and issuing them as decrees at the drop of a hat.

What were the distinguishing features of this German technocracy? In many respects these young German academics were no different from their colleagues in other countries and in other times. They were interested in securing steady funding for their research projects, privileges for themselves, and the fullest possible translation of their theoretical findings into social practice. They saw themselves as professionals and specialists in their field – not Party creatures, carrying out research to order, but men who wished to place their expertise in the service of the modernizing project that would transform society.

And yet the careers of these young academics were marked out by special historical circumstances, which favoured their social advancement and catapulted them into positions of astonishing political influence within a relatively short space of time.

In 1931–2, the years of crisis and economic stagnation, these graduates in their mid to late twenties had little chance of finding work in their chosen professions, let alone making a successful career for themselves. All that changed very quickly in 1933. The dismissal of civil servants and intellectuals who were Jews, socialists or simply members of the Centre Party created new job openings overnight for opportunistic or politically disinterested career entrants. The aspiring young professionals who benefited from these 'purges' thus became accessories to acts of injustice and crimes. And that complicity cemented their loyalty to the system that had opened up new career prospects for them in this way. In the years that followed, the opportunities for further advancement and the exercise of their professional influence grew with the state's steady encroachment on more and more areas of social and national life and with every new step along the path of territorial expansion.

It was the youngest and most flexible academic elite that had ever come to power in Germany. They swept away 'outmoded' structures, and in the first five years of the Third Reich they acquired considerable freedom of manoeuvre and scope for the exercise of authority, while the links between the scientific-academic community and the seats of political power became ever more tightly interwoven. The gap between social-reformist ideas and their translation into political praxis narrowed to the point of disappearing. These academics felt free to turn their utopias into reality. And they could do so all the more readily because they felt emboldened by the ruling ideology to put aside all moral objections and pinpricks of conscience. Their project was that of a German intelligentsia which felt itself called to restructure Germany and Europe by force within the space of just a few years. It was no coincidence that the General Plan for the East was designed to be fully implemented within a period of twenty-five to thirty years, which corresponded to the active working life that most of the planners involved could expect to enjoy.

Most of these ambitious, career-minded young professionals did not adopt the National Socialist ideology as a personal creed. It simply offered them the maximum possible freedom of action. To begin with, the content of this ideology remained sketchy and ill-defined, so there was scope for shaping it and giving it substance from within. The planners knew how to formulate their ideas and research findings in such a way that they enriched and changed Nazi ideology. By this means, vague ideological claims became principles of action and were translated into 'practicable' programmes. The notion that this young German intelligentsia simply embraced National Socialist dogma and allowed it to dictate their thoughts and actions is probably just as false as the collective excuse later offered by those involved: that they had adopted the *rhetoric* of National Socialism – for reasons of expediency and self-preservation – but not its philosophy and ideas. However overblown and anachronistic Nazi ideology seemed, it was no obstacle to the modernization of the economy and society. On the contrary. There was no contradiction between a population policy that was driven by the criteria of rational economic and social restructuring, and all the talk about the 'adjustment of ethnic national borders' or the 'conquest of living-space in the East'. It was only when ideology came together with modern scientific rationalism that a series of vague programme headings became concrete, realizable projects. Traditional concepts like 'race', 'blood' and 'soil' were gradually imbued with new meaning by social scientists, economists and agrarian experts. According to them, true Germans were no longer distinguished primarily by certain outward characteristics, but by their capacity for work and their willingness to conform. Behind this lay the ideal of a 'two-thirds society' with a high degree of social mobility. Hard workers and achievers would no longer be hindered in their advancement by the old class barriers, while the 'useless third' would be excluded and marginalized. This policy created more room for socio-political manoeuvre by wholesale redistribution, with the majority benefiting from the discriminatory treatment and dispossession of minorities.

When it came to the reordering of economic and social life in occupied Poland, racism and modernization were not conflicting tendencies but complementary ones. This only served to ensure that the resettlement schemes, deportations of forced labourers and plans for annihilation were conducted on an even larger scale than might otherwise have been the case. The German intellectuals in occupied Poland reinforced each other's arrogant belief in their own master-race supremacy. They lived and worked in the consciousness of belonging to an elite entrusted with tasks of world-historic significance. Tasks which, as they repeatedly emphasized, they wished to accomplish speedily and definitively, 'for the sake of future generations'. The sense of standing shoulder to shoulder in some forward bastion of empire, of sweeping away traditional and restrictive structures once and for all, and the ethos of an exclusive 'Germans-only' culture may well have served to reinforce the close ties between science and politics that were already a feature of National Socialism. When they wished to encourage collaboration among the local population, the new masters in their racist conceit were adept at drawing fine distinctions between the various categories of 'inferior ethnic stock'. But that same conceit also fed the delusion that all things were possible, and destroyed in them any vestige of consideration for the conditions they encountered on the ground.

The calculations carried out by the RKF or the Institute for German Development Work in the East often had very little to do with the realities of Polish village life. The plans failed in part because of the resistance of the Polish population. Nor was their efficient implementation helped by rivalry and intrigue within the occupation establishment. But the project for the annihilation of the Polish Jews did not fail, since this was one matter on which all were agreed. People like Meinhold, Gater, Kuchenbäcker, Seraphim, Oberländer, Emmerich and Arlt supplied a justification for mass murder in Poland that 'made sense' in economic and demographic terms. For years now they had been insisting on the deportation of the Jewish minority, viewing this as the first major step towards the realization of their plans.

It could be objected that they were simply opportunists who exploited the policy of annihilation – already planned and approved by others – for their own purposes and projects, legitimizing the murder of minorities after the event as an economic necessity. But this is belied by the fact that the planners themselves created the stalemate in resettlement policy, knowing full well – because they had done the studies themselves – that there was basically nowhere left for forcibly displaced 'ethnic national groups' to go. They anticipated the decisions taken by the top Party leadership and effectively determined the thrust of future 'Führerbefehle' – personal decrees issued by Hitler.

In the first chapter we sketched out how, in the wake of the pogroms of November 1938, the German state turned away decisively from the anti-Semitism of the street and the mob and delegated its 'Jewish policy' to state institutions, placing it in the hands of experts from a wide range of disciplines. Raul Hilberg cites this bureaucratic 'professionalization' as a key prerequisite for the murder of the European

Jews. And indeed the German bureaucratic machine developed its modern techniques and procedures in the 1930s and '40s with astonishing rapidity.[6] This area of study gives us an insight into the workings of the annihilation policy and its efficient functioning, but it does not answer the question 'Why?' Modern methods were used, based on the division of labour, to catalogue the victims, marginalize and dispossess them, isolate them socially and finally deport them. But no less modern were the arguments invoked by social scientists to justify the 'necessity' for reducing the size of Europe's population and changing its structure. To a very large extent the policy of annihilation was the product of rational argument taken to a mercilessly logical conclusion. This – to our mind central – aspect has been at the heart of this book.

We have attempted to outline the various arguments used by those who supplied a theoretical framework for the policy of genocide. Together they produced a blueprint in which short-term 'war imperatives' were successfully integrated with long-term policy objectives. From the plans for the military conquest of the East they developed strategies for economic exploitation and the maintenance of food supplies that went way beyond 'classic' campaigns of conquest and sadistic blood-lust and made genocide into a 'constraint', a necessary requirement for long-term domination and economic subjugation. In this way the German planners and experts, the political advisers and the 'ideas men' effectively contributed to the murder of millions of people.

The scientists, like the professional administrators, did not think of themselves as ideologues. But National Socialist ideology sat very well with their own thinking where it divided people into 'superior' and 'inferior' categories, thus setting up a value system based on racial ideology and social Darwinism under which people were to be privileged, enslaved or exterminated.

Architects of annihilation were at work in many different kinds of institutions. They either exerted a direct influence on policy in the occupied countries, or they were co-opted to the project of planning the long-term future of German-occupied Europe. While there was dissent and friction between individual Nazi bigwigs, the experts inhabited a world characterized by a common technocratic culture of rational calculation, broad consensus, close personal ties and continuity. Most of the men whose careers we have described held a plurality of offices, many of them interlinked. As typical examples one could cite Hans-Joachim Riecke, Gustav Schlotterer, Hans Kehrl, Hans

Fischböck, Konrad Meyer or Otto Ohlendorf. As the agents and representatives of ministerial thinking, who were not constrained by
ordinary departmental jurisdictions, they consolidated their own
influence not least by harnessing the professional expertise of those
who wrote scientific studies for the avowed purpose of influencing
practical policy.

The planners saw the 'new European order' as the result of a top-
down revolution. Newly installed in their jobs and already rising
rapidly through the ranks, these young technocrats made it their
ambition to 'resolve' every social contradiction and every conflict of
aims in their own way – and as 'completely' and 'definitively' as possible. Whether the analysis that underlay these plans was correct or
not was of secondary importance, as long as they persisted in their
deluded belief, encouraged by military successes and euphoric visions
of the future, that all things were possible. The mere assumption that
these analyses reflected reality was sufficient for them to start planning practical action on that basis. Once the 'problems' had been
identified and the 'constraints' defined, those who operated within
this hermetic and expediency-driven system were interested only in
the most efficient means to an end. Of course the 'tabula rasa'
scenario that so excited the imaginations of the territorial planners
and economists never existed in reality. But by declaring millions of
people to be superfluous and in the way, by regarding them as simply
non-existent in their plans for the future or suggesting that they be
'resettled', they prepared the way for the creation of a tabula rasa by
military force and police violence – and eventually by the use of
extermination camps.

As the German economy was gearing up for the Second World War,
economists had called for its speedy rationalization. Since it was necessary, in the interests of domestic political stability, to contain the
financial and social problems created by such a policy, the planners
and political advisers suggested shifting the resulting burdens on to a
particular group of people that had already been the victim of
widespread discrimination, namely the Jewish minority in Germany
and the newly-annexed Austria. The proposals for linking
'Entjudung' – the elimination of the Jews from economic life – with
economic rationalization per se accorded well with the primarily
racist orientation of the NSDAP programme, and in 1938 and 1939
they were duly implemented. This established a pattern for resolving
the latent conflict between economic and social policy by means of

racial discrimination and exclusion. Thanks to the efforts of a clever technocratic elite, what was originally a racist programme with populist appeal now 'made sense' in economic policy terms as well.

Because the social services budget was constantly being cut to finance the preparations for war and then the war itself, while adequate provision for the social needs of the German majority remained a central policy aim of the Party, the security service and Hitler himself, disadvantaged minorities, and later whole peoples, were robbed of their rights and their means of livelihood for the benefit of that same German majority. This collective profiting of one group at the expense of another was a cornerstone of the annihilation policy. It secured ongoing assent to the practice of deportation – or at least the indifference of the German population.

When the war began, the German political and economic leadership essentially took the programme that had been developed in Austria after annexation and continued it in the occupied countries of western Europe. For occupied Poland – and subsequently for the whole of eastern Europe – the German economic and demographic experts wanted 'overpopulation' reduced as a first priority, which meant getting rid of the millions whom they regarded as merely 'extra mouths to feed'. In 1939 and 1940 the German strategic planners began to change the political map of Europe and its demographic make-up by forcible means. In eastern and south-east Europe existing frontiers were redrawn, while vast resettlement projects were planned and in part implemented. These extended from Estonia to Bulgaria, and from Flanders to the Crimea.

In 1941 the German population experts identified 30–50 million – depending on how the numbers were calculated – 'superfluous' people living on the western side of the front line that now ran down through the Soviet Union. Their existence and their lack of interest in social advancement and consumption – so these experts believed – were the only things standing in the way of rapid modernization. For German industry, meanwhile, 'adjusting' the population structure of the underdeveloped countries in the German sphere of influence was a necessary precondition of its further engagement.

Added to these long-term plans for a new continental order there were more immediate strategic considerations arising out of the war which also had implications for population policy. The specialists in charge of planning food supplies proposed 'to turn [the Ukraine] around by 180 degrees', redirecting the region's grain harvests to western Europe and thus depriving workers and their families in the

Soviet industrial centres of food. The idea was to safeguard food supplies to Germany and make 'fortress Europe' immune to the effects of
blockade. At the same time the German experts responsible for war
finance planned to fund the war with the profits from the export of
Ukrainian grain, thereby 'sparing the German taxpayer'.

All these considerations and plans made it 'expedient' or 'necessary' to reduce European population numbers by many millions,
both for short-term reasons of maintaining food supplies and from
the medium- to long-term perspective of European development
policy. As the first stage in the process the population experts invariably called for the 'evacuation' or 'resettlement' of all those people
deemed to be of no productive value – and the 'evacuation' of all
Jews. In the furtherance of their population redistribution projects,
the planners exploited both the historic tradition of anti-Semitism in
Europe and the hatred of the Jews fomented by the NSDAP. The
authors of the Madagascar plan, for example, knew the score from
the beginning: they understood well enough that deportations under
these conditions would result in the deaths of many people. Even so,
resettlement schemes such as these were not yet the same thing as
the later practice of systematic mass murder. But they were a step in
that direction, and they created a situation in which the planners of a
Europe under German rule were able to factor in the 'evacuation' of
several million people as a practical and quickly achievable option
and a known quantity in their calculations. They drew up their programmes of economic reconstruction accordingly, creating new
'constraints' to be overcome.

Since the planners of the 'new order' thought it necessary to
reduce population numbers virtually everywhere, and at the same
time to resettle populations according to ethnic criteria, this led to a
situation of mutual blockade or stalemate. The visible expression of
this stalemate was the ghetto in Lódź, which was originally intended
to remain in existence for a few months only. Following the collapse
of the Madagascar project in the autumn of 1940 the first attempts
were made to exploit the economic potential of this and other
ghettos. Under the prevailing conditions, however, this was no
longer a realistic possibility – and in view of the general 'overpopulation problem' it was not even desirable.

While the 'solution of the population problem' in occupied Poland
was thus stalled, German officials and doctors were exploring the
technical and social dimensions of 'euthanasia', with particular reference to its impact on public opinion. They concluded that mass

murder was a feasible option, and that large sections of the German population were prepared to countenance such a crime. The decision to murder the European Jews had been preceded by the decision to leave many millions of POWs and civilians in the Soviet Union to starve to death. These earlier experiments and basic policy decisions on food supply and colonization on the one hand, and the murder of the European Jews on the other, were part of the same grand design: the demographic restructuring of Europe on the basis of quantitative, ethnic and racial purity criteria.

It was in this context that the decision was taken to murder European Jewry, the Sinti and Roma and sections of the Polish and Soviet populations. As for the decision-making mechanisms that preceded these crimes, it seems reasonable to suppose that it was a fairly extended process, in which the aims and targets set by various institutions were pursued in parallel – with mutually radicalizing consequences. The murder of the European Jews was one part of a much larger annihilation project; prioritized because wartime conditions allowed it, it was also the part that came closest to being fully realized.

Our study has shown that the modern praxis-oriented social sciences and the reception of their findings in the seats of political power played a significant part in the decisions that led to systematic mass murder. If the links between Auschwitz and visionary German projects of the time for a modernized and pacified Europe are denied or ignored, then Germany's crimes appear as a descent into barbarism and a break with Western civilization – rather than a potentiality inherent within it. Such an interpretation fails to engage with the larger truth, and makes the German annihilation policy of those years appear the product of a completely atypical historical situation, without context or explanation.

The aggressive ideology of National Socialism, which took up old patterns of prejudice and kept them constantly alive, needed to be crossed with the belligerency of large-scale plans for redevelopment and reconstruction before Auschwitz could become a reality. But these plans contain at least the germ of a full-blown theory of genocide. So the reasons for the murder of millions of people are not beyond thought and rational contemplation. On the contrary: it is possible to reconstruct, and put into words, the thinking that lay behind the individual stages in the process. The various programmes of mass murder that were implemented and the others that were planned all have a common utilitarian denominator.

The unique character of the Holocaust was particularly emphasized in the 'historians' dispute' of the 1980s, when many spoke up against the attempts of certain historians to relativize the past in order to ease the collective German conscience. In the course of that debate, the word 'unique' was sometimes taken to mean not only that these things had not happened before, but that they could not happen again: the possibility that these crimes could be repeated was implicitly denied. In this book we have drawn attention to the continuities in many an intellectual career and emphasized the modernity of the planning enterprise: and in doing that we are also posing the question 'Could it happen again?' After the war the planners of a new European order were not put on trial, nor were their methods subjected to analysis and reappraisal. External circumstances changed profoundly in 1945. But that change was by no means irreversible. The particular historical constellation in which such murderous plans could be carried out is no longer in place – not here, not now. Perhaps it *was* unique – in every sense of the word. But the calculating, expediency-driven thinking in which mass murder became a 'useful' instrument of structural planning and development policy – that remains very much of the present.

NOTES

Introduction

1 For a useful critical review of the current state of research, see Hans Mommsen, 'Die Realisierung des Utopischen: Die "Endlösung der Judenfrage" im "Dritten Reich"', in: *Geschichte und Gesellschaft*, Vol. 9 (1983), pp.381–420.

2 Hermann Rauschning, *Gespräche mit Hitler* (Zurich 1940), p.122.

3 Franz Neumann, *Behemoth. Struktur und Praxis des Nationalsozialismus 1933–1944* (hereinafter cited as 'Neumann, *Behemoth*'), Frankfurt a.M. 1984. The book was first published in 1942 by the Oxford University Press; an extended edition appeared in 1944.

4 Such at least was the title of the memoirs published by Hans Kehrl, head of the planning department in Göring's Four-Year Plan Authority and subsequently in Speer's Ministry of Armaments (*Krisenmanager im Dritten Reich*, 2nd edition, Düsseldorf 1973).

5 Memorandum on the remarks of the SS Reichsführer on 14 August 1942 following his visit to Kiev (Federal Archive, NS 19 neu/1446); cited hereafter Josef Ackermann, *Heinrich Himmler als Ideologe* (hereinafter cited as 'Ackermann, *Himmler*'), Göttingen/Zurich/Frankfurt a.M. 1970.

6 There is no mention in these reports, for example, of the so-called 'euthanasia campaign', which remained a highly controversial subject in domestic politics for many months. The same is largely true of the murder of the European Jews. For as Himmler put it, this was 'a glorious, unwritten and never-to-be-written chapter in our history'.

7 Martin Broszat, 'Plädoyer für eine Historisierung des Nationalsozialismus', in: *Merkur* 39 (1985), pp.373–85.

Chapter 1: 'Entjudung'

1 See note 9.

2 Said at a meeting in the Reich Air Ministry on 14 October 1938 and reprinted in: *Der Prozess gegen die Hauptkriegsverbrecher vor dem Internationalen Militärgerichtshof, Nürnberg, 14. November 1945 bis 1. Oktober 1946* (hereinafter cited as '*IMG*'), Nuremberg 1947, Vol. XXVII, p.163.

3 Unless otherwise indicated, the following quotations are taken from document No.1816–PS submitted in evidence at the trial of the major war

criminals in Nuremberg. This consists of a shorthand record, incomplete in places, of the meeting that took place on 12 November 1938. Reprinted in: *IMG*, Vol. XXVIII, pp.499–540.

4 In part this policy was also an attempt by the National Socialist state to reverse the structural consequences of the world economic crisis. In this crisis many of the unemployed had sought to make a living as 'proletarian self-employed salesmen or more often tradesmen'. 'By trying to eke out a living with a small shop, repair work or other manual skills they came into conflict with established merchants, skilled tradesmen and manufacturers.' The 'policy of Aryanization mainly served to improve the economic position of the non-Jewish middle class by removing the competition'. Esra Bennathan, 'Die demographische und wirtschaftliche Struktur der Juden' (hereinafter cited as 'Bennathan, "Struktur"'), in: Werner E. Mosse (ed.), *Entscheidungsjahr 1932. Zur Judenfrage in der Endphase der Weimarer Republik*, Tübingen 1966, pp.125, 131.

5 'Die Umschichtung in der deutschen Wirtschaft', in: *Politiken*, 28 October 1938. See also: *Jahrbuch des deutschen Handwerks 1938/39*, Berlin 1939, p.16 (here the decline in the total number of workshops for 1938 is given as 11 per cent, 'a loss in terms of numbers, but a net gain overall in terms of productivity'); Ulrich Müller, 'Die Entwicklung des Handwerks in den letzten Jahren unter besonderer Berücksichtigung der nationalsozialistischen Handwerkspolitik und Handwerksgesetzgebung' (Diss.), Berlin 1938. For a useful account of the systematic policy of business closures and concentrations during those years, including a discussion of 'Aryanization', see Herbert Block, 'Industrial Concentration versus Small Business. The Trend of Nazi Policy', in: *Social Research* 10 (1943), pp.155–99.

6 From a telephone conversation at the time between Göring and the Gauleiter of Vienna, Odilo Globocnik: '*Göring*: I forgot to say: Fischböck! Fischböck must get Trade and Commerce. *Globocnik*: Of course, that's absolutely understood!' The transcript of the telephone conversation is reprinted in: *Der Hochverratsprozess gegen Dr Guido Schmidt vor dem Wiener Volksgerichtshof. Die gerichtlichen Protokolle* [court records of the trial of Dr Guido Schmidt on a charge of high treason], Vienna 1947, p.461.

7 'Die Säuberung des Berliner Einzelhandels', in: *Wirtschaftsblatt der Industrie- und Handelskammer zu Berlin*, 36 (1938), No.32/33, p.1611.

8 *Reichsgesetzblatt* 1938/I, p.1642.

9 Teletype message of 11 November 1938 from the SD Central Office in Berlin to Stahlecker in Vienna; Federal Archive, R 58/486, p.28. Sent at the behest of Heydrich, the message calls for Eichmann 'to be marched off to Berlin forthwith', so that he could attend an important conference next day on the 'general line of policy to be pursued in future' against the Jewish population. Eichmann was to brief the conference on his own experiences 'with the practical implementation'.

10 The Reich Commissioner for the Reunification of Austria with the German Reich, Josef Bürckel, who was responsible for the progressive harmonization of Austria's administrative, legal, economic and social systems, and for the issue of the necessary transitional rulings (see below).

11 Helmut Krausnick, 'Judenverfolgung', reprinted in: Martin Broszat, Hans-Adolf Jacobsen, Helmut Krausnick, *Konzentrationslager, Kommissarbefehl, Judenverfolgung* (= *Anatomie des SS-Staates*, Vol. II) (hereinafter cited as 'Krausnick, *Judenverfolgung*'), Olten/Freiburg i.Br. 1965, p.343.

12 'Minutes of the meeting to discuss the Jewish question held in the Reich Ministry of the Interior on 16 December 1938'; Hamburg State Archive, Krogmann family archive I/C 14 VIII, pp.464–73. Reprinted in: 'Bevölkerungsstruktur und Massenmord' (= *Beiträge zur nationalsozialistischen Gesundheits- und Sozialpolitik*, Vol. 9, Berlin 1991). Those present at this follow-up meeting, apart from the two ministers mentioned, included the Minister of Finance, the head of the Reich Chancellery, Berlin's chief of police, 'plus a large number of Gauleiters, provincial government leaders, SS-Gruppenführer Heydrich, etc., etc.' Hamburg alone was represented by its 'Governing Mayor' and two aides.

13 'Der Stadtpräsident der Reichshauptstadt Berlin, Sonderbericht über die Entjudung des Einzelhandels in Berlin', drafted by Dr Ernst Schaar; Federal Archive, R 7/2170, pp.56–76. According to a report that appeared in the *Berliner Lokalanzeiger* on 25 January 1939, the number of Jewish retail businesses that had 'ceased to exist' was not just two-thirds but more than three-quarters of the total, with precisely 600 left out of 3,750; the rest had been 'shut down due to insufficient need'. See also: *Deutschlandberichte der Sozialdemokratischen Partei Deutschlands 1934–1940* (*Sopade*), Frankfurt a.M. 1980, p.1178 f. (1938), p.208 ff. (1939).

14 Hans Wagner, 'Die Überführung jüdischer Betriebe in deutschen Besitz. Unter Berücksichtigung der Verhältnisse in Baden' (Diss.), Heidelberg 1941, p.237 f. Cf. also: Bennathan, 'Struktur', p.131.

15 No.538 of 15 November 1938.

16 Heinz Boberach (ed.), *Meldungen aus dem Reich. Die geheimen Lageberichte des Sicherheitsdienstes der SS 1938 bis 1945* (hereinafter cited as '*Meldungen aus dem Reich*'), Herrsching 1984, Vol. 2, pp.20, 26.

17 'Die Judenfrage als Faktor der Aussenpolitik im Jahre 1938', written by Emil Schumburg on 25 January 1939; reprinted in: *German Foreign Policy Records*, Series D, Vol. 5, p.781.

18 'Die Entjudung der Wirtschaft in der Ostmark', the catalogue to the exhibition of the same name staged by the Property Transaction Agency in the Ministry of Economics and Labour, Vienna (no date of publication), p.3. The exhibition took place in July/August 1939, and was open to an 'interested and select circle of national comrades'. See also the report of the Reich Commissioner for Private Enterprise (a later development of the Property Transaction Agency), Walter Rafelsberger, to Goebbels, dated 6 November 1939; YIVO, OccE 6a-I.

19 Cf. Hans Kernbauer, Fritz Weber, 'Österreichs Wirtschaft 1938–1945', in: Emmerich Tálos, Ernst Hanisch, Wolfgang Neugebauer (eds.), *NS-Herrschaft in Österreich 1938–1945*, Vienna 1988, p.49. The volume also contains a number of illuminating essays on socio-economic issues which are very much in line with our own thinking.

20 'Wien, wie es exportiert und importiert', newspaper article (undated); Federal Archive, R 104/D/1–44.

21 Letter from Gater to senior civil servant Rudolf Kratz, dated 24 June 1938; General Administrative Archive (Vienna), RK/box 38. Kratz subsequently involved the future Federal Minister of Economic Affairs and Federal Chancellor Ludwig Erhard in the rationalization of the Austrian economy – 'under the command of the Gauleiter'; Erhard 'gladly agreed to help'. (Cf. 'Besprechung mit Herrn Dr Ehrhardt [sic] vom Institut für Wirtschaftsbeobachtung der deutschen Fertigware, Nürnberg', the record of a meeting with Kratz at the beginning of December 1938; ibid., box 84.)

22 'Vorschläge für das Vorgehen bei der Arisierung der Schuheinzelhandelsgeschäfte vom 24.6.1938'; General Administrative Archive (Vienna), RK/box 38.

23 General Administrative Archive (Vienna), RK/box 84. This set of documents also contains the detailed 'Report on the work of the RKW's Austria Office' from November 1938.

24 Letter of 3 June 1938; General Administrative Archive (Vienna), RK/box 84. A large number of separate reports prepared by the RKW are housed in the archive of Vienna's Chamber of Commerce and Industry, packets 2528/1 and 2.

25 RKW – Austria Office, business audit questionnaire; General Administrative Archive (Vienna), RK/box 84/2205/2.

26 Cf. Karl Schubert, 'Die Entjudung der ostmärkischen Wirtschaft und die Bemessung des Kaufpreises im Entjudungsverfahren' (Diss.), College of World Trade, Vienna 1940; State Commissioner for Private Enterprise (ed.), 'Bericht über die Entjudung der Ostmark' (status as at 1 February 1939). (The last-named report is filed under shelf mark II 32693 in the library of the Vienna Chamber of Commerce.)

27 On the South-East Europe Society, see also pp. 215–16.

28 'Bericht über die Entjudung der Ostmark', pp.13, 17. In the autumn of 1938 Rafelsberger outlined his plans at a conference of the Reich Working Party on Regional Planning in Graz. (Walter Rafelsberger, 'Die wirtschaftliche Eingliederung der Ostmark in den grossdeutschen Raum', in: *Raumforschung und Raumordnung 2* (1938), pp.481–7.)

29 General Administrative Archive (Vienna), RK/box 84.

30 Second and third supplements 'to the proposals for an effective elimination of Jewish elements from society', drafted by Walter Rafelsberger on 22 and 27 October 1938; General Administrative Archive (Vienna), RK/box 47. See also: Herbert Rosenkranz, *Verfolgung und Selbstbehauptung. Die Juden in Österreich 1938–1945*, Vienna/Munich 1978, p.208 ff.; Gerhard Botz, *Wohnungspolitik und Judendeportation in Wien 1938 bis 1945. Zur Funktion des Antisemitismus als Ersatz nationalsozialistischer Sozialpolitik* (hereinafter cited as 'Botz, *Wohnungspolitik*'), Vienna/Salzburg 1975, p.89 ff.

31 Letters from Rafelsberger and Neubacher to Göring and Funk; General Administrative Archive (Vienna), RK/box 74. (The formulations used here by Rafelsberger are repeated later in the minutes of the Wannsee conference.)

32 Memorandum of the General Directorate of Highway Engineering dated 13 March 1939; Central State Archive (Potsdam), 46.01/1200, pp.321–3.

33 'Bericht über die Entjudung der Ostmark', p.10.

34 ibid., p.21.

35 Minutes of some of the advisory board's meetings are preserved in the General Administrative Archive (Vienna), RK/boxes 47 and 74.

36 These included the Audit Office, the Omnia Trust Company, the German Auditing and Trust Company, the Property Management and Pensions Corporation (VVRA), the Household Goods Registry, the Dutch Company for the Liquidation of Business Enterprises (NAGU), the General Dutch Property Management Agency (Anbo), the Dutch Reich Office of Trade and Commerce and – charged with the cataloguing of assets – the former Jewish banking house of Lippmann & Rosenthal.

37 Letter of December 1940 from the deputy commander of the SS and police in the Netherlands, Friedrich Knolle, to his superior Wilhelm Harster; as quoted in: Luis De Jong, *Het Koninkrijk der Nederlanden en de tweede werel-doorlog* (hereinafter cited as 'De Jong'), Vol. 5, 's-Gravenhage 1974, p.1003.

38 Minutes of the meeting of the 'interministerial committee on matters relating to capital investment' held on 23 September 1941 in the Reich Ministry of Economic Affairs; Political Archive of the Foreign Office (Bonn), Inland IIg/219.

39 Dietrich Eichholtz, *Geschichte der deutschen Kriegswirtschaft 1939–1945*, Vol. I (hereinafter cited as 'Eichholtz I'), Berlin 1984, p.374.

40 See note 38. In Belgium 588 Jewish firms out of a total of 7,700 were 'Aryanized' and approximately 6,400 were wound up. Cf. Ludwig Nestler, *Europa unterm Hakenkreuz. Die faschistische Okkupationspolitik in Belgien, Luxemburg und den Niederlanden (1940–1945)*, Berlin 1990, p.62.

41 Report of the Reich Ministry of Economic Affairs for the interministerial committee, September 1941; as quoted in: Eichholtz I, p.375 f.

42 ibid., p.375.

43 Hilberg writes that Jewish capital assets did not play a major role in the Dutch economy, but that the Germans were still 'interested in every Jewish firm, every Jewish warehouse and every Jewish option, because they could never be sure that a Jewish minority interest in a particular company or market could not be combined with a German minority interest to create a controlling majority. The Netherlands were a wide-open market, and within a few months the country was awash with German businessmen looking for opportunities to invest capital.' Raul Hilberg, *Die Vernichtung der europäischen Juden. Die Gesamtgeschichte des Holocaust* (hereinafter cited as 'Hilberg'), Berlin 1982, p.398.

44 De Jong, Vol. 7, p.419.

45 ibid., p.430.

46 Jacob Presser, *Ondergang. De Vervolging en Verdelging van het Nederlandse Jodendom 1940–1945*, 's-Gravenhage 1974, Vol. 2, p.205.

47 De Jong, Vol. 6, p.41.

48 ibid., Vol. 6, p.263.

49 ibid., Vol. 5, p.602 f.

50 A suggestion proffered by H.C.H. Wohltat, Seyss-Inquart's representative at the Nederlandse Bank; ibid., p.1004.

51 The so-called 'first four-year plan' was announced by Hitler two days after

his appointment as Reich Chancellor on 1 February 1933; the Four-Year Plan as we know it was the second, which Hitler announced on 18 October 1936 at the Reich party rally of the NSDAP in Nuremberg. He appointed Göring as Commissioner for the Four-Year Plan. Göring established his own small department to administer the Plan, known as the Four-Year Plan Authority (sometimes shortened to the 'Four-Year Plan').

52 Address given before the Berlin Academy of Administration by Erich Neumann on 29 April 1941; as quoted in: Eichholtz I, p.37.

53 'Hitlers Denkschrift zum Vierjahresplan 1936', with an introduction by Wilhelm Treue, in: *Vierteljahrshefte für Zeitgeschichte* (hereinafter cited as '*VfZG*') 3 (1955), pp.184–210.

54 Otto Donner, 'Die deutsche Kriegswirtschaft', in: *Nauticus* 27 (1944), pp.397–431, here esp. p.402 f.

55 Eichholtz I, p.42.

56 *IMG*, Vol. XXVIII, p.506.

57 See note 54.

58 Otto Donner, 'Der Vierjahresplan', an address given before the Berlin Academy of Administration on 29 April 1941 (hereinafter cited as 'Donner, "Vierjahresplan"'); Secret State Archive, Berlin, Rep. 90 M/36, p.29.

59 ibid., p.34.

60 Report on a meeting with the Reichsmarschall on 7 November 1941 (minutes taken by a Dr Ritter); Federal Archive, R 25/99.

61 Carl Rachor in a letter to Robert Hallwachs, 16 May 1955; Secret State Archive, Berlin, Rep. 90/2472.

62 'Vorträge und Veröffentlichungen von Herrn Prof. Donner; Vortrag vom 16.6.1939 vor der Hochschullehrer-Tagung der Forschungsstelle für Wehrwirtschaft'; Secret State Archive, Berlin, Rep. 90 M/36.

63 ibid., p.12.

64 ibid., p.15.

65 Götz Aly, Karl Heinz Roth, *Die restlose Erfassung. Volkszählen, Identifizieren, Aussondern im Nationalsozialismus* (hereinafter cited as 'Aly/Roth'), Berlin 1984, pp.91–5.

66 Donner, 'Vierjahresplan', p.45.

67 ibid., p.46 f.

68 Announcement by Göring on the enlargement of the general council of the Four-Year Plan Authority, dated 7 December 1939; Central State Archive (Potsdam), RMEL/941, p.86. Cf. also: Dieter Petzina, *Autarkiepolitik im Dritten Reich. Der nationalsozialistische Vierjahresplan*, Stuttgart 1968, p.134 ff.

69 A classic instance of the resulting conflict was the relationship between the Reich Minister of Food and Agriculture, Walther Darré, and his undersecretary Herbert Backe (cf. Federal Archive/BDC, personal files of Herbert Backe, Walther Darré, Hans-Joachim Riecke; Federal Archive, papers of Walther Darré and Herbert Backe). The same conflict can be seen in a less acute form in the relationship between the Reich Minister of Labour, Franz Seldte, and his undersecretary Friedrich Syrup.

70 'Ein Staatssekretär der Kriegswirtschaft', in: *Deutsche Allgemeine Zeitung* of 2 October 1941.

71 'Staatssekretär im Vierjahresplan und in der Kriegswirtschaft. Zum 50. Geburtstag von Staatssekretär Körner', in: *Der Vierjahresplan* of 15 September 1943.

72 The idea had been put forward by head of section Normann in the Four-Year Plan Authority at an interministerial meeting on 8 January 1941. Normann proposed 'taking the Jews right out of German labour law and making them subject to a special arrangement, a kind of "Jewish code"'. Kurt Pätzold (ed.), *Verfolgung, Vertreibung, Vernichtung. Dokumente des faschistischen Antisemitismus* (hereinafter cited as 'Pätzold'), Leipzig 1987, p.280. Hans-Henning von Normann, whose remit at the Four-Year Plan Authority included 'Jewish affairs', later became a Federal attorney in the Federal Administrative Court.

73 Hilberg, p.652.

74 Neumann, *Behemoth*, p.565.

75 Cf. 'Personalnotizen', in: *Deutsche Allgemeine Zeitung* of 24 October 1936, *Frankfurter Zeitung* of 25 July 1938.

76 See note 18.

77 *Reich Law Gazette* 1938/I, p.415 f.

78 See note 12.

79 *IMG*, Vol. XXXI, p.230 ff.

80 As quoted in: *Faschismus, Getto, Massenmord*, published by the Jewish Historical Institute, Warsaw (hereinafter cited as 'Faschismus, Getto, Massenmord'), Berlin 1962, document 1.

81 Werner Präg, Wolfgang Jacobmeyer (eds.), *Das Diensttagebuch des deutschen Generalgouverneurs in Polen 1939–1945* (hereinafter cited as 'Diensttagebuch'), Stuttgart 1975, pp.109–11. Among those attending the meeting were Minister of Finance von Krosigk, the undersecretaries of the key ministries and the Gauleiters of the territories bordering on the Government General. The minutes of this crisis session (the so-called 'Karinhall meeting') are reprinted in: *IMG*, Vol. XXXVI, pp.299–307.

82 Copy of the minutes of the meeting on 1 April 1940, Appendix 5 to the report of the Reich Audit Office; Central State Archive (Potsdam), Reichsfinanzministerium/B 6159, p.102. Reprinted from a different source in: *Dokumenty I Materialy do dziejów okupacji niemieckiej*, Vol. III, Warszawa/Lódź/Kraków 2946, p.167 f.

83 Rademacher's memorandum of 12 August 1940: 'Gedanken über die Gründung einer intereuropäischen Bank für die Verwertung des Judenvermögens in Europa', Political Archive of the Foreign Office (Bonn), Inland IIg/177, p.228

84 Eichholtz I, p.231.

85 Danuta Czech, *Das Kalendarium von Auschwitz* (hereinafter cited as 'Czech'), Reinbek 1989, p.80.

86 'Wirtschaftsstab Ost, Beurteilung der Lage in Stichworten vom 14.7.1941'; Federal Archive/Military Archive (Freiburg), RW 31/11, p.49 f.

87 Federal Archive/Military Archive (Freiburg), RW 12/189.

88 Federal Archive/Military Archive (Freiburg), RW 31/11, p.104 f.

89 Meeting between Göring, Backe, Riecke and the senior commanders of the Wehrmacht; *IMG*, Vol. XXXVI, p.105 f.

90 Memorandum on the outcome of meeting of 2 May 1941 with the under-secretaries on the subject of Barbarossa; *IMG*, Vol. XXXI, p.84.

Chapter 2: Looking to the East

1 O.M.G.U.S., *Ermittlungen gegen die I.G. Farbenindustrie AG*, Nördlingen 1986, p.320 f.

2 Anton Reithinger, 'Das europäische Aussenhandelssystem', in: *Europäische Revue 10* (1934), No.11, p.738.

3 Anton Reithinger, 'Das europäische Bevölkerungsproblem', in: *Europäische Revue 10* (1934), No.9, p.607.

4 Anton Reithinger, 'Das europäische Agrarproblem', in: *Europäische Revue 10* (1934), No.8 (special issue 'Der Balkan'), p.553.

5 ibid.

6 Anton Reithinger, 'Bericht über eine Reise nach Polen im November 1932'; Central State Archive (Potsdam), I.G. Farben/A 622.

7 Volkswirtschaftliche Abteilung der I.G. Farben, 'Bericht über Polen (1938)'; Central State Archive (Potsdam), I.G. Farben/A 3672.

8 Raymond Leslie Buell, *Poland: Key to Europe* (hereinafter cited as 'Buell'), New York/London 1939. Buell was president of the Foreign Policy Association, which, with the Council on Foreign Relations, was one of the two key foreign policy think-tanks of the New Deal.

9 Institut d'Economie Sociale, 'La Structure Sociale des Campagnes Polonaises' (= *Questions agraires*, No.1), Warsaw 1937 (French summary of a Polish study); Hugh Seton-Watson, *Osteuropa zwischen den Kriegen 1918–1941* (hereinafter cited as 'Seton-Watson'), Paderborn 1948; Georg Kagan, 'Agrarian Regime of Pre-War Poland', in: *Journal of Central European Affairs*, No.3, October 1943; Edward Lipinski, 'Deflation als Mittel der Konjunkturpolitik in Polen' (= *Kieler Vorträge*, Vol. 42), Jena 1936.

10 Even the German statistician von Ungern-Sternberg, who could not possibly be accused of favouring a radical change in the system of land tenure, criticizes the Polish land reform as too limited. With 25 million hectares of land available for farming and 18.6 million hectares under cultivation, only 2.5 million hectares were covered by the agrarian reform programme. See Roderich von Ungern-Sternberg, *Die Bevölkerungsverhältnisse in Estland, Lettland, Litauen und Polen*, Berlin 1939, p.117.

11 Seton-Watson, p.137.

12 Madajczyk describes the close collaboration between Polish and German agrarian planners in the years after 1934. Their jointly evolved plans for reforming Polish agriculture envisaged amongst other things the 'thinning-out' of agriculture in Galicia, a controlled programme of industrialization and the relocation of the 'population surplus' to the Polish marshlands, which would first have to be drained. Czesław Madajczyk, 'Faszyzacja polityki agrarnej w Polsce w latach 1934–1939', in: *Przeglad Historyczny*, Vol. 45, No.I, Warsaw 1954, pp.56–73.

13 34 per cent of farms consisted of no more than 2 hectares, with another 31 per cent having a maximum of 5 hectares. The smallholdings in these two categories accounted for approx. 15 per cent of the available farmland. A

mere 0.6 per cent of farms were larger than 100 hectares – and these farmed 43 per cent of the country's agricultural land. According to experts, at least 5 hectares of land were needed at that time to feed a farmer and his family, while 15 hectares were considered the minimum size for a farm to return a profit. In actual fact, many families scraped a living from a smallholding of 1 to 2 hectares, often working for hire in the fields of large landowners to make ends meet.

14 Witold Lipski, *Die Landwirtschaft in Polen*, Warsaw 1964, p.7.

15 Whereas in earlier years, when the excess of births over deaths stood at 400,000, the number of people emigrating each year was 900,000, in 1937 the number of emigrants exceeded the number returning from abroad by only 20,000. ('Polens Agrarreform', in: *Berliner Börsen-Zeitung* of 13 February 1937. The following newspaper articles are nearly all taken from the collection of cuttings held by the Federal Archive in its 'Deutsche Reichsbank' holdings.)

16 Buell writes that Polish farmers felt a certain sense of guilt about selling their surpluses, having a 'natural aversion toward the exploitation of nature on a large scale' (p.203).

17 *Polen von Polen gesehen*, Berlin 1939, p.73. The book was published at the instigation of the Polish Foreign Ministry.

18 'Zur Wirtschafts- und Finanzlage Polens', in: *Osteuropäische Korrespondenz*, 21 April 1926.

19 'Polens Finanzen und Wirtschaft im Zeichen der Amerika-Anleihe', in: *Rigasche Rundschau*, 27 October 1927.

20 ibid. The 'foreign financial adviser to the government', who under the terms of the agreement exercised extensive control over Poland's economic policy for the next three years, was Charles S. Dewey, former Assistant Secretary of the United States Treasury (Buell, p.127).

21 Before the First World War a plough cost the equivalent of 134 kg of rye; by 1937 the cost had risen to 273 kg. '10 kg of sugar cost 46 kg of rye before the war, today the same amount of sugar costs 110 kg. And that is without even considering those regions where poor roads and communications, high transport costs and limited market opportunities are making the situation of farmers even more difficult.' (*Kattowitzer Zeitung*, 24/25 December 1937.)

22 On his biography see: Czesław Madajczyk, *Die Okkupationspolitik Nazideutschlands in Polen 1939–1945* (hereinafter cited as 'Madajczyk, *Okkupationspolitik*'), Berlin 1987, p.62.

23 As quoted in: 'Die Not des polnischen Dorfes', in: *Kölnische Zeitung*, 29 December 1932.

24 Buell, p.144.

25 ibid., p.vi.

26 The industrialization project was known as COP (Centralny Okreg Przemyslowy = Central Industrial Zone).

27 'Polens Bauernproblem', in: *Deutsche Zukunft*, 31 May 1938; Buell, p.161. In February 1939 the German Embassy in Warsaw reported that the Polish population had grown by 4.5 millions in the period 1928–37 inclusive, while the number of industrial workers had risen by only 20,000 over the

same period. ('Bericht über die allgemeine Wirtschaftslage in Polen im Jahre 1938'; Central State Archive (Potsdam) (now Political Archive of the Foreign Office), Auswärtiges Amt/68353, p.181 f.)

28 *Wirtschaftsdienst* (Vol. 22), 15 January 1937. This and subsequent references are taken from the journal published by the Hamburg World Economic Archive.

29 *Nachrichten für Aussenhandel* (Berlin), 25 August 1937. The People's Party had emerged from an alliance of the three 'leading groupings of Polish peasant farmers' under the leadership of Wincenty Witos.

30 Seton-Watson, p.196.

31 Founded in 1897, the Bund was the oldest Jewish workers' party in Lithuania, Russia and Poland. After the First World War the Bund was the largest Jewish political organization in Poland; it actively opposed Zionism and campaigned for equal rights and cultural autonomy for the Jewish minority.

32 'Die Judenfrage wird in Polen akut', in: *Deutsche Allgemeine Zeitung*, 22 December 1938.

33 Erich Wunderlich, 'Das moderne Polen in politisch-geographischer Betrachtung (auf Grund seiner Reisen)' (= *Stuttgarter Geographische Studien*, Vol. 33/34), Stuttgart 1933 (hereinafter cited as 'Wunderlich'), p.52. In 1917 Wunderlich had organized the publication and editing of the official 'Handbook of Poland' at the request of the German occupation authority.

34 Wunderlich, p.52.

35 Jenny Radt, *Die Juden in Polen*, Berlin 1935, p.22.

36 Simon Segal, *The New Poland and the Jews* (hereinafter cited as 'Segal'), New York 1938, p.146. Cf. also: *Sitzungsberichte des Kongresses der organisierten nationalen Gruppen in den Staaten Europas, 1925–1933*, Geneva 1926 and 1927, Vienna-Leipzig 1928, '29, '30, '31, '32, '33, '34; and Ewald Ammende (ed.), *Die Nationalitäten in den Staaten Europas*, Vienna-Leipzig 1931; (also ed.), *Die Nationalitäten in den Staaten Europas. Sammlung von Lageberichten des europäischen Nationalitäten-Kongresses. Ergänzungen*, Vienna 1932.

37 Ezra Mendelsohn, *The Jews of East Central Europe between the World Wars* (hereinafter cited as 'Mendelsohn'), Bloomington 1983, p.28.

38 Radio address by Colonel Zygmunt Wenda, chief of staff of the 'Camp of National Unity', as quoted in: 'Polen erstrebt Massenabwanderung der Juden', in: *Berliner Börsen-Zeitung*, 22 December 1938.

39 Mendelsohn, p.75.

40 'Die Judenfrage in Polen', in: *Neue Freie Presse Wien*, 14 January 1938.

41 'Die polnische Innenpolitik', in: *Danziger Neueste Nachrichten*, 17 February 1939. See also Segal, passim.

42 'Die Judenfrage in Polen', in: *Neue Freie Presse Wien*, 14 January 1938.

43 Buell, p.303.

44 Mendelsohn, p.74. The figures quoted in the Polish press are thought by Mendelsohn to be 'probably much too low'.

45 Magnus Brechtken, *'Madagaskar für die Juden'. Antisemitische Ideen und politische Praxis 1885–1945* (= *Studien zur Zeitgeschichte*, Vol. 53) (hereinafter cited as 'Brechtken, *Madagaskar*'), Munich 1997, p.88. Such demands were directed primarily at the British government, the Poles pointing out that

this would also relieve the pressure on British policy in Palestine. The emigration of Poland's Jewish minority to Palestine appeared to become impossible in 1936, following renewed – and this time particularly violent – rioting by the Arab population against Jewish settlement and the British mandate policy. The British government, fearing that the revolt might spread throughout the Near East and that the Arab national movement might be driven into the arms of the Axis powers, distanced itself from its earlier undertaking to resettle Jewish emigrants from Poland in Palestine. In 1935 a total of 30,593 people emigrated to Palestine, but following the shift in British policy this number fell to 13,256 in 1936 and 3,708 in 1937 (Mendelsohn, p.79).

46 Brechtken, p.109 ff.

47 ibid., p.124 f.

48 Mendelsohn, p.80.

49 Under the terms of the Haavara Agreement (Ha'avara is the Hebrew word for 'transfer'), which was made in 1933 between the Reich Ministry of Economic Affairs and the Jewish Agency, Jews who emigrated to Palestine from Germany paid a proportion of their assets into an account at the Reichsbank. On their arrival in Palestine a portion of that money – a smaller and smaller portion as the years went by – was paid over to them once German goods to the same value had been exported to Palestine. The advantage of the Agreement for the emigrants was that they could transfer their assets at a more favourable exchange rate than the official rate. The German government profited from the Agreement because it encouraged Jewish emigration without draining the Reich's scarce reserves of foreign exchange, and because it created an incentive for the Jewish emigrants to campaign for an end to the boycott of German goods, which had been imposed with the aim of protecting the Jewish minority in Germany. Cf. W. Feilchenfeld, W. Michaelis, L. Pinner, *Haavara-Transfer nach Palästina und Einwanderung deutscher Juden 1933–1939*, Tübingen 1972. See also *Enzyklopädie des Holocaust*.

50 Yfaat Weiss, 'Das Gespräch zwischen Jerzy Ptocki, Stephen Wise und Louis Lipsky am 31. März 1938', in: *Arbeitsemigration und Flucht. Vertreibung und Arbeitskräfteregulierung im Zwischenkriegseuropa*, Berlin/Göttingen 1993, pp.205–12, here esp. p.210. See also (by the same author): 'The Transfer Agreement and the Boycott Movement: A Jewish Dilemma on the Eve of the Holocaust', in: *Yad Vashem Studies XXVI*, Jerusalem 1998, pp.129–71, here esp. p.170.

51 'Mit einem Blankoscheck in der Tasche', in: *Kattowitzer Zeitung*, 4 April 1939.

52 'Jews of Poland', in: *The Times*, 4 April 1939.

53 One exception that is well worth reading still is Alfred Döblin's *Reise in Polen* (Munich 1987). In this book Döblin portrays his encounter with the Jewish world in Poland in 1924. Writing without the Western arrogance that characterizes most accounts, albeit with a thoroughly sexist perspective on women, he describes his own sense of not belonging in this world, and makes a genuine attempt to empathize with it and understand it.

54 Wunderlich, p.42.

55 ibid., p.43.

56 Rolf Wingendorf, *Polen – Volk zwischen Ost und West*, Berlin 1939, p.91 f.

57 Peter-Heinz Seraphim (ed.), *Polen und seine Wirtschaft* (hereinafter cited as 'Seraphim, *Polen*'), Königsberg 1937, p.4; see also (by the same author): 'Die Wanderungsbewegung des jüdischen Volkes' (= *Schriften zur Geopolitik*, No.18), Heidelberg/Berlin/Magdeburg 1940, p.8.

58 Seraphim, *Polen*, p.21.

59 ibid., p.23.

60 ibid., p.35.

61 Theodor Oberländer, *Die agrarische Überbevölkerung Polens* (hereinafter cited as 'Oberländer, *Überbevölkerung Polens*'), Berlin 1935.

62 For a critical assessment of Seraphim and 'Ostforschung' – German research on eastern Europe – see esp.: Rudi Goguel, 'Die Mitwirkung deutscher Wissenschaftler am Okkupationsregime in Polen im zweiten Weltkrieg, untersucht an drei Institutionen der deutschen Ostforschung' (Diss.), Humboldt University, Berlin 1964; Gerhard F. Volkmer, 'Die deutsche Forschung zu Osteuropa und zum osteuropäischen Judentum in den Jahren 1933 bis 1945', in: *Forschungen zur osteuropäischen Geschichte*, Vol. 42 (hereinafter cited as 'Volkmer'), Berlin 1989, pp.109–214; Michael Burleigh, *Germany Turns Eastwards. A Study of Ostforschung in the Third Reich*, Cambridge 1988. All three books examine the role of German 'Ostforschung' in the context of National Socialist expansionist policy towards Poland and the Soviet Union.

63 Peter-Heinz Seraphim, *Das Judentum im osteuropäischen Raum*, Essen 1938.

64 ibid., p.129.

65 ibid., p.556.

66 ibid., p.303.

67 ibid., p.291.

68 ibid., pp.175, 185, 266.

69 ibid., p.287.

70 ibid., p.288.

71 ibid., p.224.

72 ibid., p.320.

73 ibid., p.354.

74 ibid., p.567.

75 ibid., p.568.

76 Peter-Heinz Seraphim, 'Polen, das Land der grossen Unterschiede', in: *Frankfurter Zeitung*, 30 April 1939.

Chapter 3: Demographic Economics

1 Werner Conze, 'Die ländliche Überbevölkerung in Polen' (hereinafter cited as 'Conze, "Überbevölkerung"'), in: *Arbeiten des XIV. Internationalen Soziologen-Kongresses Bucaresti, Mitteilungen, Abteilung B – Das Dorf*, Vol. I (= D. Gusti (ed.), *Schriften zur Soziologie, Ethik und Politik. Studien und Forschung*), Bucaresti 1940, S.40. (We are grateful to Karl Heinz Roth for drawing our attention to this work.)

2 ibid., p.48.

3 Werner Conze, 'Die Strukturkrise des östlichen Mitteleuropas vor and nach 1919', in: *VfZG* I (1953), pp.319–38.

4 See note 2.

5 Carl Brinkmann, 'Das Problem der agraren Überbevölkerung in Europa', in: *Arbeitstagung des Forschungsdienstes. Dresden, October 1942* (= *Agrarpolitik-Betriebslehre, Aktuelle Probleme, Sonderheft 18*), Neudamm 1943, p.58 f. The conference at which this paper was given had been organized by Himmler's adviser on resettlement policy, Konrad Meyer (see next chapter).

6 ibid., p.61.

7 Oberländer, *Überbevölkerung Polens*, p.9.

8 Selig Sigmund Cohn, 'Die Theorie des Bevölkerungsoptimums' (Diss.) (hereinafter cited as 'Cohn'), Marburg 1934, p.16 ff. See also Susanne Heim, Ulrike Schaz, *Berechnung und Beschwörung. Überbevölkerung – Kritik einer Debatte* (hereinafter cited as 'Heim/Schaz'), Berlin/Göttingen 1996.

9 The use of mathematical formulae was very popular in general among the 'optimum theorists', who used them to invest the most banal statements with a spurious air of scientific authority, believing they could even express 'the maximum sum of happiness, and hence the political optimum', in mathematical terms. According to Gunnar Myrdal, it was to be found 'where the mathematical product of the number of people and the mean degree of happiness attains its maximum value'. Cohn, p.86.

10 'Verhandlungen des Vereins für Sozialpolitik in Wien 1926, Krisis der Weltwirtschaft. Überbevölkerung Westeuropas. Steuerüberwälzung' (= *Schriften des Vereins für Sozialpolitik*, Vol. 172), Munich/Leipzig 1926, p.170.

11 Paul Mombert, *Bevölkerungsentwicklung und Wirtschaftsgestaltung*, Leipzig 1932, p.38.

12 ibid., p.40.

13 Helmut Meinhold, 'Die Aufgaben der Sektion Wirtschaft im Institut für Deutsche Ostarbeit' (MS), January 1941; Federal Archive, R 52 IV/144, p.41.

14 Oberländer, *Überbevölkerung Polens*, p.49.

15 Helmut Meinhold, 'Die Industrialisierung des Generalgouvernements' (*Manuskriptreihe des Instituts für Deutsche Ostarbeit* – for internal use only!), December 1941; Federal Archive, R 52 IV/144d (hereinafter cited as 'Meinhold, "Industrialisierung"'), p.41 f.

16 Helmut Meinhold, 'Die Arbeiterreserven des Generalgouvernements' (hereinafter cited as 'Meinhold, "Arbeiterreserven"'), in: *Die Burg* 3 (1942), No.3, p.282.

17 ibid., p.280 f.

18 Helmut Meinhold, 'Die nichtlandwirtschaftliche Überbevölkerung im ehemaligen Polen', in: *Ostraumberichte*, Neue Folge I (1942), p.132.

19 Oberländer, *Überbevölkerung Polens*, p.51 f.

20 Meinhold, 'Industrialisierung', p.167.

21 ibid., p.168.

22 Theodor Oberländer, 'Die agrarische Überbevölkerung Ostmitteleuropas' (hereinafter cited as 'Oberländer, "Ostmitteleuropa"'), in: Hermann Aubin, Otto Brunner, Wolfgang Kohte, Johannes Papritz (eds.), *Deutsche Ostforschung, Ergebnisse und Aufgaben seit dem Ersten Weltkrieg*, Leipzig 1943, p.421 f.

23 Meinhold, 'Industrialisierung', p.213 f.

24 Hans-Kraft Nonnenmacher, 'Die Wirtschaftsstruktur des galizischen Erdölgebietes', in: *Deutsche Forschung im Osten* I (1941), No.6, p.15 ff.

25 Neumann, *Behemoth*, p.190.

26 Oberländer, 'Ostmitteleuropa', p.418.

27 In this context it is interesting to note that in 1937–8 the NSDAP Party Court had to hear a charge of 'Bolshevist sympathies' brought against Oberländer by students. He was cleared of all charges. See the correspondence from 1938, Federal Archive/BDC, personal file of Theodor Oberländer.

28 Under this system most of the land was not privately owned, but belonged to the village commune, which allocated a piece of land to individual families – usually for five years at a time – for them to farm. The size of the plot was determined either by the number of male workers in the family or by the number of mouths to feed. Anyone who left the village community automatically forfeited his right to land.

29 The figures varied according to the basis on which they were calculated. The demographer Lev J. Lubny-Gerzik, for example, whose work was also respected in the West, concluded that in the four regions alone studied by him between 14 and 18 million people were surplus to need. Other experts started from the assumption that the total 'population surplus' of the Soviet Union amounted to 7.5 millions. See Heim/Schaz, p.75 ff. Cf. also L.E. Minc, *Agrarnoe perenasesnie i rynok truda v SSSR* ('Agrarian overpopulation and the labour market in the USSR'), Moscow/Leningrad 1929; as quoted in: Michael Hoffmann, *Die agrarische Überbevölkerung Russlands*, Berlin-Wilmersdorf 1932, p.103. Also A. Jugow, *Die Volkswirtschaft der Sowjetunion und ihre Probleme*, Dresden 1929. Jugow points out that 'the intention of the resettlement authorities is to relocate 5 million people in the space of 10 years'. But he claims that there was insufficient money available to fund the project. Jugow's own estimate was that 25–30 million people needed to be resettled, but expressed doubts about the practical feasibility of this. In the final analysis 'the only radical and realistic method' in the fight against continuing population growth was a 'general industrialization and intensification of economic activity'. This alone, however, would hardly suffice – even at 'American rates of growth' – to 'absorb the overpopulation' (p.112 f.). See also Raja Silberkweit, 'Analyse und Kritik der Frage der russischen Agrarübervölkerung. Ein Beitrag zu den Problemen der russischen Agrarpolitik' (Diss.), Leipzig 1934.

30 Moshe Levin, *Russian Peasants and Soviet Power. A Study of Collectivization*, London 1968, p.507.

31 Robert Conquest, *Ernte des Todes, Stalins Holocaust in der Ukraine 1929–1933*, Munich 1988, p.305. Conquest claims that approximately 5 million people out of a Ukrainian peasant population of 20–25 millions died of starvation. It is possible that these figures are too high. In 1943 a Ukrainian writer estimated that 2–4 million people in the Ukraine had fallen victim to famine and deportation in the wake of the drive to eliminate the kulak class. See Kubijowitsch, 'Bevölkerungsverteilung', in: *Siedlungsgeschichte, Bevölkerungsverteilung und Bevölkerungsbewegung der*

Ukraine (from *Geographie der Ukraine und benachbarten Gebiete*, Vol. I, edited by Dr W. Kubijowitsch), Berlin 1943, p.80.

32 Himmler's statistician, Richard Korherr, estimated that 11.5 million people died from these causes in the Soviet Union in 1933. ('Dynamik der Zahl und der natürlichen Bevölkerungsbewegung in der UdSSR in den Jahren 1924–1941'; Federal Archive/BDC, personal file of Richard Korherr.)

33 Oberländer, 'Ostmitteleuropa', p.419.

34 Oberländer, *Überbevölkerung Polens*, p.93.

35 Helmut Meinhold, 'Die Erweiterung des Generalgouvernements nach Osten. A. Allgemeines' (*Manuskriptreihe des Instituts für Deutsche Ostarbeit* – for internal use only!), July 1941; Federal Archive, R 52 IV/144a, p.1.

36 Karl C. Thalheim, 'Die menschlichen Wanderungen in Krise und Neuaufbau der Weltwirtschaft', a speech given before the German World Economics Society in Berlin on 28 November 1941, in: *Nachrichtenblatt der Reichsstelle für das Auswanderungswesen 24* (1924), Nos.10, 11 and 12, here No.12, p.188.

37 ibid., p.186. Thalheim, born in Reval in 1900, was director of the World Economics Institute at the College of Trade and Commerce in Leipzig. After the war he built up the East European Institute at the Free University of Berlin, and acted as adviser to succeeding Federal government administrations.

38 Richard Korherr, 'Europäische Wanderungsströme', in: *Der Wirtschafts-Ring 14* (1941), No.9 (28.2.1941), pp.210–13.

39 Karl C. v. Loesch, 'Die Umsiedlungsbewegungen in Europa', in: Franz Six (ed.), *Jahrbuch der Weltpolitik 1942*, Berlin 1942, pp.36–69. For his paean to this 'work of resettlement' Loesch was given access to the secret records of the Reich Commissioner for the Strengthening of German Nationhood ('for internal use only'). Loesch was director of the Institute for Border and Foreign Studies, and had taken part in the discussions on the 'General Plan for the East' (see p.270).

40 Heinrich Gottong, 'Die Juden im Generalgouvernement', in: *Das Vorfeld* I (1940), No.3, p.20. Gottong worked initially as a specialist in Jewish affairs for the department of population management and welfare in the Government General. Immediately prior to publication of this essay he had been involved with the closure of the Warsaw ghetto; a few months later he became an assistant in the ethnic research department at the Institute for German Development Work in the East, where Meinhold and Nonnenmacher were also employed. Gottong had studied for his doctorate under Hans F.K. Günther and Bruno K. Schultz – two leading theoreticians of race and ethnicity.

Chapter 4: War and Resettlement

1 Konrad Meyer, 'Grossraumprobleme der Agrarpolitik und Betriebslehre', in: *Arbeitstagung des Forschungsdienstes. Dresden, Oktober 1942* (= *Agrarpolitik-Betriebslehre*, Sonderheft 18), Neudamm 1943, pp.5–15.

2 Reprinted in: *Der grossdeutsche Freiheitskampf*, Berlin 1942, pp.67–100.

3 Himmler on questions of resettlement, on the occasion of a visit to Madrid

on 22 October 1940; Federal Archive, R 49/20; as quoted in: Karl Heinz Roth, 'Erster "Generalplan Ost" (April/Mai 1940) von Konrad Meyer', in: *Mitteilungen der Dokumentationsstelle zur NS-Sozialpolitik I* (1985), No.4, document 4.

4 ibid.

5 Cf. Robert L. Koehl, *RKFDV: German Resettlement and Population Policy 1939–1945* (hereinafter cited as 'Koehl'), Cambridge 1957, p.45.

6 Hans Buchheim, 'Rechtsstellung und Organisation des Reichskommissars für die Festigung deutschen Volkstums' (hereinafter cited as 'Buchheim'), in: *Gutachten des Instituts für Zeitgeschichte*, Vol. I, Munich 1958, p.275.

7 Koehl, p.24.

8 Buchheim, p.276.

9 Secret note from Rudolf Creutz to the senior SS and police commander of Danzig-West Prussia, 1 March 1940; Federal Archive/BDC, personal file of Ulrich Greifelt.

10 Cf. Wolfgang Ayass, '"Ein Gebot der nationalen Arbeitsdisziplin". Die Aktion "Arbeitsscheu Reich"', in: *Feinderklärung und Prävention. Kriminalbiologie, Zigeunerforschung und Asozialenpolitik (= Beiträge zur nationalsozialistischen Gesundheits- und Sozialpolitik*, Vol. 6), Berlin 1988, pp.43–74.

11 Himmler on questions of resettlement (see note 3).

12 Greifelt writing in the journal *Siedlung und Wirtschaft*; as quoted in: *Pressedienst für Wirtschaftsaufbau* (Berlin), 13 March 1941, p.2.

13 Götz Aly, *'Endlösung'. Völkerverschiebung und der Mord an den europäischen Juden* (hereinafter cited as 'Aly, *Endlösung*'), Frankfurt a.M. 1995, p.364.

14 See Koehl, pp.84 and 236.

15 Buchheim, p.258. What this meant in practice was that the *Reichsstatthalter* (Governor) or *Oberpräsident* of each 'Gau' or province also acted as the local representative of the RKF, while his senior SS and police commander functioned as his standing deputy. The only exceptions were the Gau of Danzig-West Prussia and the Government General, where the RKF was represented directly by the senior SS and police commander (ibid., p.249).

16 As of 1 August 1942 there were RKF representatives for the following regions: Warthegau, Danzig-West Prussia, Upper Silesia, East Prussia, the Government General, Steiermark, Kärnten, Lorraine, Luxembourg, Alsace, Tirol-Vorarlberg, Salzburg, the Sudetenland, Norway, the Netherlands, the Reich Commissariat for the Ostland [the occupied Baltic states], Southern Russia (Kiev) and France (Buchheim, p.249 f.). On the work of the Reich Commissioner for the Strengthening of German Nationhood in Slovenia, see the excellent regional study by Tone Ferenc: *Quellen zur nationalsozialistischen Entnationalisierungspolitik in Slowenien 1942–1945*, Maribor 1980.

17 *Biuletyn Głównej Komisji Badania Zbrodni Hitlerowskich w Polsce* (hereinafter cited as '*Biuletyn*'), Warsaw 1960, Vol. 12, document 9F.

18 ibid., document 16F.

19 Report submitted by senior SS and police commander Warthe, 18 December 1939; ibid., document 23F.

20 Könekamp's information about the ratio of numbers was probably wrong even then. But if not, then it was not long before the number of those who

were deported to make way for the incoming ethnic Germans was
increased (see, p.95).

21 Quoted from 'Bericht von Dr Könekamp – Polenfahrt vom 29.11. bis
9.12.39' (Könekamp's report on a fact-finding trip to Poland); Federal
Archive, R 57 neu/31.

22 See, p.89.

23 See, p.92.

24 *Biuletyn*, document 71F.

25 Letter from Heydrich to the commander of the security police and SD in
Cracow and to the inspectors of the security police and SD in Breslau,
Posen, Danzig and Königsberg, dated 21 December 1939; *Biuletyn*, docu-
ment 32F.

26 Memorandum of 8 January 1940 by SS Obersturmführer Franz Abromeit;
ibid., documents 37–39F.

27 The reference here is to the rural population of Alsace-Lorraine, which
spoke a French-German dialect.

28 Memorandum on the meeting to discuss 'guidelines for the processing of
evacuated Alsatians' which took place on 4 August 1942 between representatives of the central staff office of the RKF, the head of the relocation staff
in Strasbourg, the Ethnic German Agency, the Central Office for the
Security of the Reich, the SS Central Office of Race and Resettlement and
the DUT [= German Resettlement Trust Company]; Federal Archive/BDC,
document search 'Günther Stier'.

29 Discussion between SS Gruppenführer von dem Bach and the head of the
SS Central Office of Race and Resettlement on 26 November 1939; Federal
Archive/BDC, personal file of Friedrich Brehm.

30 Letter from Sturmbannführer Brehm to a colleague, 15 November 1940;
Federal Archive/BDC, personal file of Friedrich Brehm (see, p.102 ff.).

31 Even before the occupation of France the Four-Year Plan Authority had put
the brakes on the evacuation programme pursued by Himmler and the
RKF, primarily in order to ensure 'that useful manpower resources are not
lost'. Cf. 'Sitzung über Ostfragen unter dem Vorsitz des Minister-
präsidenten Generalfeldmarschall Göring am 12.2.1940' (the so-called
'Karinhall meeting'); *IMG*, Vol. XXXVI, pp.299–307. The meeting was
attended by von Krosigk, Himmler, Frank and the Gauleiters of the
annexed eastern territories, together with all the undersecretaries of the
general council of the Four-Year Plan and the head of the Central Trust
Agency for the East.

32 Letter of 3 November 1940 from Brehm to the head of the central planning
department at the RKF, Prof. Konrad Meyer; Federal Archive/BDC, personal
file of Friedrich Brehm.

33 'Richtlinien für die Eindeutschung polnischer Familien des SS-Führers im
Rasse- und Siedlungswesen beim Höheren SS- und Polizeiführer/Südost';
Federal Archive/BDC, document search 'Günther Stier'.

34 Old and sick persons, who would otherwise have been 'suitable for
Germanization', were expressly rejected as an 'undesirable addition to the
blood stock' (Federal Archive/BDC, SS-HO/4992). To qualify as an ethnic

German, one had to speak German and have no more than 'one grandparent of foreign ethnic origin'. Such persons were 'to be naturalized as a matter of principle unless there were objections on genetic, political or security-related grounds' ('Zum Entwurf einer Dienstanweisung für die EWZ' (undated), Federal Archive/BDC, SS-HO/3180–3254).

35 'Die "Deutsche Volksliste" in Posen. Bericht über ihre Entstehung und die Entwicklung des Verfahrens', a report prepared by Herbert Strickner in the winter of 1942–3 and reprinted in: Karol Marian Pospieszalski, *Niemiecka Lista Narodowa w 'Kraju Warty'* (= *Documenta Occupationis Teutonicae*, Vol. IV), Poznan 1949, p.117; on the dating of the report, see ibid., p.326.

36 Aly/Roth, pp.105–8.

37 Memorandum of Himmler's of 28 May 1940, reprinted in: *VfZG* 5 (1957), pp.194–8.

38 ibid.

39 Himmler's notes on plans for future colonization by German farmers, 24 June 1940; Federal Archive, NS 19/184; as quoted in: Ackermann, *Himmler*, p.300 ff.

40 Record of the remarks made by the SS Reichsführer on 14 August 1942 following his visit to Kiev; Federal Archive, NS 19 neu/1446; as quoted in: ibid., p.273.

41 'Erlass für die Überprüfung und Aussonderung der Bevölkerung in den eingegliederten Ostgebieten'; State Archive of Katowice, Bodenamt/1a, p.53 ff. Cf. *Documenta Occupationis Teutonicae*, Vol. IV (see note 35).

42 People in classes 1 and 2 of the German National List were granted German nationality and Reich citizenship, while those in class 3 received only German nationality, without Reich citizen status.

43 Notes for a speech that Himmler gave at a conference of SS and police commanders in Hegewald on 16 September 1942; Federal Archive, NS 19/4009.

44 Later the Jewish and 'gypsy' population was formally excluded from the category of 'client subjects'; see for example order No.779/42 of 8 June 1942, circulated by the president of the regional labour office and Reich trustee for labour in Upper Silesia; State Archive of Katowice, Gauarbeitsamt OS/577, p.56.

45 In Slovenia the RKF granted German nationality subject to revocation to 500,000 out of a total of 800,000 residents, while in Lorraine the proportion was even higher – 500,000 out of 600,000 (cf. Czesław Madajczyk, *Die Okkupationspolitik Nazideutschlands in Polen 1939–1945*, Berlin 1987, p.469).

46 *Nbg. Dok.*, NO-5640/VIII/Rebutt A.; as quoted in: Buchheim, p.246.

47 Memorandum of 7 May 1940 'Ref.: planning maps'; State Archive of Katowice, Bodenamt/1d, p.1.

48 Notes for a speech by Himmler before a gathering of senior Party officials and Gauleiters in Berlin on 10 December 1940; Federal Archive, NS 19/4007.

49 Note for the file made by Mr Schick, employed in the Saybusch branch office of the Katowice Trust Agency, on 20 May 1942; State Archive of Katowice, HTO/9797, p.88.

50 German Foreign Institute Commission, report by Dr Quiring, No.9 ('Secret'), Litzmannstadt, 19 April 1940; Federal Archive, R 57 neu/15.

51 As quoted in: Władysław Bartoszewski, 'SS-Obersturmbannführer Karl Adolf Eichmann. Ein Beitrag zur Liste seiner Verbrechen', in: *Zachodnia Agencja Prasowa* (Warsaw), No.4, April 1961, p.13.

52 See note 21.

53 See note 50.

54 Buchheim, p.259.

55 Lorenz was also chairman of the German Expatriate Relief Mission, and from 1941 president of the Association of Germans Abroad. In 1948 he was sentenced to twenty years' imprisonment, but freed again in 1955. He died in 1974.

56 Koehl, p.64.

57 Sandberger was deputy Gruppenleiter in Section I/E of the RSHA. In December 1941 he became head of the security police and SD in Estonia. As leader of the Einsatzkommando ['special action unit'] Ia in Einsatzgruppe A, Sandberger ordered shootings of Jewish children, women and men in the Soviet Union in 1942. He remained leader of the Sonderkommando Ia [a unit with similar functions, working in support of the front-line troops] until the autumn of 1943. In 1948 he was sentenced to death at Nuremberg, but pardoned in 1951 and released.

58 Federal Archive/BDC, personal file of Ernst Fähndrich.

59 See also the annual reports of the German Resettlement Trust Company (DUT) for the years 1940–43; they are kept in the library of the World Economic Institute in Kiel.

60 See also the documents recording the activities of Leo Reichert, head of the central department of economics at the RKF; Federal Archive/BDC, personal file of Leo Reichert.

61 Political Archive of the Foreign Office, reference files Luther/Schriftverkehr L-Sch/1940/Vol. 4; film 3890, frame 2443784. On 10 December 1940 Himmler calculated that the stolen assets used to fund the work of the RKF in Poland already totalled 3.3 billion Reichsmarks. (See note 48.)

62 The composition of the supervisory board is an indication of the disparate interests that were brought together in the DUT. Those with a seat and a vote on the board were: ministerial section head Dr Hugo Fritz Berger, representing the Reich Ministry of Finance; Hans Kehrl, representing both the Four-Year Plan Authority and the Reich Ministry of Economic Affairs; chairman of the supervisory board was Wilhelm Keppler, undersecretary in the Foreign Office assigned to special duties, who for a long time had been Hitler's personal adviser on economic matters and the principal intermediary between the NSDAP and the business community, and who had co-founded the 'Heinrich Himmler Circle of Friends' (cf. Emil Helfferich, *1932–1946. Tatsachen. Ein Beitrag zur Wahrheitsfindung*, Jever 1969). Also represented of course were the NSDAP, the Reichsbank, manufacturing industry and the private banking sector and – by three members – the SS.

63 This took effect with the issue of a decree by Göring on 19 October 1939; see Ministerpräsident Generalfeldmarschall (Hermann) Göring (ed.), *Haupttreuhandstelle Ost. Materialsammlung zum inneren Dienstgebrauch* (Berlin 1940 – no place or date of publication given).

64 See for example the series of publications *Die wirtschaftlichen*

Entwicklungsmöglichkeiten in den eingegliederten Ostgebieten des deutschen Reiches, of which more than ten issues appeared. Cf. note 100.

65 Hugo Ratzmann, *Wesen und Aufgabe der Treuhandstelle Posen. Vortrag, gehalten am 28. Januar 1940 anlässlich der ersten grossen nationalsozialistischen Führertagung des Warthegaus in der Gauhauptstadt Posen*, Posen 1940, p.9.

66 'Konrad Meyer', entry in the personalia column of *Die Bewegung*, 14 January 1941.

67 'Erlass über die Reichsstelle für Raumordnung vom 26.6.1935'; *Reich Law Gazette* 1935/I, p.793.

68 Speech given by Konrad Meyer at the opening of an exhibition on 'Planning and Reconstruction in the East' in Posen on 23 October 1941; *Nbg. Dok.*, NO-3348.

69 *Nbg. Dok.*, NO-4060, p.34; NO-5546/48/VIII Rebutt A, VIII Prot. 904 ff.; as quoted in: Buchheim, p.274.

70 ibid.

71 See the letter from the resettlement office to the head of the Central Office of Race and Resettlement, f.a.o. v. Rautenfeld, dated 9 January 1943; Federal Archive/BDC, personal file of Friedrich Kann.

72 Minutes of a meeting on 15 December 1939 between SS Brigadeführer Greifelt (head of the RKF's central staff office in Berlin) and Dr Jarmer (head of the Reich Office of Regional Planning). This meeting was also attended by Prof. Dr Konrad Meyer, Dr Walter Gebert (RKF) and senior civil servant Dr Heinrich Siemer. The last-named was directed to liaise between the Reich Office of Regional Planning and the RKF (Federal Archive/BDC, personal file of Ernst Jarmer). In 1943 we read: 'The Reich Commissioner for the Strengthening of German Nationhood, in consultation with the Reich Office of Regional Planning, uses local planning officers as its appointed agents' to carry out its work. The purpose of that work was 'to actively address oneself to the necessities for the life of the nation (increased agricultural productivity, increased production of raw materials, better distribution of business enterprises, population policy based on strengthening of the race and its qualitative and quantitative increase, securing adequate supplies of food and raw materials, creation of useful employment)'. (Ernst Hamm, 'Grundsätzliches über die Raumordnung im Grossdeutschen Reich', in: *Reichsverwaltungsblatt* 64 [1943], No.3/4, p.26.)

73 Cf. Mechthild Rössler, 'Die Institutionalisierung einer neuen "Wissenschaft" im Nationalsozialismus: Raumforschung und Raumordnung 1935–1945' (hereinafter cited as 'Rössler'), in: *Geographische Zeitschrift* 75 (1987), pp.177–94.

74 SS Obersturmbannführer Fähndrich at a course for ethnic German public speakers, 6–14 September 1941; Federal Archive/BDC, personal file of Ernst Fähndrich.

75 Der Reichskommissar für die Festigung des deutschen Volkstums Stabshauptamt und der Generalinspektor für Wasser und Energie (eds.), *Richtlinien für die Elektrifizierung in den ländlichen Bereichen der eingegliederten Ostgebiete*, Berlin 1943.

76 Reichskommissar für die Festigung deutschen Volkstums, Planungshauptabteilung, *Planungsgrundlagen für den Aufbau der Ostgebiete* (no date of

publication given; circa January 1940); Federal Archive, R 49/157a, p.15; as quoted in: Karl Heinz Roth, 'Erster "Generalplan Ost"' (see note 3), here esp. document 1.

77 Walter Christaller, *Central Places in Southern Germany*, New York 1966 (German edition: Jena 1933; Darmstadt 1968).

78 Rössler, p.184.

79 Walter Christaller, *Die Zentralen Orte in den Ostgebieten und ihre Kultur- und Marktbereiche* (= *Struktur und Gestaltung der Zentralen Orte des Deutschen Ostens, Gemeinschaftswerk im Auftrage der Reichsarbeitsgemeinschaft für Raumforschung*, Teil I), Leipzig 1941, p.22 ff.

80 Memorandum on a tour of inspection, 15–17 August 1940, undertaken for the purpose of: 'I. inspecting the work carried out by the development unit of the RKF in the Warthegau, II. determining the form and method of collaboration between the regional planning authority and the development unit'; State Archive of Katowice, Land Pl GO/S/21, pp.3–5.

81 ibid., p.8.

82 'The Reich student leadership has engaged itself in the work with great idealism. A large number of students have interrupted their studies for an extended period of time in order to familiarize themselves with these matters' (ibid., p.5). Not only the development unit but also the regional planning authority relied 'very heavily on student workers, about 25 of them in all (...) They prepare plans for various model villages as study projects, and receive extensive training before they are sent out to the villages' (ibid., p.7).

83 Progress report by SS Untersturmführer Dr Heidenreich, 26 November 1940, on his work with the RKF in Posen; Federal Archive, R 69/445 (we are grateful to Matthias Hamann for drawing our attention to this document).

84 See note 80, p.6 f.

85 Letter of 21 October 1941 from the 'central planning and land department' (the former planning office run by Konrad Meyer) in the central staff office of the RKF, to the 'general department of regional planning' in Upper Silesia; State Archive of Katowice, Land Pl GO/S/212, p.98 f.

86 Letter of 15 October 1941 from the National Estate of German Craft Guilds to the central planning and land department in the central staff office of the RKF, concerning the 'location of workshops in rural areas of the annexed eastern territories'; State Archive of Katowice, Land Pl GO/S/273, p.17 ff.

87 Letter of 10 September 1942 from the administrative head of the province of Upper Silesia to the chief executive officers in Katowice and Oppeln, 'regarding application of the development order in the light of the decree of 25 April 1942 issued by the Reich Minister of Economic Affairs'; State Archive of Katowice, RK II/825, p.94 ff.

88 Letter of 13 August 1942 from the general commissioner in Reval to the Reich Commissioner for the Ostland in Riga; Historical Central Archive of Riga, P-70/5/76, p.1.

89 RMBliV. 5 (1940), column 1519 ff.

90 Cf. also Himmler's speech to the SS officer cadet college at Bad Tölz on 23 November 1942: 'And the problem of class has been resolved too. What

matters now is not class or origin, but merit and achievement!' Federal Archive, NS 19/4008.

91 In *Neues Bauerntum* 34 (1942), p.208.

92 Himmler on questions of resettlement (see note 3).

93 Details of Arlt's biography can be found in Aly/Roth, pp.71–4. The formal representative of the RKF in Upper Silesia was the Gauleiter, Fritz Bracht, but the local office was in fact run by Fritz Arlt, who also handled all business transactions with RKF central office in Berlin.

94 'Report on the development and activity of the Dept. of Resettlement during the period 10.7.1940–31.5.1941'; Dortmund public prosecutor's office, preliminary proceedings against Dr Fritz Arlt, Js 49/61, Vol. IV, p.131.

95 The head of this 'Main Office' was Arlt's deputy at the RKF, Helmut Stutzke. Letter from Arlt of 3 January 1942; Federal Archive/BDC, personal file of Helmut Stutzke.

96 Letter from Arlt's deputy Stutzke to SS Obersturmbannführer Bux, 12 February 1941; Federal Archive/BDC, personal file of Helmut Stutzke.

97 Memorandum of the Katowice Emigration Bureau attached to the chief of staff of the security police and SD: 'Reference: Organizational structure of the Katowice Emigration Bureau' (undated); State Archive of Katowice, RK/4088, p.1 ff.

98 Report of the Katowice sector of the SD on a conference with Dr Arlt on 8 May 1941, in: *Documenta Occupationis*, Vol. XI, Poznan 1983, p.62 ff.

99 Cf. the memorandum written on 11 January 1944 by the administrative head of the province of Upper Silesia on a visit to the SS Reichsführer on 5 and 6 January 1944; State Archive of Katowice, OPK/140, p.92 f.

100 Fritz Arlt, *Siedlung und Landwirtschaft in den eingegliederten Gebieten Oberschlesiens* (hereinafter cited as 'Arlt, *Siedlung*'), Berlin 1942, p.43. This work appeared as Vol. 10 in the series *Die wirtschaftlichen Entwicklungsmöglichkeiten in den eingegliederten Ostgebieten des deutschen Reiches*, which the geographer Walter Geisler edited on behalf of the Central Trust Agency for the East and the RKF.

101 ibid., p.36.

102 ibid., p.31.

103 ibid., p.52.

104 Regional planner Gerhard Ziegler in a letter to the members of 'Working Party II' (undated); State Archive of Katowice, Land Pl GO/S/213, p.19.

105 Cf. Ziegler's letter of 13 July 1943 to Dr Gerhard Isenberg of the Reich Office of Regional Planning; State Archive of Katowice, Land Pl GO/S/234, p.19 f.; 109 passim and 14, p.32 f.

106 Gerhard Ziegler, 'Kurzblicke auf meinen Lebenslauf' (unpublished manuscript). Ziegler was sent as regional planner to the Sudeten district by the Reich Office of Regional Planning in October 1938. He gives the date of his transfer to Katowice – and his promotion to civil service rank – as 1 July 1941. However, the records held in the State Archive of Katowice show that Ziegler was regional planner for Upper Silesia by December 1940 at the latest. See State Archive of Katowice, Land Pl GO/S/467. (We are grateful to Niels Gutschow for providing a copy of Ziegler's handwritten resumé.)

107 The terms of this collaboration were discussed at a meeting on 9 April 1941; see State Archive of Katowice, Land Pl GO/S/212, p.158.

108 Memorandum from the 'Upper Silesia regional planning association' of October 1941 (the exact date is not given on the document), 'ref.: preparation of maps on the regional economic organization of Upper Silesia'; State Archive of Katowice, Land Pl GO/S/71, p.4.

109 Cf. the talk given by Ziegler in early 1943 to a gathering of economic staff and advisers for Upper Silesia; State Archive of Katowice, Land Pl GO/S/37, pp.1–16. On the role of Ziegler and other regional planning experts, see Joachim Wolschke and Gerd Gröning, 'Regionalistische Freiraumgestaltung als Ausdruck autoritären Gesellschaftsverständnisses? Ein historischer Versuch', in: *Kritische Berichte* 12 (1984), No.1, pp.5–45.

110 'Übersicht über die oberschlesische Bevölkerungsstruktur als erster Beitrag zum Problem des West-Ost-Gefälles', a confidential report drafted by Fritz Arlt; State Archive of Katowice, OPK/385, p.42.

111 Although none of it has survived, it is worth noting that Arlt insisted on signing in person the correspondence with Greifelt, Heydrich, Ehlich, Hoffmann, Lorenz and Behrends – i.e. the key SS functionaries responsible for racial and resettlement policy and other policy issues in the occupied eastern territories. See memorandum of 3 June 1942, State Archive of Katowice, OPK/140, p.1.

112 In the villages of Neuberun (Bierun), Bobrek and Grojetz, for example, or alternatively (and this was the preferred choice of Arlt, who wanted to retain the fertile soils of Grojetz for agricultural use) in Wlosenitz and Zaborze. See the note written by district planner Udo Froese on 10 March 1943 on a meeting that took place two days previously in the Auschwitz mayor's office 'regarding the boundaries of the I.G. Farben site and the Auschwitz municipal district'; State Archive of Katowice, Land Pl GO/S/467, p.50. The meeting was attended by twelve men, including Dr Arlt and two representatives of the RKF's central land office, the town planner of Auschwitz, Dr Ing. Hans Stosberg, and Froese himself.

113 Minutes of the meeting held on 15 and 16 January 1943 in the inspectorate of the Reich Housing Commissioner in Berlin, Kanonierstrasse 9; ibid., p.65. The minutes were taken by government architect Töpler from Katowice; among those who had travelled to Berlin for the meeting was the town architect of Auschwitz, Hans Stosberg.

114 The concentration camp inmates who worked for I.G. Auschwitz had clearly not been included in this calculation, since no allowance had to be made for their accommodation needs. Between the end of 1941 and the end of 1944 their numbers rose from 1,000 to 11,000, at which point they accounted for a third of the plant's entire workforce. See Karl Heinz Roth, 'I.G. Auschwitz. Normalität oder Anomalie eines kapitalistischen Entwicklungssprungs' (hereinafter cited as 'Roth, "I.G. Auschwitz"'), in: *1999*, 4 (1989), No.4, p.23.

115 See note 112, p.61.

116 Letter of 29 May 1943 from the head of the regional council in Katowice 'concerning planning issues in Auschwitz'; ibid., p.15.

117 Otto Ambros at a meeting held on 16 January 1941 in Ludwigshafen; NI-

11784; as quoted in: Dieter Maier, 'Die Mitwirkung der Arbeitsverwaltung beim Bau der I.G. Farben Auschwitz' (hereinafter cited as 'Maier, "Arbeitsverwaltung"'), in: *Arbeitsmarkt und Sondererlass* (= *Beiträge zur nationalsozialistischen Gesundheits- und Sozialpolitik*, Vol. 8), Berlin 1990, p.176.

118 Letter from Bergwerksverwaltung Oberschlesien GmbH, the operating company running the mines in Upper Silesia for the Hermann Göring Works Corporation (the date and addressee are not indicated in the document); State Archive of Katowice, Land Pl GO/S/467, p.83.

119 Letter of 22 December 1942 from the district administrator [*Landrat*] to the head of the regional council in Katowice; ibid., p.78.

120 In a New Year's greetings card sent to his 'patrons and friends' for the 1942 New Year, Stosberg included the following text: 'In 1341 Silesian warriors defeated the Mongol hordes near Wahlstatt and became the saviours of the Reich. In the same century Auschwitz came into being as a German town. 600 years later the Führer Adolf Hitler is successfully defending Europe against the Bolshevist peril. In this year of 1941 work began on the planning and construction of a new German town and the restoration of the historic Silesian market square.' Ibid., p.151.

121 Letter of 31 December 1940 from the camp commandant, Höss, to regional planner Ziegler; ibid., p.301.

122 The meeting on 28 June 1941, for instance, which was attended by Höss, Ziegler, Froese and the mayor of Auschwitz, Heinrich Gutsche; ibid., pp.180–83. From time to time these meetings were also attended by Fritz Arlt and SS functionaries and construction experts from Berlin.

123 See the letter of 25 February 1943 from Stosberg to the head of the regional council in Katowice, ibid., pp.38–40; also the minutes of the meeting held on 15 and 16 January 1943 in the inspectorate of the Reich Housing Commissioner in Berlin, ibid., p.62. On the environmental arguments, see Ziegler's letter to Höss of 23 December 1941; ibid., p.304 f.; Ziegler's letter to the RKF central planning and land office of 18 February 1942; ibid., pp.130–32. (Ziegler was concerned that a proposed sewage treatment plant for the concentration camp on the Vistula might pollute the local drinking water supply.)

124 The representative of the SS Reichsführer in his capacity as Reich Commissioner for the Strengthening of German Nationhood, SS Relocation Office South, 'Die Möglichkeiten der Siedlung 1941' (no date, circa December 1940–January 1941); Federal Archive, R 49/Anh. III/26, pp.96–100.

125 I.G. Farben was certainly one of the 'interested parties', having made it clear from December 1940 onwards that it was interested in building a production plant at Auschwitz, not least because of the manpower resources to which the RKF's population policies gave it access. I.G. Farben needed to maintain a close and harmonious relationship with the RKF because the site it had in mind for its new plant was administered by the RKF. In other words, the land in question had been confiscated – stolen – from its original owners, who had been evicted beforehand. See Roth, 'I.G. Auschwitz', pp.14 and 17.

126 For the explanatory sketch accompanying the paper, see note 124, loc. cit., p.102.

127 ibid., p.98.

128 ibid., p.102.

129 Maier, 'Arbeitsverwaltung', p.175.

130 Archive of the Auschwitz Memorial Centre, 'Maurerprozess', Dpr. Mau/7/25398 (= *Nbg. Dok.*, NI-1240), p.13 f.

131 See Roth, 'I.G. Auschwitz', p.18. On 4 March 1941 Karl Krauch, a member of the supervisory board of I.G. Farben and 'executive manager for special aspects of chemical production to the Commissioner for the Four-Year Plan', boasted that Göring's order to Himmler and the instructions issued by the latter on 26 February 1941 were the result of his, Krauch's, recommendation. (ibid.)

132 The president of the Silesian regional employment office in a letter of 12 March 1941 to the Reich Minister of Labour, for the attention of head of section Dr Richter (as quoted in: Maier, 'Arbeitsverwaltung', p.179 f.). The letter from the regional employment office essentially passes on a report from the Bielitz employment office, but without giving its date or the date of the meeting to which it relates. The author of the report notes that he took the initiative to contact the commandant of the Auschwitz concentration camp 'some time ago in order to discuss the deployment of the camp inmates on labour duties' and that they 'reached complete agreement'.

133 Note made by Butschek on a meeting in Berlin on 19 March 1941; see note 112, loc. cit., p.104.

134 Czech, p.79.

135 See note 94, loc. cit., p.123. The broad background to the halt on deportations and the establishment of reservations is covered in greater detail in: Aly, *Endlösung*, pp.207–79.

136 See note 112, loc. cit., p.14.

137 Gerhard Ziegler, 'Kurzblicke auf meinen Lebenslauf', p.4.

138 Koehl, p.236.

139 Cf. Rössler, p.180.

140 In 1961 Schauroth wrote in these terms about Frankfurt's Opernplatz: 'Here at the red traffic lights, not so long ago, drivers in a hurry and passers-by with no time to spare could not but be acutely aware of a bygone era. And then it was there: a brave new world that was absolutely and completely *now*, like a fanfare ringing out across the open space – bright, clear, unmistakable.' *Frankfurt aus Stahl und Beton – ein neues Gesicht*, Frankfurt a.M. 1961, p.14.

Chapter 5: Living Life as a Member of the Master Race

1 Karl Baedeker, *Das Generalgouvernement. Reisehandbuch*, Leipzig, p.V f.

2 ibid., p.XXVII f.

3 ibid., p.50; authors' emphasis.

4 Dietrich Troschke, 'Polen – "Nebenland des Deutschen Reiches". Tagebuchblätter 1940–1945' (manuscript); Federal Archive, Ost-Dok.

13/234. It is quite apparent that the author revised his notes after the war, casting himself in the role of one who was 'really against it all' from the outset. It was only then that Troschke lodged his 'diaries' with the Federal Archive. But his attempts to paint himself in a better light are only superficially successful; the impressions he records – and we have quoted the ones that he probably regarded as completely harmless and uncompromising – are all the more revealing as a guide to how German intellectuals, economists and administrators viewed occupied Poland. (Omitted passages have not been specifically marked as such.)

5 Report of the town commandant in Reichshof (Rzeszów) for the month of October 1940 on the elimination of the Jews from economic life, in: *Faschismus, Getto, Massenmord*, p.186 f.

6 'Deutsche Ostarbeit', in: *Frankfurter Zeitung*, 24 May 1941.

7 See Meinhold's personal file, Federal Archive, R 52 IV/89. In common with all the other surviving personal files held by the Institute for German Development Work in the East, Meinhold's file was purged of incriminating material, closed and handed over to the Americans by the Institute's director, Wilhelm Coblitz, in order to demonstrate that the Institute was engaged in harmless academic pursuits. So heads of department in charge of racial research suddenly became 'historians', etc.

8 From a reference written by Meinhold for his assistant, Erika Bochdam-Löptien; Federal Archive, R 52 IV/144.

9 Helmut Meinhold, in the representations he made in support of his department's draft budget submission for the 1942/43 financial year; Federal Archive, R 52 IV/135.

10 'Die Aufgaben der Sektion Wirtschaft im Institut für Deutsche Ostarbeit' (manuscript), January 1941; Federal Archive, R 52 IV/144.

11 Report of the Cracow town commandant ('signed: Dr Krämer') to the governor of the district, dated 10 August 1944; Warsaw Archive for New Documents, Reg. GG/1344, pp.204–9.

12 Meinhold's spoken recollection of 23 November 1985.

13 Helmut Meinhold, review of August Lösch, *Die räumliche Ordnung der Wirtschaft* (Jena 1940), in: *Die Burg* 3 (1942), No.3, p.360.

14 Archive of the University of Vienna, personal file of Dorothea Kahlich.

15 Letter from Plügel to Kahlich of 22 October 1941 (Anton Plügel was Fliethmann's superior); Archive of the University of Cracow, 'Institut für Deutsche Ostarbeit'/70.

16 Letter from Kahlich to Plügel of 3 November 1941; ibid.

17 Letter from Fliethmann to Kahlich (undated); ibid.

18 Elfriede Fliethmann, 'Vorläufiger Bericht über anthropologische Aufnahmen an Judenfamilien in Tarnów', in: *Deutsche Forschung im Osten* 2 (1942), No.3, pp.92–111.

19 Letter from Kahlich to Fliethmann (undated copy); see note 15.

20 Letter from the commander of the security police and SD in Lvov to Fliethmann, 28 April 1942; ibid.

21 Letter from Plügel to SS Hauptsturmführer Schenk, 23 April 1942; ibid.

22 ibid.

23 Letter from Kahlich to Fliethmann, 11 March 1942; ibid.

24 Letter from Fliethmann to Kahlich, 13 May 1942; ibid.

25 Letter from Kahlich to Fliethmann, 8 April 1942; ibid.

26 Letter from Fliethmann to Kahlich, 13 May 1942; ibid.

27 ibid.

28 Letter from Kahlich to Fliethmann, 4 June 1942; ibid.

29 ibid.; Fliethmann left the Institute on 31 December 1943, following her marriage. Thereafter she used the double-barrelled name Fliethmann-Henseling.

30 Prague State Archive, URP/dod II/57.

31 Federal Archive, R 57 neu/31. The French occupying power appointed Könekamp as deputy mayor of Stuttgart in 1945.

32 As quoted in: 'Das Posener Tagebuch des Anatomen Hermann Voss. Erläutert von Götz Aly', in: *Biedermann und Schreibtischtäter. Materialien zur deutschen Täterbiographie* (= *Beiträge zur nationalsozialistischen Gesundheits- und Sozialpolitik*, Vol. 4), Berlin 1987, pp.15–66. After the war Voss became the most highly regarded German anatomist, teaching in Halle and Jena.

Chapter 6: The Government General

1 The patients in the psychiatric hospital at Chełm, for example, were killed on 12 January 1940; Henry Friedlander, 'Jüdische Anstaltspatienten in Deutschland', in: Götz Aly (ed.), *Aktion T4 1939–1945. Die 'Euthanasie'-Zentrale in der Tiergartenstrasse 4* (hereinafter cited as 'Aly, *Aktion T4*'), Berlin 1987, p.40.

2 'Dr. Frank verabschiedet Gauamtsleiter Arlt', in: *Krakauer Zeitung*, 22/23 September 1940.

3 'Bericht über den Aufbau der Verwaltung im Generalgouvernement vom Juni 1940' (hereinafter cited as 'Bericht'); Federal Archive, R 52 II/247, p.182.

4 Fritz Arlt, 'Vom Sinn und Aufbau des Gruppendezernats Bevölke-rungswesen und Fürsorge', in: Fritz Arlt (ed.), *Die Ordnung der Fürsorge und Wohlfahrt im Generalgouvernement*, Cracow 1940, p.3 ff.

5 Fritz Arlt, 'Übersicht über die Bevölkerungsverhältnisse im General-gouvernement' (hereinafter cited as 'Arlt, "Übersicht"'), Cracow 1940, p.41. (This issue appeared in September 1940.)

6 Lothar Weirauch, 'Die Volksgruppen im Generalgouvernement', in: *Europäische Revue* 18 (1942), p.251.

7 As for example when Arlt, together with the governor of the district of Lublin, 'gave back' the cathedral of Chełm to the Greek Orthodox Church 'on the occasion of the Führer's birthday'. See *Krakauer Zeitung*, 21 May 1940.

8 'Bericht', p.182.

9 Arlt, 'Übersicht', p.19.

10 *Krakauer Zeitung*, 2 August 1940.

11 Arlt, 'Übersicht', p.9.

12 'Bericht', p.201.

13 'Ein Jahr Aufbauarbeit im Distrikt Krakau' (section on the department of

population management and welfare; hereinafter cited as 'Aufbauarbeit'), Cracow 1940, p.29.

14 'Bericht', p.196.

15 Arlt, 'Übersicht', p.24.

16 ibid., p.21.

17 'Die ukrainische Volksgruppe im deutschen Generalgouvernement Polen', Cracow 1940, p.17.

18 'Aufbauarbeit', p.30.

19 Circular from Gottong, dated 6 April 1940, to the governors of the various districts 'concerning guidelines for the treatment of the Jewish population' (reprinted in: *Faschismus, Getto, Massenmord*, p.55). Gottong was a Jewish specialist in the Government General's department of population management and welfare.

20 Ibid. Gottong's proposals for distinguishing between 'half-Jews' and 'full Jews' carried particular weight because 'keeping a record of Jews and deciding who was to be classed as a Jew' was essentially his full-time job (ibid., p.88).

21 In a memorandum on the first deportation of Jews from Vienna, written on 18 October 1939 by Brunner, a member of Eichmann's staff, we read: 'As part of the whole resettlement operation the gypsies currently in the Ostmark [= Austria] are also being put on separate trucks and added to the transport.' As quoted in: Peter Longerich (ed.), *Die Ermordung der europäischen Juden. Eine umfassende Dokumentation des Holocaust 1941–1945* (hereinafter cited as 'Longerich'), Munich/Zurich 1989, p.52 f.

22 'Zeugnis für Dr Fritz Arlt vom 1.9.1940'; Federal Archive/BDC, personal file of Fritz Arlt.

23 Personal file of Heinz Auerswald; State Archive of Warsaw, Amt des Distriktchefs/318/319. Auerswald was evidently present at discussions on the 'final solution of the Jewish problem' which took place in Berlin on 20 January 1942. On 19 January 1942 the chairman of the Jewish Council in Warsaw, Adam Czerniaków, noted: 'I heard that A[uerswald] had been summoned to Berlin. I have this constant fear that the Jews in Warsaw may be deported en masse.' Four days later, when Auerswald was back in Warsaw, Czerniaków asked him 'whether there were any new orders or instructions from Berlin'. Auerswald lied, saying he had been to Berlin 'on private business'. Three days later Auerswald turned up at the offices of the Jewish community leaders, accompanied by a number of SS men 'who asked questions about the ghetto'. *Im Warschauer Ghetto. Das Tagebuch des Adam Czerniaków 1939–1942* (hereinafter cited as 'Czerniaków'), Munich 1986, pp.219–21.

24 Letter from Weirauch to the senior SS and police commander in Cracow 'in the matter of Dr Hagen', 4 February 1943; Federal Archive, NS 19/1210.

25 Statement given by Herbert Heinrich on 8 October 1962; Hamburg public prosecutor's office, 141 Js 573/60.

26 Tatiana Brustin-Berenstein, 'Die Jüdische Soziale Selbsthilfe' (hereinafter cited as 'Berenstein'), in: *Arbeitsamt und Sondererlass* (= *Beiträge zur nationalsozialistischen Gesundheits- und Sozialpolitik*, Vol. 8), Berlin 1990, p.172.

27 Report by Richard Türk, head of the department of population management and welfare in the Lublin district, dated 7 April 1942; as quoted in:
Faschismus, Getto, Massenmord, p.271.

28 Letter from Föhl to his 'SS comrades' in Berlin, 21 June 1942; Federal
Archive/BDC, personal file of Walter Föhl. In the minutes of the Wannsee
conference we read: '... the able-bodied Jews will be taken off to build roads
in these territories, where large numbers will undoubtedly be lost through
natural wastage'.

29 Hilberg, p.299. Weirauch later represented his work as purely charitable in
nature (Federal Archive, Ost-Dok. 13/248). After the war he became a head
of section in the Federal Ministry of Defence, where he also procured a job
for Herbert Heinrich, a former specialist in 'Jewish questions' at the department of population management and welfare. Germany's public prosecutors subsequently dropped all judicial inquiries into former members of the
department of population management and welfare.

30 Statement given by Wilhelm Hagen on 1 August 1962; Hamburg public
prosecutor's office, 141 Js 192/62, p.8932 ff.

31 Letter from Hagen to Hitler, 7 December 1942; Federal Archive, NS
19/1210. Hagen's protest was directed not against the treatment of the Jews
as such, but against the fact that the Poles were being treated in the same
way. Extensive reflection on population policy issues had led him to conclude 'that a reduction in the size of the Polish population is not in our
interests'. As a Social Democrat, Hagen had initially been removed from
public service in 1933. He set up in practice as a registered doctor, became
chief medical officer of Warsaw in 1941, and in 1956 was appointed to the
presidency of the Federal Office of Public Health.

32 'Der Parteigenosse ist Repräsentant des Reiches', in: *Krakauer Zeitung*, 7
August 1940.

33 Letter from Arlt to Hanns von Krannhals of 16 September 1964; Federal
Archive, ZSg 122/8.

34 'Der Gauschulungsleiter', in: *Kattowitzer Zeitung*, 19 February 1941.

35 'Bericht', p.207.

36 See above, p.71 and p.133.

37 Josef Sommerfeldt, '200 Jahre Abwehrkampf gegen das Ostjudentum', in:
Deutsche Post aus dem Osten 15 (1943), No.2/3, p.12.

38 This is documented not only by the (now missing) study that Helmut
Meinhold co-wrote with Anton Plügel, a racial research specialist at the
Institute – 'Die Bereinigung der Volkstumsgrenzen' (*Manuskriptreihe des
Instituts für deutsche Ostarbeit*), referred to in: *Die Burg* 3 (1942), No.3, p.357
– but also by Meinhold's responsibility for numerous statistical tables in
which Jews, Ukrainians and Poles are listed separately.

39 Report by Manfred Grisebach on his trip from 11 to 19 February 1943;
Federal Archive, R 57/1074, Berichte Grisebach, 11–19.2.1943.

40 Work report from the department of racial and ethnic studies, 21 June 1944
(Archive of the Central Board in Warsaw, IDO/Sektion Rassen- und
Volkstumsforschung/Korrespondenz/2).

41 Letter from Arlt to Konrad Meyer, 18 March 1941; Federal Archive/BDC,
personal file of Klemens Kleppik. The opening of the Institute was marked

by an inaugural conference (26–28 March 1941).

42 Report by Otmar von Verschuer on the foundation of the Institute, in: *Der Erbarzt* 9 (1941), p.91 f.

43 Peter-Heinz Seraphim, 'Arbeitstagung des Instituts für deutsche Ostarbeit', in: *Weltkampf. Die Judenfrage in Geschichte und Gegenwart* I (1941), No.1/2, p.177. See also the article by Wilhelm Grau in the same issue (p.20).

44 'Mitteilung', in: *Weltkampf* I (1941), No.3, p.182.

45 Wilhelm Coblitz, 'Das Institut für Deutsche Ostarbeit in Krakau', in: *Der Deutsche im Osten* 4 (1941), No.2, p.90.

46 Organizational plan of the Upper East Armaments Inspectorate, 20 June 1940; Federal Archive/Military Archive (Freiburg), RW 23/6a, p.8.

47 'Die Polen machten Warschau zur Judenmetropole', in: *Krakauer Zeitung*, 22 July 1940.

48 Peter-Heinz Seraphim, *Die Wirtschaftsstruktur des Generalgouvernements*, Cracow 1941, p.5.

49 ibid., p.34.

50 Arlt, 'Übersicht', foreword.

51 Michael Weichert, *Milchrome (Der Krieg)*, Tel Aviv 1963, p.61; as quoted in: Berenstein, p.174.

52 Order of 9 April 1940. Emmerich had been received by Frank the same day and took up his new post immediately; see Frank's diary, entry for 9 April 1940. We refer to the original as 'Frank's diary', giving the date of the entry only where the passage quoted is not included in the printed edition of the diary (Werner Präg, Wolfgang Jacobmeyer [eds.], *Das Diensttagebuch des deutschen Generalgouverneurs in Polen*, Stuttgart 1975). References to this edition will be cited as '*Diensttagebuch*', giving the page number.

53 Max Biehl, 'Ausgangspunkte des deutschen Aufbauwerkes im General-gouvernement', in: *Wirtschaftsdienst* 26 (1941), No.1, pp.18–19.

54 *Diensttagebuch*, p.244.

55 ibid., p.91. This explains why the Four-Year Plan Authority was so keen to see Emmerich appointed to the post. Cf. Robert Bührmann, 'Wirtschaftsplanung und Wirtschaftslenkung im Generalgouvernement Polen', in: *Der Südosten* 19 (1940), No.4, pp.80–82.

56 According to the spoken testimony of Helmut Meinhold, Harald Hansen and Gerhard Emmerich. After the war Emmerich was interned for two years in Neuengamme. Poland's request for extradition was blocked by the British military government.

57 *Diensttagebuch*, p.252.

58 Frank's diary, entry of 1 August 1940.

59 1st plenary session of the Economic Council for the Government General, 31 October 1940; ibid.

60 Walter Emmerich, 'Aufbau im neuen Wirtschaftsraum', in: *Berliner Börsenzeitung*, 30 November 1940.

61 Frank's speech to the Economic Conference of the Government General, 6 and 7 June 1940; see Frank's diary.

62 Briefing given by Hitler to the German High Command on 17 October 1939; *IMG*, Vol. XXVI, p.378 ff.

63 A similar view was taken by the commander of the security police in the

Government General, the Hamburg businessman Bruno Streckenbach; *Diensttagebuch*, p.261 f.

64 Discussion between Hitler, Bormann, Schirach, Frank and Koch on 2 October 1940; *IMG*, Vol. XXXIX, p.425 ff.

65 Letter dated 3 December 1940; *IMG*, Vol. XXIX, p.175 f.

66 The document is reprinted in Gerhard Botz, *Wohnungspolitik und Judendeportation in Wien 1938 bis 1945. Zur Funktion des Antisemitismus als Ersatz nationalsozialistischer Sozialpolitik*, Vienna/Salzburg 1975, p. 199.

67 Frank on a conversation with Hitler on 4 November 1940; *Diensttagebuch*, p.302. See also: Gerhard Eisenblätter, 'Grundlinien der Politik des Reiches gegenüber dem Generalgouvernement, 1939–1945' (Diss.), Frankfurt a.M. 1969, p.108.

68 Cf. the personal files of Meinhold/Bochdam-Löptien/Nonnenmacher; Federal Archive, R 52 IV/89/69/82.

69 Personal file of Dr Helmut Seifert; Warsaw Archive for New Documents, Reg. GG/1324/I.

70 Undated statement made by Emmerich during the extradition proceedings started against him by Communist Poland in 1946 (Archive of the Central Board in Warsaw, No.105, p.34); statement by Günther Bergemann in the denazification court proceedings against Emmerich (Federal Archive, Z 42/IV/3801, p.13); letter from the Reich Ministry of Economic Affairs, 7 March 1940 (Federal Archive, R 7/3460, p.271).

71 Letter from Messrs. Wolfers & Pontt, 27 May 1940; State Archive of Warsaw, Deutsche Handelskammer für Polen/117, p.2.

72 Letter from the same firm of 13 December 1939; ibid., Vol. 72, p.6.

73 *Diensttagebuch*, p.226.

74 Frank's diary, 1st plenary session of the Economic Council for the Government General, 31 October 1940.

75 From a speech by Emmerich (summer of 1940); Central State Archive (Potsdam), film 59757, frame 817.

76 Cf. Hilberg, p.178.

77 *Ostdeutscher Beobachter* (undated copy), circa May 1940.

78 Walter Emmerich, 'Die Wirtschaft des Generalgouvernements', in: *Danziger Wirtschaftszeitung* 22 (1942), No.11, p.246.

79 A. Günther (executive secretary of the 'Gruppe Handel', a regulatory body and lobby group representing the interests of German traders in the Government General), 'Einsatz deutscher Grosshändler im General-gouvernement', in: *Deutsche Wirtschaftszeitung* 39 (1942), No.35/36, p.469.

80 Cf. the letter from Emmerich to all town commandants and district admin-istrators, 18 July 1940; Central State Archive (Potsdam), film 59757, frame 845 ff.

81 Police pressure culminated in the 'Order for safeguarding the collection of harvested produce' of 31 July 1942 (Gazette of ordinances for the Government General, No.61). 'Paragraph 2 states: The following will be punished by death: 1. Persons who wilfully and maliciously damage or destroy agricultural produce of any kind intended for the feeding of humans or animals; 2. Persons who wilfully and maliciously fail to fulfil

their duty to deliver agricultural produce to the designated collection points; 3. Persons who withhold by their own culpable action significant quantities of agricultural produce from the authorities; 4. Persons who incite or direct others to commit any of the punishable crimes listed above under 1-3.'

82 Cornelius Witt, 'Überseefirmen versorgen Europa', in: *Der freie Aussenhandel*, issue 79/80, January 1944, p.428 ff. The practice of systematically plundering whole countries with the aid of German firms was duly continued during the occupation of the Soviet Union. In the 'Reich Commissariats for the occupied Baltic states and the Ukraine' the Germans also planned to involve Dutch, Danish, French, Belgian and even Swiss wholesale companies.

83 ibid., p.431.

84 Reich Board for Industrial Rationalization, Office for the Government General, 'Die wirtschaftlichen Grundlagen des Generalgouvernements' (hereinafter cited as 'RKW, "Grundlagen"'), p.6; Federal Archive/Military Archive (Freiburg), RW 19 Anh. I/1349.

85 See Chapter 3, 'Demographic Economics – the Emergence of a New Science', p.63 f., here especially p.64.

86 Meinhold, 'Industrialisierung', p.43.

87 Meinhold, 'Arbeiterreserven', in: *Die Burg* 3 (1942), No.3, p.280.

88 Erika (Löptien-)Bochdam, 'Die Handelsbetriebe im ehemaligen Polen', in: *Deutsche Forschung im Osten* 2 (1942), No.1/2, p.10–20.

89 Erika (Löptien-)Bochdam, 'Das Generalgouvernement in statistischen Angaben', in: *Zeitschrift für Erdkunde* 10 (1942), No.6, p.394.

90 RKW, 'Grundlagen', p.30 f. Frank was more sceptical than his experts. Back in September 1940 he had pointed out that 'not all the Jews in the Government General can be written off as down-and-outs … as skilled tradesmen they make an essential contribution to the life of the Polish nation. (…) We cannot teach the Poles the enterprise, drive and skills they would need to take the place of the Jews' (Frank's diary, entry of 12 September 1940).

91 See note 88.

92 Federal Archive/BDC, personal file of Karl Kuchenbäcker.

93 Karl Kuchenbäcker, 'Änderung der Ordnung der Agrarstruktur im Generalgouvernement', in: *Neues Bauerntum* 33 (1941), No.7, pp.257–62.

94 Karl Kuchenbäcker, 'Bodenordnung im Generalgouvernement'; the programme was unveiled on 20 May 1941, and is reprinted in: *Najnowsze Dzieje Polski* 8/1965, pp.112–38.

95 Meinhold, 'Industrialisierung', p.161. Similar arguments, albeit often formulated in less specific terms, can be found in much of the literature on this theme. See for example Hans Bernhard v. Grünberg, 'Die Regionale Frage', in: *Neues Bauerntum* 36 (1944), No.1/2, pp.76–86. The argument also makes a very early appearance (in January 1940) in a memorandum entitled 'Rechtsgestaltung deutscher Polenpolitik nach volkspolitischen Gesichtspunkten' (see esp. p.17), which was drafted for the 'nationality law committee' of Frank's Academy for German Law. Federal Archive, R 61/243 (also: *IMG*, Vol. XXVI, p.206 ff.).

96 Helmut Meinhold, 'Materialien zum Vergleich der Lohnhöhe im Gebiet des Generalgouvernements und im Altreich' (hereinafter cited as 'Meinhold, "Lohnhöhe"'), May 1941, p.6; Federal Archive, R 52 IV/144c.

97 ibid., p.4.

98 RKW, 'Grundlagen', p.6.

99 ibid., p.7.

100 Heinrich Gottong, 'Die Juden im Generalgouvernement', in: *Das Vorfeld* I (1940), No.3, p.20. See also Chapter 3, 'Demographic Economics – the Emergence of a New Science', p.71 f.

101 *Wirtschaftsdienst* 26 (1941), pp.18/19.

102 The memorandum may well have been commissioned by the RKF in connection with the preliminary studies for the General Plan for the East. Certainly the department of regional studies at the Institute for German Development Work in the East received such commissions from the RKF at a later date (Federal Archive/BDC, personal file of Hans Graul).

103 Helmut Meinhold, 'Die Erweiterung des Generalgouvernements nach Osten. A. Allgemeines', July 1941 (hereinafter cited as 'Meinhold, "Erweiterung"'); Federal Archive, R 52 IV/144a, p.11.

104 Spoken testimony of Helmut Meinhold, 23 November 1985.

105 Meinhold, 'Erweiterung', p.19.

106 Werner Jochmann (ed.), *Monologe im Führerhauptquartier 1941–1944. Die Aufzeichnungen Heinrich Heims* (hereinafter cited as '*Monologe*'), Hamburg 1980, p.74; entry for 28 September 1941.

107 'Even in the relatively sparsely inhabited north-east [of the Government General], including the Rokitno Marshes, there are too many people working in agriculture, so that (...) we can reasonably speak in terms of agricultural overpopulation here.' Helmut Meinhold, 'Das Generalgouvernement als Transitland', in: *Die Burg* 2 (1941), No.4, p.42.

108 Prior to 1918 Galicia embraced the entire southern and south-eastern regions of what was later to become the Polish state, including Cracow. The province was under Austrian rule. The 'administrative district of Galicia', with its capital at Lvov, was annexed to the Government General on 1 August 1941, and took in the eastern part of the old Galicia. It now became the fifth district of the Government General alongside Warsaw, Cracow, Lublin and Radom.

109 Draft notes for an initial administrative report on the district of Galicia, 26 August 1941; State Archive of Lvov, R-35/12/30, p.33.

110 Report of the head of the department of food and agriculture in Lvov, 15 October 1941; State Archive of Lvov, R-35/12/27, p.2.

111 In 1960 Meinhold concocted the story of a 'vacation trip' which had allegedly given him an opportunity 'to study a number of recently collectivized farms (...) immediately following the occupation by German troops'. Helmut Meinhold, 'Marktwirtschaft und zentrale Planwirtschaft', a lecture given at the 8th conference of German Student Fraternities (5–8 January 1960), in: *Die Bedeutung der Wirtschaftspolitik in der Auseinandersetzung zwischen Ost und West* (= *Burschenschaftliche Bücherei*, No.17), Frankfurt a.M. 1960, p.15.

112 Helmut Meinhold, 'Die Betriebsgrössenverhältnisse im polnischen Gewerbe', in: *Deutsche Forschung im Osten* 2 (1942), No.4, p.139.

113 According to the head of the department of regional planning in the Government General, Hans-Julius Schepers, who in October 1941 also became head of the economic council for the district of Galicia; *Diensttagebuch*, p.463.

114 Hans-Kraft Nonnenmacher, 'Die Wirtschaftsstruktur des galizischen Erdölgebietes', in: *Deutsche Forschung im Osten* 1 (1941), No.6, p.27.

Chapter 7: 1940: Plans, Experiments and Lessons Learned

1 Peter-Heinz Seraphim, *Das Judentum. Seine Rolle und Bedeutung in Vergangenheit und Gegenwart*, Munich 1942, p.52.

2 Cf. Seev Goshen, 'Eichmann und die Nisko-Aktion im November 1939', in: *VfZG* 29 (1981), pp.74–96.

3 Pätzold, p.350.

4 Memorandum of Rademacher's, 3 July 1940; *Nbg. Dok.*, NG-2586–B-cont'd.

5 On the genesis and significance of the Madagascar project, see Brechtken, *Madagaskar*.

6 'Reichssicherheitshauptamt: Madagaskar-Projekt' (sent to the Foreign Office on 15 August 1940; hereinafter cited as '"Reichssicherheitshauptamt"'); Political Archive of the Foreign Office (Bonn), Inland IIg/177, pp.199–219, here esp. p.201.

7 Meeting of departmental heads, 12 July 1940; *Diensttagebuch*, p.252.

8 Andreas Hillgruber, *Hitlers Strategie, Politik und Kriegsführung 1940–1941* (hereinafter cited as 'Hillgruber, *Strategie*'), Frankfurt a.M. 1965, p.254.

9 The Madagascar plan was formulated 'at the instigation of and in close consultation with' the Foreign Office, under the personal direction of Franz Rademacher. (See Rademacher's memorandum of 30 August 1940 on the 'progress to date on the Madagascar plan by Section D III' in the Foreign Office; Political Archive of the Foreign Office (Bonn), Inland IIg/177, p.195.)

10 See Rademacher's memorandum of 12 August 1940: 'Gedanken über die Gründung einer intereuropäischen Bank für die Verwertung des Judenvermögens in Europa'; Political Archive of the Foreign Office (Bonn), Inland IIg/177, p.228.

11 ibid.

12 Hillgruber, *Strategie*, pp.246, 252.

13 'Zusammenstellung der mineralischen Bodenschätze von Madagaskar (gez. Schumacher)'; Political Archive of the Foreign Office (Bonn), Inland IIg/177, pp.222–4.

14 The Foreign Office sent Schumacher's report, and presumably Burgdörfer's report as well, to the Anti-Semitic Campaign, the Central Office for the Security of the Reich, the Four-Year Plan Authority and the Reich Institute for the History of the New Germany; ibid.

15 The point is not made by the report itself, but by Seraphim in an observation on the Madagascar project; cf. Volkmer, p.191.

16 Friedrich Burgdörfer's report of 17 July 1940, 'Zur Frage der Umsiedlung der Juden'; Central State Archive (Potsdam), film 15806, frames 612577–612581. Brechtken reviews a report on the Madagascar project that historians have long ignored. It was commissioned by Göring in the summer of 1940 from the Reich Office of Regional Planning, and sent to Göring by its author, Ernst Jarmer, on 22 August 1940. See Brechtken, pp.254–9.

17 For a detailed discussion see Hillgruber, *Strategie*, pp.242–55, here esp. p.249.

18 Rademacher's memorandum of 10 February 1942; as quoted in: Hillgruber, *Strategie*, p.254.

19 Himmler's decree on 'The settlement of the gypsy question' of 8 December 1938, reprinted in: *Ministerialblatt des Reichs- und Preussischen Ministeriums des Innern* 3 (1938), columns 2105–10.

20 Letter from the head of the SS Central Office of Race and Resettlement, Günther Pancke, to Heinrich Himmler, dated 19 December 1938; Federal Archive/BDC, SS-HO/2250.

21 Letter from Astel to Himmler of 14 June 1937 and Himmler's reply; as quoted in: Ackermann, *Himmler*, p.284 ff.

22 As quoted in: Friedrich Karl Kaul, *Nazimordaktion T4. Ein Bericht über die erste industriemässig durchgeführte Mordaktion des Naziregimes*, Berlin 1973, p.63.

23 Reprinted in: Götz Aly, 'Medizin gegen Unbrauchbare', in: *Aussonderung und Tod. Die klinische Hinrichtung der Unbrauchbaren* (= *Beiträge zur national-sozialistischen Gesundheits- und Sozialpolitik*, Vol. 1), Berlin 1985, p.32 f. Evidently the mayor of Plauen, Eugen Wörner, typed these notes himself (with numerous typing errors in the German original) as an aide-memoire. Wörner's candour will have been the exception. The corresponding entry in the diary of the Governing Mayor of Hamburg is terse and matter-of-fact: '3.4.1941: morning session on hospitals and nursing homes at the local authorities' conference.'

24 Alfred Döblin, 'Die Fahrt ins Blaue', in: *Badische Zeitung*, 3 May 1946; as quoted in: H.D. Heilmann, 'Döblins Fahrt ins Blaue', in: Aly, *Aktion T4*, 1989, p.209.

25 Aly/Roth, p.93 f.

26 Schedule of departmental functions at the Reich Ministry of the Interior for 1943; Secret State Archive, Berlin, Rep. 151/381.

27 Ludwig Schaich, *Lebensunwert? Kirche und Innere Mission Württembergs im Kampf gegen die 'Vernichtung lebensunwerten Lebens'*, Stuttgart 1947, p.79.

28 Report by the T4 doctor Robert Müller on the nursing home at Rastatt (July 1942); as quoted in: Aly, *Aktion T4*, p.16.

29 Ewald Meltzer, *Das Problem der Abkürzung 'lebensunwerten' Lebens*, Halle 1925. The replies to which Morell referred included the following: 'What am I supposed to do as a single parent? I leave it to you, do what you think best. Better if you hadn't said anything to me, and had just put the child to sleep.'

    'Would rather not have been bothered with this question. If the news of his death had been broken to us suddenly we would have accepted it. How much better for the child if something had been done right at the beginning!'

'I'd rather not have known anything about it.'

'Agreed in principle, but parents shouldn't be asked; it's hard for them to confirm a death sentence on their own flesh and blood. But if they are told the child has died from some illness or other, then anyone would accept that.'

Melzter interpreted this attitude thus: 'People are glad to release themselves, and perhaps the child too, from the burden, but they don't want their conscience to be troubled' (ibid., p.90).

30 Morell's unpublished papers, No.81, undated drafts; NAW, T 253/Roll 44.
31 As quoted by Aly (see note 23), p.16.
32 Brief notes on the meeting taken by higher court judge Alexander Bergmann; ibid., p.26 f.
33 See also Aly, *Endlösung*, pp.312–16.

Chapter 8: Interim Reflection

1 From a discussion between Hitler and Keitel on 17 October 1939 'on the future shaping of Polish relations with Germany' (transcript of 20 October 1939); *IMG*, Vol. XXVI, p.377 ff.
2 Peter-Heinz Seraphim, 'Die Judenfrage im Generalgouvernement als Bevölkerungsproblem', in: *Die Burg* 1 (1940), No.1, p.63.
3 Speech given by Himmler to a gathering of Gauleiters and other Party functionaries on 29 January 1940; as quoted in: Bradley E. Smith, Agnes E. Peterson (eds.), *Heinrich Himmler. Geheimreden 1933 bis 1945* (hereinafter cited as 'Himmler, *Geheimreden*'), Frankfurt a.M./Berlin/Vienna 1974, p.130.
4 Hitler in an interview with the journalist Colin Ross on 12 March 1940; as quoted in: *ADAP* (Documents on German Foreign Policy), Series D, Vol.8, p.716.
5 Transcript by Martin Bormann, dated 2 October 1940, of a meeting in Hitler's Berlin apartment attended by Frank, Koch, von Schirach and others; *IMG*, Vol. XXXIX, p.425 ff.
6 Frank reported on statements to this effect from Hitler on 4 November 1940 and in December 1940 at a 'meeting to discuss issues arising from the relocation of Poles and Jews to the Government General' on 15 January 1941; *Diensttagebuch*, p.327.
7 *Diensttagebuch*, p.335.
8 From a discussion between Hitler, Field Marshal Keitel and General Zeitzler on 8 June 1943; Federal Archive/Military Archive (Freiburg), RW 4/507, p.32.
9 'Studentenarbeit im Generalgouvernement', in: *Die Bewegung* 9 (1941), issue 20/21, p.1.
10 Walter Emmerich, Helmut Meinhold, 'Die Aufgaben der Sektion Wirtschaft im Institut für Deutsche Ostarbeit', in: *Deutsche Forschung im Osten* I (1941), No.4, p.39 ff.
11 'Grundlinien des industriellen Wiederaufbaus von Gross-Hamburg' (here-

inafter cited as 'Grundlinien'), prepared at the World Economic Institute at the University of Kiel by Dr Helmut Meinhold, November 1945.

12　ibid., p.12.

13　ibid., p.16.

14　Meinhold, 'Industrialisierung', p.213 f.

15　'Grundlinien', p.16 f.

16　Born in Stargard, Pomerania, in 1914, Helmut Meinhold was a key figure in German post-war reconstruction. His second career began in the weeks prior to Germany's capitulation in the place where his first career had also been launched – at the World Economic Institute in Kiel. In 1947–8 he worked in the British occupation zone's Central Office of Economic Affairs, from 1949 to 1952 he headed the economic policy unit in the Federal Ministry of Economic Affairs. Thereafter he became a full professor at Heidelberg University, and from 1962 onwards he was teaching economics and social policy at the university in Frankfurt am Main. From 1959 to 1986 Meinhold was the most important adviser on social policy to successive Federal German governments. In 1988 Federal President Richard von Weizsäcker awarded him the Order of Merit of the Federal Republic, in the full knowledge of Helmut Meinhold's past.

Chapter 9: The Economic Exploitation of the Ghettos

1　The coffee wholesaler Hans Biebow was born in Bremen in 1902 and executed in Lódź in 1947. He secured his post as head of the Lódź ghetto administration through the intervention of the Lódź Chamber of Industry and Commerce and of the undersecretary in the Reich Ministry of Economic Affairs. Note for the files by Alexander Palfinger, 7 April 1941; State Archive of Warsaw, Der Kommissar für den jüdischen Wohnbezirk in Warschau/125.

2　On the history of the ghetto, see also 'Niederschrift der Beauftragten des Rechnungshofs des Deutschen Reichs über die örtliche Prüfung der Ernährungs- und Wirtschaftsstelle Getto des Oberbürgermeisters der Stadt Litzmannstadt [= Lódź] in Litzmannstadt, Hermann-Göring-Strasse Nr.21' (the report of the Reich Audit Office referred to above – hereinafter cited as 'Gutachten des Reichsrechnungshofes'); Federal Archive, Reichsfinanzministerium/B 6159, pp.84–103 (reprinted in: *Beiträge zur nationalsozialistischen Gesundheits- und Sozialpolitik*, Vol. 9, Berlin 1991).

3　Karl Weber, 'Litzmannstadt. Geschichte und Probleme eines Wirtschaftszentrums im deutschen Osten' (= *Kieler Vorträge*, Vol. 70), Jena 1943, p.10. Weber was president of the Lódź Chamber of Commerce, and he delivered this speech on 9 December 1942 at the Kiel World Economic Institute. In the course of two years the number of businesses in Lódź had been reduced from 43,000 to just 3,000 (Hilberg, p.171).

4　Helge Grabitz, Wolfgang Scheffler, *Letzte Spuren* (hereinafter cited as 'Grabitz/Scheffler'), Berlin 1988, p.281.

5　Letter from Reich Minister of Finance Schwerin von Krosigk to the Reich Minister of the Interior, 9 November 1940; Federal Archive, Reichsfinanzministerium/B 6158, p.87 f. The Reich Minister of Finance also worried in this letter that the ghetto population would not be 'contributing to the public purse', i.e. would not be paying taxes.

6 'Gutachten des Reichsrechnungshofes', p.92 f.

7 See note 5.

8 Letter from the Reich Ministry of Finance to the Reich Ministry of the Interior, 29 August 1940; Federal Archive, Reichsfinanzministerium/B 6030, p.14. The meeting at which the 'credit' had been approved had taken place at the Reich Ministry of the Interior on 1 April 1940, a month before the ghetto was sealed off, albeit on the understanding that the Jewish population of Łódź would be evacuated very quickly. The figure of 25 million does not appear in the minutes, but it can be inferred from the report of the Reich Audit Office (Appendix 5, p.102).

9 'Gutachten des Reichsrechnungshofes', p.86. In November the central district tax office in Łódź had already carried out an audit of the books, the results of which had evidently prompted the Reich Minister of Finance to investigate further; ibid., p.91.

10 ibid.

11 ibid., p.88.

12 ibid., p.97.

13 This demolition process was the necessary precursor to the high-flown plans of the German city administration, which proposed to build a new 'totally German central city' in place of the old Łódź. 'The present city on the site would have to be completely demolished' (memorandum on a tour of inspection of the redevelopment works in Łódź, 22 August 1940; State Archive of Katowice, Land Pl GO/21, p.1 f.). In December 1939 Wilhelm Hallbauer was appointed head of town planning in Łódź. His brief: 'Make Łódź a German city!' To that end he insisted that 'the Łódź city centre must be systematically cleansed of foreign peoples and the suburbs in question heavily Germanized'. As quoted in: Niels Gutschow, 'Stadtplanung im Warthegau 1939–1944', in: Mechthild Rössler, Sabine Schleiermacher (eds.), *Der 'Generalplan Ost'. Hauptlinien der nationalsozialistischen Planungs- und Vernichtungspolitik* (hereinafter cited as 'Rössler, Schleiermacher'), Berlin 1993, p.239 f. In October 1941 Hallbauer became municipal surveyor and deputy town commandant of Lvov.

14 'Gutachten des Reichsrechnungshofes', p.89 f.

15 ibid., p.98.

16 Heydrich had announced the deportation of 813,000 persons to the Government General at a meeting that took place at the Central Office for the Security of the Reich on 8 January 1941. Among those present were the regional planning and population experts from the Government General. Another 200,000 people inside the Government General would have to be relocated, they were told, to make room for military training areas. Frank had sought to block these resettlement proposals, in part with the argument that 'these people are being dispossessed in Germany and coming here as the dispossessed, to a region where they basically have no prospect of rebuilding their lives again' (*Diensttagebuch*, p.326 f.).

17 As quoted in: Grabitz/Scheffler, p.281 f.

18 Letter of 16 July 1941 from SS Sturmbannführer Höppner in Posen to the

Central Office for the Security of the Reich, marked 'for the attention of Adolf Eichmann', with enclosure 'Solution of the Jewish question in the Reichsgau Wartheland'; as quoted in: Pätzold, p.295.

19 Memorandum on a departmental meeting 'on the subject of Jewish labour', which took place on 28 November 1941 in the Reich Ministry of Labour, attended by representatives from the annexed Polish territories; as quoted in: Pätzold, p.322.

20 Isaiah Trunk, *Lodzher geto*, New York 1962, pp.251–7. Deteriorating conditions within the ghetto also increased the number of those who met the selection criteria. The first ghetto occupants to be selected for deportation were those who were not from Lódź, who consequently had little influence – and for the most part little money. The quota of women in every age-group was disproportionately high. Cf. Joan Ringelheim, 'Verschleppung, Tod und Überleben. Nationalsozialistische Ghettopolitik gegen Frauen und Männer im besetzten Polen', in: Theresa Wobbe (ed.), *Nach Osten. Verdeckte Spuren nationalsozialistischer Verbrechen*, Frankfurt a.M. 1992, pp.135–60.

21 'Reichskuratorium für Wirtschaftlichkeit, Dienststelle General-gouvernement, Bericht über die wirtschaftlichen Auswirkungen der Bildung eines jüdischen Wohnbezirks in Warschau', Cracow, 19 December 1940; Federal Archive/Military Archive (Freiburg), RW 19/1499. The report was written by Gater's deputy, Meder.

22 'Reichskuratorium für Wirtschaftlichkeit, Dienststelle General-gouvernement, Die Wirtschaftsbilanz des jüdischen Wohnbezirks in Warschau', Cracow, March 1941 (hereinafter cited as 'Die Wirt-schaftsbilanz'); State Archive of Warsaw, Der Kommissar für den jüdischen Wohnbezirk in Warschau/125. The report runs to 53 pages and 10 appendices (reprinted in: *Beiträge zur nationalsozialistischen Gesundheits- und Sozialpolitik*, Vol. 9, Berlin 1991).

23 'A report on the establishment of the Jewish quarter in Warsaw', presented on 21 January 1941 by section head Waldemar Schön from the department of resettlement (Warsaw district); Federal Archive/Military Archive (Freiburg), RW 19/1499.

24 'Die Wirtschaftsbilanz', p.1 ('Zusammenfassung').

25 ibid., p. 13.

26 ibid., p.2.

27 ibid., p.8.

28 ibid., p.6.

29 ibid., p.17.

30 ibid., p.20.

31 Abraham I. Katsh (ed.), *Buch der Agonie. Das Warschauer Tagebuch des Chaim A. Kaplan*, Frankfurt a.M. 1967, p.226.

32 'Die Wirtschaftsbilanz', p.21. Gater failed to mention in his report that lack of food, proper clothing and equipment for the workers also contributed to this outcome.

33 ibid., p.20.

34 ibid., p.23.

35 ibid., p.10.

36 ibid., p.12.

37 ibid., p.26.

38 ibid., p.28.

39 ibid., p.47.

40 ibid., p.51.

41 ibid., 'Zusammenfassung'.

42 ibid., p.53.

43 ibid.

44 Minutes of the government meeting of 3 April 1941; *Diensttagebuch*, p.344 f.

45 Cf. the remarks by district governor Fischer and undersecretary Kundt in the minutes of the government meeting of 19 April 1941, *Diensttagebuch*, p.360; Frank's diary.

46 Government meeting of 3 April 1941; *Diensttagebuch*, p.344.

47 These detailed 'implementing regulations' – 'Durchführungsbestimmungen zur Anordnung des Chefs des Distrikts Krakau vom 3.3.1941 über die Bildung eines jüdischen Wohnbezirks in der Stadt Krakau vom 15.4.1941' – were published in the *Krakauer Zeitung* of 20/21 April 1941.

48 *Czerniaków*, p.151 (entry for 21 May 1941). Here he writes: 'In Cracow a substantial number of the Jewish population have passes and business interests outside the ghetto.' See also the memorable account of living conditions inside the Cracow ghetto by Roman Polanski; *Roman Polanski*, Munich 1984.

49 Palfinger had protested against Gater's report in a lengthy memorandum, but his protest went unheeded. One of the arguments used by Palfinger to discredit Gater's calculations was that 'the Jews [were] beasts of burden', whose pattern of eating was determined by nature, so that calculations of their needs were a waste of time. State Archive of Warsaw, Der Kommissar für den jüdischen Wohnbezirk in Warschau/125 (fragment). On the tensions between Palfinger and Gater, see also *Czerniaków*, p.143. (Unfortunately the key period between 14 December 1940 and 22 April 1941 is missing from Czerniaków's diary notes.)

50 Brief announcement in the *Krakauer Zeitung* of 21 May 1941.

51 See Bischof's memorandum of 30 April 1941; State Archive of Warsaw, Der Kommissar für den jüdischen Wohnbezirk in Warschau/11, p.9. In a statement to district governor Fischer, Bischof describes the RKW report as 'correct in its conclusions' and 'an authoritative basis for further discussion'.

52 Archive of the Central Commission, Warsaw, Reg. GG/Hauptabteilung Arbeit/Abt. Arbeitseinsatz, IX/12, p.20.

53 Archive for New Documents, Warsaw, Reg. GG/1414/7 (undated fragment, circa March 1941).

54 See for example the letter headed 'The Jewish labour market in the Government General' that Bischof circulated to all the Chambers of Industry and Commerce in the Reich from August 1941 onwards; Federal Archive, R II/1220. One of the arguments he used was that 'the economy as a whole must not be held back by having to feed useless mouths'. The contents of this letter were also published in various daily newspapers, such as the *Nationalzeitung* in Essen of 26 August 1941 ('Jüdischer Arbeitsmarkt im

Generalgouvernement').

55 Memorandum of 20 November 1941 by the Statistical Office of the Government General; Archive of the Central Statistical Office of the Republic of Poland, Statistisches Amt 1940–1944/255.

56 Log of confidential documents received by the department of regional planning in the district of Warsaw; State Archive of Warsaw, Abteilung Raumordnung/872.

57 Tatiana Berenstein, 'O hitlerowskich metodach eksploatacji gospodarczej getta warszawskiego' ['National Socialist methods for the economic exploitation of the Warsaw ghetto'], in: *Biuletyn Zydowskiego Instytutu Historycznego*, Warsaw 1953, No.4. Selected extracts translated into German and reprinted in: *Beiträge zur nationalsozialistischen Gesundheits- und Sozialpolitik*, Vol. 9, Berlin 1991.

58 ibid.

59 State Archive of Warsaw, Der Kommissar für den jüdischen in Wohnbezirk Warschau/1, p.7. To that extent there is no factual basis for the distinction drawn by Christopher Browning when he divides the German experts and politicians responsible for running the ghetto into 'productivists' (Gater, Emmerich, Bischof) and 'starvers' (Palfinger, Schön, Fischer), emphasizing the disagreements between the two groups. It is our belief that the different policy options listed by Gater in his report were not intended as *alternatives*, and that they were in actual fact implemented in combination: productivity increases *and* starvation. See Christopher R. Browning, 'Vernichtung und Arbeit', in: *konkret*, 32 (1989), No.12, pp.64–9.

60 Charter of the Warsaw transfer agency, 14 May 1941; Political Archive of the Foreign Office (Bonn), Inland IIg/199, p.2.

61 Economic conference of 22 July 1941, see esp. Frank's opening address and the paper given by the executive director of the Central Department of Food and Agriculture; Frank's diary.

62 Papers given at the government meeting in Warsaw on 15 October 1941; State Archive of Warsaw, Amt des Distrikts Warschau/132, p.26.

63 Letter of 11 November 1941 from the Reich Minister of Labour to the Association of Chambers of Industry and Commerce in the Reich Chamber for Economic Affairs; Federal Archive, R II/1220, p.237.

64 Government meeting of 15 October 1941, p.10.

65 ibid., p.5.

66 ibid., p.12.

67 ibid., p.18.

68 Cf. the remarks made by Emmerich at the meeting of 16 October 1941; Frank's diary.

69 Cf. the letter of 27 May 1942 written by the Jewish community of the city of Lvov to municipal surveyor and deputy town commandant Wilhelm Hallbauer; State Archive of Lvov, R-37/4/140, p.21.

70 Memorandum of 20 January 1942 from the Lvov municipal administration; State Archive of Lvov, R-37/4/516, p.32.

71 Such reclassification and downgrading of the work done by Jews often antagonized the local authorities, who then complained that 'their' Jews had been taken away from them. Not that they had any objections to

deportation and murder as such; but they saw the withdrawal of Jewish labour as an attack on their own authority and autonomy.

72 Order issued by town commandant Höller on 25 March 1942; State Archive of Lvov, R-37/4/140, p.41 f. Cf. Hilberg, p.152.

73 Stefan Szende, *Der letzte Jude in Polen* (hereinafter cited as 'Szende'), Stockholm 1944, p.241.

74 Reports of the department of population management and welfare; State Archive of Lvov, R-24/1/123.

75 State Archive of Lvov, R-24/1/123, p.98.

76 See note 72, p.41. Before he came to Lvov in February 1942, Höller had been district administrator for the area around Cracow.

77 This was also reflected in the fact that when a deportation was imminent the ghetto population – here and in other Galician towns – was required to assemble for 'registration' in the yard of the employment office, where the victims of the next 'resettlement operation' were then selected; as for example on 7 September 1942 in the district town of Kolomyya in south-eastern Galicia. See the report of a police lieutenant to the police commander of the Galicia district, 14 November 1942; as quoted in: Raul Hilberg, *Sonderzüge nach Auschwitz*, Mainz 1981, p.194 ff.

78 Szende, p.240.

79 Szende reported that up to 5,000 marks were paid for a relatively secure job in waste collection; ibid., p.210.

80 Gerald Reitlinger, *Die Endlösung. Hitlers Versuch der Ausrottung der Juden Europas 1939–1945*, Berlin 1956, p.306. Those who sought to evade deportation with the aid of forged work papers received 'special treatment' at the hands of the German authorities; ibid., p.285.

81 Report of SS and police commander Friedrich Katzmann to the senior SS and police commander Friedrich-Wilhelm Krüger, 30 June 1943; *IMG*, Vol. XXXVII, p.394.

82 Frank's diary, minutes of the government meeting of 3 April 1941.

83 Federal Archive/Military Archive (Freiburg), RW-23/3.

84 See the 'Provisional collection of material on the question of the rationalization of trade and commerce in the Government General', compiled by senior civil servant Schulte-Wissermann in September 1942; Archive of the Central Commission, Warsaw, Reg. GG/Staatssekretariat/I/48.

85 Federal Archive/Military Archive (Freiburg), RW-23/2.

86 Rudolf Gater, Rudolf Wittich, Fritz Gerlach, *Der Einheitskostenplan für Industriebetriebe im Generalgouvernement. Leitfaden für die Einführung eines geordneten Rechnungsverkehrs*, Berlin 1942.

87 'Refa' stands for 'Reichsausschuss für Arbeitszeitermittlung' (roughly, 'Reich Committee for Time and Motion Studies'). Its work was used as a basis for rationalizing production and setting piecework rates.

88 See numerous articles in: *Die wirtschaftliche Leistung* 1 (1942) – 3 (1944); the journal was initially edited by Biehl, then – from No.4/1943 onwards – by Gater.

89 August Heinrichsbauer (executive secretary of the South-East Europe Society), 'Zur Lage im Generalgouvernement. Bericht über einen Aufenthalt im Generalgouvernement vom 30.9.–6.10.1942'; Federal

Archive, R 63/206, pp.129–48. Exactly the same arguments are used by Rudolf Gater in his article 'Warum arbeitet die Industrie im GG so teuer?', in: *Die wirtschaftliche Leistung* 1 (1942), No.5, pp.138–41.

90 It is interesting to note in this context the survey of agricultural enterprises carried out by the Statistical Office of the Government General in the spring of 1941. The area of land under cultivation was calculated and all the people living on each farm were listed by name. They had to state their age, the trade they had learned and their present job, in the case of those who had a job off the farm. From the raw data of the survey an 'agricultural registry' was immediately compiled. This was sent direct to the regional employment offices, which were then able to calculate the number of 'surplus mouths to feed' on each farm and earmark specific individuals for forced labour. (Archive of the Central Statistical Office of the Republic of Poland, document collection 'Statistisches Amt 1939–1945', passim.)

91 'Planmässige Steigerung der wirtschaftlichen Leistung', in: *Die wirtschaftliche Leistung* 2 (1943), No.1, pp.7–9.

92 Georg Robert, 'Industrielle Rationalisierung im Generalgouvernement', in: *Der deutsche Volkswirt* 17 (1942/43), No.29/30 of 17 April 1943. Robert was a colleague of Gater's in Cracow.

93 Of these 112,000 businesses 109,000 had been closed down and only 3,000 'Aryanized'; Hilberg, p.177.

94 *Die wirtschaftliche Leistung* 3 (1944), No.7, July, p.1.

95 Speech given by Himmler to a gathering of senior Party officials and Gauleiters in Posen on 6 October 1943; as quoted in: Himmler, *Geheimreden*, p.170.

96 '100 Einwohner je qkm und doch zuviel. Generalgouvernement hat über 1,5 Mill. überschüssige Arbeitskräfte in Reserve', in: *Brüsseler Zeitung* of 10 November 1942. The article reviews a study by Meinhold that had appeared in *Die Burg* on the number of 'surplus' workers in the Government General, and clearly draws in part on a separate interview with him.

97 Rudolf Bräuning, 'Die Landwirtschaft im Generalgouvernement auf der Schwelle einer neuen Zeit', in: *Die Burg* 4 (1943), No.1, p.23.

Chapter 10: 'Population Surpluses' in the European Trading Area

1 The term was in general use by 1942 at the latest. It was used, for instance, as the title for a series of lectures jointly organized in the early months of 1942 by the NSDAP's economic adviser for the Berlin district, the Berlin Chamber of Industry and Commerce, the Berlin School of Economics and the Association of Berlin Businessmen. The lectures are published in: Walther Funk et al., *Europäische Wirtschaftsgemeinschaft*, Berlin 1942.

2 *Europäische Grossraumwirtschaft. Vorträge gehalten auf der Tagung zu Weimar vom 9.-11.10.1941*, Leipzig (no date of publication), p.iv.

3 Hermann Gross, 'Zur Geschichte der wirtschaftswissenschaftlichen Südosteuropa-Forschung', in: *Osteuropa-Wirtschaft* 24 (1979), p.129.

4 The institutions represented on the committee, in addition to the South-East Europe Society and the Central European Economic Conference, were

I.G. Farben, the German and Viennese Institutes for Economic Research, the Reich Ministry of Economic Affairs, the Kiel Institute of World Economic Studies, the South-East Association of German Universities and the Central Federation of Industry of Bohemia and Moravia.

5 Secret protocol of 27 June 1942; Federal Archive, R 63/303, pp.53–70.

6 Cf. Wolfgang Schumann (ed.), *Griff nach Südosteuropa* (hereinafter cited as 'Schumann'), Berlin 1973. One of the team of economic specialists working for the board of the Central European Economic Conference, Alfred Sohn-Rethel, later wrote the book *Ökonomie und Klassenstruktur des deutschen Faschismus* (hereinafter cited as 'Sohn-Rethel'), Frankfurt a.M. 1975.

7 Tilo von Wilmowsky, 'Aufgaben und Ziele des Mitteleuropäischen Wirtschaftstages', in: *Wiener Tagung des Mitteleuropäischen Wirtschaftstages am 2. September 1940*, Vienna 1940, p.9.

8 Cf. *Monatsberichte des Wiener Instituts für Wirtschaftsforschung*, 15 (1941), No.5/6, p.92; Hans Radandt, 'Die Interessen der I.G. Farbenindustrie AG in Bulgarien bis 1944', in: *1999* 3 (1988), No.4, pp.10–30.

9 'Die Bedeutung der südosteuropäischen Getreidewirtschaft und ihre wehrwirtschaftliche Beurteilung, Geheimbericht des Instituts für Weltwirtschaft an der Universität Kiel' (hereinafter cited as 'Getreidewirtschaft'), April 1939, p.21; Federal Archive/Military Archive (Freiburg), RW 19/Anh. I/572. In bad harvest years the supply of grain in Yugoslavia, Romania and Bulgaria was not even sufficient to feed the indigenous population. See Otto von Frangeš, 'Die Bevölkerungsdichte als Triebkraft der Wirtschaftspolitik der südosteuropäischen Bauernstaaten' (= *Kieler Vorträge*, Vol. 59; hereinafter cited as 'Frangeš, "Bevölkerungsdichte"'), Jena 1939, pp.13, 15.

10 ibid., p.25.

11 Otto von Frangeš, 'Die Donaustaaten Südosteuropas und der deutsche Grosswirtschaftsraum', in: *Weltwirtschaftliches Archiv* 53 (1941), p.285. Frangeš (1870–1945) was Yugoslavia's Minister of Agriculture from 1929 to 1931, and as the essay cited here reveals, he maintained close ties with German economic experts and 'hands-on practitioners'. Like the economist Mihail Manoilescu, who became Romania's Foreign Minister for about a year in 1940, he regarded himself as one of the 'voices in the wilderness' who had long been calling for 'the closest possible ties between the agrarian countries of south-east Europe on the one hand and Germany and Italy on the other'.

12 'Konzept der Reichsstelle für Wirtschaftsausbau im Vierjahresplan vom August 1939'; Federal Archive, R 25/53, pp.1–15.

13 ibid.

14 Press conference on the economy, held on the evening of 24 July 1940; Federal Archive, Backe's unpublished papers Nachlass Backe/9.

15 From the minutes of the meeting of the senior advisory board of the Reich Federation of Industrialists on 3 October 1940, as quoted in: Eichholtz I, p.368 ff.

16 'Ausarbeitung des Deutschen Instituts für Bankwissenschaft und Bankwesen vom 27.8.1940 zu Fragen der Aussenwirtschaft und der Währungspolitik nach dem Kriege', reprinted in: *Bulletin des Arbeitskreises*

'*Zweiter Weltkrieg*', No.1/2, 1971, p.70. In Serbia, Bulgaria, Romania, Slovakia and Croatia social attachés were installed in collaboration with the local German Embassy, their activities coordinated by a Berlin-based 'central office for international social engineering' set up by the German Labour Front. The benefits of their experience were then passed on to the Labour Science Institute of the German Labour Front 'to be incorporated into the general planning process for Europe as a whole'. Their remit included 'acquainting foreign governments, leading figures, public authorities (...) the press, etc., with (...) German social policy; making proposals to the individual governments for, and securing the adoption of, specific social policy objectives that would have to be carefully coordinated with the economic condition of the countries concerned, the character of the people (...) and various German interests'. (Memorandum by Hans Felix Zeck, 'concerning conversation with SS Obersturmbannführer Smagon on 6 January 1944'; Federal Archive, R 63/124, pp.33–4.)

17 Wolfgang Peters, 'Soziale Zukunftsperspektiven', in: *Donaueuropa* 3 (1943), p.327.

18 *Monologe*, p.56, entry for 10 August 1941.

19 Gustav Schlotterer, 'Wirtschaftliche Zusammenarbeit in Europa', in: *Die Deutsche Volkswirtschaft* 9 (1940), p.944 ff.

20 In Yugoslavia the average size of agricultural smallholdings following the agrarian reform was 6.61 hectares, in Bulgaria it was 5 hectares. In 1934 as many as 89.3 per cent of the smallholdings in Yugoslavia were said to be under 10 hectares in size (*Monatsberichte des Wiener Instituts für Wirtschaftsforschung* 15 (1941), No.3/4, p.83). Detailed statistical material can be found in the report by the Labour Science Institute of the German Labour Front, 'Deutschland und Südosteuropa' (hereinafter cited as 'Deutschland und Südosteuropa'), Berlin 1940, reprinted in: Michael Hepp and Karl Heinz Roth (eds.), *Sozialstrategien der Deutschen Arbeitsfront*, published by the Hamburg Foundation for Social History of the 20th Century with an introduction by the editors, Munich/New York/Oxford/Paris 1987 ff.

21 Food exports, German experts complained, remained 'far below the projected figures'. ('Deutschland und Südosteuropa', p.89.)

22 ibid. p.97.

23 'Die Wirtschaftsstruktur Rumäniens unter Berücksichtigung der Gebietsabtretungen', in: *Ländernachrichten. Kriegsausgabe*, 9.4.1941, Vowi 4316; Central State Archive (Potsdam), IG-Farben/A 366, p.370 ff.

24 'Wirtschaftsbericht Bulgarien', 2.3.1939, Vowi 3216 (published by I.G. Farben); Central State Archive (Potsdam), IG-Farben/A 597/1.

25 Todor D. Zotschew, 'Landvolk in Bulgarien', in: *Neues Bauerntum* 35 (1943), p. 231.

26 'Die volkswirtschaftliche Struktur der Slowakei', in: *Monatsberichte des Wiener Instituts für Wirtschaftsforschung* 15 (1941), No.3/4, p.44. Two-thirds of the land under cultivation was divided among farm units of under 20 hectares. Another source tells us that 'the majority of agricultural enterprises (65.6 per cent) were tiny smallholdings of up to 5 hectares' (Hermann

Gross, 'Die Slowakei in der Grossraumwirtschaft Europas', in: *Nachrichten für Aussenhandel vom 13.1.1944*, No.19).

27 See for example Peter Zatko, 'Die Entwicklung der slowakischen Industrie' (Federal Archive, R 63/218, pp.21–30); 'Slowakei braucht neue Industrien. 325,000 Menschen in der Landwirtschaft überzählig', in: *Neues Wiener Tagblatt*, 18 June 1939.

28 'Deutschland und Südosteuropa', p.59.

29 See above, p.64.

30 'Deutschland und Südosteuropa', p.60.

31 *Der Donau-Karpatenraum (Kartenwerk für den Dienstgebrauch)*, a collection of maps published by the Reich Research Council, Regional Planning Section/Reich Commissioner for the Strengthening of German Nationhood and the Ethnic German Agency [now incorporated into the Central Office for the Security of the Reich], Stuttgart 1943, notes to map sheets 5 and 6.

32 'Deutschland und Südosteuropa', pp.26–8.

33 ibid., p.31.

34 ibid., p.72.

35 ibid., p.62.

36 ibid., p.76.

37 Andreas Predöhl, 'Stabilisierung und Weltwirtschaft', in: *Europäische Grossraumwirtschaft, Vorträge gehalten auf der Tagung zu Weimar vom 9.-11. Oktober 1941*, Leipzig (no date of publication), p.172.

38 'Zur Frage der künftigen Wirtschaftspolitik gegenüber Südosteuropa. Ausarbeitung der Forschungsstelle für Wehrwirtschaft beim Amt des Beauftragten für den Vierjahresplan vom 15.1.1941'; Federal Archive, R 2/10382, p.27 ff.; excerpts reprinted in Schumann, p.109 f.

39 Federal Archive, R 63/293, p.189. In all probability this was a paper drafted by the 'committee of twelve'; see above, p.215.

40 'Stand und wehrwirtschaftliche Bedeutung der rumänischen Getreidewirtschaft, Geheimstudie für das OKW, ausgearbeitet vom Institut für Weltwirtschaft im April 1939'; Federal Archive/Military Archive (Freiburg), RW 15/Anh. I/689, p.21.

41 Report dated 1 September 1942; Federal Archive, R 63/253, p.72 ff. Janowsky was head of the foreign trade section of the 'Business group for the wholesale, import and export trades' in Berlin, and toured south-east Europe in this capacity. He was viewed as 'a supporter of the idea of liquidating selected branches of industry in the South-East' (from the transcript of an industrial planning meeting on 30 March 1942; Federal Archive, R 63/295, p.104).

42 According to Janowsky, it was not 'just a matter of grain, breadfruit, maize and oil-producing plants', but also of 'animals reared for slaughter and animal products, such as beef cattle and pigs, plus poultry, eggs, feathers, down, animal hair and that kind of thing' (ibid.).

43 Seraphim, *Das Judentum im osteuropäischen Raum*, p.175, p.187 f., p.206, p.266 f. In the summer of 1940 the economic research department of I.G. Farben also analysed 'rural overpopulation' and 'the Jewish presence' in

Bessarabia, concluding that 'the Jews [were] for the most part agents of Russian-Communist ideas'. 'Die wirtschaftlichen Kräfte Bessarabiens und der nördlichen Bukowina und ihre Bedeutung für Rumänien', in: *Ländernachrichten. Kriegsausgabe*, 15.7.1940, published by the economic research department of I.G. Farben.

44   Political report of the German legation in Bucharest on a conversation with King Carol on the 'Jewish question', 26 June 1937 (Political Archive of the Foreign Office (Bonn), Politische Abteilung/Akten betreffend Judenfragen/ Rumänien, Pol IV/347, pp.41–6); German legation in Bucharest to Chief Inspector Hoppe of the Reichsbank at the office of the Commissioner for the Four-Year Plan, 12 August 1941 (Political Archive of the Foreign Office (Bonn), Inland IIg/203, p.3 f.). There is a note in the file stating that 'the German legation has advised the deputy prime minister to proceed with the elimination of Jewish elements *slowly and methodically*'. Rademacher and Hoppe had already had dealings with each other in connection with the Madagascar project. See the political report of the German legation in Hungary (signed 'Werkmüller'), 20 April 1937 (Political Archive of the Foreign Office (Bonn), Politische Abteilung/Pol IV/512); and the report of 26 July 1937 on the influence of the Jews in the national life of Hungary (ibid.).

45   'Deutschland und Südosteuropa', p.32.

46   Janowsky's report, p.16.

47   'Deutschland und Südosteuropa', p.32 f.

48   Note of 2 December 1942; Political Archive of the Foreign Office (Bonn), Akten betreffend Judenfrage in Ungarn 1942–43, Inland IIg/208, pp.45–52.

49   Telegram No.133 of 24 April 1944 from the senior SS and police commander; Political Archive of the Foreign Office (Bonn), Akten betreffend Judenfrage in Ungarn/Sonderaktion 1944/Inland IIg/210, p.14 f.

50   Walter Christiansen, in: *Wirtschaftsdienst* 26 (1941), p.669.

51   'Bericht Slov. Nr.15 vom 16.10.1941 zur Lage in der Slowakei', p.2; Federal Archive/Military Archive (Freiburg), RW 29/2. The report was written by an unnamed agent of the Business Information Committee. The latter was founded by the business communities in Hamburg and Bremen to gather information about conditions in other countries. Its 'Confidential Reports' were made available to a select circle of recipients, who were instructed to destroy these documents as soon as they had read them. The report cited here is one of the few whose existence has so far been documented. It is safe to assume that the reports of the Business Information Committee would be an important source for studying the economic motives that led Germany into the Second World War. The Business Information Committee collaborated closely with the Hamburg World Economic Institute, which had been officially cooperating with the security service (SD) since August 1939 at the latest, furnishing regular reports about 'observing the Jews' to the head of the SD department concerned, Franz Six. These reports have likewise disappeared without trace; their existence can be inferred from the correspondence between the Hamburg Institute and the Central Office for the Security of the Reich (Federal Archive, R 58/565, pp.3–7, p.104 f.).

52 Max Biehl, 'Slowakei. Ein neuer Staat richtet sich ein', in: *Wirtschaftsdienst* 24 (1939), p.1026. (Biehl too had begun his career at the Hamburg World Economic Institute.)

53 'Juden im Südosten', in: *Berliner Börsenzeitung*, 11 June 1941.

54 'Deutschland und Südosteuropa', p.71.

55 'Rumäniens Kampf gegen die Juden', in: *Frankfurter Zeitung*, 22 July 1943.

56 'Bericht des Präsidenten des Bayerischen Statistischen Landesamts Prof. Dr Burgdörfer über die Tätigkeit als Beobachter der Allgemeinen Rumänischen Volkszählung 1941'; Political Archive of the Foreign Office (Bonn), Abt.III/HaPol IVb/Akten betreffend Bevölkerungsfragen in Rumänien, p.14. See also: Aly/Roth, p.82 f. Burgdörfer's report went on to say that in the wake of the census Romania's system of registration and the keeping of a population register were to be reviewed and overhauled. The statistician entrusted with this task, Dr med. P. Vlad, would be 'coming to Germany in the near future to study the German system of registration' ('Bericht', p.8). The conduct and results of the Romanian census of 1941 are the subject of a book published by the Vienna Publications Office in collaboration with the SD under the title *Die Bevölkerungszählung in Rumänien 1941* ('For limited distribution', Vienna 1943). According to the authors, the purpose of the census was to assemble the basic statistical material for 'more extensive resettlement programmes and migratory movements'; of 'special importance' here was the 'separate census of the population of Jewish origin', while 'separate counts were also made of agricultural businesses and of commercial and industrial enterprises'. The lists of questions on which these statistical counts were based were likewise said to 'go into very great detail' (pp.5–11).

57 Peter-Heinz Seraphim, 'Bevölkerungs- und Wirtschaftsprobleme einer europäischen Gesamtlösung der Judenfrage', in: *Weltkampf* 1 (1941), No.1/2, p.45. Max Biehl writes in similar vein: 'The removal of the Jews from the civil service and public services as well as from the liberal professions (principally lawyers, doctors, apothecaries) was very quickly accomplished. (...) Now that opportunities for advancement in the civil service and the liberal professions have been opened up for Slovaks, young people have been heading off to the colleges and universities in large numbers.' (Max Biehl, 'Slowakei. Einrichtung im eigenen Staat', in: *Wirtschaftsdienst* 25 (1940), p.750.)

58 Reich Office for Economic Development at the Four-Year Plan Authority, 'Die künftigen Aufgaben der einzelnen europäischen Länder im Rahmen des Grosswirtschaftsraums' (5 May1941); Federal Archive, R 25/94.

59 Record of the conversation between Hitler and the Hungarian Regent, Admiral Horthy, on 18 April 1943; *ADAP* (Documents on German Foreign Policy), Series E, Vol. 5, Göttingen 1978, pp.621–40.

60 'Lagebericht. Beiblatt zum Politischen Dienst für SS und Polizei' (published by the SS Reichsführer, SS Central Office), No.1, May 1944.

61 *Deutsche Aussenwirtschaft* (published on behalf of the Reich Ministry of Economic Affairs) I (1944), No.1, 1 September 1944, p.24.

62 Alfred Maelicke, 'Fortschreitende Entjudung Europas', in: *Die Deutsche Volkswirtschaft* 17 (1942/43), pp.1272–6.

63 Maelicke had obtained his doctorate in 1936 with a dissertation on the city of Berlin's economic advisory bureau. During his time as district economic adviser he took a close interest in December 1938 in the 'disposal of Jewish businesses'. In a series of articles for the 'Economic Bulletin of the Berlin Chamber of Industry and Commerce' he explained – writing on 7 December 1938 – the newly created legal position regarding 'Aryanizations', outlining to 'prospective Aryan purchasers' with an eye to the main chance the criteria by which their applications to take over Jewish businesses would be judged: the district economic adviser, German Labour Front and Chamber of Industry and Commerce would decide in 'exemplary collaboration' which applicants were suited, in terms of their business and political credentials, to take over such enterprises, and which businesses ought to be closed down rather than 'Aryanized' in the interests of reducing 'overcrowding' in certain sectors of the economy. Alfred Maelicke, 'Zur Veräusserung jüdischer Gewerbebetriebe', in: *Wirtschaftsblatt der Industrie- und Handelskammer zu Berlin* 36 (1938), No.34, pp.1634–6.

64 Cf. Donald Kenrick, Gratton Puxon, *Sinti und Roma – die Vernichtung eines Volkes im NS-Staat*, Göttingen 1981, pp.93–105 and p.135. The figure cited is based in part on estimates (for Slovakia and Serbia), and the authors point out that the real figures could turn out to be much higher if further documentary evidence becomes available.

65 Report of the head of the civilian administration in Serbia, Turner, to the Wehrmacht commander for the South-East, Löhr, on 29 August 1942; *Nbg. Dok.*, NOKW-1486. As quoted in: Longerich, p.294 f.

66 Economic research department of I.G. Farben, 'Die Wirtschaftsstruktur Kroatiens' (Vowi 4479), report of 23 March 1942, signed by 'Dr Br'; Central State Archive (Potsdam), film 10796. We are grateful to Dr Martin Seckendorf of the State Archive Administration of the former GDR, an acknowledged expert on Nazi policy in south-east Europe, for drawing our attention to this document. A 1941 study produced the following figures for Zagoria: the total labour resource available amounted to 61,000,000 man-hours, of which only 17,712,000 were utilized in agriculture and industry. The conclusion reached: 'Surplus labour resource 43,200,000 man-hours = 70.9 per cent'. (Milan Fister, 'Kroatien und der europäische Wirtschaftsraum', in: *Auswärtige Politik* 9 (1942), p.938.)

67 Cf. Radandt (see note 8).

68 'Die Wiedereingliederung der Süddobrudscha nach dem Vertrag von Craiova und ihre wirtschaftlichen und finanziellen Probleme', in: *Ländernachrichten. Kriegsausgabe*, 24.10.1940, published by the economic research department of I.G. Farben.

69 'Das Siedlungswerk von 1942 in Rumänien', in: *Raumforschung und Raumordnung* 7 (1943), No.1/2, p.62 ff. In all, some 80,000 ethnic Germans from the Bukovina and Dobrudja regions were relocated.

70 Cf. Aly, *Endlösung*, p.166 ff.

Chapter 11: The War against the Soviet Union

1 Göring in November 1941, in conversation with the Italian Foreign

Minister, Count Ciano, in: *Les Archives Secrètes du Comte Ciano 1936–1942*, Paris 1948, p.478; as quoted in: Madajczyk, *Okkupationspolitik*, p.92. Göring discussed the famine in Greece with Ciano, and advised him 'not to take this matter so seriously; we wouldn't get worked up in Germany over the fact that Soviet prisoners of war are starving' (ibid.).

2 Supplies were already running short by 1940, and in a report of 14 December 1940 on 'The first war harvest in Europe' the Reich Ministry of Food and Agriculture put the grain shortage for continental Europe (excluding Great Britain and the Soviet Union) at 21.7 million tonnes – equivalent to the food requirements of nearly 50 million people; Central State Archive (Potsdam), RMEL/2360.

3 See in particular: Joachim Lehmann, 'Faschistische Agrarpolitik im zweiten Weltkrieg. Zur Konzeption von Herbert Backe' (hereinafter cited as 'Lehmann, "Faschistische Agrarpolitik"'), in: *Zeitschrift für Geschichtswissenschaft* 28 (1980), pp.948–56; Martin Kutz, 'Kriegserfahrung und Kriegsvorbereitung. Die agrarwirtschaftliche Vorbereitung des Zweiten Weltkrieges in Deutschland vor dem Hintergrund der Weltkrieg-I-Erfahrung', in: *Zeitschrift für Agrargeschichte und Agrarsoziologie* 32 (1984), pp.59–82 and 135–64; Hans Erich Volkmann, 'Die NS-Wirtschaft in Vorbereitung des Krieges', in: *Ursachen und Voraussetzungen der deutschen Kriegspolitik* (= *Das Deutsche Reich und der Zweite Weltkrieg*, Vol. 1), Stuttgart 1979; Rolf-Dieter Müller, 'Von der Wirtschaftsallianz zum kolonialen Ausbeutungskrieg', in: *Der Angriff auf die Sowjetunion* (= *Das Deutsche Reich und der Zweite Weltkrieg*, Vol. 4; hereinafter cited as 'Müller, "Ausbeutungskrieg"'), Stuttgart 1983.

4 Joachim Lehmann, 'Untersuchungen zur Agrarpolitik und Landwirtschaft im faschistischen Deutschland während des zweiten Weltkrieges (1942–1945)' (Diss.), Rostock 1977, p.11.

5 *Diensttagebuch*, p.186.

6 This figure is based on Backe's calculations of Russia's population growth since 1914; it is confirmed in Göring's remark to Ciano, cited at the head of this chapter. Herbert Backe's advisers Joachim Riecke and Alfons Moritz also played a key role in the development and coordination of these plans.

7 *IMG*, Vol. IV, p.535 f.

8 Lecture given by Neumann to the Berlin Academy of Public Administration on 29 April 1941; *Nbg. Dok.*, NID-13844.

9 'Vorträge und Veröffentlichungen von Herrn O. Donner, Vortrag vor der Verwaltungsakademie Berlin am 29.4.1941'; Secret State Archive, Berlin, Rep. 90 M/33, pp.25–48.

10 Draft of a speech 'for Monday 20 May 1940'; Federal Archive, Backe's unpublished papers (Nachlass Backe/5). Concealed behind a somewhat unwieldy title is a persuasive account of these events in: Rolf Melzer, 'Studien zur Agrarpolitik der faschistischen deutschen Imperialisten in Deutschland im System der Kriegsplanung und Kriegsführung 1933 bis 1941' (Diss.), Rostock 1966, p.268 ff.

11 Frangeš gives the minimum food requirement of a Yugoslavian peasant farmer as 300 kg of cereals per year (Frangeš, 'Bevölkerungsdichte', p.12); in 1941 the Four-Year Plan Authority reckoned on 250 kg per year for a Soviet

peasant farmer. Converted into equivalent 'cereal units', the annual food intake of a German must have amounted to 400–500 kg per year.

12 Goebbels' diary, entry for 1 May 1941.

13 See above, p.38.

14 Goebbels' diary, entry for 6 May 1941.

15 See also: Müller, 'Ausbeutungskrieg', p.157.

16 Reprinted in: *IMG*, Vol. XXXVI, pp.135–57. The quotations that follow are taken – unless otherwise indicated – from these guidelines. Backe published these views – without specific reference to the genocidal dimension – in the foreword to the 1941 internal departmental reprint of his 1926 dissertation, which had been failed by Göttingen University: 'Europe is dependent on overseas corn markets not only in wartime: this is a fundamental, underlying condition. This Europe must look to the East to supplement its needs. (...) In order to succeed in this task we must learn about the structure of the Russian economy prior to the [First] World War. We must understand the means that led to the surpluses. (...) The long-term goal must be to increase production, but the short-term task stands inexorably before us: to supply adequate surpluses for Europe's needs.' Herbert Backe, 'Die russische Getreidewirtschaft als Grundlage der Land- und Volkswirtschaft Russlands', Berlin 1941 (= reprint; no date or place of original publication).

17 As quoted in: Christian Streit, *Keine Kameraden. Die Wehrmacht und die sowjetischen Kriegsgefangenen 1941–1945* (hereinafter cited as 'Streit'), Stuttgart 1978, p.65.

18 Letter written from the front by second lieutenant Dr Friedrich Richter, the official in charge of 'Eastern questions' at the Four-Year Plan Authority, on 26 May 1943. In the wake of successive German defeats the letter calls for a policy that seeks 'to win the hearts and minds' of the people in the occupied territories of the Soviet Union, so that Germany would not be tied down in its pursuit of 'better power-political solutions'. Federal Archive, R 6/60a, pp.1–4.

19 Shorthand report of the meeting between Reichsmarschall Göring and the Reich commissioners for the occupied territories and the military commanders to discuss the food supply situation on 6 August 1942; *IMG*, Vol. XXIX, p.385.

20 Guidelines (see note 16).

21 As quoted in: Dietrich Eichholtz, 'Die Richtlinien Görings für die Wirtschaftspolitik auf dem besetzten sowjetischen Territorium vom 8. November 1941', in: *Bulletin des Arbeitskreises 'Zweiter Weltkrieg'*, No.1–2/1977, pp.73–111.

22 *Monologe*, p.58 f. Hitler also aligned himself totally with Backe's thinking in a letter to Mussolini of 21 June 1941 (see Müller, 'Ausbeutungskrieg', p.157) and in a conversation with the Romanian deputy prime minister and foreign minister Mihai Antonescu in Berlin on 28 September 1941; cf. Andreas Hillgruber (ed.), *Staatsmänner und Diplomaten bei Hitler. Vertrauliche Aufzeichnungen über Unterredungen mit Vertretern des Auslandes 1939–1941*, Frankfurt a.M. 1967, Vol. 1, p.670.

23 *Monologe*, p.63; entry for 17/18 September 1941.

24 Speech given by Rosenberg on 20 June 1941 to a gathering of those most closely involved with the 'eastern problem'; *IMG*, Vol. XXVI, p.610 ff.

25 Eleventh meeting of the general council on 24 June 1941, under the chairmanship of undersecretary Körner; *Nbg. Dok.*, NI-7474.

26 Goebbels' diary, entry for 28 June 1941.

27 *IMG*, Vol. XXXVIII, p.86 ff.

28 Decree of Göring's of 27 July 1941; Historical Central Archive of Riga, P-70/5/1, pp.2–4. A member of staff at the Central Trading Company (East) told us: 'Of course it was our job to get as much out of the Soviet Union as possible. We had lots of different options, we were juggling with four different letterheads: depending on the circumstances we could be the Central Trading Company (East), the Economic Policy Unit for the East, the Four-Year Plan Authority or the Reich Ministry of Food and Agriculture.' After the war the German Corn Exchange funded the defence of Walter Emmerich when Poland's Communist government sought to initiate extradition proceedings against him (information supplied by Harald Hansen, 15 August 1986).

29 Meeting of the Economic Policy Unit for the East on 31 July 1941; Federal Archive/Military Archive (Freiburg), RW 31/11, p.104 f.

30 Notes on the meeting taken by ministerial official Görnert; as quoted in: Streit, p.143.

31 Notes on the same meeting recorded on 16 September 1941 by Major-General Hans Nagel; *IMG*, Vol. XXXVI, p.105 ff.

32 *Der grossdeutsche Freiheitskampf. Reden Adolf Hitlers*, Vol. 3, Munich 1943, p.97.

33 As quoted in: Eichholtz (see note 21), p.93.

34 State Archive of Hamburg, Familie Krogmann I/Carl Vincent Krogmann/Tagesberichte/chronologische Serie/C 14 IX, 1941. The report referred to was evidently made by Hans Glade, a senior revenue officer.

35 Ales Adamowitsch, Danil Granin, *Das Blockadebuch*, Part 1, Berlin 1987, p.49 f.

36 R.-D. Müller also notes 'that the German occupation authorities were not caught off guard by the problem of how to feed all these people. Instead, as in the case of the extermination of the Jews, the war and the constraints that seemingly arose from it were to be deliberately exploited in order to commit genocide.' R.-D. Müller, 'Das "Unternehmen Barbarossa" als wirtschaftlicher Raubkrieg', in: Gerd Ueberschär, Wolfram Wette (eds.), *'Unternehmen Barbarossa'. Der deutsche Überfall auf die Sowjetunion 1941*, Paderborn 1984, p.187.

37 Teletype message from Einsatzgruppe A in Reval to the Central Office for the Security of the Reich, departments III and IV, 6 November 1941; Historical Central Archive of Riga, P-1026/1/12a.

38 Secret decree issued by the Commissioner for the Four-Year Plan on 1 December 1942, concerning distribution of agricultural produce in the occupied eastern territories; Historical Central Archive of Riga, P-69/1²/10, p.188.

39 War management supremo Riecke at the economic press briefing on 3 February 1942; Central State Archive (Potsdam), 24.01 (Beauftragter für den

Vierjahresplan)/22/1.

40　Secret State Archive, Berlin, Rep. 90 M/45, pp.65–8.

41　Joachim Riecke, 'Aufgaben der Landwirtschaft', in: *Ostaufgaben der Wissenschaft. Vorträge der Osttagung deutscher Wissenschaftler*, published by the Central Office for Science in Rosenberg's Ministry, Munich 1943, p.31 f. The lecture cited here was given on 24 March 1942 in Berlin.

42　Otto Bräutigam, *Die Landwirtschaft in der Sowjetunion*, Berlin 1942 (published in the series *Bücherei des Ostraums*, ed. Georg Leibbrandt), p.61.

43　Theodor Bühler, *Die Sozialstruktur der Feinde. Ein zusammenfassender Überblick* (= *Schriftenreihe zur weltanschaulichen Schulung der NSDAP*, No.32), Munich 1943, p.3; Bühler worked as a general adviser in the Labour Science Institute of the German Labour Front.

44　This section relies entirely on material from the excellent book by Christian Streit, *Keine Kameraden* (here: p.128). The labour deployment unit at the Four-Year Plan Authority was headed by Werner Mansfeld.

45　Letter of 26 August 1941; as quoted in: Streit, p.131.

46　ibid., p.134.

47　ibid., p.135.

48　ibid., p.142.

49　ibid., p.144.

50　According to the half-monthly report of the Economic Policy Unit for the East for the period 16–30 September 1941; ibid., p.145.

51　ibid., p.157 f. Eduard Wagner later joined the ranks of the conspirators in the 20 July 1944 bomb plot.

52　Streit, p.143.

53　Herbert Backe, *Um die Nahrungsfreiheit Europas. Wirtschaftsraum oder Grossraum*, Leipzig 1941, p.11; second enlarged edition, Leipzig 1943; the third, abridged edition appeared in 1957 under the imprint of the Institute for Geosociology and Politics as: *Kapitalismus und Nahrungsfreiheit*, with an introduction by Rolf Hinder, Bad Godesberg 1957.

54　Federal Archive, Backe's unpublished papers (Nachlass Backe/5).

55　'Die Zukunftsmöglichkeiten in der Ukraine und in den Gebieten zwischen Don und Kaukasus', a paper prepared by the Reich Office for Economic Expansion (a division of the Four-Year Plan Authority), dated 26 October 1942; Federal Archive, R 25/42.

56　Istvan Csöppüs, 'Die Entwicklung des ungarischen Agrarexports nach Deutschland zur Zeit des Zweiten Weltkrieges 1938 bis 1944', in: *Zeitschrift für Agrargeschichte und Agrarsoziologie* 31 (1983), No.1, pp.57–69.

57　See also Lothar Kettenacker, 'Hitler's Final Solution and its Rationalization', in: Gerhard Hirschfeld (ed.), *The Policies of Genocide. Jews and Soviet Prisoners of War in Nazi Germany*, London/Boston/Sydney 1986, pp.73–96. Recent research has served to endorse this view. See for example Christian Gerlach, *Krieg, Ernährung, Völkermord. Forschungen zur deutschen Vernichtungspolitik im Zweiten Weltkrieg*, Hamburg 1998, pp.13–30, 167–257.

58　Report submitted by the armaments inspector (Ukraine) to the head of the War Economy and Armaments Office at the Armed Forces High Command on 2 December 1941 ('The report was written by senior war administration officer Prof. Seraphim'); *IMG*, Vol. XXXII, p.71 ff. Possibly ignorant of the

German resettlement plans that had already been drawn up, and which extended far beyond the Ukraine, but perhaps also because he wanted to retain at least a part of the indigenous population as a source of labour for future colonists, Seraphim was moved to wonder 'who exactly is going to produce the wealth here (…) if we shoot the Jews, allow the POWs to die, leave most of the population of the larger cities to starve' and 'next year look like losing a portion of the rural population as well to hunger' (ibid.).

59 Draft of speech 'for Monday 20 May 1940'; Federal Archive, Backe's unpublished papers (Nachlass Backe/5).

60 Memorandum of the meeting with undersecretary Backe on 6 March 1937; Federal Archive/BDC, personal file of Herbert Backe. A very different verdict was passed in 1949 by the executive board of the Max Planck Society (known as the Kaiser Wilhelm Society until 1945), as whose senior vice-president Backe had served from 1941 to 1945: '… a man of blameless and noble character … selfless in his personal dealings … dedicated to the cause of research and the preservation of its independence … highly respected in all scientific circles …' (letter of 3 January 1949 from the executive board of the Max Planck Society, signed by Dr Ernst Telschow; Federal Archive, Nachlass Backe/9).

Chapter 12: The 'General Plan for the East'

1 See above, p. 156.

2 The professor in question was Wolfgang Abel in Berlin, a pupil of Eugen Fischer; cf. 'Der Generalplan Ost', with introduction and commentary by Helmut Heiber (hereinafter cited as 'Heiber'), in: *VfZG* 6 (1958), pp.281–325, here esp. p.312 ff.

3 Appendix to a paper written by the Wehrmacht's representative on the staff of the Reich Protector in Bohemia and Moravia, General Erich Friderici, on the subject of 'the Czech problem'; as quoted in: *Die Vergangenheit warnt. Dokumente über die Germanisierungspolitik der Naziokkupanten in der Tschechoslowakei*, compiled by Václav Král, Prague 1960, p.45.

4 Memorandum from the department of agriculture and food in the Office of the Reich Protector, 11 February 1941; as quoted in: ibid., p.118 f.

5 Speech by senior Nazi Party functionary Nutzenberger at a rally in Iglau on 8 August 1941; as quoted in: Jaroslava Milotová, Miroslav Kárný, 'Od Neuratha k Heydrichovi', in: *Sborník Archivních Prací* 39 (1989), p.342 f.

6 Konrad Meyer, 'Neues Landvolk. Verwirklichung im neuen Osten', in: *Neues Bauerntum* 33 (1941), No.3, pp.93–9.

7 ibid.

8 Bulletin No.1 on the conditions in the new eastern territories, issued by the Armed Forces High Command on 16 May 1941; *Heeres-Verordnungsblatt* 23 (16.6.1941), Part C, No.508, published in: Rolf-Dieter Müller, 'Industrielle Interessenpolitik im Rahmen des "Generalplans Ost"', in: *Militärgeschichtliche Mitteilungen* 29 (1981), No.1, p.117.

9 Udo von Schauroth, 'Aufgaben und Ziele der Reichsplanung', in: *Reich, Volksordnung, Lebensraum* 5 (1943), p.127.

10 Cf. Heiber; the documents reprinted here reflect a portion of what was undoubtedly very widespread discussion of the plan in the Central Office for the Security of the Reich and the Ministry for the Occupied Eastern Territories.

11 Czesław Madajczyk, 'Generalplan Ost' (hereinafter cited as 'Madajczyk'), in: *Polish Western Affairs* 3 (1962), pp.391–442; the document is reprinted here in its entirety.

12 RKF, 'Kurzer Überblick über Osteuropa'; Archive of the Federal Institute for Geosciences and Raw Materials (Hanover), Sowjetunion/63017.

13 Wladimir von Poletika, 'Naturverhältnisse und Agrargeographie in der Sowjetunion' (no date of publication); Federal Archive/Military Archive (Freiburg), RW 19, Anh. I/1550.

14 Konrad Meyer, 'Bodenordnung als volkspolitische Aufgabe und Zielsetzung nationalsozialistischen Ordnungswillens' (= *Preussische Akademie der Wissenschaften. Vorträge und Schriften*, No.2), Berlin 1940.

15 Herbert Backe, 'Stand und Aussichten der deutschen Ernährungswirtschaft', in: *Niederlande* 8 (1942), No.15, p.10. Backe and Himmler were in full agreement on the policy of Germanization in the occupied 'Ostraum': Backe specifically welcomed the fact 'that SS Reichsführer Himmler, by virtue of the task entrusted to him as Reich Commissioner for the Strengthening of German Nationhood by the Führer, is taking a keen interest in the role of the farming community in the great enterprise of recolonizing the East'. Himmler returned the compliment at the conference of SS Gruppenführer in Posen in 1943: 'If the SS together with the farmers, and we together with our friend Backe, carry out the work of colonization in the East with vision, energy and revolutionary fervour, then in twenty years' time we will have pushed the frontiers of our nation 500 kilometres further to the east.' (As quoted in: Lehmann, 'Faschistische Agrarpolitik', p.954).

16 *Monologe*, p.59; entry for 19 August 1941.

17 'Die Durchdringung des Ostens in Rohstoff- und Landwirtschaft' (a paper prepared by the Labour Science Institute of the German Labour Front and marked 'Secret'), Berlin, December 1941; reprinted with an introduction by Michael Hepp in: *1999* 2 (1987), No.4, pp.96–134.

18 As quoted in: Madajczyk, p.437. Back in 1940 Meyer had already commissioned the Reich Working Party on Regional Planning to conduct an extensive research project on this subject under the title: 'Untersuchung der Aussiedlungsmöglichkeiten aus dem Klein- und Zwergbauerntum der Realteilungsgebiete Mittel- und Westdeutschlands sowie der Siedlerreserven an nachgeborenen Bauernsöhnen und Landarbeitern'. A study carried out for the Rhine Province calculated that there were 165,280 potential colonists in this region alone. This study examined in very specific detail the domestic political conditions on which the General Plan for the East was predicated, and the implications it would have for domestic policy; cf. Wilhelm Busch, 'Raumordnung durch landwirtschaftliche Umsiedlung in der Rheinprovinz' (= *Berichte zur Raumforschung und Raumordnung*, Vol. IX), Leipzig 1943, p.137. A similar purpose underlies the other essays cited below by way of example, which are essentially outlines written for the purpose of obtaining research grants or for more large-scale

studies: Heinz Sauermann, 'Voraussetzungen und Möglichkeiten der Verlagerung von Industriegebieten aus dem rhein-mainischen Ballungskern in den Osten'; Carl Brinkmann, 'Gesundung der bäuerlichen Verhältnisse und Siedlerreserve in Nordbaden'; Paul Hesse, 'Zur Frage der Gesundung des schwäbischen Lebensraumes im Zusammenhang mit der Kolonisation der neuen Ostgebiete'; Fritz Klute, 'Die Beurteilung der Ackernahrung als Voraussetzung der Umsiedlung und Gesundung der bäuerlichen Verhältnisse in Hessen'; all in: *Raumforschung und Raumordnung* 4 (1940), No.3/4, pp.183–99.

19 Dr Gottfried Müller, '(Geheimer) Entwurf (Raumordnungsskizze) zur Aufstellung eines Raumordnungsplanes für das Ostland' (17 November 1942); Historical Central Archive of Riga, P-69/1a/3, p.161.

20 As quoted in: Heiber, p.314 f.

21 As quoted in: Madajczyk, p.436.

22 'Raumordnungsskizze' (see note 19), p.170 f.

23 This can be inferred from Wetzel's comments on the General Plan for the East; as quoted in: Heiber, p.297.

24 As quoted in: Madajczyk, p.409.

25 Hitler intervened at least twice in the dispute between the Ministry for the Occupied Eastern Territories and the authors of the General Plan for the East, on both occasions in order to strengthen Himmler's powers in the area of colonization policy: in September 1941, when he explicitly confirmed that Himmler's remit as Reich Commissioner for the Strengthening of German Nationhood extended also to the occupied Soviet territories (secret communiqué from the head of the security police and SD to the head of the SS administrative office, SS Gruppenführer Pohl, dated 12 September 1941; Historical Central Archive of Riga, P-70/5/8, p.4); and in March 1942, when he placed the Racial Policy Office of the NSDAP under the control of the RKF. The 'decree of the Führer' states: 'In accordance with Order A 7/41 of 26 February 1941 SS Reichsführer Heinrich Himmler, in his capacity as commissioner of the NSDAP for all matters relating to national identity and ethnicity, also has overall responsibility for dealing with such matters.' (*Nationalsozialistische Deutsche Arbeiterpartei. Reichsverfügungsblatt*, Munich, 16 March 1942, Issue A, 11/42.)

26 As quoted in: Madajczyk, p.411.

27 As quoted in: Madajczyk, p.413.

28 Speech given by Himmler to a gathering of senior departmental heads in Berlin on 9 June 1942; as quoted in: Himmler, *Geheimreden*, p.159.

29 Report by the head of the Economic Policy Unit for the East, Lieutenant-General Schubert; as quoted in: Streit, p.144.

30 Brief summary of the memorandum on the General Plan for the East (28 May 1942); Federal Archive, NS 19/1739, p.5.

31 As quoted in: Madajczyk, p.433.

32 *Monologe*, p.55 (entries for 8/11 August 1941); see also esp.: Federal Archive, R 6/23.

33 As quoted in: Madajczyk, p.435.

34 See also ibid., p.433.

35 As quoted in: ibid., p.435.

36 As quoted in: ibid., p.437.

37 Record of the meeting on 4 February 1942 in the Ministry for the Occupied Eastern Territories 'on the issues of Germanization, with particular reference to the Baltic states'; as quoted in: Heiber, p.296.

38 Cf. Madajczyk, p.440. Without the additional Estonians and Letts the number of volunteer colonists was thus estimated at 4.15 million. From Wetzel's critique we learn that in an earlier draft of the General Plan for the East – or in a report thereon prepared by the Central Office for the Security of the Reich – the projected number of German volunteer colonists was still 4.5 million, a figure that would increase to ten million in the course of thirty years. Wetzel thought this figure unrealistic, believing that eight million was the most that could be expected (cf. Heiber, p.300). So in the July 1942 version of the General Plan the estimates of colonist numbers were much lower – and the projected time-scale for Germanization had been reduced from thirty to twenty-five years, presumably at Himmler's insistence.

39 As quoted in: Heiber, loc. cit.

40 Cf. the record of the meeting of 29 January 1942, chaired by Otto Bräutigam; *Nbg. Dok.*, NG-5035.

41 Dr Erhard Wetzel (born 1903) had studied law, joined the NSDAP in May 1933, was appointed a district court judge in Potsdam in 1936 and then joined the staff of the Party's Racial Policy Office, before transferring to the Ministry for the Occupied Eastern Territories in 1941 as head of department for racial policy. See Heiber, p.286.

42 As quoted in: ibid., pp.300–306.

43 See above, p.250.

44 Heiber, p.318 f.

45 Henry Picker, *Hitlers Tischgespräche im Führerhauptquartier. Hitler, wie er wirklich war*, Stuttgart 1976, p.453.

46 Discussion on 'the final solution of the Jewish question' in the Central Office for the Security of the Reich, 6 March 1942; *Nbg. Dok.*, NG-2586.

47 Minutes of meeting on 27 October 1942; *Nbg. Dok.*, NG-2586–M.

48 Notes on a 'research institute for reproductive biology' drafted by Clauberg and presented to Himmler on 27 May 1941; Federal Archive/BDC, personal file of Carl Clauberg.

49 As quoted in: *SS im Einsatz. Eine Dokumentation über die Verbrechen der SS* (hereinafter cited as 'SS im Einsatz' – published by the Committee of Anti-Fascist Resistance Fighters in the GDR), Berlin 1957, p.357 ff.

50 Cf. Gisela Bock, *Zwangssterilisation im Nationalsozialismus. Studien zur Rassenpolitik und Frauenpolitik*, Opladen 1986, pp.452–6.

51 As quoted in: Alexander Mitscherlich, Fred Mielke, *Medizin ohne Menschlichkeit. Dokumente des Nürnberger Ärzteprozesses* (hereinafter cited as 'Mitscherlich/Mielke'), Frankfurt a.M. 1983, p.237. A few days later another doctor committed to the doctrines of 'racial hygiene' drew Himmler's attention to the same drug, commending it for the same reasons: 'Given that one of the first priorities of our National Socialist racial and population policy is to prevent genetically unsuitable and racially inferior persons from reproducing ...' (ibid., p.239).

52 Letter from Brandt to Clauberg of 10 July 1942; *SS im Einsatz*, p.361.

53 Mitscherlich/Mielke, p.238.

54 Letter from Clauberg to Himmler of 7 July 1943; as quoted in: *SS im Einsatz*, p.362 ff.

55 Mitscherlich/Mielke, p.242.

56 Statement given by Bertus Gerdes (a senior official in the Gau administration) on 20 November 1945; *IMG*, Vol. XXXII, p.297.

57 As quoted in: *Auschwitz. Faschistisches Vernichtungslager*, Warsaw 1981 (2nd edition), p.135. Also quoted here is the statement by Rudolf Höss claiming that 'Himmler wanted to use the Clauberg method for the liquidation and biological destruction of the Polish and Czech people'.

58 Heiber, p.308.

59 ibid., p.316 f.

60 ibid., p.311 f.

61 ibid., p.307. In November 1942 Wetzel wrote a memorandum 'On the suitability of the peoples from the East for Germanization', followed in March 1943 by his 'Guidelines on the suitability of the Estonians, Letts and Lithuanians for Germanization'; both papers set out targets and time-scales for the Germanization of the Baltic peoples that were notably more tentative and long-term, reflecting the way the war was now going. In his correspondence with Wetzel the head of the special 'German Eastern Policy' unit in the Ministry for the Occupied Eastern Territories, Werner Hasselblatt, put it thus on 21 December 1942: 'I am so glad that you and I both take a different view from our many impatient colleagues ...' (Federal Archive, R 6/160, p.21). No less important here is the shared understanding with regard to selection criteria, the acknowledgement that a 'positive racial exterior' is not enough by itself, that it is also 'essential' to examine 'the capability and attitude' of the potential 'candidate' for Germanization (ibid., p.8).

62 Cf. Heiber, p.293 f. Here Heiber notes: 'Dr Gerhard Teich was assistant director of this institute. In the study of "peoples, ethnic groups and tribes in the former territory of the USSR" compiled by him the assistance of the following persons is gratefully acknowledged: the Racial Affairs Office at the Central Office of Race and Resettlement, Prof. v. Mende, SS Standartenführer B.K. Schultz and finally Dr Wetzel.' The director of the Institute for Border and Foreign Studies in Berlin-Steglitz was Prof. Karl C. v. Loesch, who maintained close ties with the RKF (see above, p.71). On Teich's position in the Ministry for the Occupied Eastern Territories, see the internal schedule of departmental functions for 1942.

63 ibid., p.296.

64 The Armed Forces High Command (OKW) maintained the office of 'OKW representative for resettlement questions', which liaised closely with the RKF and the Four-Year Plan Authority. Little is known about the activities of this agency, but its overall purpose was to facilitate and develop resettlement opportunities for members of the German armed forces. The agency's staff are listed in the Wehrmacht telephone directory, issue of 1 January 1943; Federal Archive/Military Archive (Freiburg), RHD 46/3.

65 Historical Central Archive of Riga, P-1018c/1/2, pp.26–33 (hereinafter cited as 'Trampedach'). On the first page of this report, Reich Commissioner Hinrich Lohse had noted: 'This is an excellent report. It should be brought to the notice of the Reich Minister for the Occupied Eastern Territories and the General Commissioners in Kaunas and Riga!' Trampedach was a senior civil servant [*Regierungsrat*] in the political department of the Reich Commissariat.

66 The head of a racial commission, Dr Günther Holtz, thought that over half the population of Estonia and Latvia was 'capable of Germanization', while in Lithuania the proportion was 'at best a third' (from the secret minutes [*Geheimprotokoll*] of a talk given by Holtz on 26 October 1942 and the ensuing discussion on the results of an inspection of Reich Labour Service volunteers; Historical Central Archive of Riga, P-68/1a/19, p.95 – hereinafter cited as 'Geheimprotokoll'). In addition to Dr Holtz from the special racial policy section of the Ministry for the Occupied Eastern Territories, the discussion was attended by a further thirteen men, including the aforementioned Friedrich Trampedach, Dr Werner Essen, head of section within the department of regional planning in the Reich Commissariat for the occupied Baltic states, and Messrs. Lutter, Buchholz, Dr Steiniger and Dr Lenz from the political department of the Reich Commissariat.

67 Hermann Schlau, 'Rassenpolitische Erwägungen zur Umvolkung der Letten', a study paper of 15 February 1942 (hereinafter cited as 'Schlau'); Historical Central Archive of Riga, P-70ds/5s/89, p.3. Schlau was a lieutenant in the medical corps serving with the Wehrmacht in Posen.

68 Report of 20 August 1941 by the district leader for racial policy, SS Obersturmbannführer Dr med. Hans Thomas Meyer (hereinafter cited as 'Meyer'); Historical Central Archive of Riga, P-70ds/5s/89, p.16. Meyer believed that western Latvia had 'areas for absorbing racially superior stock', while the eastern part of the country he designated as 'areas for the expulsion of racially inferior stock' (ibid., p.15).

69 Report of the district commissioner in Daugavpils, 15 February 1944; Historical Central Archive of Riga, P-1018/1/43, pp.74–86. The report goes on: 'There are over 90,000 farms in the district, including some 40,000 "single-milker" enterprises, which effectively contribute nothing to agricultural production, since they barely grow and produce enough to meet their own needs.' Because mass evacuations had to be handled more carefully during the second half of the war, and because there was also a shortage of manpower in the Reich at this time, the consequence of this policy was that unusually large numbers of people were deported from Latgallia to Germany as forced labourers.

70 Geheimprotokoll, p.95.

71 Schlau, p.2.

72 ibid., p.4.

73 Volkspolitische Überlegungen zur Frage der Eindeutschung der Völker des Ostlands; Historical Central Archive of Riga, P-70/5/8, pp.111–21. This 'important memorandum' was sent by section head Dr Werner Essen to the Reich Commissioner for the occupied Baltic states on 8 February 1943. It

was written by an unidentified 'acquaintance' of Essen's who was 'well-versed in matters of ethnic policy'.

74 Meyer, p.17.

75 Memorandum from Friedrich Gollert on 'the future fate of the Government General', 29 March 1943; YIVO, OccE 2–74.

76 Letter of 15 February 1943 from the head of the propaganda staff – written in his name by a Dr Prause – to Goebbels on 'the treatment of the Poles in the Government General'; YIVO, OccE 2–12.

77 Cf. Barbara Klain, 'Stadtplaner im Krieg: Warschau 1939–1945', in: Rössler, Schleiermacher, pp.294–307, here esp. p.305 f.

78 Letter from Himmler to Greifelt of 12 June 1942; Federal Archive, NS 19/1739, p.13.

79 Letter from the commander of the SS and police in Lublin (SS Hauptsturmführer Helmut Müller) to the head of the Office of Race and Resettlement in Berlin, 15 October 1941; as quoted in: *Biuletyn*, Vol. XIII, pp.13–16. See also Himmler's remarks on 13/14 March 1942 in Cracow on what he planned to achieve in the 'first five-year resettlement plan after the end of the war'; *IMG*, Vol. XXVI, p.410.

80 Letter from the head of the security police (IV B 4) to the Zamosc office of the Posen Emigration Bureau (UWZ); *Biuletyn*, Vol. XIII, p.8.

81 Letter from the head of the security police and SD (IV B 4a/Müller) to Heinrich Himmler, 31 October 1942; *Biuletyn*, Vol. III, p.6F-7F.

82 See above, p.132.

83 Cf. Czech, p.358 ff.

84 ibid., p.427 ff.

85 See also Krausnick, 'Judenverfolgung', pp.283–448, here esp. p.439. See also Hans-Günther Adler, *Der verwaltete Mensch. Studien zur Deportation der Juden aus Deutschland*, Tübingen 1974, p.224 ff. Both writers drew attention to this specific connection early on, but did not pursue the point in a more detailed study.

86 The timetable is reprinted – without further interpretation or comment – in: Raul Hilberg, *Sonderzüge nach Auschwitz*, Mainz 1981, p.212. A second train also served this route – the Zamosc/Berlin/Auschwitz triangle – while other trains in the same timetable shuttled back and forth between the ghettos and extermination camps, and yet others transported ethnic German colonists to the resettlement areas designated in the General Plan for the East.

87 Report of SS Untersturmführer Heinrich Kinna 'on the transport of 644 Poles (from Zamosc) to the Auschwitz labour camp on 10 December 1942', reprinted in: *Biuletyn Głównej Komisji Badania Zbrodni Hitlerowskich w Polsce* XIII (1960), p.18 ff.

88 'Ein Dorf erwacht zu neuem Leben. Auslandsdeutsche Bauern werden im Gebiet von Zamosc angesiedelt', in: *Warschauer Zeitung*, 3 January 1943; as quoted in the excellent standard work: Czesław Madajczyk (ed.), *Zamojszczyzna – Sonderlaboratorium SS. Zbiór dokumentów polskich in niemieckich z okresu okupacji hitlerlowskiej*, 2 vols., Warsaw 1977. This bilingual edition contains nearly five hundred documents relating to this criminal act of displacement.

A similar resettlement operation took place on a smaller scale in the vicinity of Schitomir (German 'Hegewald'); see Alexander Dallin, *Deutsche Herrschaft in Russland 1941–1945*, Düsseldorf 1958. In 1941–2 exactly 1,655 German colonists were relocated to the 'base settlement' of Kherson/ Nikolayev, and 5,376 Germans were settled in Dnepropetrovsk, which was evidently also designated a 'base settlement' in 1942 (Federal Archive/BDC, research, SS-HO, 5645).

89 Letter from Meyer to SS Oberführer Prof. Mentzel, 13 April 1942; Federal Archive, R 73/13127 (Konrad Meyer).

90 Federal Archive, R 73/13230 (Herbert Morgen).

91 Federal Archive, R 73/1037.

92 See note 89 (Boesler is named therein as Meyer's representative).

93 Teletype message from Himmler to Greifelt, 18 May 1943; Federal Archive, R 26 IV/vorl. 33, p.65.

Chapter 13: Conclusions

1 Tadeusz Kudyba, 'Die strukturelle Veränderung der polnischen Wirtschaft während der Besatzungszeit', staatswissenschaftliche Diss. (manuscript), Bonn 1950, p.158.

2 Hannah Arendt, *Elemente totaler Herrschaft*, Frankfurt a.M. 1958, p.256.

3 Zygmunt Baumann, *Modernity and the Holocaust*, Ithaca/New York 1989, p.66.

4 Edward Lipinski, 'Deflation als Mittel der Konjunkturpolitik' (= *Kieler Vorträge*, Vol. 42), Jena 1936.

5 Meinhold's spoken recollection of 23 November 1985.

6 Cf. Aly/Roth.

BIBLIOGRAPHY

Abelshauser, Werner: *Wirtschaftsgeschichte der Bundesrepublik Deutschland 1945–1980.* Frankfurt a.M. 1983

Abelshauser, Werner: *Die langen fünfziger Jahre. Wirtschaft und Gesellschaft der Bundesrepublik Deutschland 1945–1966.* Düsseldorf 1987

Abs, Hermann J.: 'The Structure of the Western German Monetary System'. In: *The Economic Journal* 80 (1950), pp.481–488

Abs, Hermann J.: *Zeitfragen der Geld- und Wirtschaftspolitik. Aus Vortrögen und Aufsötzen.* Frankfurt a.M. 1959

Abs, Hermann J.: 'Deutschlands wirtschaftlicher und finanzieller Aufbau'. In: Carstens, Karl et al. (eds.): *Franz Josef Strauss. Erkenntnisse, Standpunkte, Ausblicke.* Munich 1985, pp.351–370

Abs, Hermann J.: 'Der Weg zum Londoner Schuldenabkommen'. In: Mückl, Wolfgang J. (ed.): *Fîderalismus und Finanzpolitik. Gedenkschrift für Fritz Schöffer.* Paderborn 1990, pp.81–93

Abs, Hermann J.: *Entscheidungen 1949–1953. Die Entstehung des Londoner Schuldenabkommens.* Mainz/Munich 1991

Achterberg, Erich: 'Hermann Wallich'. In: *Zeitschrift für das gesamte Kreditwesen* 16 (1963), pp.228–231

Achterberg, Erich: *Berliner Hochfinanz. Kaiser, Fürsten, Millionöre um 1900.* Frankfurt a.M. 1965

Achterberg, Erich/Müller-Jabusch, Maximilian: *Lebensbilder deutscher Bankiers aus fünf Jahrhunderten.* Frankfurt a.M. 1963

Adamsen, Heiner R.: *Investitionshilfe für die Ruhr. Wiederaufbau, Verbönde und soziale Marktwirtschaft 1948–1952.* Wuppertal 1981

Adenauer, Konrad: *Briefe 1945–1947.* Berlin 1983

Adler, Hans A.: The Post-War Reorganization of the German Banking System. In: *The Quarterly Journal of Economics* 63 (1949), pp.322–341

Akten der Reichskanzlei. Kabinette Brüning. 3 vols. Boppard am Rhein 1990

Allgemeine Elektricitöts-Gesellschaft (ed.): 50 Jahre AEG. Berlin 1956

Ambrosius, Gerold: *Die Durchsetzung der Sozialen Marktwirtschaft in Westdeutschland 1945–1949.* Stuttgart 1977

Aubin, Hermann/Zorn, Wolfgang (eds.): *Handbuch der Deutschen Wirtschafts- und Sozialgeschichte.* Vol.2. Stuttgart 1976

Backer, John H.: *Priming the German Economy. American Occupational Policies 1945–1948*. Durham, N.C. 1971

Balderston, Theodore: 'War Finance and Inflation in Germany 1914–1918'. In: *Economic History Review* 42 (1989), pp.222–244

Balderston, Theodore: 'German Banking Between the Wars. The Crisis of the Credit Banks'. In: *Business History Review* 65 (1991), pp.554–605

Balderston, Theodore: The Origins and Course of the German Economic Crisis 1923–1932. (= *Schriften der Historischen Kommission zu Berlin 2*). Berlin 1993

Balogh, Thomas: *Studies in Financial Organization*. Cambridge 1947

Bamberger, Ludwig: *Erinnerungen*. Edited by Paul Nathan. Berlin 1899

Bank deutscher Länder (ed.): *Statistisches Handbuch der Bank deutscher Länder 1948–1954*. Frankfurt a.M. 1955

Barkai, Avraham: Sozialdarwinismus und Antiliberalismus in Hitlers Wirtschaftskonzept. Zu Henry A. Turner Jr. 'Hitlers Einstellung zu Wirtschaft und Gesellschaft vor 1933'. In: *Geschichte und Gesellschaft* 3 (1977), pp.406–417

Barkai, Avraham: *From Boycott to Elimination. The economic struggle of German Jews, 1933–1943*. Hannover/London 1989

Barkai, Avraham: *Das Wirtschaftssystem des Nationalsozialismus*. Stuttgart 1988

Barkai, Avraham: 'Die deutschen Unternehmer und die Judenpolitik im Dritten Reich'. In: *Geschichte und Gesellschaft* 15 (1989), pp.227–247

Bauer, Walter: *Die westdeutsche Bankreform. Eine Studie zur Entwicklung des Grossbank- und Zentralbankwesens seit dem Jahre 1945 bis zur Gegenwart*. Thesis Tübingen 1954

Behrens, Bolke/Müller, Mario: Insel der Seligen. Interview: Kopper über Konjunktur und Banken. In: *Wirtschaftswoche* 44 (1990), No.39, pp.226–230

Bennett, Edward W.: *Germany and the Diplomacy of the Financial Crisis 1931*. Cambridge, Mass. 1962

Benz, Wolfgang: *Von der Besatzungsherrschaft zur Bundesrepublik. Stationen einer Staatsgründung 1946–1949*. Frankfurt a.M. 1984

Berghahn, Volker: *Unternehmer und Politik in der Bundesrepublik*. Frankfurt a.M. 1985

Berghahn, Volker: *The Americanisation of West German Industry 1945–1973*. Leamington Spa 1986

Berghoff, Hartmut/Müller, Roland: 'Unternehmer in Deutschland und England'. In: *Historische Zeitschrift* 256 (1993), pp.353–386

Bernhard, Georg: 'Anklagen in der Generalversammlung': In: *Magazin der Wirtschaft* (Mai 1930), pp.970–971

Besier, Gerhard: *Die Mittwochs-Gesellschaft im Kaiserreich*. Berlin 1990

Bessell, Georg: *Norddeutscher Lloyd 1857–1957. Geschichte einer bremischen Reederei*. Bremen 1957

Blaich, Fritz: *Staat und Verbände in Deutschland zwischen 1871 und 1945*. Wiesbaden 1979

Blume, Herbert: *Gründungszeit und Gründungskrach mit Beziehung auf das deutsche Bankwesen*. Danzig 1914

Boelcke, Willi A.: *Die deutsche Wirtschaft 1930–1945. Interna des Reichswirtschaftsministeriums*. Düsseldorf 1983

Boelcke, Willi A. (ed.): *Kriegspropaganda 1939–1941*. Stuttgart 1966

Bîhme, Helmut: *Deutschlands Weg zur Grossmacht. Studien zum Verhöltnis von Wirtschaft und Staat wöhrend der Reichsgründungszeit 1848–1881.* Cologne 21972

Booker, John: *Temples of Mammon. The Architecture of Banking.* Edinburgh 1990

Booms, Hans (ed.): *Die Kabinettsprotokolle der Bundesregierung.* Vol.1. 1949. Boppard am Rhein 1982

Borchardt, Knut: 'Realkredit- und Pfandbriefmarkt im Wandel von 100 Jahren'. In: *100 Jahre Rheinische Hypothekenbank.* Frankfurt a.M. 1971, pp.105–196

Borchardt, Knut: 'Zur Frage des Kapitalmangels in der ersten Hölfte des 19. Jahrhunderts in Deutschland'. In: Braun, Rudolf et al. (eds.): *Industrielle Revolution. Wirtschaftliche Aspekte.* Cologne/Berlin 1972, pp.216–236

Borchardt, Knut: *Perspectives on Modern German Economic History and Policy.* Cambridge 1991

Borchardt, Knut: 'Germany 1700–1914'. In: Cipolla, Carlo M. (ed.): *The Fontana Economic History of Europe. Vol.4. The Emergence of Industrial Societies,* part 1. Glasgow 1973, pp.76–160

Born, Karl Erich: *Die Deutsche Bankenkrise 1931: Finanzen und Politik.* Munich 1967

Born, Karl Erich: *International Banking in the 19th and 20th Centuries.* New York 1983

Born, Karl Erich: 'Die Hauptentwicklungslinien des mitteleuropöischen Universalbankensystems'. In: *Universalbankensystem als historisches und politisches Problem.* (= *Bankhistorisches Archiv Beiheft 2*). Frankfurt a.M. 1977, pp.13–18

Born, Karl Erich: 'Deutsche Bank during Germanys Great Inflation after the First World War'. In: *Studies on Economic and Monetary Problems and on Banking History* 17 (1979), pp.11–27. Reprinted Mainz 1988, pp.495–514

Born, Karl Erich: 'Vom Beginn des Ersten Weltkrieges bis zum Ende der Weimarer Republik (1918–1933)'. In: *Deutsche Bankengeschichte.* Edited by the Wissenschaftliche Beirat des Instituts für bankhistorische Forschung. Vol.3. Frankfurt a.M. 1983, pp.11–146

Bower, Tom: *The Pledge Betrayed. America and Britain and the Denazification of Postwar Germany.* Garden City, N.Y. 1982

Brackmann, Michael: *Vom totalen Krieg zum Wirtschaftswunder. Die Vorgeschichte der westdeutschen Wöhrungsreform 1948.* Essen 1993

Bredrow, Wilhelm: *Friedrich Krupp der Erfinder und Gründer. Leben und Briefe.* Berlin 1923

Breuer, Rolf-E.: 'Europa ist total overbanked' [Interview]. In: *Finanz und Wirtschaft* (1990), No.41, pp.33–39

Brüning, Heinrich: *Memoiren 1918–1934.* Stuttgart 1970

Buchheim, Christoph: 'Der Ausgangspunkt des westdeutschen Wirtschaftswunders. Zur neueren Diskussion über die Wirkungen von Wöhrungs- und Bewirtschaftungsreform 1948'. In: *IFO-Studien 34* (1988), pp.69–77

Buchheim, Christoph: 'Die Wöhrungsreform 1948 in Westdeutschland'. In: *Vierteljahrshefte für Zeitgeschichte* 36 (1988), pp.189–231

Buchheim, Christoph: 'Die Wöhrungsreform in Westdeutschland im Jahre 1948. Einige îkonomische Aspekte'. In: Fischer, Wolfram (ed.):

Wöhrungsreform und Soziale Marktwirtschaft. Erfahrungen und Perspektiven nach 40 Jahren. Berlin 1989, pp.391–402

Buchheim, Christoph: *Die Wiedereingliederung Westdeutschlands in die Weltwirtschaft 1945–1958.* Munich 1990

Buchheim, Christoph: 'Marshall Plan and Currency Reform'. In: Diefendorf, Jeffry et al. (eds.): *American Policy and the Reconstruction of West Germany 1945–1955.* Cambridge 1993, pp.69–83

Bührer, Werner: *Ruhrstahl und Europa. Die Wirtschaftsvereinigung Eisen- und Stahlindustrie und die Anfönge der europöischen Integration 1945–1952.* Munich 1986

Bülow, Bernhard Fürst von: *Denkwürdigkeiten.* Vol.3. Berlin 1930

Bungeroth, Rudolf: *50 Jahre Mannesmannrîhren 1884–1934.* Berlin 1934

Burchardt, Lothar: *Wissenschaftspolitik im Wilhelminischen Deutschland. Vorgeschichte, Gründung und Aufbau der Kaiser-Wilhelm-Gesellschaft zur Fîrderung der Wissenschaften.* (= *Studien zu Naturwissenschaft, Technik und Wirtschaft im Neunzehnten Jahrhundert 1*). Gîttingen 1975

Büschgen, Hans E.: *Universalbanken oder spezialisierte Banken als Ordnungsalternativen für das Bankgewerbe der Bundesrepublik Deutschland unter besonderer Berücksichtigung der Sammlung und Verwertung von Kapital.* 2 parts. Cologne 1970

Büschgen, Hans E.: *Die Grossbanken.* Frankfurt a.M. 1983

Büschgen, Hans E.: 'Zeitgeschichtliche Problemfelder des Bankwesens der Bundesrepublik Deutschland'. In: *Deutsche Bankengeschichte.* Edited by the Wissenschaftliche Beirat des Instituts für bankhistorische Forschung. Vol.3. Frankfurt a.M. 1983, pp.351–405

Büschgen, Hans E.: 'Entwicklungsphasen des internationalen Bankgeschöftes'. In: Büschgen, Hans E./Richolt, Kurt (eds.): *Handbuch des internationalen Bankgeschöfts.* Wiesbaden 1989, pp.1–23

Büschgen, Hans E.: *Bankbetriebslehre. Bankmanagement.* Wiesbaden 41993

Büschgen, Hans E.: 'Geld und Banken nach dem Zweiten Weltkrieg. Internationale Kapitalbewegungen, Bankensysteme, grenzüberschreitende Kooperation'. In: Pohl, Hans (ed.): *Europöische Bankengeschichte.* Frankfurt a.M. 1993, pp.455–485

Büschgen, Hans E.: *Internationales Finanzmanagement.* Frankfurt a.M. 21993

Cahn-Garnier, Fritz: 'Dekartellierung der Banken'. In: *Deutsche Finanzwirtschaft* 1 (1947), No.6, pp.9–14

Carosso, Vincent P.: *The Morgans. Private International Bankers 1854–1913.* (= *Harvard Studies in Business History* 38). Cambridge, Mass./London 1987

Cassier, Siegfried C.: *Biographie einer Unternehmerbank.* Frankfurt a.M. 1977

Christopeit, Joachim: *Hermes-Deckungen.* Munich 1968

Clay, Lucius D.: *Decision in Germany.* London 1950

Commerzbank (ed.): *Wer gehîrt zu Wem? Mutter- und Tochtergesellschaften von A-Z.* Jge. 1954–1957

Döbritz, Walther: *Denkschrift zum fünfzigjöhrigen Bestehen der Essener Credit-Anstalt in Essen.* Essen 1922

Deckers, Josef: *Die Transformation des Bankensystems in der sowjetischen Besatzungszone/DDR.* Berlin 1974

Delbrück, Adelbert: *Aufzeichnungen unseres Vaters Adelbert Delbrück. Für die Enkel und Urenkel gedruckt.* Leipzig 1922

Deutsche Bank (ed.): *Sonderausgabe '30 Jahre Privatkundengeschöft'.* Frankfurt a.M. 1989

Deutsche Bankengeschichte. Edited by the Wissenschaftliche Beirat des Instituts für bankhistorische Forschung. 3 vols. Frankfurt a.M. 1982–1983

Deutsche Bundesbank (ed.): *Deutsches Geld- und Bankwesen in Zahlen 1876–1975.* Frankfurt a.M. 1976

Deutsche Bundesbank (ed.): *Wöhrung und Wirtschaft in Deutschland 1876–1975.* Frankfurt a.M. 21976

Deutsche Bundesbank (ed.): *40 Jahre Deutsche Mark. Monetöre Statistiken 1948–1987.* Frankfurt a.M. 1988

Diefendorf, Jeffry M./Frohn, Axel/Pupieper, Hermann-J. (eds.): *American Policy and the Reconstruction of West Germany 1945–1955.* Cambridge 1993

Dietrich, Yorck: *Die Mannesmannrîhren Werke 1888 bis 1920.* (= Zeitschrift für Unternehmensgeschichte Beiheft 66). Stuttgart 1991

Donnison, Frank S.V.: *Civil Affairs and Military Government North-West Europe 1944–1946.* London 1961

Dorendorf, Annelies: *Der Zonenbeirat der britisch besetzten Zone. Ein Rückblick auf seine Tötigkeit.* Gîttingen 1953

Dormanns, Albert: 'Die amerikanischen Banken – das System und die derzeitigen Reformbestrebungen'. In: *Bank-Betrieb* 6 (1976), pp.191–196, 241–245

Eichengreen, Barry: *Golden Fetters. The Gold Standard and the Great Depression 1919–1939.* Oxford 1991

Eichholtz, Dietrich: *Geschichte der deutschen Kriegswirtschaft 1939–1945.* Vol.1. East Berlin 1971

Eichholtz, D./Schumann, W.: *Neue Dokumente zur Rolle des deutschen Monopolkapitals bei der Vorbereitung und Durchführung des Zweiten Weltkrieges.* East Berlin 1969

Emminger, Otmar: *D-Mark, Dollar, Wöhrungskrisen. Erinnerungen eines ehemaligen Bundesbankpräsidenten.* Stuttgart 1986

Endres, Michael: 'Die europöische Bankenwelt – Entwicklungslinien und Zukunftstrends'. In: *Bank-Archiv* 38 (1990), No.9, pp.658–664

Epstein, Gerald/Ferguson, Thomas: 'Monetary Policy, Loan Liquidation, and Industrial Conflict. The Federal Reserve and the Open Market Operations of 1932'. In: *Journal of Economic History* 44 (1984), pp.957–983

Erhard, Ludwig: *Deutschlands Rückkehr zum Weltmarkt.* Düsseldorf 1953

Erhard, Ludwig: 'Die deutsche Wirtschaftspolitik im Blickfeld europöischer Politik'. In: Hunold, Albert (ed.): *Wirtschaft ohne Wunder.* Erlenbach-Zürich 1953, pp.128–157

Erhard, Ludwig: *Deutsche Wirtschaftspolitik. Der Weg der Sozialen Marktwirtschaft.* Düsseldorf/Vienna 1962

Eschenburg, Theodor: 'Deutschland in der Politik der Alliierten': In: Foschepoth, Josef (ed.): *Kalter Krieg und Deutsche Frage. Deutschland im Widerstreit der Möchte 1945–1952.* Gîttingen/Zürich 1985, pp.35–197

Eschenburg, Theodor/Bracher, Karl Dietrich et al. (eds.): *Geschichte der Bundesrepublik Deutschland.* 5 vols. Stuttgart/Wiesbaden 1981–1987

Feder, Ernst: *Heute sprach ich mit... Tagebücher eines Berliner Publizisten 1926–1932.* Stuttgart 1971

Feldenkirchen, Wilfried: 'Die Rolle der Banken bei der Sanierung von Industrieunternehmen (1850–1914)'. In: *Die Rolle der Banken bei der Unternehmenssanierung.* (= *Bankhistorisches Archiv Beiheft* 22). Frankfurt a.M. 1993, pp.14–39

Feldenkirchen, Wilfried: 'Banken und Stahlindustrie im Ruhrgebiet. Zur Entwicklung ihrer Beziehungen 1873–1914'. In: *Bankhistorisches Archiv* 5 (1979), No.2, pp.26–52

Feldman, Gerald D.: *The Great Disorder: Politics, Economics, and Society in the German Inflation 1914–1924.* Oxford 1993

Feldman, Gerald D.: Jakob Goldschmidt, the History of the Banking Crisis of 1931, and the Problem of Freedom of Manoeuvre in the Weimar Economy. In: Buchheim, Christoph/Hutter, Michael/James, Harold (eds.): *Zerrissene Zwischenkriegszeit. Wirtschaftshistorische Beiträge. Knut Borchardt zum 65. Geburtstag.* Baden-Baden 1994

Fisch, Jörg: *Reparationen nach dem Zweiten Weltkrieg.* Munich 1992

Fischer, Fritz: *Griff nach der Weltmacht. Die Kriegszielpolitik des kaiserlichen Deutschland 1914/18.* Düsseldorf 1961

Fohlen, Claude: 'France 1700–1914'. In: Cipolla, Carlo M. (ed.): *The Fontana Economic History of Europe. Vol.4. The Emergence of Industrial Societies,* part 1. Glasgow 1973, pp.7–75

Frederiksen, Oliver J.: *The American Military Occupation of Germany 1945–1953.* Edited by the Historical Division, Headquarters, United States Army, Europe. o.O. 1953

Fricke, Dieter (ed.): *Die bürgerlichen Parteien in Deutschland.* 2 vols. Berlin 1970

Friedjung, Heinrich: *Das Zeitalter des Imperialismus 1884–1914.* 3 vols. Berlin 1919–1922

Friedrich, Carl J.: *American Experiences in Military Government in World War II.* New York 1948

Fürstenberg, Carl: *Die Lebensgeschichte eines deutschen Bankiers.* Edited by Hans Fürstenberg. Berlin 1931

Gaddis, John Lewis: *The United States and the Origins of the Cold War 1941–1947.* New York/London 1972

Gall, Lothar: *Bismarck. The white revolutionary.* London 1986

Gall, Lothar: *Europa auf dem Weg in die Moderne 1850–1890.* (= *Oldenbourg-Grundriss der Geschichte* 14). Munich/Vienna 1984

Gelber, Harry G.: 'Der Morgenthau-Plan'. In: *Vierteljahrshefte für Zeitgeschichte* 13 (1965), pp.372–402

Gellately, Robert: *The Gestapo and German Society. Enforcing Racial Policy 1933–1945.* Oxford 1990

Gerhards, Michael: 'Die westdeutschen Banken'. In: *WSI Mitteilungen* 28 (1975), pp.391–398

Gerschenkron, Alexander: 'Wirtschaftliche Rückständigkeit in historischer Perspektive'. In: Braun, Rudolf et al. (eds.): *Industrielle Revolution. Wirtschaftliche Aspekte.* Cologne/Berlin 1972, pp.59–78

Giersch, Herbert/Paqué, Karl-Heinz/Schmieding, Holger: *The Fading Miracle. Four Decades of Market Economy in Germany.* New York 1992

Gille, Bertrand: 'Banking and Industrialisation in Europe 1730–1914'. In: Cipolla, Carlo M. (ed.): *The Fontana Economic History of Europe. Vol.3. The Industrial Revolution.* Glasgow 1973, pp.255–300

Gillingham, John: 'The Baron de Launoit. A Case Study in the "Politics of Production" of Belgian Industry during Nazi Occupation'. In: *Revue belge d'histoire contemporaine* 5 (1974), pp.1–59

Gimbel, John: *Amerikanische Besatzungspolitik in Deutschland 1945–1949.* Frankfurt a.M. 1971

Gimbel, John: *The Origins of the Marshall-Plan.* Stanford 1976

Glum, Friedrich: *Zwischen Wissenschaft und Politik. Erlebtes und Erdachtes in vier Reichen.* Bonn 1964

Gneist, Rudolf: *Die nationale Rechtsidee von den Stönden und das preussische Dreiklassenwahlsystem.* Darmstadt 1962

Gottlieb, Manuel: 'Failure of Quadripartite Monetary Reform 1945–1947'. In: *Finanzarchiv* 17 (1956/57), pp.398–417

Graml, Hermann: 'Zwischen Jalta und Potsdam. Zur amerikanischen Deutschlandplanung im Frühjahr 1945'. In: *Vierteljahrshefte für Zeitgeschichte* 24 (1976), pp.308–323

Graml, Hermann: *Die Alliierten und die Teilung Deutschlands. Konflikte und Entscheidungen 1941–1948.* Frankfurt a.M. 1985

Grotkopp, Wilhelm et al. (eds.): *Germany 1945–1954.* Cologne 1955

Guth, Wilfried: 'Verantwortung der Banken – heute'. In: Guth, Wilfried: *Weltwirtschaft und Wöhrung. Aufsötze und Vortröge 1967–1989.* Mainz 1989, pp.373–398

Gwinner, Arthur von: *Lebenserinnerungen.* Edited by Manfred Pohl on behalf of the Historische Gesellschaft der Deutschen Bank. Frankfurt a.M. 21992

Habedank, Heinz: *Die Reichsbank in der Weimarer Republik. Zur Rolle der Zentralbank in der Politik des deutschen Imperialismus.* East Berlin 1981

Hallgarten, George: *Imperialismus vor 1914,* Vol.1. Munich 21963

Hammond, Paul Y.: 'Directives for the Occupation of Germany: The Washington Controversy'. In: Stein, Harold (ed.): *American Civil-Military Decisions. A Book of Case Studies.* Birmingham, Alabama 1963, pp.311–364

Hörtel, Lia: *Der Lönderrat des amerikanischen Besatzungsgebietes.* Stuttgart/Cologne 1951

Hayes, Peter: *Industry and Ideology. IG Farben in the Nazi Era.* New York 1987

Hayes, Peter: 'State Policy and Corporate Involvement in the Holocaust'. In: US Holocaust Museum (ed.): *The Holocaust. The Known, the Unknown, the Disputed and the Reexamined.* Washington D.C. 1994

Helfferich, Emil: *Tatsachen 1932–1946. Ein Beitrag zur Wahrheitsfindung.* Oldenburg 1968

Helfferich, Karl: Georg von Siemens. *Ein Lebensbild aus Deutschlands grosser Zeit.* 3 vols. Berlin 1921–1923

Henke, Klaus-Dietmar: *Die amerikanische Besetzung Deutschlands.* Vol. 2. Ins Innere des Reiches. Munich 1994

Henning, Friedrich-Wilhelm: *Die Industrialisierung in Deutschland 1800 bis 1914.* Paderborn et al. 1989

Herbst, Ludolf: *Der totale Krieg und die Ordnung der Wirtschaft. Die Kriegswirtschaft im Spannungsfeld von Politik, Ideologie und Propaganda 1939–1945.* Stuttgart 1982

Herbst, Ludolf (ed.): *Westdeutschland 1945–1955. Unterwerfung, Kontrolle, Integration*. Munich 1986

Herbst, Ludolf/Bührer, Werner/Sowade, Hanno (eds.): *Vom Marshallplan zur EWG. Die Eingliederung der Bundesrepublik Deutschland in die westliche Welt*. Munich 1990

Herold, Hermann: 'Die Neuordnung der Grossbanken im Bundesgebiet'. In: *Neue Juristische Wochenschrift* 5 (1952), pp.481–484, 566–568

Herrhausen, Alfred: 'Zielvorstellungen und Gestaltungsmîglichkeiten einer Langfristplanung in Kreditinstituten'. In: *Bank-Betrieb* 11 (1971), No.10, pp.354–359.

Herrhausen, Alfred: 'Strategische Führung – Mehr als nur Strategie'. In: Henzler, Herbert A. (ed.): *Handbuch Strategische Führung*. Wiesbaden 1988, pp.59–68

Hertner, Peter: 'German Banks abroad before 1914'. In: Jones, Geoffrey (ed.): *Banks as multinationals*. London/New York 1990, pp.99–119

Hess, Hermann: *Ritter von Halt. Der Sportler und Soldat*. Berlin 1936

Hildebrand, Klaus: *Vom Reich zum Weltreich. Hitler, NSDAP und koloniale Frage 1919–1945*. Munich 1969

Hildebrand, Klaus: *Deutsche Aussenpolitik 1871 – 1918. (= Enzyklopödie Deutscher Geschichte 2)*. Munich 1989

Hilferding, Rudolf: *Das Finanzkapital. Eine Studie über die jüngste Entwicklung des Kapitalismus*. Reprint of the 1st edition of 1910. Berlin 1947

Hillgruber, Andreas: *Hitler, Kînig Carol und Marschal Antonescu. Die deutsch-rumönischen Beziehungen 1938–44*. Wiesbaden 1954

Hilpert, Werner/Stahlberg, Max: 'Wirtschaftsfreiheit und Bankpolitik'. In: *Frankfurter Hefte* 4 (1951), pp.101–112

Hintner, Otto: 'Der amerikanische Einfluss auf die Organisation des deutschen Bankwesens'. In: *ôsterreichisches Bankarchiv* 1 (1953), pp.332–339

Hobson, J. A.: *Imperialism. A Study*. London/Boston/Sydney 31988

Hohorst, Gerd/Kocka, Jürgen/Ritter, Gerhard A.: *Sozialgeschichtliches Arbeitsbuch*. Vol.2. Materialien zur Statistik des Kaiserreichs 1870–1914. Munich 1978

Holborn, Hajo: *American Military Government. Its Organization and Policies*. Washington, D.C. 1947

Holtfrerich, Carl-Ludwig: *Die deutsche Inflation 1914–1923. Ursachen und Folgen in internationaler Perspektive*. Berlin/New York 1980

Holtfrerich, Carl-Ludwig: 'Zur Entwicklung der deutschen Bankenstruktur'. In: Deutscher Sparkassen- und Giroverband (ed.): *Standortbestimmung. Entwicklungslinien der deutschen Kreditwirtschaft*. Stuttgart 1984, pp.13–42

Holtfrerich, Carl-Ludwig: 'Auswirkungen der Inflation auf die Struktur des deutschen Kreditgewerbes'. In: Feldman, Gerald D./Müller-Luckner, Elisabeth: *Die Nachwirkungen der Inflation auf die Deutsche Geschichte*. Munich 1985, pp.187–209

Hook, Walter: *Die wirtschaftliche Entwicklung der ehemaligen Deutschen Bank im Spiegel ihrer Bilanzen*. Heidelberg 1954

Hooven, Eckart van: 'Changes in Banking Business with Personal Customers'. In: *Studies on Economic and Monetary Problems and on Banking History* 12 (1974), pp.3–13. Reprinted Mainz 1988, pp.297–309

Horstmann, Theo: 'Die Angst vor dem finanziellen Kollaps. Banken- und Kreditpolitik in der britischen Zone 1945–1948'. In: Petzina,

Dietmar/Euchner, Walter (eds.): *Wirtschaftspolitik im Britischen Besatzungsgebiet*. Düsseldorf 1984, pp.215–233

Horstmann, Theo: 'Um "das schlechteste Bankensystem der Welt". Die interalliierten Auseinandersetzungen über amerikanische Plöne zur Reform des deutschen Bankwesens 1945/46'. In: *Bankhistorisches Archiv* 11 (1985), pp.3–27

Horstmann, Theo: 'Kontinuitöt und Wandel im deutschen Notenbanksystem. Die Bank deutscher Lönder als Ergebnis alliierter Besatzungspolitik nach dem Zweiten Weltkrieg'. In: Pirker, Theo (ed.): *Autonomie und Kontrolle. Beitröge zur Soziologie des Finanz- und Steuerstaates*. Berlin 1989, pp.135–154

Horstmann, Theo: 'Die Entstehung der Bank deutscher Lönder als geldpolitische Lenkungsinstanz in der Bundesrepublik Deutschland'. In: Riese, Hajo/Spahn, Heinz-Peter (eds.): *Geldpolitik und îkonomische Entwicklung. Ein Symposion*. Regensburg 1990, pp.202–218

Horstmann, Theo: *Die Alliierten und die deutschen Grossbanken. Bankenpolitik nach dem Zweiten Weltkrieg in Westdeutschland*. Bonn 1991

Horwood, Cleve/Goetz, Sebastian: 'The battle plans of Hilmar Kopper' [Interview]. In: *Euromoney* (January 1994), pp.28–44

Hübner, Otto: *Die Banken*. Leipzig 1854

Hummer, Waldemar: 'Wirtschaft'. In: *Argentinien. 100 Jahre Deutsche Bank am Rio de la Plata*. Katalog zur Ausstellung der Deutschen Bank AG. Mainz 1987

Hunger, Anton/Müller, Reinhold: 'Die Funkstille war nicht gewollt'. [Interview with Hilmar Kopper]. In: *Industriemagazin* (1991), No.2, pp.25–28

Hunke, Heinrich: 'Verstaatlichung der Grossbanken'. In: *Die Deutsche Volkswirtschaft* 3 (1934), No.1, pp.3–6

Islamoglu-Inan, H. (ed.): *The Ottoman Empire and the World Economy*. Cambridge 1987

Jacobsen, Hans-Adolf: *'Spiegelbild einer Verschwîrung'. Die Opposition gegen Hitler und der Staatsstreich vom 20. Juli 1944 in der SD-Berichterstattu*ng. Vol.1. Stuttgart 1984

Jacobsson, Erin J.: *A Life for Sound Money. Per Jacobsson. His Biography*. Oxford 1979

Jaeger, Hans: *Unternehmer in der deutschen Politik 1890–1918*. Bonn 1967

James, Harold: 'The Causes of the German Banking Crisis of 1931'. In: *Economic History Review* 45 (1984), pp.68–87

James, Harold: *The Reichsbank and Public Finance in Germany 1924–1933. A Study of the Politics of Economics during the Great Depression*. (= *Schriftenreihe des Instituts für bankhistorische Forschung* 5). Frankfurt a.M. 1985

James, Harold: 'Did the Reichsbank draw the Right Conclusions from the Great Inflation?' In: Feldman, Gerald D./Müller-Luckner, Elisabeth: *Die Nachwirkungen der Inflation auf die Deutsche Geschichte*. Munich 1985, pp.211–231

James, Harold: *The German Slump. Politics and Economics, 1924–1936*. Oxford 1986

Janberg, Hans: *Die Bankangestellten. Eine soziologische Studie*. Wiesbaden 1958

Jeidels, Otto: *Das Verhöltnis der deutschen Grossbanken zur Industrie mit besonderer Berücksichtigung der Eisenindustrie*. Munich/Leipzig 21913

Jelinek, Yeshayahu A.: 'Die Krise der Shilumim/Wiedergutmachungs-Verhandlungen im Sommer 1952'. In: *Vierteljahrshefte für Zeitgeschichte* 38 (1990), pp.113–139

Jerchow, Friedrich: *Deutschland in der Weltwirtschaft 1944–1947. Alliierte Deutschland- und Reparationspolitik und die Anfänge der westdeutschen Aussenwirtschaft*. Düsseldorf 1978

Jones, Larry E.: *German Liberalism and the Dissolution of the Weimar Party System*. Chapel Hill 1988

Kaiser, David E.: *Economic Diplomacy and the Origins of the Second World War. Germany, Britain, France and Eastern Europe 1930–39*. Princeton 1980

Kampen, Wilhelm von: *Studien zur deutschen Türkeipolitik in der Zeit Wilhelms II*. PhD Thesis Kiel 1968

Karlsch, Rainer: 'Die Garantie- und Kreditbank AG – Hausbank der Besatzungsmacht in der SBZ/DDR von 1946 bis 1956'. In: *Bankhistorisches Archiv* 18 (1992), pp.69–84

Karlsch, Rainer: *Allein bezahlt? Die Reparationsleistungen der SBZ/DDR 1945–53*. Berlin 1993

Kent, Bruce: *The Spoils of War. The Politics, Economics, and Diplomacy of Reparations 1918–1932*. Oxford 1989

Kern, Werner: *Zentralismus und Föderalismus im Bankwesen*. Thesis Darmstadt 1957

Kiesewetter, Hubert: *Industrielle Revolution in Deutschland 1815–1914*. Frankfurt a.M. 1989

Klein, Ernst: 'The Deutsche Bank's South American Business before the First World War'. In: *Studies on Economic and Monetary Problems and on Banking History* 16 (1978), pp.11–22. Reprinted Mainz 1988, pp.471–483

Klopstock, Fred H.: 'Monetary Reform in Western Germany'. In: *Journal of Political Economy* 57 (1949), pp.277–292

Klump, Rainer: 'Die Wöhrungsreform von 1948. Ihre Bedeutung aus wachstumstheoretischer und ordnungspolitischer Sicht'. In: Fischer, Wolfram (ed.): *Wöhrungsreform und Soziale Marktwirtschaft. Erfahrungen und Perspektiven nach 40 Jahren*. Berlin 1989, pp.403–422

Klump, Rainer (ed.): *40 Jahre Deutsche Mark. Die politische und îkonomische Bedeutung der westdeutschen Wöhrungsreform von 1948*. Wiesbaden 1989

Koch, Heinrich: *75 Jahre Mannesmann. Geschichte einer Erfindung und eines Unternehmens*. Düsseldorf 1965

Kocka, Jürgen: *Unternehmensverwaltung und Angestelltenschaft am Beispiel Siemens 1847–1914. Zum Verhöltnis zwischen Kapitalismus und Bürokratie in der deutschen Industrialisierung*. Stuttgart 1969

Kocka, Jürgen: 'Angestellter'. In: Brunner, Otto/Conze, Werner/Koselleck, Reinhart (eds.): *Geschichtliche Grundbegriffe. Historisches Lexikon zur politisch-sozialen Sprache in Deutschland*. Vol.1. Stuttgart 1972, pp.110–128

Kocka, Jürgen: *Die Angestellten in der deutschen Geschichte 1850–1980*. Gîttingen 1981

Kopper, Christopher: *Zwischen Marktwirtschaft und Dirigismus. Staat, Banken und Bankenpolitik im 'Dritten Reich' von 1933 bis 1939*. Unpublished PhD Thesis Bochum 1992

Kopper, Hilmar: 'Strategische Ausrichtung einer Universalbank auf einen gemeinsamen EG-Finanzmarkt'. In: *Bank-Archiv* 38 (1990), No.2, pp.67–72

Kopper, Hilmar: 'Wir verkaufen, was dem Kunden Freude macht'. In: *Cash* (1991), No.6, pp.19–25

Kopper, Hilmar: 'Zu warten, dass ein Kunde kommt – das hat sich längst geöndert'. [Interview]. In: *Cash* (1992), No.1, pp.21–25

Kopper, Hilmar: 'Neue Aufgaben und Ziele im Marketing einer internationalen Bank'. In: Kolbeck, Rosemarie (ed.): *Bankmarketing vor neuen Aufgaben.* Frankfurt a.M. 1992, pp.107–117

Kopper, Hilmar: 'Die Zeit ist reif. Neue Leitlinien und Ziele für die Deutsche Bank'. In: *Forum* (1993), No.1, pp.2–3

Krebs, Paul: 'Schuldenabkommen'. In: Seischab, Hans/Schwantag, Karl (eds.): *Handwîrterbuch der Betriebswirtschaft.* Vol. 3. Stuttgart 1960, Sp.4816–4829

Kreimeier, Klaus: *Die Ufa-Story. Geschichte eines Filmkonzerns.* Munich/Vienna 1992

Krieger, Leonard: 'The Inter-Regnum in Germany: March – August 1945'. In: *Political Science Quarterly* 64 (1949), pp.507–532

Krieger, Wolfgang: *General Lucius D. Clay und die amerikanische Deutschlandpolitik 1945–1949.* Stuttgart 1987

Krüger, Peter: *Deutschland und die Reparationen 1918/19. Die Genesis des Reparationsproblems in Deutschland zwischen Waffenstillstand und Versailler Friedensschluss.* Stuttgart 1973

Krüger, Peter: *Die Aussenpolitik der Republik von Weimar.* Darmstadt 1985

Krumnow, Jürgen: 'Operatives Controlling im Bankkonzern'. In: Krumnow, Jürgen/Metz, Matthias (eds.): *Rechnungswesen im Dienste der Bankpolitik.* Stuttgart 1987, pp.127–143

Krumnow, Jürgen: 'Finanzdienstleistungen und EG-Binnenmarkt'. In: Büschgen, Hans E. (ed.): *Der Finanzdienstleistungsmarkt in der Europöischen Gemeinschaft.* Frankfurt a.M. 1990, pp.67–79

Krumnow, Jürgen: 'Strategisches Bankencontrolling. Organisatorische und instrumentelle Führungsunterstützung in einem Bankkonzern'. In: Horvarth, Peter (ed.): *Strategieunterstützung durch das Controlling. Revolution im Rechnungswesen?* Stuttgart 1990, pp.333–351

Krumnow, Jürgen: 'Ideal wöre eine franzîsische Investmentbank'. [Interview]. In: *Bîrse Online* (1990), No.40, pp.25–26

Krumnow, Jürgen: 'Das Betriebsergebnis der Banken – ein aussageföhiger Erfolgsindikator?' In: *Zeitschrift für das gesamte Kreditwesen* 46 (1993), No.2, pp.64–68

Krupp, Georg: 'Bankpreise zwischen wirtschaftlichen und 'politischen' Notwendigkeiten'. In: *Die Bank* (1993), No.2, pp.78–81

Krupp, Georg: 'Bankstrategien im Versicherungsgeschöft'. In: *Die Bank* (1993), No.6, pp.332–337

Langen, Eugen: *Die neuen Wöhrungsgesetze.* Essen 1948

Lanner, J.: 'Changes in the Structure of the German Banking System'. In: *Economica* 18 (1951), pp.169–183

Lansburgh, Alfred: 'Zur Kapitalserhîhung der Deutschen Bank'. In: *Die Bank* 10 (1917), pp.185–196

Latour, Conrad F./Vogelsang, Thilo: *Okkupation und Wiederaufbau. Die Tötigkeit der Militörregierung in der amerikanischen Besatzungszone Deutschlands 1944–1947.* Stuttgart 1973

Lederer, Emil: *Die Privatangestellten in der modernen Wirtschaftsentwicklung.* Tübingen 1912

Lederer, Emil: 'Kritische öbersichten der Sozialen Bewegung. Die Bewegung der Privatangestellten seit dem Herbst 1918, die Entwicklung der Organisationen, die Gestaltung der Lebenshaltung und der Besoldung; die Umformung des sozialen Habitus und der Ideologien'. In: *Archiv für Sozialwissenschaft* 47 (1920–1921), pp.585–619

Lehmann, Karin: *The Reaction of the Deutsche Bank and Disconto-Gesellschaft to the Banking Crisis of 1931.* [Unpublished Manuscript]

Leitner, Bernhard: 'Geld und Raum'. In: Leitner, Bernhard/Pohl, Manfred/Becker, Gilbert: *Taunusanlage 12.* Frankfurt a.M. 1985, pp.11–95

List, Friedrich: *Der internationale Handel, die Handelspolitik und der deutsche Zollverein.* Stuttgart 21842

Loehr, Rodney C.: *The West German Banking System.* Edited by the Office of the U.S. High Commissioner for Germany, Office of the Executive Secretary, Historical Division. o.O. 1952

Lîvinson, Köthe: *Frauenarbeit in Bankbetrieben. Ein Beitrag zur Wirtschaftsgeschichte unserer Zeit.* Berlin 1926

Lüke, Rolf E.: *Von der Stabilisierung zur Krise.* Zürich 1958

Lüke, Rolf E.: *13. Juli 1931. Das Geheimnis der deutschen Bankenkrise.* Frankfurt a.M. 1981

MacDonogh, Giles: *A Good German. Adam von Trott zu Solz.* London 1989

Maier, Charles/Bischof, Günter (eds.): *The Marshall Plan and Germany. West German Development within the Framework of the European Recovery Program.* New York/Oxford 1991

Marguerat, Philippe: *Le IIIe Reich et le pétrole roumaine 1938–1940. Contribution à l'étude de la pénétration économique allemande dans les Balkans a la veille et au début de la Seconde Guerre Mondiale.* Geneva 1977

Martin, Rudolf: *Handbuch des Vermîgens und Einkommens der Millionöre in Preussen.* Berlin 1912

McNeil, William C.: *American Money and the Weimar Republic. Economics and Politics on the Eve of the Great Depression.* New York 1986

Meier, Johann Christian: *Die Entstehung des Bîrsengesetzes vom 22. Juni 1896.* St. Katharinen 1992

Mejcher, Helmut: 'Die Bagdadbahn als Instrument deutschen wirtschaftlichen Einflusses im Osmanischen Reich'. In: *Geschichte und Gesellschaft* 1 (1975), pp.447–481

Merkl, Peter-Hans: *Die Entstehung der Bundesrepublik Deutschland.* Stuttgart 1965

Mertin, Klaus: 'Das Rechnungswesen einer Grossbank im Spannungsbereich verönderter Umfeldbedingungen'. In: *Wirtschaft und Wissenschaft im Wandel. Festschrift für Dr. Carl Zimmerer zum 60. Geburtstag.* Frankfurt a.M. 1986, pp.233–245

Meyer, F.W.: 'Der Aussenhandel der westlichen Besatzungszonen Deutschlands und der Bundesrepublik 1945–1952'. In: Hunold, Albert (ed.): *Wirtschaft ohne Wunder.* Erlenbach-Zürich 1953, pp.258–285

Meyer, Ulrich: 'Die Verwalter der Grossbanken'. In: *Deutsche Rechts-Zeitschrift* 4 (1949), No.2, pp.25–29

Milward, Alan S.: *The German Economy at War*. London 1965

Minutes of Evidence taken before the Committee on Finance and Industry. 2 vols. London 1931

Model, Paul: *Die grossen Berliner Effektenbanken*. Jena 1896

Mîhring, Philipp: 'Rechtsprobleme der Grossbanken-Dezentralisation'. In: *Zeitschrift für das gesamte Kreditwesen* 5 (1949), pp.14–16

Mîller, Hans (ed..): *Zur Vorgeschichte der Deutschen Mark. Die Wöhrungsreformplöne 1945–1948*. Tübingen 1961

Mîller, Hans: 'Die westdeutsche Wöhrungsreform von 1948'. In: Deutsche Bundesbank (ed.): *Wöhrung und Wirtschaft in Deutschland 1876–1975*. Frankfurt a.M. 21976, pp.433–483

Moltmann, Günther: 'Zur Formulierung der amerikanischen Besatzungspolitik in Deutschland am Ende des Zweiten Weltkrieges'. In: *Vierteljahrshefte für Zeitgeschichte* 15 (1967), pp.299–322

Mommsen, Hans: *Die verspielte Freiheit. Der Weg der Republik von Weimar in den Untergang 1918–1932*. Frankfurt a.M./Berlin 1989

Mommsen, Hans et al. (eds.): *Industrielles System und Politische Entwicklung in der Weimarer Republik*. Düsseldorf 1974

Morgenthau, Henry Jr.: *Germany Is Our Problem*. New York/London 1945

Morsey, Rudolf: *Die Bundesrepublik Deutschland. Entstehung und Entwicklung bis 1969*. Munich 1987

Moser, Hubertus: 'Von der Sparkasse der Stadt Berlin zur Landesbank Berlin. Geschichte der Sparkasse in Berlin seit dem Ende des Zweiten Weltkriegs'. In: Fischer, Wolfram/Böhr, Johannes (eds.): *Wirtschaft im geteilten Berlin 1945–1990. Forschungsansötze und Zeitzeugen*. Munich 1994, pp.289–299

Mosse, Werner E.: *Jews in the German Economy. The German-Jewish Economic Elite 1820–1935*. Oxford 1987

Mosse, Werner E.: 'Problems and Limits of Assimilation. Hermann and Paul Wallich 1833–1938'. In: *Leo Baeck Institute Year Book* 33 (1988), pp.43–65

Muehring, Kevin: 'The Kopper era at Deutsche Bank'. In: *Institutional Investor* (December 1990), pp.43–51

Müller, Rolf-Dieter: 'Von der Wirtschaftsallianz zum kolonialen Ausbeutungskrieg'. In: *Das Deutsche Reich und der Zweite Weltkrieg*, Vol. IV. Edited by the Militörgeschichtliche Forschungsamt Freiburg. Stuttgart 1983

Müller-Jabusch, Maximilian: *Fünfzig Jahre Deutsch-Asiatische Bank 1890–1939*. Berlin 1940

Müller-Jabusch, Maximilian: *Franz Urbig*. o.O. 1954.

Murphy, Robert: *Diplomat Among Warriors*. London 1964

Neebe, Reinhard: 'Technologietransfer und Aussenhandel in den Anfangsjahren der Bundesrepublik Deutschland'. In: *Vierteljahrschrift für Sozial- und Wirtschaftsgeschichte* 76 (1989), pp.49–75

Neuburger, Hugh/Stokes, Houston H.: 'German Banks and German Growth, 1883–1913. An Empirical View'. In: *The Journal of Economic History* 34 (1974), pp.710–731

Neuburger, Hugh: 'The Industrial Politics of the Kreditbanken 1880–1914'. In: *The Business History Review* 51 (1977), pp.190–207

Neue Deutsche Biographie. Edited by the Historische Kommission der Bayerischen Akademie der Wissenschaften. Vols.1–17. Berlin 1953–1994

Niethammer, Lutz: *Entnazifizierung in Bayern. Söuberung und Rehabilitierung unter amerikanischer Besatzung*. Frankfurt a.M. 1972

Nipperdey, Thomas: *Deutsche Geschichte 1866–1918*. Vol.1. Arbeitswelt und Bürgergeist. Munich 1990

Nipperdey, Thomas: *Deutsche Geschichte 1866–1918*. Vol.2. Machtstaat vor der Demokratie. Munich 1992

Nîrr, Knut Wolfgang: *Zwischen den Mühlsteinen. Eine Privatrechtsgeschichte der Weimarer Republik*. Tübingen 1988

Obst, Georg: *Der Bankberuf. Stellungen im Bankwesen, Aussichten im Bankberuf, Fortbildung der Bankbeamten*. Stuttgart 1921

OMGUS: *Ermittlungen gegen die Deutsche Bank 1946/47*. Nîrdlingen 1985

OMGUS: *Ermittlungen gegen die Dresdner Bank 1946*. Nîrdlingen 1986

Osthoff, Michael: 'Das Bankwesen in den USA'. In: *Die Bank* 8 (1980), pp.371–375

Ott, Hugo/Schöfer, Hermann (eds.): *Wirtschafts-Ploetz. Die Wirtschaftsgeschichte zum Nachschlagen*. Freiburg/Würzburg 21984

Palyi, Michael: *The Twilight of Gold 1914–1936. Myths and Realities*. Chicago 1972

Pamuk, S.: *The Ottoman Empire and European Capitalism 1820–1913. Trade, Investment and Production*. Cambridge 1987

Panten, Hans-Joachim: 'The Growth and Activity of the West German Successor Banks'. In: *The Bankers' Magazine* 177 (1954), pp.113–122

Panten, Hans-Joachim: 'The Come-back of the German Big Three Banks'. In: *The Bankers' Magazine* 184 (1957), pp.280–283

Pauluhn, Burkhardt: 'Everything from one Source – a Strategy for the Future'. In: *Bank und Markt und Technik* 20 (1991), No.6, pp.21–23

Peter, Matthias: *John Maynard Keynes und die deutsche Frage. Strukturprobleme der britischen Deutschlandpolitik zwischen politischem Machtanspruch und îkonomischer Realitöt in der ersten Hölfte des 20. Jahrhunderts*. Munich 1994

Peteranderl, Martin: *Die Welt der Deutschen Bank 1870 – 1914. Ein Beitrag zur 'Betriebs-Organisation' im deutschen Kaiserreich. Unverîffentlichte Magisterarbeit im Fach Neuere und Neueste Geschichte an der Ludwig-Maximilians-Universitöt*, Munich 1993

Petzlin, Heinz: *Hjalmar Schacht. Leben und Wirken einer umstrittenen Persînlichkeit*. Berlin 1980

Pierenkemper, Toni: *Arbeitsmarkt und Angestellte im Deutschen Kaiserreich 1880–1913. Interessen und Strategien als Elemente der Integration eines segmentierten Arbeitsmarktes. (= Vierteljahrschrift für Sozial- und Wirtschaftsgeschichte Beiheft* 82). Stuttgart 1987

Pierenkemper, Toni: 'Zur Finanzierung von industriellen Unternehmensgründungen im 19. Jahrhundert – mit einigen Bemerkungen über die Bedeutung der Familie'. In: Petzina, Dietmar (ed.): *Zur Geschichte der Unternehmensfinanzierung*. Berlin 1990, pp.69–97

Pingel, Falk: 'Politik deutscher Institutionen in den westlichen Besatzungszonen 1945–1948'. In: *Neue politische Literatur* 25 (1980), pp.341–359

Pingel, Falk: '"Die Russen am Rhein?" Zur Wende der britischen Besatzungspolitik im Frühjahr 1946'. In: *Vierteljahrshefte für Zeitgeschichte* 30 (1982), pp.98–116

Pinner, Felix: *Emil Rathenau und das elektrische Zeitalter*. Leipzig 1918

Pinner, Felix: *Deutsche Wirtschaftsführer*. Berlin 1925

Plischke, Elmer: *The Allied High Commission for Germany*. Edited by the Office of the U.S. High Commissioner for Germany, Office of the Executive Secretary, Historical Division. o.O. 1953

Pogge von Strandmann, Hartmut: *Unternehmenspolitik und Unternehmensführung. Der Dialog zwischen Vorstand und Aufsichtsrat bei Mannesmann 1900 bis 1919*. Düsseldorf/Vienna 1978

Pohl, Hans: 'The Steaua Romana and the Deutsche Bank (1903–1920)'. In: *Studies on Economic and Monetary Problems and on Banking History* 24 (1989), pp.77–94

Pohl, Hans/Habeth, Stephanie/Brüninghaus, Beate: *Die Daimler-Benz AG in den Jahren 1933 bis 1944*. Wiesbaden 1986

Pohl, Manfred: *Wiederaufbau. Kunst und Technik der Finanzierung 1947–1953. Die ersten Jahre der Kreditanstalt für Wiederaufbau*. Frankfurt a.M. 1973

Pohl, Manfred: 'Deutsche Bank London Agency founded 100 years ago'. In: *Studies on Economic and Monetary Problems and on Banking History* 10 (1973), pp.17–35. Reprinted Mainz 1988, pp.233–253

Pohl, Manfred: 'Deutsche Bank during the "Company Promotion" Crisis (1873–1876)'. In: *Studies on Economic and Monetary Problems and on Banking History* 11 (1973), pp.19–33. Reprinted Mainz 1988, S.277–293

Pohl, Manfred: 'Dismemberment and Reconstruction of Germany's Big Banks, 1945–1957'. In: *Studies on Economic and Monetary Problems and on Banking History* 13 (1974), pp.18–27. Reprinted Mainz 1988, pp.343–353

Pohl, Manfred: *Die Finanzierung der Russengeschäfte zwischen den beiden Weltkriegen. Die Entwicklung der 12 grossen Russlandkonsortien. (= Tradition Beiheft 9)*. Frankfurt a.M. 1975

Pohl, Manfred: *Einführung in die Deutsche Bankengeschichte*. Frankfurt a.M. 1976

Pohl, Manfred: 'Deutsche Bank's East Asia Business (1870–1875). A Contribution to the Economic History of China and Japan'. In: *Studies on Economic and Monetary Problems and on Banking History* 15 (1977), pp.25–57. Reprinted Mainz 1988, pp.423–459

Pohl, Manfred: 'Die Situation der Banken in der Inflationszeit'. In: Büsch, Otto/Feldman, Gerald D. (eds.): *Historische Prozesse der Deutschen Inflation 1914–1924. Ein Tagungsbericht. (= Einzelveröffentlichungen der Historischen Kommission zu Berlin* 21). Berlin 1978, pp.83–95, 115–126

Pohl, Manfred: 'The Amalgamation of Deutsche Bank and Disconto-Gesellschaft in October 1929'. In: *Studies on Economic and Monetary Problems and on Banking History* 18 (1980), pp.27–52. Reprinted Mainz 1988, pp.543–570

Pohl, Manfred: *Konzentration im deutschen Bankwesen 1848–1980. (= Schriftenreihe des Instituts für bankhistorische Forschung* 4). Frankfurt a.M. 1982

Pohl, Manfred: 'The Deutsche Bank's Entry into the Industrial Area in the Rhineland and Westphalia. The Merger with the Bergisch Märkinsche Bank and the Essener Credit-Anstalt in 1914 and 1925'. In: *Studies on Economic and*

Monetary Problems and on Banking History 20 (1983), pp.13–24. Reprinted Mainz 1988, pp.637–654

Pohl, Manfred: 'Die Entwicklung des privaten Bankwesens nach 1945. Die Kreditgenossenschaften nach 1945'. In: *Deutsche Bankengeschichte*. Edited by the Wissenschaftliche Beirat des Instituts für bankhistorische Forschung. Vol.3. Frankfurt a.M. 1983, pp.207–276

Pohl, Manfred: 'Die Gebäude der Deutschen Bank. Ein Rückblick'. In: Leitner, Bernhard/Pohl, Manfred/Becker, Gilbert: *Taunusanlage* 12. Frankfurt a.M. 1985, pp.97–131

Pohl, Manfred: *Entstehung und Entwicklung des Universalbankensystems. Konzentration und Krise als wichtige Faktoren.* (= *Schriftenreihe des Instituts für bankhistorische Forschung* 7). Frankfurt a M. 1986

Pohl, Manfred: *Deutsche Bank Buenos Aires 1887–1987.* Mainz 1987

Pohl, Manfred: *Emil Rathenau und die AEG.* Berlin/Frankfurt a.M. 1988

Pohl, Manfred: *Geschöft und Politik. Deutsch-russisch/sowjetische Wirtschaftsbeziehungen 1850–1988.* Mainz 1988

Pohl, Manfred: 'Die öberlebenschancen von Unternehmensgründungen in der Zeit von 1870 bis 1918'. In: Pohl, Hans (ed.): *öberlebenschancen von Unternehmensgründungen.* (= *Zeitschrift für Unternehmensgeschichte Beiheft* 63). Stuttgart 1991, pp.29–47

Pohl, Manfred: *Baden-Württembergische Bankgeschichte.* Stuttgart/Berlin/Cologne 1992

Pohl, Manfred (ed.): *Hermann J. Abs. A Biography in Text and Pictures.* Mainz 1983

Pohl, Manfred/Lodemann, Jürgen: *Die Bagdadbahn. Geschichte und Gegenwart einer berühmten Eisenbahnlinie.* Mainz 1989

Pollock, James K.: *Besatzung und Staatsaufbau nach 1945. Occupation Diary and Private Correspondence 1945–1948.* Edited by Ingrid Krüger-Bulcke. Munich 1994

Pollock, James K./Meisel, James H.: *Germany under Occupation. Illustrative Materials and Documents.* Ann Arbor, Michigan 1947

Priester, H.E.: *Das Geheimnis des 13. Juli. Ein Tatsachenbericht von der Bankenkrise.* Berlin 1932

Prinz, Arthur: *Juden im Deutschen Wirtschaftsleben 1850–1914.* (= *Schriftenreihe wissenschaftlicher Abhandlungen des Leo Baeck Instituts* 43). Tübingen 1984

Pritzkoleit, Kurt: *Bosse, Banken, Bîrsen. Herren über Geld und Wirtschaft.* Vienna 1954

Pritzkoleit, Kurt: *Mönner, Möchte, Monopole. Hinter den Türen der westdeutschen Wirtschaft.* Düsseldorf 21960

Quataert, Donald: 'Limited Revolution: The Impact of the Anatolian Railway on Turkish Transportation and the Provisioning of Istanbul 1890–1908'. In: *Business History Review* 51 (1977), pp.139–160

Raschdau, Ludwig: *Unter Bismarck und Caprivi. Erinnerungen eines deutschen Diplomaten 1885–1894.* Berlin 1939

Riesser, Jacob: *Die deutschen Grossbanken und ihre Konzentration im Zusammenhang mit der Entwicklung der Gesamtwirtschaft in Deutschland.* Jena 1912

Ritschl, Albrecht: 'Die Wöhrungsreform von 1948 und der Wiederaufstieg der westdeutschen Industrie. Zu den Thesen von Mathias Manz und Werner

Abelshauser über die Produktionswirkungen der Wöhrungsreform'. In: *Vierteljahrshefte für Zeitgeschichte* 33 (1985), pp.136–163

Rosenbaum, Eduard/Sherman, A.J.: *M.M. Warburg & Co. 1798–1938. Merchant Bankers of Hamburg.* London 1979

Rosenberg, Hans: *Grosse Depression und Bismarckzeit. Wirtschaftsablauf, Gesellschaft und Politik in Mitteleuropa.* Berlin 1967

Rostow, Walt Whitman: *Stadien wirtschaftlichen Wachstums. Eine Alternative zur marxistischen Entwicklungstheorie.* Gîttingen 1960

Ruhl, Hans-Jîrg (ed.): *Neubeginn und Restauration. Dokumente zur Vorgeschichte der Bundesrepublik Deutschland 1945–1949.* Munich 1982

Ruhm von Oppen, Beate (ed.): *Documents on Germany under Occupation 1945–1954.* London 1955

Ruhm von Oppen, Beate (ed.): *Helmuth James von Moltke. Briefe an Freya 1939–1945.* Munich 1988

Rummel, Hans: 'Die Rentabilitötsfrage der Banken, ihre Unkosten und die Kalkulation'. In: *Untersuchung des Bankwesens* 1933. Part I. Vol.1. Berlin 1933, pp.421–475

Rupieper, Hermann-Josef: *Der besetzte Verbündete. Die amerikanische Deutschland-Politik 1949–1955.* Opladen 1991

Rupieper, Hermann-Josef: *Die Wurzeln der westdeutschen Nachkriegsdemokratie. Der amerikanische Beitrag 1945–1952.* Opladen 1993

Schaffner, Peter F.: *Die Regelung der verbrieften Auslandsschulden des Deutschen Reichs innerhalb des Londoner Schuldenabkommens – ein taugliches Modell zur Bereinigung gouvernementaler Auslandsschulden?* Thesis Würzburg 1987

Scharf, Claus/Schrîder, Hans-Jürgen (eds.): *Die Deutschlandpolitik Grossbritanniens und die Britische Zone 1945–1949.* Wiesbaden 1979

Scherpenberg, Jens van: *ôffentliche Finanzwirtschaft in Westdeutschland 1944–1948.* Munich 1984

Schieder, Theodor (ed.): *Handbuch der Europöischen Geschichte.* Vol.6. Europa im Zeitalter der Nationalstaaten und Europöische Weltpolitik bis zum Weltkrieg. Stuttgart 1968. Reprinted 1973

Schlarp, Karl-Heinz/Windelen, Markus: 'Das Dilemma des westdeutschen Osthandels und die Entstehung des Ost-Ausschusses der Deutschen Wirtschaft 1950–1952'. In: *Vierteljahrshefte für Zeitgeschichte* 41 (1993), pp.223–276

Schmiale, Bernd: *Zur Tötigkeit der Philipp Holzmann AG im Rahmen der Nahostexpansion der Deutschen Bank AG. Eine wirtschaftshistorische Betrachtung unter besonderer Berücksichtigung des Zeitraumes zwischen 1888 und 1918.* Unpublished Thesis East Berlin 1987

Schmidt, Ernst Wilhelm: *Mönner der Deutschen Bank und der Disconto-Gesellschaft.* Düsseldorf 1957

Schîllgen, Gregor: *Imperialismus und Gleichgewicht. Deutschland, England und die orientalische Frage 1871–1914.* Munich 1984

Schîllgen, Gregor: *Das Zeitalter des Imperialismus.* (= Oldenbourg Grundriss der Geschichte 15). Munich 1994

Schîllgen, Gregor (ed.): *Flucht in den Krieg? Die Aussenpolitik des kaiserlichen Deutschland.* Darmstadt 1991

Schrîder, Hans-Jürgen (ed.): *Marshallplan und Westdeutscher Wiederaufstieg.* Stuttgart 1990

Schubert, Aurel: *The Credit-Anstalt Crisis of 1931.* Cambridge 1991

Schulz, Gerhard: *Von Brüning zu Hitler. Zwischen Demokratie und Diktatur.* 3 vols. Berlin/New York 1992.

Schulz, Gerhard et al.: *Politik und Wirtschaft in der Krise. Quellen zur éra Brüning.* 2 vols. Düsseldorf 1980

Schulz, Günther: *Die Arbeiter und Angestellten bei Felten & Guilleaume.* (= *Zeitschrift für Unternehmensgeschichte Beiheft* 13). Wiesbaden 1979

Schulz, Günther: 'Die weiblichen Angestellten vom 19. Jahrhundert bis 1945'. In: Pohl, Hans (ed.): *Die Frau in der deutschen Wirtschaft.* Referate und Diskussionsbeitröge des 8. Wissenschaftlichen Symposiums der Gesellschaft für Unternehmensgeschichte am 8. und 9. Dezember 1983 in Essen. (= *Zeitschrift für Unternehmensgeschichte Beiheft* 35). Stuttgart 1985, pp.179–215

Schwartz, Thomas Alan: *America's Germany. John J. McCloy and the Federal Republic of Germany.* Cambridge/London 1991

Schwarz, Hans-Peter: *Vom Reich zur Bundesrepublik. Deutschland im Widerstreit der aussenpolitischen Konzeptionen in den Jahren der Besatzungsherrschaft 1945–1949.* Stuttgart 1980

Schwarz, Hans-Peter: *Adenauer. Der Aufstieg: 1876–1952.* Stuttgart 1986

Schwarz, Hans-Peter (ed.): *Die Wiederherstellung des deutschen Kredits. Das Londoner Schuldenabkommen.* Stuttgart/Zürich 1982

Seidel, Franz: *Die Nachfolgebanken in Westdeutschland. Ihre Entstehung und Entwicklung auf Grund ihrer Bilanzen.* Vienna 1955

Seidel, Franz: 'Die Nachfolgebanken in Westdeutschland'. In: *ôsterreichisches Bankarchiv* 3 (1955), pp.398–409

Seidenzahl, Fritz: 'The Agreement concerning the Turkish Petroleum Company. The Deutsche Bank and the Anglo-German Understanding of the 19th March, 1914'. In: *Studies on Economic and Monetary Problems and on Banking History*, 5 (1967), pp.14–36. Reprinted Mainz 1988, pp.95–120

Seidenzahl, Fritz: 'The Beginnings of the Deutsch-öberseeische Elektricitöts-Gesellschaft'. In: *Studies on Economic and Monetary Problems and on Banking History* 7 (1968), pp.15–21. Reprinted Mainz 1988, pp.163–169

Seidenzahl, Fritz: 'Das Spannungsfeld zwischen Staat und Bankier im wilhelminischen Zeitalter'. In: *Tradition* 13 (1968), pp.142–150

Seidenzahl, Fritz: 'A Forgotten Pamphlet by Georg Siemens'. In: *Studies on Economic and Monetary Problems and on Banking History* 8 (1969), pp.17–21. Reprinted Mainz 1988, pp.187–192

Seidenzahl, Fritz: *100 Jahre Deutsche Bank 1870–1970.* Frankfurt a.M. 1970

Sewering, Karl: 'Zum Neubau der Banken'. In: *Betriebswirtschaftliche Forschung und Praxis* 1 (1949), pp.449–460, 708–711

Shonfield, Andrew: *Modern Capitalism. The Changing Balance of Public and Private Power.* London 1967

Siemens, Georg: *Geschichte des Hauses Siemens.* 3 vols. Freiburg/Munich 1947–1951

Smith, Jean Edward: *Lucius D. Clay. An American Life.* New York 1990

Smith, Jean Edward (ed.): *The Papers of General Lucius D. Clay. Germany 1945–1949*. 2 vols. Bloomington, Indiana 1974

Sombart, Werner: *Die deutsche Volkswirtschaft im Neunzehnten Jahrhundert*. Berlin 1903

Sommerfeldt, Martin H.: *Ich war dabei. Die Verschwîrung der Dömonen 1933–1939*. Darmstadt o.J.

Soutou, Georges-Henri: *L'or et le sang. Les buts de guerre économiques de la Première Guerre mondiale*. Paris 1989

Steinberg, Jonathan: *All or Nothing. The Axis and the Holocaust*. London 1990

Steininger, Rolf: *Deutsche Geschichte 1945–1961. Darstellung und Dokumente*. 2 vols. Frankfurt a.M. 1983

Stern, Fritz: Gold and Iron. *Bismarck, Bleichrîder and the Building of the German Empire*. New York 1977

Stillich, Oskar: *Soziale Strukturverönderungen im Bankwesen*. Berlin 1916

Stillich, Oskar: 'Die Schulbildung der Bankbeamten'. In: *Zeitschrift für die gesamte Staatswissenschaft* 72 (1916), pp.103–113

Stolper, Gustav/Höuser, Karl/Borchardt, Knut: *Deutsche Wirtschaft seit 1870*. Tübingen 1966

Strasser, Karl: *Die deutschen Banken im Ausland*. Munich 1924

Strauss, Willi: *Die Konzentrationsbewegung im deutschen Bankgewerbe. Ein Beitrag zur Organisationsentwicklung der Wirtschaft unter dem Einfluss der Konzentration des Kapitals. Mit besonderer Berücksichtigung der Nachkriegszeit*. Berlin/Leipzig 1928

Stucken, Rudolf: *Deutsche Geld- und Kreditpolitik 1914 bis 1963*. Tübingen 1964

Stützel, Wolfgang: 'Banken, Kapital und Kredit in der zweiten Hölfte des 20. Jahrhunderts'. In: Neumark, Fritz (ed.): *Strukturwandlungen einer wachsenden Wirtschaft*. Vol.2. Berlin 1964, S.527–575

Taylor, Graham D.: 'The Rise and Fall of Antitrust in Occupied Germany 1945–48'. In: *Prologue. The Journal of the National Archives* 11 (1979), pp.23–39

'The Banks and the Gold Standard in the German Financial Crisis of 1931'. In: *University of Manchester Working Papers in Economic and Social History* 24 (1993)

Tilly, Richard H.: 'Los von England. Probleme des Nationalismus in der deutschen Wirtschaftsgeschichte'. In: *Zeitschrift für die gesamte Staatswissenschaft* 124 (1968), pp.179–196

Tilly, Richard H.: *Vom Zollverein zum Industriestaat. Die wirtschaftlich-soziale Entwicklung Deutschlands 1834 bis 1914*. Munich 1990

Treue, Wilhelm: 'Die Juden in der Wirtschaftsgeschichte des rheinischen Raumes 1648 – 1945'. In: Treue, Wilhelm: *Unternehmens- und Unternehmergeschichte aus fünf Jahrzehnten*. (= *Zeitschrift für Unternehmensgeschichte Beiheft* 50). Stuttgart 1989, pp.113–160

Trumpener, Ulrich: *Germany and the Ottoman Empire 1914–1918*. Princeton 1968

Turner, Jr., Henry A.: 'Hitlers Einstellung zu Wirtschaft und Gesellschaft vor 1933'. In: *Geschichte und Gesellschaft* 2 (1976), pp.89–117

Turner, Jr., Henry A.: *German Business and the Rise of Hitler*. New York/Oxford 1985

Turner, Jan D. (ed.): *Reconstruction in Post-War Germany. British Occupation Policy and the Western Zones 1945–55*. Oxford 1989

U.S. Department of State: *Foreign Relations of the United States. Diplomatic Papers. The Conferences of Malta and Yalta 1945.* Washington, D.C. 1955

U.S. Department of State: *Documents on Germany 1944–1985.* Washington, D.C. 1985

Umbreit, Hans: 'Auf dem Weg zur Kontinentalherrschaft'. In: *Das Deutsche Reich und der Zweite Weltkrieg.* Vol.V/1. Edited by the Militörgeschichtliche Forschungsamt Freiburg. Stuttgart 1988

Untersuchung des Bankwesens 1933. Part I. Vol.2. Berlin 1933

Varain, Heinz Josef: 'Verböndeeinfluss auf Gesetzgebung und Parlament'. In: Varain, Heinz Josef (ed.): *Interessenverbönde in Deutschland.* Cologne 1973, pp.305–319

'Verhandlungen des I. Allgemeinen Deutschen Bankiertages zu Frankfurt am Main am 19. und 20. September 1902'. Frankfurt a.M. 1902

'Verhandlungen des IV. Allgemeinen Deutschen Bankiertages zu München am 17. und 18. September 1912'. Berlin 1912

'Verhandlungen des VI. Allgemeinen Deutschen Bankiertages zu Berlin in der "Oper am Kînigsplatz" (Kroll), am 14., 15. und 16. September 1925'. Berlin/Leipzig 1925

'Verhandlungen des VII. Allgemeinen Deutschen Bankiertages zu Kîln am Rhein am 9., 10. und 11. September 1928'. Berlin/Leipzig 1928

Verhoeyen, Etienne: 'Les grands industriels belges entre collaboration et résistance. Le moindre mal'. In: *Centre de Recherches et d'études historiques de la seconde guerre mondiale* 10 (1986), pp.57–114

Vocke, Wilhelm: *Memoiren.* Stuttgart 1973

Volkmann, Hans-Erich: 'Die NS-Wirtschaft in Vorbereitung des Krieges'. In: *Das Deutsche Reich und der Zweite Weltkrieg.* Vol.I. Edited by the Militörgeschichtliche Forschungsamt Freiburg. Stuttgart 1979

Vollnhals, Clemens (ed.): *Entnazifizierung. Politische Söuberung und Rehabilitierung in den vier Besatzungszonen 1945–1949.* Munich 1991

Wagner, Kurt: *Stationen deutscher Bankengeschichte. 75 Jahre Bankenverband.* Cologne 1976.

Wallich, Henry C.: *Triebkröfte des deutschen Wiederaufstiegs.* Frankfurt a.M. 1955

Wallich, Hermann: 'Aus meinem Leben'. In: Wallich, Hermann/Wallich, Paul: *Zwei Generationen im deutschen Bankwesen 1833–1914.* (= *Schriftenreihe des Instituts für bankhistorische Forschung* 2). Frankfurt a.M. 1978, pp.29–158

Wallich, Paul: 'Lehr- und Wanderjahre eines Bankiers'. In: Wallich, Hermann/Wallich, Paul: *Zwei Generationen im deutschen Bankwesen 1833–1914.* (= *Schriftenreihe des Instituts für bankhistorische Forschung* 2). Frankfurt a.M. 1978, S.159–426

Walter, Rolf: 'Jüdische Bankiers in Deutschland bis 1932'. In: Mosse, Werner E./Pohl, Hans (eds.): *Jüdische Unternehmer in Deutschland im 19. und 20. Jahrhundert.* (= *Zeitschrift für Unternehmensgeschichte Beiheft* 64). Stuttgart 1992, pp.78–99

Wandel, Eckhard: *Hans Schöffer. Steuermann in wirtschaftlichen und politischen Krisen.* Stuttgart 1974

Wandel, Eckhard: *Die Entstehung der Bank deutscher Lönder und die deutsche Wöhrungsreform 1948.* Frankfurt a.M. 1980

Weber, Adolf: *Depositenbanken und Spekulationsbanken. Ein Vergleich deutschen und englischen Bankwesens*. Munich 1938

Weber, Hans: *Der Bankplatz Berlin*. Cologne/Opladen 1957

Weber, Marie-Lise: *Ludwig Bamberger. Ideologie statt Realpolitik*. Stuttgart 1987

Weber, Werner/Jahn, Werner: *Synopse zur Deutschlandpolitik 1941 bis 1973*. Gîttingen 1973

Wehler, Hans-Ulrich: *Bismarck und der Imperialismus*. Cologne/Berlin 1969

Wehler, Hans-Ulrich: *Das Deutsche Kaiserreich 1871–1918*. Gîttingen 1983

Weiss, Ulrich: 'Sparmarketing in der Inflation'. Part 1. In: *Bank-Betrieb* 14 (1974), No.12, pp.490–495

Weiss, Ulrich.: 'Aufbauorganisation einer Europabank'. In: *Mitteilungen und Berichte des Instituts für Bankwirtschaft und Bankrecht der Universitöt zu Kîln. Abt. Bankwirtschaft* 21 (1990), No.63

Weiss, Ulrich: 'Menschen in der Bank'. In: *Zeitschrift für das gesamte Kreditwesen* 43 (1990), No.17, pp.872–876

Weiss, Ulrich: 'Warum brauchen wir die Leitlinien?' In: *Forum* (1993), No.1, pp.4–5

Weiternweber, Andreas: 'Das System Goldschmidt'. In: *Die Bank* 34 (1941), pp.549–566, 576–582

Welch, David: *Propaganda and the German Cinema 1933–1945*. Oxford 1983

Wellhîner, Volker: *Grossbanken und Grossindustrie im Kaiserreich*. (= *Kritische Studien zur Geschichtswissenschaft* 85). Gîttingen 1989

Wellhîner, Volker/Wixforth, Harald: 'Unternehmensfinanzierung durch Banken – ein Hebel zur Etablierung der Bankenherrschaft? Ein Beitrag zum Verhöltnis von Banken und Schwerindustrie wöhrend des Kaiserreiches und der Weimarer Republik'. In: Petzina, Dietmar (ed.): *Zur Geschichte der Unternehmensfinanzierung*. Berlin 1990, pp.11–33

Wengenroth, Ulrich: 'Iron and Steel'. In: Cameron, Rondo/Bovykin, V.I. (eds.): *International Banking 1870–1914*. New York/Oxford 1991, pp.485–498

Wessel, Horst A.: *Kontinuitöt im Wandel. 100 Jahre Mannesmann 1890–1990*. Düsseldorf 1990

Wessel, Horst A.: 'Finanzierungsprobleme in der Gründungs- und Ausbauphase der Deutsch-îsterreichischen Mannesmannrîhren-Werke AG. 1890–1907'. In: Petzina, Dietmar (ed.): *Zur Geschichte der Unternehmensfinanzierung*. Berlin 1990, pp.119–171

Whale, P. Barrett: *Joint Stock Banking in Germany. A Study of the German Creditbanks Before and After the War*. London 1930

Wiegand, Gerhard (ed.): *Halbmond im letzten Viertel. Briefe und Reiseberichte aus der alten Türkei von Theodor und Marie Wiegand 1895 bis 1918*. Munich 1970

Wilkins, Mira: *The history of foreign investment in the United States to 1914*. Cambridge, Mass./London 1989

Williamson, John G.: *Karl Helfferich 1872–1924. Economist, Financier, Politician*. Princeton, New Jersey 1971

Willis, F. Roy: *France, Germany, and the New Europe 1945–1967*. Stanford 1968

Winkel, Harald: *Die Wirtschaft im geteilten Deutschland 1945–1970*. Wiesbaden 1974

Winkler, Dîrte: 'Die amerikanische Sozialisierungspolitik in Deutschland

1945–1948'. In: Winkler, Heinrich A. (ed.): *Politische Weichenstellungen im Nachkriegsdeutschland 1945–1953*. Gîttingen 1979, pp.88–110

Winkler, Heinrich August: *Weimar 1918–1933. Die Geschichte der ersten deutschen Demokratie*. Munich 1993

Wolf, Herbert: *30 Jahre Nachkriegsentwicklung im deutschen Bankwesen*. Mainz 1980

Wolf, Herbert: 'Die Dreier-Lîsung. Marginalien zum Niederlassungsgesetz von 1952'. In: *Bankhistorisches Archiv* 19 (1993), pp.26–42

Wolf, Herbert: 'Geld und Banken nach dem Zweiten Weltkrieg. Internationale Kapitalbewegungen, Bankensysteme, grenzüberschreitende Kooperation. Lönderkapitel Deutschland'. In: Pohl, Hans (ed.): *Europöische Bankengeschichte*. Frankfurt a.M. 1993, pp.517–550

Wolff, Michael W.: *Die Wöhrungsreform in Berlin 1948/49*. Berlin/New York 1991

Wulf, Peter: *Hugo Stinnes. Wirtschaft und Politik 1918–1924*. Stuttgart 1979

Zechlin, Egmont: 'Deutschland zwischen Kabinettskrieg und Wirtschaftskrieg. Politik und Kriegführung in den ersten Monaten des Weltkrieges 1914'. In: *Historische Zeitschrift* 199 (1964), pp.347–458

Zehle, Sybille: 'Der Erbe'. In: *Manager Magazin* 20 (1990), No.9, p.77

Ziemke, Earl F.: *The U.S. Army in the Occupation of Germany 1944–1946*. Washington, D.C. 1975

Zilch, Reinhold: 'Zum Plan einer Zwangsregulierung im deutschen Bankwesen vor dem ersten Weltkrieg und zu seinen Ursachen. Dokumentation'. In: Aisin, B.A./Gutsche, W. (eds.): *Forschungsergebnisse zur Geschichte des deutschen Imperialismus vor 1917*. East Berlin 1980, pp.229–256

Zink, Harold: *The United States in Germany 1944–1955*. Princeton 1957

Zitelmann, Rainer: Hitler. Selbstverstöndnis eines Revolutionörs. Stuttgart 21991

Zorn, Wolfgang: 'Wirtschaft und Politik im deutschen Imperialismus'. In: Abel, Wilhelm et al. (eds.): *Wirtschaft, Geschichte und Wirtschaftsgeschichte. Festschrift zum 65. Geburtstag von Friedrich Lütge*. Stuttgart 1966, pp.340–354

Zschaler, Frank: 'Von der Emissions- und Girobank zur Deutschen Notenbank. Zu den Umstönden der Gründung einer Staatsbank für Ostdeutschland'. In: *Bankhistorisches Archiv* 18 (1992), pp.59–68

Zucker, Stanley: *Ludwig Bamberger. German Politician and Social Critic 1823–1899*. Pittsburgh 1975